Contemporary
Economic
Issues

THE IRWIN SERIES IN ECONOMICS

Consulting Editor
LLOYD G. REYNOLDS
Yale University

Contemporary Economic Issues

Edited by

NEIL W. CHAMBERLAIN

Armand G. Erpf Professor of the Modern Corporation
Graduate School of Business
Columbia University

Revised Edition · 1973
RICHARD D. IRWIN, INC. *Homewood, Illinois 60430*
IRWIN-DORSEY LIMITED *Georgetown, Ontario*

Revised Edition

First Printing, January 1973

ISBN 0-256-01427-2
Library of Congress Catalog Card No. 72–92423
Printed in the United States of America

Editor's Preface to the First Edition

Both the citizen on the street and the professional economist in his study often refer to "the economic system." Neither very often takes the time to examine what he means by that term. With only a little reflection, agreement could probably be reached on a definition that would read something like: "a national unit whose component parts are so functionally related to each other as collectively to realize certain desired economic results."

If we dug a little below the surface, we could probably also agree on certain necessary ingredients for an economic system. Since the results it achieves are neither precisely repetitive nor mechanically reproducible, but on the contrary are the purposive behavior of men, there must be some way of insuring that the myriad of individual decisions being taken throughout the economic system are guided by a common set of values. These are partly reflected in laws but also embodied in traditional modes of conduct.

At the same time, if the economic system is to realize certain objectives, there must be something more than the unrelated decisions of many functionaries, however similar their values. There must be specific system objectives, such as full employment (however defined); a specific rate of increase in gross national product; or national programs relating to highway construction, the rehabilitation of cities, the improvement of education, or even putting a man on the moon. These are objectives which the relevant parts of the system seek to achieve by making their particular functional contributions.

To insure the coordination of the parts of this human system in the pursuit of specific objectives, some form of organization and management is necessary. The organization consists of a network of political subunits— a federal government, state governments, city governments, and a variety of special districts. It also includes a network of private producing units in the form of business establishments, as well as nonprofit activities such as universities and hospitals. As a kind of elemental unit in the system, there is also a population of households. All these units—governments, establishments, households—are both producers and consumers of their own and each other's outputs.

If we think of the economic system as geographically or politically defined by the national state, then the management of that system resides, at the apex, in the federal government. The federal administration constitutes in effect the top management whose function is to coordinate the parts so that the overall results—the specific objectives which are wanted —are realized. In doing this it must make use of the nation's real assets— its natural resources and its population, in all their diversity, and its public and private producing units. In order to mobilize these assets to secure the goals which are sought, the government, as manager, must have available to it certain inducements or coercions; these may take the form of tax levies or tax credits, subsidies or fines, control over access to funds and influence over rates of interest, and certainly a public purse and the means of continually refilling it. With these the federal management must do as well as it can to secure the responses which it needs from all the system components in order to meet the objectives which the system has set for itself.

We speak of this as an economic system because the parts are purposefully (functionally) related. This implies that if we were to take a cross section view of our society at work, at a point in time, we should be able to discern how all the parts are connected, like the works of a clock. This is the view of the economy which is typically presented by the textbooks on economic theory: each chapter deals with behavior which is functionally related to the behavior discussed in every other chapter. The parts all hang together; the system works.

Indeed, not only does the system work, but generally speaking there are pressures either built in or consciously being applied to perfect the working of the system. In government and private establishment alike there is a continuing drive to increase the efficiency of performance. We have regulatory agencies to restrain anticompetitive practices, for example, and industrial engineers to ferret out cost-saving procedures. We have information systems which make available, ever faster and more accurately, the data we need to tie our multitude of operations together into a more smoothly integrated system.

But with all these actions designed to improve the systematic nature of our economic activity, there are always other pressures at work disrupting the smoothness of operation of the economy. As a consequence of technological change, organizational innovations, discoveries of natural phenomena, political disruption, or widespread popular movements assaulting traditional values; sometimes also as a consequence of indifference, inertia, obtuseness, or wilfullness on a grand scale; or changes in the numbers, composition, and location of population—as a consequence of any or all of these, the smooth functioning of the system is disrupted. The system stutters, is unable to achieve the objectives it has spelled out for itself or cannot achieve them with the expected efficiency, may even have difficulty in defining its economic objectives.

In these instances, the system managers (either the top managers in the federal administration or the managers of the appropriate subsystem units, such as local governments and corporations) must take such steps as are possible to restore the system to functioning efficiency, or more likely, to redesign the system in a way that takes account of the cause of the malfunctioning. Sometimes this requires a change in values or a new set of specific objectives; sometimes it requires organizational change and a new management. In any event, such interferences with the efficiency of system operation are just as persistent as the pressures to improve system efficiency. The student of economics cannot afford to ignore them.

This book attempts to analyze some of the trouble spots in the contemporary economic system of the United States, and to explore some of the less well understood parts of that system. The chapters speak for themselves; their contents are too detailed and subtle to lend themselves to easy summary. These are the subjects which are not often included in the standard economics text because they do not fit so readily into the system as it now functions, because they involve pressures for some kind of change in that system, or require a modification or elaboration in our understanding of how that system works.

All the authors are professors in major universities, and some have other duties as well. All are recognized authorities on the issues about which they write. Their knowledge constitutes in large part the tools we must use in any reconditioning of our economic system.

Neil W. Chamberlain

Preface to the Revised Edition

The essays contained in this volume are surveys of and insights into six problem areas of major concern to thoughtful Americans these days—the survival of our cities, the amelioration of poverty, the care of health, the place of education, the improvement of transportation, and the impact of population changes. Each has been revised and updated from the first edition. The authors are the same recognized authorities in their fields, with one exception. The essay on education is entirely new. Allan Cartter, whose schedule did not permit him to undertake a re-writing of his essay in the first edition, has been succeeded by Douglas Windham.

January 1973   Neil W. Chamberlain

Contents

1

The Economic Base
of Urban Problems*

WILBUR R. THOMPSON

Professor of Economics
Wayne State University

The principal applied or policy fields of economics change from time to time, reflecting the leading public issues of the day. The new field of urban economics has important roots in "regional economics" and "location theory," but it differs from both in its very heavy problem and policy orientation. Urban economics takes from regional economics the context of the open economy—wide-open, to flows of migrants as well as trade and capital flows. The urban area as a subunit of the national economy hosts only a few of the countless industries that diversify the national economy; the distinctive industry mix of the local economy is, in fact, the principal determinant of its economic performance and an important determinant of its physical form as well. One of the major themes of this chapter is that a city *is* what a city *does:* "Tell me your industry mix and I will tell your fortune."

* While this essay on urban economics draws heavily on materials which appeared first in *A Preface to Urban Economics* (Baltimore: The Johns Hopkins Press, 1965), the organization of these ideas follows more closely the form of a subsequent article, "Toward an Urban Economics," *Urban Research and Policy Planning,* Leo F. Schnore and Henry Fagin, eds. (Beverly Hills, Calif.: Sage Publications, Inc., 1967). The basic economic model or "system" introduced in that article has been greatly expanded and enriched with selected materials synthesized from various other short works appearing since *The Preface:* "Urban Economic Development," *Regional Accounting for Policy Decisions,* Werner Z. Hirsch, ed. (Baltimore:

In urban economics, location and space are central. Conventional (national) economics in its preoccupation with "what to produce, how to produce it, and for whom it is produced" has virtually ignored the question of "where." The city is a creation in space, and vivid word pictures such as the suburban sprawl, dying cores, traffic tangles, the black ghetto and the white noose, and political balkanization convey the critical spatial dimension.

A third distinguishing characteristic of urban economics is that rigorous but static traditional partial equilibrium analyses are often inferior to more rough-and-ready dynamic systems analyses. This may be because urban economics stresses public goods and services more than does conventional (national) economics. In the public economy, partial equiibrium analysis falls short for many reasons: interdependencies are fundamental, as in urban land use and transportation; spillovers are commonplace, as in suburban traffic flows through the central city; and cumulative processes (cumulative disequilibria) are debilitating, as in various population movements (flight).

Or perhaps the need for a framework of analysis broader than the conventional approach of microeconomics (price theory) lies in the fact that urban economics resembles development economics, where the relevant time period is so long that almost everything changes. The critical (public) capital stock, for example, has a much longer amortization period than does, say, manufacturing plant, and the basic land-use pattern is locked in for that same period. The recycling of the city takes so long that one most often measures time in decades.

An important part of the argument of this chapter is that the city is a system—an ecology—and while partial equilibrium analysis is useful and will be used throughout, the greatest contribution of the economist will come when he joins with other specialists to rationalize a broad urban system. An attempt will be made to present the material below in a systematic way. An early overview is, therefore, more important to this work than most.

We begin with a brief review of the export base theory of regional development in Section 1. Care is taken to distinguish between short and long periods of time when establishing lines of causation.

The Johns Hopkins Press, 1966); "Toward a Framework for Urban Public Management," *Planning for a Nation of Cities,* S. B. Werner, ed. (Cambridge, Mass.: The M.I.T. Press, 1966); "Urban Economics," *Taming Megalopolis, Vol. I.,* H. Wentworth Eldredge, ed. (Garden City, N.Y.: Doubleday-Anchor, 1967); "On Urban Goals and Problems," *Urban America Goals and Problems,* Subcommittee on Urban Affairs, Joint Economic Committee of the Congress of the United States (U.S. Government Printing Office, Washington, D.C., 1967); and, with John M. Mattila, "Internal and External Factors in the Development of Urban Economies," *Issues in Urban Economics,* Harvey S. Perloff and Lowdon Wingo Jr., ed. (Baltimore: The Johns Hopkins Press, 1968). An earlier version of this paper was presented at various seminars in the Urban Journalism Program of the Medill School of Journalism of Northwestern University in the spring and summer, 1968.

Section 2 launches the interrelated analysis that extends through the remainder of the paper. We move from the local industry mix to the rate of local growth in employment and population, and then extend the analysis to show how growing size feeds back to restructure the local economy so as to virtually ensure further growth.

Section 3 returns to the local industry mix as the foundation of the local income pattern. The level, distribution, and stability of local income are drawn out of the distinctive wage and employment characteristics of the basic industries.

Section 4 turns from the positive economics of what is to normative economics and asks what ought to be the local rate of growth. We reach for some guidelines to a city-size policy.

Section 5 takes the great leap from urban-regional economics to intra-urban analysis. In what must surely become, in time, the principal contribution of the economist, we undertake to stretch some strands from the economic base—industry mix—to the internal form and functioning of the city. The case made here is that in land-use and transportation patterns a city is what it does.

Section 6 continues the work of translating the basic economic characteristics of a locality into the language of local public policymakers and managers by drawing out the connection between the growth rate and the housing problem.

Section 7 picks up city size as a major source of urban problems, emphasizing residential patterns, population density, and political fragmentation.

Section 8 brings into focus a very distinctive perspective of economics—choice and opportunity cost. A trade off is posed among three goals—residential-social amenities, political values, and socioeconomic responsibility. The intellectual clarity and emotional maturity to frame and face hard choices are at issue, with special reference to political fragmentation.

Section 9 emphasizes the residential spatial pattern by socioeconomic class. The argument here is that houses are not just filler separating key locations of stores, offices, and plants; rather, neighborhood arrangements underlie many urban problems.

Finally, Section 10 considers the organization of the local public economy in space. The economics of the case for political consolidation in the larger metropolitan area is the closing theme of the chapter.

1. *The export and local service sectors: a not-so-simple dichotomy*

From the uncertain date of the first systematic inquiry into the subject matter sometime in the early twenties up to the present time, urban-regional growth theory has subsisted on just one simple but powerful idea—the export base concept. Economic geographers, economic historians, urban planners, and urban land economists have long noted the need to distinguish between those local industries which sell outside the local labor market and those which sell within the local economy. The export industries prime the local economy with a net flow of income with which the necessary imports can be financed. In this most immediate sense of current money flow, the export sector is basic and the local service sector is derivative in origin and is dependent in function.

In the postwar period, a few economists took notice of the export base concept and tried to identify it with the "new economics" of cyclical fluctuations, portraying it as a special case of the export multiplier concept in Keynesian economics. In so doing, they reinfoced the notion of the primacy of the local export sector; the multiplier analogy brought a subtle and largely unnoticed shift in emphasis from secular growth to the expansion and contraction of output and employment within given plant facilities. The direction of causation in local business cycles is clear: change pulses through the portal of the local export sector and establishes a responsive rhythm in the more passive stores and offices engaged in local trade.

While economists refined the measurement, they blurred the concept of the export base. Those with a deeper and more sustained involvement with the city—urban planners especially—did not have in mind the direction of causation of variations in *per capita* income of a (nearly) fixed population and labor force over the brief period of the business cycle. Urbanists in general care much more about the process of growth of *total* population and its economic consequences over decades. Physical planners, for example, were usually much more interested in a very different kind of multiplier: one that defined long-run *locational* linkages between, say, new manufacturing plants and derivative investment in homes, streets, and stores.

In the exchanges between economists and urbanists, it has not always been clear when a given discussion pertained to cyclical changes in local output, income, and employment of deep concern to both the local tax commissioner and welfare commissioner, or when near-permanent public investments in streets, utilities, and schools were at issue. Both the projecting of next year's tax revenue and the pouring of cement are important to the well-managed city, but the very different time horizons impose quite different contexts for decisions.

Quite understandably, many urban planners rose to reject, even denounce, the terms "basic industry" and "local services" because they implied a higher priority for the needs of the export sector. To them, the export sector was those drab manufacturing plants on the edge of town or, worse, those plants in the very process of fleeing the central city to suburban havens. The local service sector was visualized by urbanists as the elegant office buildings rising high from favored downtown sites and symbolizing city itself. Usually, the urban planner lacked the sophistication in economics to defend his intuition that in *his* world of the very long run (locational economics), the local service sector was more often enduring (basic) and the manufacturing plant more often transitory.

In the long-run, locational-developmental context, interest shifts to the comparative costs of one city relative to competing urban centers in the production of goods for outside markets. The lines of causation are then turned inside out. To the degree that comparative costs rest on the efficiency of local transportaion systems, public uilities, banks and other financial institutions, schools and universiites and other training and retraining centers, and a host of other critical supporting services, the local service sector is basic. A long-lived electric utility and a commercial bank that have efficiently served first a carriagemaker then an early automobile firm and then an airframe manufacturer have a strong claim to be counted basic in the local economy. Factories come and go.

The effect of time period on the lines of causation in urban change becomes clearer when we examine more precisely the simplistic dichotomy of export and local service. The concept of the export sector has been extended beyond direct exports to other regions to include local firms which supply intormodiato produoto to looal oxportoro. Ao ono movoc, howovor, from the more obvious linked industries (e.g., tire manufacturers in Detroit) farther and farther back in the stages of production to trucking firms hauling inputs and outputs, to accounting, financial and promotional sorvicos, and even back to technical and vocational schools, a near continuum of export-oriented activity emerges. Even in an immediate sense, it becomes very difficult to dichotomize local activity; the very same banks, schools, and utilities serve both the exporter-manufacturers and the local households.

Finally, with greater urban size comes a tendency toward greater local self-sufficiency. More than a decade ago, critics of the early, more simplistic form of the export base theory noted the tendency for the base-to-service ratio to decrease with increased size. Surely, few if any students of the city would have insisted, on being pressed, that the ratio of export to local service workers was fixed, but they did all too easily fall into the habit of multiplying the change in the number of, say, manufacturing workers by some fixed (rule-of-thumb) coefficient to derive the change in total employment, and then remultiplying that employment figure by the (inverse of the) labor force participation rate to derive the change in total population of a community. Perhaps the number of retail food store clerks or barbers per thousand population is nearly constant across the spectrum of urban areas, but with increasing size the threshold (break-even point) of local production for the local market is passed for one new activity after another. First come those activities which are tightly bound to local markets by modest economies of scale and high transportation costs (e.g., routine dentistry and pediatrics), but with larger size even those activities with considerable scale economies and low transportation costs (infrequent contact) come to be performed locally for local use (e.g., brain surgery).

An export sector that accounts for half of all local activity in a city of 10,000 population unquestionably dominates that city, but in a metropolitan area of a half million or over, the export sector slips to perhaps a quarter of all activity.[1] The relative importance and roles of the export and local service sectors change with the relevant time period and the size of the urban region under analysis: the longer and the larger, the more important the local service sector.

In the analysis to follow, an all-embracing term will be used—the local industry mix. In static or very short period analysis of a small urban area, the distinctive and determining part of the local industry mix is the current export mix, and the impact of the current local industrial specialization on local economic welfare will be traced through—on the pattern of income as well as on the growth rate. But as we extend time and expand city size, we will come to stress the way in which structural change in the local industry mix takes place, with special reference to local innovation and import substitution. Emphasis shifts then to the capacity of the local service sector to induce progressive change in the export sector and to the normal evolution toward greater regional self-sufficiency.

2.   The urban-regional growth loop: industry mix, growth and size

To the economist used to working with industries rather than areas, the most obvious major determinant of the local rate of growth in employment and population is the local industry mix. A national system of cities can also been seen as an overlay of nationwide industry locational patterns. Let us begin, then, by characterizing each urban area as a distinctive bundle of industries in space. We would expect greater-than-average expansion of output and demand for labor in those areas producing either new products or products subject to income-elastic demands. New industries are virtually unbounded in potential growth rate in the early stage of exploitation of a new market; in sharp contrast, mature industries tend to find growth limited to replacement purchases plus the slow increase in population. Centers of innovation tend, therefore, to be fast-growing places.

Still, even areas specializing in established products may attain average and even above-average rates of growth if their principal exports are income-elastic—that is, if a given increase in per capita income leads to a more than proportionate increase in the consumption of their export products. The increasing talk about a "zero growth" economy notwith-

---

[1] In the larger metropolitan areas, changes in local investment expenditures and shifts in the "local consumption of local production" function probably come to rival local export multipliers as sources of local cyclical instability. See Thompson, *A Preface to Urban Economics,* pp. 164–72.

standing, few dimensions of the future seem to be as foreseeable as the extrapolations of the seemingly inexorable rise in per capita income. We have, therefore, few qualms about projecting a steady growth of population at an average rate or better in (old) state capitals, university towns, and medical centers, to mention a few more obvious income-sensitive activities.

We see in the Detroit area through the first half of the 20th century, for example, an economy that boomed on the basis of a product—automobiles —which was both a new product and one for which there was an income-elastic demand. Detroit is still growing and probably will continue to grow throughout the remainder of the century, at about an average rate, on the strength of the income elasticity of demand factor alone, now that the newness of its product has worn off. We see in the Boston area a dramatic shift from specialization in an old, income-inelastic product—textiles—to a new growth industry—electronics—which could raise the rate of growth in employment and population from about half the national rate to near parity in the near future.

With rapid growth and large size comes a structural transformation in the local economy that virtually ensures further growth at a near national average rate. The simplest and certainly the most widely appreciated structural change accompanying large size is industrial diversification. Chicago or Philadelphia, with perhaps a dozen or more important current exports, can hardly avoid having some appreciable scatter across the full spectrum: young and fast-growing, mature and slow-growing, and even a few dying industries. So large a sample would, moreover, ordinarily blend an industry mix of income elastic and income inelastic products. We would not, then, expect the large diversified urban areas to exhibit either very rapid or very slow growth. We would, in fact, expect urban areas to regress toward the national average growth rate with larger size.

But the long view of urban history teaches us that no competitive open economy can stand pat. All industries are dying from the moment they are born. An urban area can ensure its economic future only by continually reaching for new industries. Again, who would not extrapolate our current rapid rate of technological change with its implications for an unending rise and fall of individual industries? Five-year projections may be drawn from the prospects of the given industry mix, but perhaps 10-year and certainly 20-year forecasts would seem to call for a theory of local industrial evolution. Consider for a moment the folly of projecting the Los Angeles economy of a few decades ago on the basis of the growth trends in movies and citrus fruits, or projecting Detroit of 1900 to 1930 along the growth curve of horseless carriages. How does one make the difficult transition from, say, a five-year projection of the current industry mix to the difficult business of projecting changes in the industry mix itself?

Again, great scale would seem to simplify the problem. Suppose stable growth over decades is traceable more to local capability to invent and innovate and otherwise acquire new export bases, decade after decade, than it is to the sheer number of exports amassed at any point in time. Can we establish that larger places are more than proportionately centers of invention and innovation? Does the metropolis respond well to change originating elsewhere?

The true *economic* base of the great city-region would, then, be the creativity of its universities and research parks, the sophistication of its engineering firms and financial institutions, the persuasiveness of its public relations and advertising agencies, the flexibility of its transportation networks and utility systems, and all the other dimensions of infrastructure that facilitate the quick and orderly transfer from old dying bases to new growing ones. A diversified set of current exports—breadth—softens the shock of exogenous change, while a rich infrastructure—depth—facilitates the adjustment to change by providing the socioeconomic institutions and physical facilities needed to initiate new enterprises, transfer capital from old to new forms, and retrain labor.

Large places are also better based to adapt to innovations originating elsewhere. With a wider assortment of educational institutions and more professional counseling, local workers may be more quickly retrained from declining to expanding occupations Reemployment can often be achieved within the same local labor market, eliminating the very difficult residential relocation characteristic of smaller places. Finally, in the most general way, urban scale extends the range of consumer and occupational choice, consistent with high and rising levels of income and education, luring and holding the more creative and urbane individuals.

To argue that the larger urban areas are more than proportionately places of innovation and that new products tend to exhibit greater-than-average rates of growth in output and employment would seem to imply that the larger urban areas attain greater-than-average population growth. But this is not so. The decennial rates of growth in population since 1940 show virtually no correlation with size—through the range over 50,000 population. The resolution of this seeming paradox is, I think, simply this: the larger places find their fast-growing industry mix dampened by a steady loss of share in these industries, netting out to a roughly average performance.

In national perspective, industries filter down through the system of cities, from places of greater to lesser industrial sophistication. Most often, the highest skills are needed in the difficult, early stage of mastering a new process, and skill requirements decline steadily as the production process is rationalized and routinized with experience. As the industry slides down the learning curve, the high wage rates of the more industrially sophisticated innovating areas become superfluous. The aging industry seeks out industrial backwaters where the cheaper labor is now up to the lesser demands of the simplified process.

The New York study [2] pointed out that New York has lost nearly every industry it has ever had—flour mills, foundries, meat-packing plants, textile mills, and tanneries. More recently, this most dynamic economy has spun off apparel and printing while retaining its share of the higher functions of designing and selling garments and publishing. Such a pattern befits a high-wage, high-rent area that can continue to earn these high returns to labor and land only by ceaselessly exploiting the newest industries during their early (precompetitive) high-price, high-profit-margin stages. In the long run, the larger, more sophisticated urban economies can, of course, continue to earn above-average incomes only by continually performing the more difficult newer work.

A filter-down theory of industrial location would go far toward explaining the isolated small town's lament that it always gets the slow-growing industries. They find they must run to stand still, as their industrial catches seem only to come to these out-of-the-way places to die. These smaller, industrial novices also struggle to raise per capita income over the hurdle of industries which pay the lowest wage rates. Clearly, the twin characteristics of slow growth and low wage rates (low skills) might be viewed as two facets of the aging industry. The smaller, less industrially advanced area struggles to achieve an average rate of growth out of enlarging shares of slow-growth industries, which were attracted by the area's low wage rates. It would seem then, that both the larger industrial centers from which, and the smaller areas to which, industries filter down must run to stand still (at the national average growth rate); the larger areas do, however, run for higher stakes.

The economic development of the smaller, less developed urban area would seem to require that it receive each successive industry a little earlier in its life cycle, to acquire the industry at a point in time when it still has both substantial job-forming potential and high-skill work. Only by upgrading the labor force on the job and by generating the higher incomes (fiscal capacity) needed to finance better schools can the area hope to break out of its underdevelopment trap. Moving back up the learning curve and back toward higher growth rates for a given industry will tend to create the tight and demanding local labor market that will keep the better young adults home, lure good new ones in, and up-grade the less able ones. The alternative facing the industrially underdeveloped urban region is to run along a treadmill, trading low-skill, dying industries for increased shares of other almost as low-skill, mature industries, already beginning to show their age. Regional economics needs the theoretical support of a more dynamic location theory.

---

[2] See particularly the concluding and summary volume of the study, Raymond Vernon, *Metropolis 1985* (New York: Doubleday & Co., Inc., 1960).

Toward a new location theory

Looking to the future, will equilibrating tendencies arise to slow the growth of the larger places or revitalize the smaller ones? Do prospective trends in technology and economic organization favor the larger or smaller places? Let us examine the coming importance of scale with respect to the classic factors of production: entrepreneurship, capital, labor, and land, in that order.

The stabilization and even institutionalization of entrepreneurship may be the principal strength of the large urban area. In an earlier work, the argument was advanced that a large population operated to ensure a steady flow of gifted persons, native to the area. A population of 50,000 that gives birth to only one commercial or industrial genius every decade might get caught between geniuses at a time of great economic trial, such as the loss of a large employer. But in a population cluster of 5 million, with an average flow of 10 per year, a serious and prolonged crisis in economic leadership seems highly improbable. Reinforcing the advantage of the larger places is the tendency of entrepreneurs with experience and success to move toward bigger arenas.

On further thought, the great viability of the large aggregate in a time of quick and sharp change seems to lie even more in the institutionalization of the many entrepreneurial functions. The very large metropolitan area typically hosts a large university with well-developed programs in basic research and in graduate, professional, and continuing education. The main medical centers grow up to serve the nearby population, and the many advantages of scale draw medical research personnel and funds. As we become more a service-oriented economy, the city itself becomes the very product which is being redesigned and reengineered—becomes the object of the experiment as well as the living laboratory.

When we turn to consider the cooperating factors of production, the case for the large urban area does not suffer. Money capital has long been recognized as the most spatially mobile factor. Moreover, the advent of the modern large corporation, financed internally from depreciation reserves and retained earnings and externally in a national money market, further weakens the locational attraction of *local* capital supplies for the large, well-established, national market business. The small urban area is, therefore, not seriously disadvantaged by its meager supply of capital funds. But existing real capital is highly immobile—most often permanently fixed in space. The large urban area has, by definition, the largest and most varied supply of existing real capital—infrastructure.[3] It is, in fact,

---

[3] To the extent that larger is equivalent to older, the possibility of obsolete urban infrastructure presents an offsetting—dampening—force. But the thesis here has been that large urban areas tend to grow at a near national average rate, ensuring both the continued addition of new capital as well as the regular replacement of old capital. Old, small places are much more likely to be plagued by inefficient, blighting obsolescence.

difficult to define the boundaries between institutionalized entrepreneurship and capital; consider the case of the university research laboratory with tenure faculty and elaborate equipment.

The local endowment in transportation capital may be most critical in the locational decision of the large, multiproduct corporation. The theoretical solution of the least-cost location of a multiple-input, multiple-output operation may even be indeterminate, but a practical approximation to the best location is to be at, or very near, a multiple-mode transportation center. Big cities are transportation nodes (and/or transportation nodes tend to become big cities). Expensive, indivisible railroad faciilities, such as terminals and yards, give rise to heavy fixed costs that can be borne only when spread over the large volumes of traffic generated by large population centers. These bigger places tend also to be served by both a number of carriers of a given mode and a number of different modes to the end that flexibility is greater, risk is lessened, and rivalry ensures that much or most of the reduced cost of volume operations will be passed on to the shipper. Most important, rapid technological change creates uncertainty; the corporation often does not know what products it will be producing from one year to the next, and therefore which transportation modes will best serve it. Changes in transportation technology itself adds to the uncertainty. The minimum-risk strategy is clear: locate near a transportation center . . . hedge!

Turning to labor as a locational factor, the case for the large urban area is again reinforced. With the spread of unionism comes the drive for a uniform wage rate throughout the country in order to cut off flight from unions and to buttress labor's bargaining power. An industry-wide wage rate in a given industry is a big step toward spatially invariant labor costs, although regional differences in productivity may remain, due to regional differences in skill and motivaiton. But evermore automated production processes probably operate, on net, to reduce the opportunity for variations in worker skill or effort large enough to alter in significant measure the quantity or quality of output.

For workers to quote the same wage for all places is for them to give up all influence on the selection of the place of work. If blue-collar, middle-income workers should happen to prefer small towns or medium-size cities as places to live and to fish, such a preference is irrelevant as a locational factor. What could be most relevant is that the wives of the corporate managers prefer the theater. Under unionism, managers become increasingly free to locate where *they* would like to live. Plant location as a personal, consumption decision of the head of the business is not a new phenomenon.[4] Many, perhaps most, family firms were initiated in the hometown

---

[4] Melvin L. Greenhut, *Plant Location in Theory and Practice* (Chapel Hill, N.C.: The University of North Carolina Press, 1956), especially Chapter 9.

and stayed there because the owner preferred to live there. The difference would seem to be that the manager (not owner) group now chooses the place to live and work, with income and education rather than birthplace and family ties determining that choice.

The declining role of land and the rising role of access also acts to reinforce the advantage of the larger urban area in the competitive struggle for industry. While the trend to market orientation may well have been up to now largely a result of the shift in emphasis from material processing to product fabricating within manufacturing, the locational power of the mass market may in coming decades rest more on the coming dominance of the high services. Extractive industries gain from being dispersed to avoid the diminishing returns of very intensive cultivation or extraction, while manufacturing operations, and services even more, seem to experience a rather long stage of increasing returns with higher densities. Manufacturing at large scale requires the assembling of large work forces, and the movement of persons (job commuting) is, on the whole, much more expensive than the transportation of materials or product. But service industries need to weigh the costs of movement of both the producer (lawyer, doctor, teacher) and the consumer (client, patient, student), although these are sometimes substitutive (the house call). A dense cluster of people—a city —is almost by definition a physical manifestation of a planned arrangement for the heavy personal interaction especially characteristic of the service industries.

Out of all this, one gets a very strong feeling for near-inexorable urban growth through the population range from 200,000 to 16 million. (The New York region becomes, of course, a special case of growth into a new range with which we have had no experience.) The argument is, in sum, that metropolitan areas of a million and over develop industrial structures especially suited to give birth to *new industries,* and they amass markets especially attractive to the *income-elastic high services.* With possession of both kinds of high-growth industries, it will be extremely difficult to restrain their growth, and it is far from clear that we should even try to do so. Of course, a national average (= natural) rate of local populaiton growth would, in a state of zero national population growth, stabilize large-city size. It is family planning which is most likely to slow the growth of large cities.

3.   Urban-regional income analysis

The level of income

Since the level of income is the single most meaningful measure of economic welfare, regional income analysis becomes the keystone of any comprehensive urban study. The major point of departure from conventional income analysis is that no attempt need be made here to discuss the general level of income or the general degree of inequality or overall national income stability. Rather, our concern here is with the pattern of regional deviations about the national average. Our charge in urban-regional economics is then to determine why some urban areas are richer or more egalitarian or more unstable than others—or all three (e.g., the automobile city of Flint, Michigan). Urban-regional economics, freed from explaining the general state of the economy, becomes the study of variations within the system of cities. While urban-regional income analysis is more than industrial analysis, it is surprising how far one can go in explaining the level, distribution, and stability of local income as direct extensions of the local industry mix. How could a highly specialized economy fail to reflect in its income pattern and growth rate its distinctive industry mix?

A high local per capita income, originating in a favorable industry mix, may derive from either skill or power. Industries that blend a distinctive mix of high-education occupations will, of course, tend to generate a higher-than-average per capita income in the urban area so favored. State capitals, especially ones that are also sites of large state universities, gather together relatively large numbers of lawyers, financiers, professors, technical consultants, and other high-skill, high-income persons.

But local affluence may follow, instead, from sheer market power, originating in pronounced internal economies of scale relative to the size of the market. Heavy investment in plant and equipment gives rise to high fixed costs; these lead to substantially lower unit costs at very large outputs; this leads, in turn, to fewer plants (firms) and collusion (explicit or implicit) in pricing. Large investments tend to reinforce this market power by impeding the entry of new firms; potential competitors need to marshal large sums of capital and need to master a complex technology.

But the power to administer product prices and to reap large profits over long periods does not enrich a community if the local plant is run by an absentee firm, or even if the management lives in town but ownership is absentee (e.g., widely scattered stockholders) In either case, profits are drained from the local economy; wage payments alone are germane. The presence of a few large employers—oligopsony in the local labor market—does, however, tend to induce the formation of monopoly power on the seller's side of the labor market—labor unions. To the extent, then, that (a) monopoly power in product markets turns into monopsonistic power in local labor markets, and is then matched with the countervailing power of trade unionism, and to the extent that (b) the unions are aggressive in their wage demands, and that (c) the employers are operating off large profit margins and face consumers who will not much reduce the quantity purchased in response to significant price increases (price-inelastic product demands), local employers are virtually certain to be paying relatively high wage rates for given skills, generating a relatively high median family income in the area.

Perhaps the best deductive case of all can be made for the urban area which hosts a new industry, for here skill and power are combined. If almost all tasks are more difficult in the beginning and become simpler and easier in time and with practice, we would expect to find more talented work forces in urban areas that are innovating. Further, in the beginning firms are few and competition is weak, so that high profits tend also to be characteristic of new industries. Insofar as these new firms were locally promoted and are locally owned, these high profits will be paid out to local entrepreneurs and venture capitalists. In any event, wages reflect not only skill but also ability to pay, and local labor may therefore share the temporary monopoly power of the early lead in the form of higher-than-scale wage rates.

In time, as the innovating firm slides down the learning curve and work becomes simpler, and as entry occurs and the industry becomes more competitive, local firms must meet the competition, either by paying relatively lower wages or by seeking out low-skill, low-wage areas that can now also perform the (simpler) work. Still, we can identify urban areas that continue indefinitely to earn much higher-than-average wage rates because they do not stick with products to the bitter end, but rather make *innovating* their business. New York has, for example, lost—delegated to others—virtually every industry it has ever had, but it retains its high wage rates by continually developing new products.

Before leaving this very static analysis running from the industry mix to the level of income, it would be instructive to explore a little the likely long-run consequences of local monopoly power. In some very complex and unclear way, the past is prologue in urban-regional development. Each stage or process of growth alters the local stock and/or cost of land, labor, or entrepreneurship, and predetermines, in part, the next stage. Even a single illustration which highlights the delicate balance between equilibrating and disequilibrating sequences in regional change is useful, if for no other reason than to avoid giving the impression of simple determinacy in regional income analysis.

In static terms, we argued above that a locality could parlay an oligopolistic export industry and a strong union—market power—into high wage rates and high incomes. A locality that achieves relative wage rates that exceed its relative productivity lives well, but dangerously, on overpriced labor. As the beneficent industry matures, its national rate of job formation will tend to slow, and the rate of *local* job formation fares even worse because a substantial locational decentralizaiton ordinarily comes with maturation.[5] The locality comes to face a rate of local job formation inadequate

---

[5] Even if we assume that the industry faces a nationwide union and a spatially invariant wage, and we thereby rule out relocation into lower wage areas as operations become more routine, as argued under the filtering hypothesis above, decentralization to reduce transportation costs is a common pattern in maturing industries.

to absorb the natural increase in the local labor force, and the search for new industries is greatly hindered by its overpriced labor.

The power to exploit the rest of the country may, in the very long run, backfire in another way Strong unions may set rigid work standards and work rules that become more binding and expensive as time passes and technology progresses. Historically, new processes that permitted a worker to tend more spindles at one time or drill more holes in a given time period, with no more effort than before, often could not be introduced locally. New processes will be innovated, elsewhere if need be, leaving the locality with a sharply declining share of what could still be a rapidly growing industry. Thus, the classic advantages of an early start—a pool of labor where "the skill is in the air" and bankers who know the industry and identify with it— all may be undone by rigid work rules in a world of rapid technological change. In either event, chronic unemployment will force the locality through a painful wage deflation before it can rebuild. In short, there may be a day of retribution.

Then, again, there may not. If the beneficent oligopoly exhibits a very. prolonged stage of strong growth and is slow to decentralize, for example, if it sells a very income-elastic product, and it experiences substantial agglomeration economies, it could enrich its host area for a full generation or more. (The case of the automobile industry in Detroit comes to mind.) That locality may come in time to acquire the education and skill which merits a relatively high local wage rate. High wage rates, however acquired, provide the personal income and the tax base needed to build superior social overhead and thereby to provide a wholly new local *economic base* to support new *export bases.* By the time the moment of truth arrives, the local labor force could have matured in education and skill to the point where it is no longer significantly overpriced, and has become, in fact, a scarce factor and the principal local attraction.

Thus, in this case, no equilibrating force would ever come into play. The original nexus of market power could lead, instead, to a set of disequilibrating forces, as power leads to affluence, and affluence leads to education and skill, and on ot further affluence. Clearly, whether equilibrating or disequilibrating forces prevail is a matter of timing: the longer a locality holds market power, the more likely it is that there will be no day of retribution.

The distribution of income

The virtual neglect of the distribution of local income is hard to explain, considering its critical importance to urban problems and the ease of applying conventional economic concepts to its understanding. Differences in income inequality among the 200-odd metropolitan areas are, moreover, not trivial, with the most unequal areas exhibiting twice the inequality of the least unequal ones.[6] The first regularity in the pattern of urban-regional income distribution that catches the economist's eye is the clear tendency for manufacturing places to show much less inequality than nonmanufacturing places. Factory work calls for a relatively narrow range of skills, and imposes similar levels of effort, especially in the more routine assembly plant operations where operations are keyed to one another. In addition, the egalitarianism of the trade union further compresses wage rate variation within the given industry and the host area. The periodic threat by the skilled workers to break away and create their own union is indirect evidence that union ideology is much more egalitarian than the free competitive market.

Industry mix shapes income distribution in another way: through the local occupation mix and demographic balance (or imbalance) in the demand for labor. A set of industries that produces a derived set of occupational demands that matches the supply of labor by age, sex, color, physical fitness, and whatever else is relevant to clearing the labor market will tend to reduce the degree of income inequality. For example, a high female labor force participation rate is significantly associated with a low degree of family income inequality. To the degree that working wives come more than proportionately from the lower-income families, industries that produce ample jobs for women tend ot both raise and equalize family incomes, with the latter more significant, both quantitatively and socially. In sum, we find tendencies toward greater income equality in such diverse places as (a) highly unionized centers of heavy industry, (b) female-employing light industry towns (e.g., textile towns), and (c) female-employing commercial-professional-governmental centers. Washington, D.C., and Ottawa, Ontario, with their heavy demands for secretaries and clerks, show much less family income inequality than might be expected, even considering their egalitarian civil service salary structures.

The stability of employment and income

Nothing could seem more certain, deductively, than a close, causal relationship between the local industry mix and the cyclical instability of that area. Local business cycles would seem to reflect in large part the cyclical characteristics of its principal exports: (a) durable or nondurable goods, (b) producer or consumer goods, and (c) sensitive or insensitive to changes in per capita income (income elastic or inelastic).

Because the replacement of durables can be easily postponed—we can make do with the old car or refrigerator a little longer—retrenchments in spending on durables impose the least sacrifice in a recession. And this

---

[6] Using as an index the interquartile deviation of family income divided by the arithmetic mean. This degree of interurban variation in income inequality approximates the variation in income level, which also registers a high of roughly twice the lowest value.

rule applies with equal force to either business or households; the replacement of old (repairable) lathes can be postponed but not the purchase of new power to run them, and in parallel fashion we would expect much greater fluctuations in spending on automobiles than on gasoline.

To this insight, we add the fact that investment expenditures tend to vary much more sharply over the business cycle than do consumption expenditures. This may be, in part, because durables make up a larger share of business investment expenditures than do durables in household consumption expenditures. But beyond this, business investment is probably more speculative than household consumption; the sharp changes in expectations that follow the swings of business activity do seem to have more influence on investment. In sum, we expect and find, nationally, *producer durables* to be the most volatile and *consumer nondurables* to be the most stable.

Within the more stable consumer nondurables we have those for which consumers typically spend a larger share of their income as income rises, and those for which a larger share of a smaller income is spent. Clearly, goods which have income-elastic demands would enjoy more rapid increases in sales, production, and employment in the prosperity phase and suffer sharper slumps in recession. Conversely, spending on income-inelastic products changes relatively little over the cycle. Food-processing towns would therefore tend to be more stable than tourist towns, and those canning peas more stable than those packaging TV dinners.

The characteristics of durability and income elasticity are also additive. The replacement of an aging furnace or washing machine has a higher priority than does the purchase of a new boat or automatic ironer, such that a town producing furnaces or washing machines should experience less drastic reductions in sales in recessions, and, with less backlog demand to make up, climb more slowly during the ensuing recovery period. The most stable areas should then be those places specializing in consumer nondurable necessities (e.g., food and otbacco), and the most unstable places those producing consumer durable luxuries (e.g., outboard motors) or, integrating this with the discussion above, producer durables (e.g., lathes and trucks). Nondurable luxuries (e.g., entertainment) and durable necessities (e.g., washing machines) would occupy an intermediate position in the ranks of cyclical instability.

Still, preliminary empirical work here has produced puzzling results. We find, as expected, that on a *national* basis durables exhibited average peak-to-trough declines of 3.6 and 10.8 percent in the 1953-54 and 1957-58 recessions, respectively; nondurables remained nearly constant in both; consumer expenditures on services exhibited average *increases* of 5.3 and 3.2 percent, respectively, despite the recessions. We would then be quite surprised if those *areas* specializing in durable goods were not substantially more unstable over the cycle than those emphasizing nondurables.

And surprising it is to find, for example, no significant correlation between the percent of total local manufacturing employment engaged in durable goods production and the percent peak-to-trough decline in total employment, 1957-58, for the larger 135 of the 200-odd standard metropolitan areas. The data used does not, admittedly, permit the separation of producers' durables from consumer durables. While it would be premature to reject an industry mix explanation of the local business cycle, urban areas are, it would seem, something more than simple bundles of industries in space, and urban economics something more than industry location theory.

A knowledge of the local industry mix and the cycle patterns of the products in question is apparently not enough. We should, perhaps, appraise the characteristics of the local firms and the markets in which they sell. The local impact on employment of a given decrease in demand for a local export depends, in part, on the degree of competition that characterizes that industry. If the industry is highly competitive, the product price will decline, and buyers will not cut back their purchases quite so much in physical units. Conversely, an oligopolist that administers its price in tacit collusion with a few nonprice competitors will be more likely to meet a decrease in demand with rigid prices, and the full impact of the decrease would then be absorbed by a reduction in production and employment. Other things equal, local employment should hold up much better in competitive industries than in oligopolistic ones, given parallel declines in demand for the two.

This conclusion follows only if firm failure rates are approximately equal under both market structures. But the oligopoly is more likely to survive a protracted or deep depression, both because its price power probably enabled it to build up cash reserves in the previous prosperity period and also because of its easier access to sources of credit. Economic power is again relevant to local income patterns.

An industry-mix approach which imputes to a *locality* the average cycle of a given *industry* will, of course, not be sufficient if the local firms are the marginal suppliers in that industry. To illustrate, semifinished parts are often purchased by large final-product plants from a number of small suppliers, including one of their own divisions or subsidiaries. The buyer's practice of supplying part of its own needs—tapered vertical integration—results in extreme instability for the small seller of the marginal supply. Obviously, when final sales decline the full cutback will normally be passed on to the outside firm, while output in the captive source of supply will be maintained.

Local firms may occupy a marginal position in the industry and experience significant changes in their share of industry sales for other reasons. A local economy is not only an atypical bundle of industries, it tends also to be a biased sample of plants by age. Older industrial areas tend to have older plants, and these higher cost facilities are cut back first and brought back last over the cycle. If, moreover, the newer plants are more capital intensive (automated), the higher ratio of fixed to variable (labor) cost lowers marginal cost and reinforces the tendency for the newer facilities to absorb more than their share of the smaller recession market and a lesser share of the larger boom output. Automated production facilities tend to run at a more constant rate.

Marginal supplies and the asymmetry of national and regional cycles may also be traceable to spatial position A locality may have the marginal high-cost facilities not because of age but by virtue of its out-of-the-way location. Remoteness from the market (higher transportation costs) raises marginal costs and amplifies output variations in response to demand and price fluctuations.

The local growth rate as an additive factor

The local income pattern is shaped by the rate of local growth in employment and population almost as much as by the local industry mix. It was argued above, for example, that an oligopolistic export industry plus a strong, aggressive union add up to the power to exploit the world outside. This power is, of course, limited by the elasticity of demand for the local export—by the degree to which consumers resist higher prices by reducing their purchases. But even a moderately high degree of price elasticity of demand is not likely to constrain local income if the adverse employment effects of high wage rates and high product prices can be worked off in an expanding market (e g , a new or income-elastic product)—one in which the demand curve for labor is rapidly shifting upward and to the right.

Besides, If the oligopolistic export industry is a growth industry the community will enjoy the benefits of economic power to the fullest as the monopoly wage rate of the export sector rolls out into the local service sector, increasing the demand for local teachers, bus drivers, and bankers, and raising their wages, too. Wage roll-out assumes that there is some appreciable labor mobility between the export and import sectors and some appreciable immobility into the community from the outside, so that the high export wage is shared largely by insiders, for a while.

The serious, even anxious, way in which localities seek to promote industrial expansion testifies to their conviction that local growth has the most beneficial effects on local Income patterns. Clearly, very rapid growth and the very tight national labor market of World War II days did greatly reduce income inequality; almost all of the lessening of income inequality since the Depression came about then, and little or no reduction in income inequality has occurred since. But the impact of growth on the distribution of income within an urban area is more complex. In common with the na-

tion, a greater than average increase in the local demand for labor interacts with an average increase in the local supply of labor (average birth,
death, and labor force participation rates) to create rising wage rates,
overtime, upgrading, part-time jobs, jobs for women and youth, relaxed
job requirements, and other reflections of a tight labor market. A greater-
than-average rate of growth in the demand for local labor should then lead
to a relatively rapid increase in median family income, but even more
surely to a lessening income inequality. The marginal worker who finds a
full-time job will, of course, experience the greatest rate of increase in
income, and second earners come more than proportionately from the
lower income households.

The distinction between the part and the whole is, however, that the
nation may well face an almost fixed supply of low-skilled labor, but urban
areas are open economies, and the surrounding farms and stagnant small
towns abound with potential in-migrants who await only a tightening of the
local labor market. In-migration of unemployed and underemployed low-
skilled workers will tend to add households to the lower income classes
almost as fast as occupational upgrading withdraws them. The degree of
local income inequality may therefore revert to its original, higher level, and
the principal *long-run* effect of a greater-than-average rate of growth in
local employment opportunities may be a larger local population, spanning
as before the full range of education, productivity, and income. In general,
growth industries and temporarily tight local labor markets do not, in the
long run, make a locality richer—only bigger. (Larger size does, however,
tend to enrich the local skillmix and produce an above-average per capita
income.)

One might begin a deductive analysis of the relationship between
growth and stability by recalling that construction is one of the more unstable industries and that a rapidly growing area would normally have a
relatively large construction sector. The upswings, therefore, would tend
to be sharp as the building of factories, houses, stores, and schools
booms, and the cutbacks could be equally sharp and sizable. Buildings
are not only easily postponable durable goods but as investments are
more subject to speculation. Thus, we might expect a rapidly growing
area to have a local cycle of relatively large amplitude. And we do find
that the rate of local aggregative growth is significantly associated with
the local business cycle. The percent increase in total population (or employment), 1950-60, exhibits a correlation coefficient of .49, with the percent decline in total employment from the 1957 peak to the 1958 trough,
in a sample of 135 of the larger metropolitan areas.

Still, one feels intuitively that a rapid rate of aggregate growth in an
urban area could be stabilizing, if for no other reason than that rapid
growth would swamp the local cycle. This would seem to follow most
convincingly now that modern fiscal and monetary policies have greatly

softened the national cycle. The resolution of this apparent paradox would seem to lie in a subtle measurement problem. While the amplitude of the local cycle, measured around a rapidly rising trend, may be very large in absolute terms, a cycle trough that is barely lower than the preceding prosperity peak is a depression in only a very limited sense of the word. The concrete manifestation of such a depression is probably a reduced rate of in-migration of labor, with local employment holding steady.

While it is quite useful, analytically, to isolate the trend and cycle components of a time series, it is also quite important in a policy context to put them back together again. A local recession which takes the harsh form of unemployment has very different implications to local tax receipts, unemployment compensation claims, public assistance payments, and other income-sensitive payments than does a local recession which takes the mild form of a reduced rate of in-migration. A "recession" in net in-migration would certainly be welcomed by harassed local school and traffic planners.

4.   Toward a policy on urban growth and size

Students of urban economic development have been very hesitant to suggest an optimum rate of local growth, or even their preferred one. Given the state of our knowledge, some reasonable degree of humility is well taken, but surely there are rates clearly too slow or too fast to be easily assimilated. To form jobs locally at less than the natural rate of increase of the local labor force (the birth rate of roughly two decades earlier minus current retirements and deaths) is to invite either heavy chronic unemployment or to force net out-migration. Certainly, it is hard to argue against out-migration—the natural free-market corrective—when a redundant local labor force piles up heavy public welfare loads and creates a culture of poverty and dependency. But out-migration may only solve the problem of the out-migrants; the lot of the remaining residents may improve or deteriorate, depending on whether the local contraction turns out to be an equilibrating adjustment in the quantity of labor or a disequilibrating force operating through the quality of labor.

Out-migrants tend to be the more mobile members of the labor force—the young adults, almost certainly, and often the more skilled persons. Thus, a corrective net out-migration that is adversely selective of local human resources—a brain drain—can become a cure that is worse than the disease. Each wave of out-migration could easily weaken the *long-run* productivity of the local economy, requiring further out-migration, even as it is adjusting the *short-run* supply of labor to the inadequate current demand. If, moreover, net out-migration comes to surpass natural increase so that an absolute decline in local population and employment results, idle capacity in public plant will appear, reflected in a rising per capita cost of government. High taxes fall heavily on a population that is laboring under a static or even falling per capita income. To the extent, moreover, that contradiction or even slow growth slows capital replacement, the town begins to wear out, and a shabby, poorly serviced community is unlikely to attract the more desirable industries. Absolute decline also narrows the range of consumer and occupation choice, weakening the attraction of the place to the more affluent and educated. A community that *grows* at much less than the natural rate of increase in its labor force runs the risk, therefore, of not developing, and so decline or even slow growth requires local management of the highest order to prevent a process of cumulative contraction from forming.

Local job formation and population growth much in excess of the natural (national average) rate, with the attendant rapid net in-migration, also bring strains, even if less severe. Overloaded facilities deteriorate rapidly, creating urban blight; congestion, delays, and shortages raise the cost of doing business and lower living amenities in the booming place. Who would argue that the social costs of housing shortages and crowded schools on half-day sessions do not, in the long run, inflict social costs that rival those of too-slow local growth? To be sure, there will be strong voices in the community all too ready to risk erring on the side of too-fast growth as the lesser evil; rapidly rising local sales and property values are healing salve to local merchants, landlords, and landowners. But the local economy pays, as well as receives, high rents and land prices in a set of pure fiscal transfers that redistribute but do not create new wealth or income; growthmanship need not be blindly served.

While it is much too early to offer axioms, it does not seem too heroic to strike the hypothesis that a local rate of growth at near the natural (national average) rate of population increase is the easiest to assimilate. A complementary hypothesis might be that small deviations from that rate are nearly as good, but that substantial deterioration in local well-being begins to set in at about half or twice the rate of natural increase (the zero net migration rate). The relationship between the local growth rate and economic welfare would then assume the shape of an inverted U with near-average growth favored.

Strengthening this first impression is the hard fact that an above-average rate of growth in one place is by definition offset by a below-average rate of growth in some other place. One of the two deviations from average is almost certain to lower economic welfare, and both deviations will inflict serious social costs in most cases. (None of this argues for government subsidies to achieve an average rate of increase in urban areas that lack the long-run economic potential to ultimately justify the continuing existence of the locality, much less the larger size which results from growth.)

A rigorous concept of optimum city size is as elusive as optimum urban growth, but again some operational formulation may be manageable. Quite likely there is some fairly wide range of city sizes which are not markedly superior or inferior to each other as production or residential sites, and where choice would be determined by taste. Those who enjoy movies and fishing, and who have more ubiquitous occupations (accountants, for example) would probably find a given money income yields a higher real income in urban areas of, say, 50,000 population, while the museum and theatre-going financial analyst would seek an urban area of a million or over to maximize consumer satisfaction and occupational expression.

But city size may not be strictly a matter of taste over the full range of cities; there may be a pathology of the extremes. Urban areas of less than, say 50,000 population may typically be too small to provide the wide range of choice in consumer goods and occupations and the technological base sufficient unto the day. Urban areas of over, say, 8 million may face exceedingly difficult natural resource and management problems. Again, we might hypothesize a U-shaped welfare curve, with the middle size urban area favored.

Finally, policies on growth and size must be consistent. Not infrequently, we find communities behaving as if they would like to grow but not get bigger; other communities behave as if they would like to be bigger but do not want to bear the pains of growth—temporary shortages, congestion, waves of strangers, and so forth. City planning literature too narrowly discussed the optimum size of cities without integrating this discussion with a considered position on the desired rate of growth of these places. New towns were idealized at a set size, with little thought given to the implications of an adversely selective net out-migration that would leave behind an aging and increasingly obsolete labor force.

It is quite possible that the preferred set of city sizes has been increasing through time in response to: (a) rising incomes that incline us more toward greater range of consumer choice, (b) rising levels of education that bring greater occupational specialization and require greater occupational variety, and (c) a rapidly advancing technology that both demands greater city size (for graduate schools and technical centers) and permits greater city size (e.g., advances in transportation systems and pollution controls). Perhaps we have been lucky over the past few decades; broad national forces may have been moving the preferred city size(s) upward at a rate very near the natural rate of increase in the population and labor force—about 15 to 20 percent increase per decade. In this case, a standoff in interurban competition that left almost all places holding their natural increase with a near-zero rate of net migration would align itself nicely with the desired increase in city size over time. Everything would be for in best in the best of all possible worlds. But, this would be a most fortuitous alignment of desired growth rate and aggregate size.

Finally, just as generals are always accused of fighting the last war, we must today continually guard against implicitly predicting rapid population growth. If the nation should approach a state of zero population growth (ZPG), an optimum (static) city size could be joined to the zero average rate of natural increase (= zero net migration). But this could come to mean trading one set of development problems for another. The salvation of many smaller places may lie in a rapid rate of natural increase that will quickly carry them upward to a viable size. From what new source will they add to their stock of population in a state of ZPG? Note that large cities will also not be growing, and they might come to master their large size as long as they were not getting larger. Perhaps our local public sectors are not so much plagued by diseconomies of size as by sluggishness. If, in a state of ZPG, cities which are where their citizens want them to be are better off, towns which need to be bigger are surely worse off.

Room at the top?

From the viewpoint of business and industry, the larger cities have clear advantages: cheaper and more flexible transportation and utility systems, better research and development facilities, a more skilled and varied labor supply, and better facilities for educating and retraining workers. These economies of scale are captured by private business as lower private costs; many of the attendant social costs, such as additional traffic congestion and air pollution, are sloughed off on society. In themselves, these factors would tend to promote urban growth and great size.

But other forces work in the opposite direction. They originate for the most part in the household sector. Alarms of an urban crisis are almost invariably couched in the color words of amenities: congestion, pollution, and other aspects of bigness, or at least poorly managed bigness. It is, in fact, not at all clear from this largely impressionistic (and frequently impassioned) literature whether the hypothesized rising costs and/or deteriorating quality of urban life with greater scale is due to some naturally scarce factor, such as fresh air or clean water, or due instead to the probable or demonstrated failure of urban public policy and management.

To date, the most that can be made of these well-publicized problems of great city size is that they have slightly slowed the growth of the largest urban areas—in the United States probably New York and less clearly Chicago. But paradoxically, the loss of amenities with great size may redound to support the growth of the second echelon of metropolitan areas. Metropolitan areas with over a million population but less than Chicago's 8 million offer substantial infrastructure in support of modern business, although they do not rival New York and Chicago on this score. But then neither are their problems quite so big.

We could argue that New York must wrestle with a somewhat more advanced form of each of the classic urban problems, or we could argue alternatively the equivalent: New York must face each new problem in urban management first. Thus, New York was the first to have to learn how to handle 10 million people and must soon be the first to master the problems posed by 20 million. Each successively smaller city, roughly in its rank order, has one more example from which to profit, whether the examples be good or bad. Chicago finds the path a little easier because New York has done it before, and Detroit profits from the pioneering of both. Detroit, that is, should be able to offer in 1970 a better organized version of the 5-million population cluster, as a partial offset to the disadvantages it suffers by living in the shadow of the greater choice and urbanity of Chicago.

A good case can be made that each of the two dozen or so urban areas with a million to 5 million population will net out to about an average growth rate over the next 50 years, and more than double in size. New York and Chicago will pave the way, perhaps at a slowing rate. All this assumes, of course, the absence of national policy that would restrict the continued growth of big cities. And at this time and vantage point, it seems likely that our national policy will be directed more toward mastering the management of large population clusters than toward preventing their growth.

The viability of small places

No cliché is more widespread than the call for "urban-rural balance," and no urban policy would seem harder to formulate than an appropriate industrial development strategy for the isolated, smaller urban area (less than 50,000 population). Industry diversification sufficient to ensure stable growth is out of reach. Small places usually depend on a single industry and often on a single firm, exposing them to uncertainties ranging from dying products to shifting brand loyalties to incompetent management. Lacking the scale for diversification, the small place might instead pursue viability through adaptability.

A strategy of industrial adaptability (flexibility)) is much easier to recommend broadly than to detail operationally. The local labor force should be prepared to shift frequently from one type of semiskilled work to another as the local shoe factory fails or moves out and the shirt factory moves in, tentatively.

A local labor force that has a reasonably good basic general education would seem better prepared for uncertainty than one with a specialized, vocational training in depth. (Even so, the educational strategy adopted in most of our depressed area programs leans heavily toward a vocational education. The acquisition of specific skills would seem more to prepare a worker for Cleveland than to be a jack-of-all-trades in a small Appalachian town.) Labor-management rapport to prevent mutually destructive jurisdictional disputes would seem to be a prerequisite to achieving the necessary occupational flexibility. Occupational counseling in depth would contribute to untangling the unending series of labor reassignment puzzles.

Wage rate policy needs also to be well handled. If local wage rate increases outstrip local productivity, rising local unit costs will discourage new entry and weaken the competitive position of local firms. On the other hand, the lower, the better is not a good wage policy. If most profit, interest, and rent income is lost to absentee property owners, wages become almost the sole source of local value added and local income. A wage rate too low impoverishes the community, and poor communities do not attract market-oriented firms. Perhaps even more damaging, depressed wage rates starve the local *public* economy, debilitating schools and other public services essential to area development. The prospects are not bright for an area that can attract only those industries and personnel who will tolerate a low-quality environment. The ratio of local wage rates to those elsewhere should keep up with the ratio of local productivity to productivity elsewhere if competitive position in both business efficiency and household amenities are considered.

The availability of local equity capital for small, struggling businesses, known only locally, has been widely recognized and institutionalized in community industrial development funds. The critical importance of short-term working capital to the new firm is less well recognized and points to the need for a mildly venturesome local banking group. Recent studies,[7] moreover, have emphasized the availability of vacant plants for immediate occupancy. Rising per capita income leads to discretionary spending and impulse buying. The ability to get into production quickly to exploit a transitory market (remember hula hoops?) often overshadows comparative cost considerations. A community with a vacant multipurpose (shell) plant will often win out over rivals with lower tax rates, lower wage rates, or better transportation facilities.

Certainly, a strategy of industrial flexibility is a euphemism—a call for the smaller urban area to live dangerously in a battle of wits in a world of great uncertainty. But often the small town has little choice but to live like a small businessman, gleaning the fields for opportunities temporarily missed or ignored by the economic giants. Some new forms of quasi-public etrepreneurship seem to be indicated; the more successful variants of the increasingly common nonprofit, local development corporation will probably be continually refined.

The small urban area might, instead or in addition, simulate greater scale. A number of small- and medium-size urban areas, connected by good highways and/or rail lines may form a loose network of interrelated labor markets. With widespread ownership of automobiles and a well-developed bus system on expressways permitting average speeds of 50

---

[7] See, for example, *Community Economic Development Efforts: Five Case Studies,* Committee for Economic Development, Supplementary Paper No. 18, December 1964.

miles an hour, the effective local labor market would extend radially for 25 to 30 miles around one of the larger urban places. A couple of small cities of, say, 25,000 population, with two or three main industries each, plus a half-dozen small one- or two-industry towns of half that size add up to a 100,000 to 200,000 population, extended local labor market, built on the moderately broad base of more than a dozen important industries.

The case for the federated local labor market can be made more programmatically by promoting a comprehensive and coordinated employment service. The local labor market could then achieve the scale necessary to offer the counseling and teaching so critical in our rapidly changing economy. Area industrial development efforts could be coordinated, including common research and industrial parks. In North Carolina, a state filled with small- and medium-size urban areas, a research and development triangle has been created in the Chapel Hill–Durham–Raleigh area, which is 15 to 30 miles on a side and encloses about a quarter of a million people.

In such complexes, both public and private investments could be planned strategically. Instead of many small, bare community halls sprinkled across the area, one spacious, acoustically pleasing auditorium could be built. In place of a couple of two-year community colleges staffed as extensions of the local high schools, a strong four-year college could be supported. Nearby and inexpensive higher education—commuter colleges —may be critical in holding in the area talented young from middle- and low-income homes, and perhaps in attracting those families in the first place. Again, museums, professional athletic teams, complete medical facilities, and other accoutrements of modern urban life could be supported collectively. The smaller urban places could become analogous to the dormitory suburbs of the large metropolitan area, with their central business districts serving as regional shopping centers. The largest or most centrally located town could become the central business district—downtown—for the whole network of urban places, with travel times not significantly greater than those which now exist in the typical million population metropolitan areas. As these federated places grew and prospered, the interstices would, of course, begin to fill in, moving the area closer to the large metropolitan area form. But alert action in land planning and zoning could preserve open spaces in a pattern superior to those found in most large urban areas.

The fate of whole regions—the West North Central wheat belt and the Appalachian Mountain area, for example—may rest on the ability of conurbations of smaller urban places to emulate the spatial-funcitonal form of the large metropolitan areas. While local jealousies and capital gains and losses in real property pose real obstacles, the depth of the local crises which attend inaction may prompt bold measures. Often, the largest place easily assumes a leadership role. Or rivalry between near-equals might be resolved by resorting to the price mechanism. Suppose each community wants the regional auditorium and resists being the site for the new jail. Each community might bid for the auditorium by offering to assume some disproportionate share of the cost, with the prize going to the highest bidder—biggest contributor. The highest bidder might also acquire the right to assign the jail.

While cooperation among separate political entities is never easy, it is not obvious a priori why the rationalization of a set of too-small, separate economies in a sparsely populated region would be more difficult to arrange than cooperation among contiguous municipalities in the politically fragmented larger metropolitan areas. If contiguity sharpens the sense of interdependence and community of interest, so too it gives rise to more spillover effects and potential conflicts of interests. Finally, the constituent political entities are the creations of and subject to the state. Without predicting that it will move into this vacuum, the state could, at will, undertake the broad regional planning suggested here.

5.   *"Form follows function" for whole cities, too: from industry mix to land use*

Everyone favors beginning with an economic base study of his locality to guide planning and policy, and no one knows quite what to do with the report on completion. Seldom, if ever, does the analyst carry his work forward far enough to connect with the real issues and choices—to turn on the decision makers. Certainly, projections of the likely trends in employment and population of the local economy are useful as broad guidelines for public and private investment. How many new houses, shopping centers, and schools will we need over the next decade or two? Occasionally, the economic base study is extended to manpower planning: the changing demand for and supply of the various kinds of labor, and the anticipated need to retrain or relocate labor. But seldom is the connection made between the current and evolving mix of local industries and occupations and the resulting level and distribution of income, and almost never is this latter analysis carried through to questions of housing, land use, transportation networks, and the like—traditional city (physical) planning.

How does the current local industry mix affect the prospects for downtown, and what do current trends in that mix imply for the appropriateness of the downtown redevelopment plan proposed by the city planning department and/or the central business district merchants association? Able and articulate urban planner-designers unfold colorful prints and plans to introduce exciting new urbanity into dying downtowns, but usually regardless of the very different economic bases of the urban areas in mind. Often, these plans would transplant the heart of a European national capital or regional metropolis—elegant central plazas and museums—into the body of a midwestern manufacturing city. The risk of rejection is great if these designs recapture too well an earlier day of much greater income inequality, *noblesse oblige,* and much slower means of transportation that kept activity tightly clustered in a central place.

Suppose that the local economic base study describes a heavy industry town: a local economy dominated by a few very large plants of national market oligopolists, and a local labor force dominantly one of highly organized, medium to highly skilled, blue-collar workers. Such a coalition of economic power could easily raise administered prices to yield both high profits and high wages and a higher-than-average median family income. The narrow range of medium-high blue-collar skills would, moreover, be further compressed by union egalitarianism into an even narrower spread of incomes. Suppose, further, that the adult population of this metal fabricating, machinery, or motor vehicle assembling area has a relatively low level of formal education. Would, then, the proposed downtown redevelopment plan still be appropriate?

A community populated predominantly by upper middle income persons, with a relatively low level of formal education, would seem to evoke a clear picture of single-family dwellings, sited on large lots, with at least one car in the driveway. This image is hardly consistent with or supportive of the large, centrally located, urbane, pedestrian malls that dominate the currently fashionable designs for great cities. An above-average income associated with a below-average level of formal education evokes stronger images of outdoor recreation and motor trips than it does of coffeehouses and art museums.[8] Centrifugal forces would seem destined to prevail over centripetal ones in heavy manufacturing areas, and multiple-nuclei land forms would seem more relevant than the single-nucleus, star-shaped forms all too often assumed to be universally applicable.

All of this is, moreover, strongly reinforced by the evolving locational pattern of manufacturing plants. The urbane observer who predicts that these skilled workers will tire of the ever-longer, more expensive, and more burdensome journey to work, and who is waiting for them to move back in close to their jobs, may have a long wait because their jobs are moving out to them. Thus, the journey to work for the worker in the suburban manufacturing plant is not only tolerable but is today usually shorter in time if not in distance than it would be if he lived in the core area.

Conversely, one can be much more sanguine about the outlook for the conventional downtown in cities that specialize in commerce, finance, and/

---

[8] Cross-section multiple correlation and regression analysis of U.S. standard metropolitan areas for the period 1940–60 does indicate: a significantly higher median income, lesser income inequality and a lower "median number of school years completed by adults" in heavy industry urban areas. See W. R. Thompson and J. M. Mattila, "Internal and External Factors in the Development of Urban Economics," *Issues in Urban Economics,* Appendix. Whether the high wage rate in heavy industries reflects the parlay of strong union-big business price power or a greater trade school and/or on-the-job training found in this work is less at issue here than the assumption that it is primarily the formal education of a person which inclines him toward theaters, art museums, and similar centers of urbanity.

or government. Professional service centers bring together persons with greater ranges of skill and, accordingly, these places exhibit much greater disparities in income. High-income (highly educated) households can afford to live well in the core, despite very high land values and rents. Attracted by easy access to theaters, museums, and gourmet restaurants, they gather and attain the critical mass necessary to make these pleasures profitable. The unorganized, low-income service workers are kept massed near-in by their dependence on the better mass transit and the large supply of very old (cheap) housing characteristic of central cities and especially their core areas. Further, the major workplaces are tall office buildings, which need centrality and can afford expensive downtown sites by building upward. Again, the location of workplace reinforces residential preferences.

The point to be made is a simple one. Urban plans and, by implication, goals are often drawn up in splendid isolation of the context in which they are to be implemented. Urban design literature is rightly critical of our contemporary cities, but the new forms proposed seem to be all of one mold or, at best, modest variations on a few themes, seemingly unaware of or insensitive to the very different character of the economic and social bases on which the proposed new form must be built. The old adage of architecture, "form follows function," applies to whole cities as well as single buildings. But as of this writing few, if any, urban planner-designers have established rapport with urban economists.

None of this argues that midwestern manufacturing cities are destined (doomed?) to retain their current form forever, even in the absence of architectural leadership. All urban areas are experiencing, to varying degrees, the national shift from manufacturing toward the high services, just as the 19th century saw an inexorable structural shift from agriculture to manufacturing. Whether almost all urban areas will in, say, the year 2000 be dominated by the high services—education, health, government, especially—and be highly nucleated and mass transit-oriented is beyond the context and perspective of this chapter. In any event, Dayton will probably arrive at this stage behind Columbus, Ohio, and Detroit will trail Chicago. It is not the path of urban change but rather the timing of movement along it which is at issue.

Further, our projections of local income levels and trends in the distribution of that income may carry very different implications than the current pattern implies. Our hypothetical upper middle income manufacturing community would probably be willing and able to support better-than-average schools, and the next generation of workers may exhibit much higher levels of formal education, much different occupational mixes and very different taste patterns. Specifically, the next generation may well be core-area-employed professionals that prefer museums to fishing.

None of this argues that some urban planner-elitist does not have a much better design to offer than the one that the current economic base, free markets, and the democratic process are producing. Even if steadily rising levels of income and education are leading us in the planned direction, there are those who would, however, hurry such a trend, and perhaps bend it a little. But they must, in a democracy, be willing to compete in the market of ideas. To be effective, the planner-designer will have to become more knowledgeable about his product—the city—and his clientele—the citizen-voter—and become a much better tactician. The attendance explosion at our art museums and concert halls is not a random harvest; countless art and music teachers have patiently cultivated the next generation over the years. How have the urban planner-designers prepared the public for great architecture? Who has labored to instill a sense of community and civic-mindedness in the next generation, in sharp contrast to the lifeless "civics" we teach?

And on to transportation, access, and choice

As we come to know better the relationship between the local economic base and the land-use pattern it precipitates, we will be able to move much more surely in our transportation planning. If specialization in commercial, financial, and/or governmental activities does build strong downtowns, we would expect to find higher quality and financially stronger mass transit operations in those places. Conversely, spread cities spawned by the much more dispersed manufacturing plants and their auto-owning, outdoor-recreation-oriented workers would seem to offer formidable, if not insurmountable, obstacles to achieveing the heavy trunk-line operations necessary to justify mass transit. The most highly developed systems of mass transit are, indeed, found in New York, London, and Paris, with recent adoptions in Toronto, Montreal, and San Francisco—all notable commercial, financial, and governmental centers.

The long chain that links together the local industry mix, income characteristics, land-use pattern, and transportation system is more than an intellectual exercise. Access is critical to full participation in urban life: job choice, comparative shopping, cultural and social interaction, and so forth. The problem of access in the big city is that public goods are often indivisible—lumpy. In the private economy, if four fifths of the consumers prefer orange juice, apple juice is still available at a reasonable price because it can be produced economically at small scale. If, however, four fifths of the urban residents prefer automobile movement, public mass transit deteriorates badly because it cannot be produced at small scale, at reasonable cost. Would you have buses that service only one fifth of the residents run only every hour instead of every 10 to 15 minutes, or would you cover only one fifth of the city! A strong case can be made that one of the costs of turning on the ignition of a private vehicle should be a contribution (perhaps only a little less than the alternative bus fare) to the public transit system, if access (opportunity) for all is a sincere goal of our society. And it is not only the poor whose mobility is at stake; the elderly, the handicapped, and the young are vulnerable to majority rule in urban transportation.

Finally, if different mixes of industry do create different kinds of cities, we should welcome and exploit the advantages of variety and choice. The federal government should tailor its grant-in-aid programs so as to accentuate these differences by giving Los Angeles more than its share of the federal highway money and less than its share of the mass transit aid, and reverse this practice in San Francisco. Let Los Angeles pioneer with the spread city and San Francisco search for amenity out of high-density nucleation. We assume here that a marked reduction in automobile emissions is both technologically possible and economically feasible, or that the automobile-dominant system comes to be some form of 'park-n-ride" combination of buses on freeways with the automobile largely confined to short collector and distributor trips between dispersed homes and transit-stop parking lots. Given our great and growing mobility, our national system of cities should offer wide choice for diverse tastes. From a longer range viewpoint, moreover, variation becomes experimentation as we test the long-run viability of alternative urban forms.

Much that we do not now know about cities will not come easily, if at all, through deductive analysis or statistical inference drawn from existing data. The social science of the city will surely need to incorporate experimental methods to a much greater degree than economists, sociologists, and political scientists now practice. Because the benefits from experimentation accrue to all cities, we should not expect individual cities to pay the full costs of these experiments. This practice would not only be inequitable but also highly inefficient—that is, we would get, are getting, far too little of this much needed social invention and innovation.

The federal government's role here is very clear and pressing. We may differ on the degree of obligation of the federal government to rebuild, all across the country, central business districts in conventional forms, but the case for federal financial support of bold (and expensive) experiments in new urban forms (e.g., new towns, new towns-in-town) is very persuasive. It is hard to think of any urban goal superior to that of gaining deeper insight into this most complex creation of man—the great city. Surely, all other urban goals must derive from this central one. And federal government could be most instrumental in this pursuit. A small step in this direction was taken in the Urban Growth and New Community Development Act of 1970 which makes provision for federal grants for planning, limited grants for public services for short periods in the early years, and federal guarantees of the financial obligations of new communities, as well as direct lending.

6. Rapid growth can be a mixed blessing: the housing crush

We must also come to appreciate the long lines of linkage running from the local industry mix to the rate of local job creation and household formation and on to the problem of urban blight. Specialization in fast-growing industries increases the demand for labor in the local market, boosts labor income through higher wage rates and more overtime hours, and attracts in-migrants. A high rate of net in-migration piled on top of the natural increase in the local labor force would almost surely outrun the increase in the local stock of housing. We need not assume that the in-migrants are more than proportionately from the lower income groups (lower skilled or young and inexperienced), even though this may be generally so, to predict that the shortage will be most severe and persist the longest in low-income housing.

The supply of high-income housing can be greatly increased in a single building period—a year or so—and the price rise will be modest and short-lived. But low-income families live in old houses that have filtered down from the original owners, and at any given time the supply of 30- to 50-year-old houses is limited—virtually fixed in supply. How would you increase the supply of 50-year-old houses! The very poor can, of course, bid away some of the 40-year-old dwellings from the near-poor, who can replace these by competing with the low middle income class for the 30-year-old units. Even so, the low-skill, poor immigrants and natives face a sharply increasing supply price for housing, and they are forced to spend a larger proportion of their income for shelter. Discrimination further intensifies the housing shortage for many insofar as it slows the normal filtering down of houses from white to black occupants.

The paradox is clear. Growth industries and a tight, prosperous labor market are not unmixed blessings. The marginal members of the local labor force are called back to work again, and the distribution of income becomes less unequal. But these minimum-wage workers face a serious housing crush, which at least partly offsets their income gains. And those not in the labor force—the elderly, handicapped, and female heads of households—suffer rent increases with no income offset. Local prosperity through rapid growth can impoverish some.

The other side of this coin is urban blight. Rapid postwar migration from rural areas and small towns to the big cities has kept the pressure on core area housing, overcrowding and overloading it. Thus, the oldest part of the housing stock is aged prematurely, and then this blighted housing is kept in service unusually long. By the same token, the depopulation of small towns has left them with a redundant housing supply and their blight of vacant, dilapidated houses. Thus, the great migration to the larger cities has created housing blight at both ends.

Rapid growth in population also greatly influences the spatial pattern of urban blight. Ordinarily, the city has grown centrifugally, so that the oldest housing is in the innermost concentric zone that surrounds the central business district. Rapid local growth and heavy in-migration funnels large numbers of low-income newcomers into these close-in residential areas. Poor households can be amassed in numbers so great that the inner edge of the inner city ghetto is held in place even as the outer edge is moving away from downtown. There is no growing hole in the doughnut; a solid spot of poverty enlarges.

A second paradox is seen in the downtown merchants association pushing, with their right hand, area industrial development programs that promise faster growth, heavier in-migration (more customers), all the while blind to the side-effects that this heavy in-migration promises for the neighborhoods adjacent to their stores. An increasingly crowded, more rapidly deteriorating surrounding residential area is quite at odds with the inner-city slum clearance programs that they have been pushing with their left hand. And these downtown merchants will register dismay when inner-city political coalitions form to block core area urban renewal programs that are making an already very tight low-income housing market even tighter. "Urban Renewal is Negro Removal." Rapid regional growth has its costs; one is that the clearance of blighted areas surrounding downtown may be appreciably slowed.

If, conversely, the rate of local job (household) formation is less than the rate of depreciation in the local housing stock, such that houses in the next concentric ring out from the center filter down to prices within reach of the lowest income group in amounts equal to or in excess of the number of such houses needed, the very lowest income group will move *outward* in space from the innermost ring of housing, as they move to stand still in housing quality (age). The most sanguine outlook for the inner city is that a reduced rate of in-migration in the future, now that our rural areas have been largely emptied out, offers the possibility that the rate of filtering down of the housing in successive rings out from the central business district may more than accommodate net new household formation in the lowest income class and permit blight to pull away from downtown.

The opening up of the inner ring is, moreover, more likely the closer we move to a zero rate of natural increase. No urban population figures of the day are more arresting than the precipitous decline in the central city: population losses from 1960 to 1970 reaching levels of over 10 percent in Detroit, over 15 percent in Cleveland and Pittsburgh, and nearly 20 percent in St. Louis. The most sanguine view of this phenomenon is that the central city is undergoing the depopulation that prepares the way for repopulation.

The great dilemma of the local growth rate and the inner city seems to be that a slow rate of job formation creates unemployment, which falls more than proportionately on the unskilled inner city labor force, and thus creates poverty and blight, and that a rapid rate of growth brings immigrants, crowding, and blight. Of more than passing interest is that right up to the tragic summer of 1967 Detroit was in a prolonged boom, with unemployment low and housing tight. The inhabitants of Detroit's black ghettos were better able to buy good housing at precisely the time when it was relatively the most scarce. What could be more frustrating than to be (housing) poor *with* money?

7. City size is more than just a difference of degree

Sheer population size is a major source of many, even most, urban problems. A growing population is accommodated, in part, by horizontal expansion, sweeping over the surrounding rural areas. Greater distances must then be traversed if any semblance of economic and social unity are to be preserved— if, that is, the urban area is to be more than a collection of urban villagers in accidental proximity. Population growth leads, then, to a more than proportionate expansion in transportation demands (as *per capita* movement increases). To the extent, therefore, that government plays asignificant role in supplying transportation facilities and services, the public sector tends also to expand more than proportionately.

And it is almost inevitable that local government will be forced to assume a greater responsibility for internal transportation as the volume of movement mounts. Transportation arteries need to be widened, and bordering private property must be taken. Larger operations often dictate transportation forms that employ much larger initial investments resulting in heavy fixed cost, unit costs that decrease over long ranges of output, and very long amortization periods. Decreasing unit cost lead to monopoly, which must be either publicly owned or regulated, and long payoff periods tend to discourage private enterprise.

The horizontal extension of the city also operates to increase the distance and lessen communication between the various socioeconomic population clusters that seem always to form in cities. Perhaps in a relative sense, residential segregation by income, and to a lesser extent by occupation, was just as true of urban places a century ago as it is the iron law of urban living today.

The poor have nearly always lived on the other side of the tracks, but the distances were short and contacts frequent, as in the schoolrooms and town halls. But the all-slum block becomes first the all-slum school, next the all-slum community—the ghetto—and threatens now to become the all-slum municipality. What was once, if not benign, at least digestible *apartheid* at small scale portends on a larger scale unemployability, antisocial behavior, and, ultimately, recourse to even more centralization of authority. Slum schools that graduate unemployables and political enclaves of the poor that lack the tax base to support minimum public standards of health and safety (vice havens, perhaps) invite either state or federal intervention.

The horizontal extension of the city has, therefore, laid on the public sector new responsibilities in effecting greater intergroup communication, reflected in the burgeoning poverty programs. We are learning the lesson that a social structure, such as residential segregation by income, which may be viable at small scale is not necessarily viable at very large scale.

A growing population is also accommodated in part by vertical expansion and by sheer crowding. Higher land rents in the ever denser core area are a substitute for the higher cost of traveling ever farther to the receding edge of town. Those activities which interact frequently with others in the core or those which need to command the full sweep of the urban area from a single base often find that bearing the rising cost of constructing higher floors while economizing on space below is the most economical course.

Greater urban densities generate greater interpersonal interactions, both planned contact and unplanned friction. Greater density and interaction is perhaps the principal objective of city building. Still, densely packed populations get in each other's way (e.g., traffic delay—congestion) or annoy each other (e.g., noise, noxious odors—pollution) or otherwise impose neighborhood effects, as in driving automobiles or burning garbage. Spillover costs and benefits require the mediation of some impartial third force, such as government. Clearly, increasing density intensifies spillovers and leads inexorably to more pervasive government.

Finally, we have the now classic problem in metropolitan area public finance: political fragmentation into the haves and have-nots. While sheer population size may not change the basic concentric spatial pattern, in which income and wealth vary directly with distance from the central city, the fact that political boundaries, especially those of the central city, are usually fixed means that great size can impoverish the central city. To oversimplify and exaggerate, when the central city accommodated virtually everyone it mixed the rich and the poor. A decade ago, with about one half of the metropolitan area population living in the suburban ring in the typical large urban area, the central city housed a population drawn largely from the lower half of the income earners. Today, with the suburbs accounting for about two thirds of the metropolitan area population, the central city houses largely the lowest third of the income earners.

It is interesting to reflect on what difference it would have made if the boundaries of the first municipal corporation—the central city—had been defined originally as "the edge of town." Some performance guides, such as minimum population density or job commuting criteria, could have given us a floating boundary that updated itself automatically, instead of the fixed geographical boundaries that lead to political fragmentation through policy drift if not planned flight.

Let us bring together the arguments from above. A rising standard of living increases both the absolute and relative size of the public sector, assuming an income elasticity of demand for public services of greater than one. The persistence of an impoverished group left behind in the climb to general affluence reinforces the expansion of the public role. The growing population size of the urban area extends its horizontal dimension, forcing the public sector to take on the added task of holding it together with new programs in transportation and intergroup communication. Size also leads to greater density, turning previously free goods into public goods (e.g., fresh air and community development), and causes interpersonal spillovers that require the impartial mediation of government. This growing role of the public sector is thrust on local government at just the time when its financial, decision-making, and production functions have been weakened by political fragmentation—when it is least able to respond.

8. Wanted: the maturity to face hard choices

Even when we do come to see clearly the evolution of cities, we seem to lack the courage and maturity to face up to the hard tradeoffs required. On the great issue of political fragmentation, it is not so much new knowledge as it is moral and intellectual integrity which is at issue. Casual observation is enough to establish the preferences of the typical citizen-voter of our large metropolitan areas, and casual reflection is enough to establish their incompatibility.

1. We endorse an efficient, dynamic, but harsh economic system, which generates a substantial degree of income inequality, but one appreciably softened by the redistribution of income and opportunity through the public sector (federal, state and local). A very significant part of that redistribution is effected through minimum public service standards at the local level.

2. We prefer residential segregation by socioeconomic class, with income (house values) serving as a simple device for arranging culturally homogeneous neighborhoods. We zone for one-acre lots and require minimum floor area to ensure exclusiveness.

3. We defend small local government as a means of ensuring personal political participation, highly responsive local government, and economy in government.

One needs to reflect on these three goals only a few moments to realize that they are not fully compatible. The citizen-voter can have only two of the three in full measure, and must trade off significant amounts of one he holds to gain some minimal quantity of the third. We can choose to live clustered with others of like income, but if we then proceed to draw and defend political boundaries between these clusters to achieve small local government, we divorce tax base and public service needs and undermine the minimum public service standards critical to income redistribution and equality of opportunity. Again, we could hold tightly to current residential patterns that segregate households by income but still avoid default on our social responsibilities if we were willing to consolidate financing and at least some public services at the metropolitan area level. Such action would, of course, sacrifice the goal of small government with local fiscal autonomy. Or we could accept at the local level the responsibility to arrange transfers between households of different incomes and retain a vital and viable small local government by rearranging land-use patterns so that each political fragment of the metropolitan area encompassed a nearly full cross-section of the population. But mixing populations across income levels, and perforce across ethnic and racial lines, is also stoutly resisted.

To decide which of these various paths is the right one, or even which mixed strategy is preferred, is not the purpose of this discussion. The point to be made is simply that no one is willing or forced to assume the responsibility for clarifying the issues, sharpening the public debate, and forcing a public decision. Politicians, newsmen, and community leaders have not seemed able to pose this great tradeoff clearly and incisively, or to hold the attention of a public that does not want to stand up and be counted. Which would you sacrifice: equal opportunity? small local government? or income-segregated communities? Hard decisions cannot be evaded for long; we move inexorably toward implicit decisions and unplanned goals.

For example, our current practice is to try to hold fast to "nice neighborhoods" and "grass roots democracy" and fiscal autonomy and then to find minimum public service levels slipping away in the poorer municipalities. Reluctantly we transfer financial responsibility for the poor to higher levels of government, first to the state as in the shared state income or sales tax for education and then to the federal government, as in the poverty program. As more and more strings become attached to these grants-in-aid of local programs designed to equalize opportunity, local government becomes more nominal in respect to the more significant functions and political participation more illusory. All that is truly left untouched is the "nice neighborhood," the latest version of "Fortress America." [9]

Just as we cannot expect to formulate realistic goals from a base of misinformation or shallow understanding, so, too, we cannot expect to make intelligent public decisions on hard tradeoffs without rigorous frameworks and good data.

How large would local governments have to be in our politically fragmented large metropolitan areas to mix income classes, given our current housing practices? Some preliminary study of the Detroit metropolitan area indicates that little averaging out of the rich and poor occurs short of the county level, but most of the inter-area variation in income is removed at the county level. But this conclusion does not apply to many other large metropolitan areas, where substantial inequality transcends the county level.

---

[9] Wilbur R. Thompson, "Toward an Urban Economics," pp. 152–53.

How fast is political participation lost with the enlarged scale of local government? How does one, moreover, balance the loss of close control over a relatively impotent, small local government whose jurisdiction is inadequate to deal effectively with the problem (e.g., air or water pollution) against less control over a larger and more competent consolidated government? [10]

More often than not we just do not know enough about the functional and spatial organization of urban life ot make good urban policy or to set up viable urban programs. And when we do know we do not get the message through.

Our media of mass communication have not risen to the challenge of articulating the urban issues of the day. Rambling narratives on urban problems, cursory surverys of the extent of welfare cheating, and photographs in full color of architectural triumphs do not suffice to sharpen the critical issues for incisive public debate and explicit democratic decisionmaking. One bright note here is a current program, financed by the Ford Foundation, under which "urban journalists" are gathered at the Medill School of Journalism of Northwestern University, to study urban affairs for periods of up to 3 months. But by and large newspapers and television have not stimulated really meaningful public consideration of urban problems or urban goals. There will be a lot of bond issue referendums defeated on the way to "Great Cities." [11]

9. Residential patterns are what it's about

Our interest in the spatial pattern of the large metropolitan area is not confined to problems of political fragmentation and public finance. The residential pattern by income (socioeconomic class) is critical to the most basic goal of all—high and equal opportunity. Too long have urban studies concentrated on commercial and industrial land-use patterns: Is downtown dying? Strip developments or shopping centers and industrial parks? Residences simply filled the gaps between the key office, store, and factory sites. At long last we have come to appreciate the great social significance of the residential spatial pattern, especially by socioeconomic class.

The more one reflects on the web of urban problems, the more one is struck with the central importance of the typical pattern of residential clustering by income. Since the separation of slums from nice neighborhoods is a very old urban form (although far from universal in either time or space), it is the scale of the separation which is at issue. As the distance between homes and neighborhoods of different socioeconomic classes has increased from a few blocks to many miles, the erosion of intergroup access and interaction has had an adverse effect on employment opportunities, formal and informal education, public safety, and, indeed, almost every facet of urban life. There is a very great impressionistic literature on the debilitating effects of tough neighborhoods, repressive slum schools and dead-end jobs.

---

[10] Ibid., p. 153.
[11] Wilbur R. Thompson, "On Urban Goals and Problems," p. 124.

What is the optimum size of a slum? We need not be afraid to ask this question so bluntly if our purpose is to arrive at that slum size which is most likely to reduce if not eliminate environments that destroy aspiration, inhibit expression, and generally degrade urban life. Perhaps slums can be too small to create the minimal clustering of one's own kind that produces a base of emotional security from which one can venture more safely and experiment more tentatively. Again, certain public services rendered especially to the poor may be performed more efficiently if the poor are clustered a little—for example, community development activity stressing political participation and leadership experience.

But surely slums are most often far too big. A slum that exhausts a grade school district puts the child about two grades behind by the end of the sixth grade, so that even if he transfers to a mixed junior high school he carries a handicap from which he probably will never fully recover. Now that our biggest city slums have grown to high school district size, chronic unemployment for many and, for some, near unemployability is almost ensured. A neighborhood, moreover, which breeds a conniving, mistrusting youth who seeks only the quick payoff and self-preservation will hardly prepare him to be a disciplined laboratory technician in a cooperative scientific venture, or for other "jobs with a future."

Besides, from whom will he hear of these new fields? Which neighbor can provide him with the informal job contacts and "pull" that provide the entering wedge into the better job markets? The slum youth finds, moreover, few nearby part-time jobs which he may bump into on a chance stroll and to which he could easily and cheaply commute. Few in absolute number, for what neighbor can afford to have his grass cut, or even has grass? Fewer still in relative measure, for he must compete with desperate adults for the few jobs that do exist nearby.

A national television audience was treated to the incredible spectacle of the controlled demolition of almost one half of the housing units of the massive Pruitt Igoe housing project in St. Louis. It was too big, too crowded—a jungle. Wholesale destruction of very scarce, relatively new low-income housing units was thought not too great a price to pay to shrink a much too big ghetto.

Perhaps no challenge confronting urban public managers is as grave or as difficult as that of rearranging the residential form of the large metropolitan area to regain some reasonable momentum toward the goal of equal opportunity. One strategy would be to retrace our steps: attract some of the affluent back into the central city and move some of the poor to the fringe. A promising set of tactics to achieve this is not so clear. We might, for example, experiment with renewing public facilities—social overhead —in our core areas. Better public schools, parks, and libraries—not just better than before but better than those existing in suburbia—might induce the return of those families that place the least premium on cultural homogeneity and are least afraid of strangers. If we are to use taxpayers' money to subsidize core area renewal, a better case can be made for buying the pioneering of hardier souls by offering superior public services to all core area residents than for subsidizing luxury apartments (via the writedown of land values). Those who are most adverse to living near low-income families should be made aware of the need to provide some cross-cultural contacts and should at least be willing to support extra rewards in the form of extra-high-quality public services for those less disinclined than they to take on the serious responsibility of serving as leaders and models. To be blunt: the timid should at least be willing to hire mercenaries to take the risks of social innovation.

New towns hold some potential for creating mixed-income communities, especially if the integrated planning of house and community could produce a new living arrangement so attractive (or at least so fashionable) that socioeconomic heterogeneity is accepted as a price worth paying for a superior environment. If, then, the state or its agent—a newly created metropolitan housing authority, perhaps—were to approve large-tract new towns only if they embraced a very wide range of housing values, we might make considerable progress toward socioeconomic reintegration within a few decades.

The tactics of establishing and maintaining balanced communities would need to be quite sophisticated. Since we have not learned how to build new houses priced within reach of the low-income family, do we resort to public housing or rent subsidies to house the poor? Or should we be content to begin with a slightly truncated range of high to low middle income housing and fill out the income spectrum in time as the houses age and filter down to lower income families? Such a strategy would have the virtue of being more acceptable during the critical early stages and provide a more grateful transition to an all-inclusive population. The new towns would have to be built in stages, so that new housing would be added at all times to ensure the retention of the more affluent. In addition, continual construction and demolition—a widespread age distribution of housing—ensures that the community will not be left with all old housing —massive blight— at some future time. In any event, the objective of creating socioeconomic heterogeneity at some meaningful level, such as the high school district level, is certainly not new and untried nor radical. If anything, such a program may be a bit romantic—a call to return to turn-of-the-century, small-town America.

Houses are a most durable good, so that even if hardened attitudes about socioeconomic mixing of residences could be softened overnight it would take years to attain integrated neighborhood schools. As a transitional device, we are experimenting with busing of students to schools in neighborhoods culturally different from their own. Too much should not be expected of this tactic, for our big-city ghettoes have grown so large that very long hauls are necessary to go much beyond token mixing at the margins. Also, the low-income nonwhite school population has already attained majority status in many central cities, so that student exchanges between municipalities would be required to achieve significant mixing, a far more difficult objective. And our core area ghettoes are still growing in size.

Still, even if busing is only a palliative in itself it is a beginning, and a good experience in the few mixed schools that do evolve would serve to reduce unfounded fears of the unknown and soften resistance to the basic land reforms discussed above (e.g., income-balanced new towns). Besides, if segregated housing no longer ensures segregated schools, one of the bases for resisting socioeconomic mixing is eliminated. And if we could desegregate housing we would not need to bus school children to mix. Busing, by removing one major objective of segregation, becomes a means to the end of achieving integrated neighborhood schools.

Another spatial strategy designed to diversify student bodies is the creation of very large educational parks, which would draw students from school districts so large that no single socioeconomic group would be large enough to fill so extensive an area. Because we seek to promote not only *more equal* educational opportunity but also *greater* opportunity for all, we might establish superior, specialized high schools that would draw from the whole metropolitan area, one emphasizing natural science, another social science, a third humanities, a fourth vocational education. Granting a tendency toward segregation in occupational orientaiton that reflects cultural background, as upper class youths choose science, and lower class ones choose vocational education, more than proportionately, the prospect still remains that such cultural patterning would be less sharp than the residential patterning on which base we now segregate.[12] Moreover, the natural science high school could run the gamut from advanced physics to routine laboratory technique and achieve some cross-cultural contact in laboratories, music and drama classes, the gymnasium, and extracurricular activities at the very minimum. The inducement to suffer longer bus rides to school would be the simple but powerful fact that these schools would provide better preparation for college than do the comprehensive high schools with which they would compete. This is not trivial in a time for growing competition to gain entrance to favored colleges.

10.   *Rationalizing the local public economy in space*

In the minds of many, original sin in urban affairs goes by the name "political fragmentation." The presumption most often conveyed is that the

---

[12] This would be a different twist to an old idea. The Bronx High School of Science draws students from a very wide area and was, in fact, changed from a comprehensive to a specialized high school to prevent its becoming dominated by a single ethnic group in the school district.

case for regionwide political consolidation is so obvious and overpowering that only extreme apathy or vested interest or plain cussedness could explain the persistence of political fragmentation. Because any reasonably full treatment of the local public economy would require much more space than we can devote to that subject here, this section will be built around a single theme: the relative merits of many small or one large local government in the large metropolitan area, or rationalizing the local public economy in space.

The general case for political consolidation in the metropolitan area embraces at least three major dimensions: (1) a more efficient provision of public services, (2) a more equitable sharing and financing of those services, and (3) a more creative and responsive formulation of public policy. Let us take up each of the three in turn.

Efficiency in the provision of public services

A metropolitan area is substantially a single *economic* entity: the primary labor market, a unified transportation surface, and a closely interrelated set of housing submarkets (if not literally an indivisible housing market). When this close-knit economic entity is broken up into many separate and largely autonomous local *public economies* (or local public service segments), two distinct inefficiencies tend to arise. First, the several independent political subdivisions duplicate each other's too-small, high-cost facilities, instead of jointly supporting a high-volume, low-unit-cost, regionwide facility. The sharp contrast in scale (and efficiency) between the typically large, regionwide, *private* gas or electric utility and the many small *public* water, sewer, and bus systems is all too obvious and is damaging to the reputation of the public sector.

Second, the efficiency of the local public sector is further threatened by the reduction of *coverage* that comes with political fragmentation, regardless of the absolute scale or total volume of operations. Large autonomous municipalities may have enough buses or police cars to be efficient, but if these vehicles do not have access to and serve the full reaches of the urban region, the cost and quality of the operation is impaired. Transportation and protection attain high quality more out of comprehensiveness than out of sheer volume or scale of operations.

In sum, duplication of local public facilities and services prevents the achievement of internal economies of scale, and atonomous municipalities complicate and inhibit the spatial coordination needed to lower the cost or raise the quality of public services in contiguous service units that share areawide flows of vehicles, water, and wastes that crisscross their common and largely arbitrary boundaries.

Why, then, has the political consolidation of our politically fragmented metropolitan areas been so slow in coming? The answer lies, in part, in both ineffectual mass communication and the natural (or at least familiar) sluggishness of social change. But beyond this, many close and articulate observers of city life have risen of late to argue the case *for* political fragmentation—to argue against regionwide political consolidation. Let us begin with the newest line of defense of political fragmentation—namely, that small local government need not come at the expense of technical efficiency in local public services.

The (fragile) virtue of competition in local public services

Some political scientists have recently come up with a sophisticated new defense of political fragmentation: internal economies of scale can be achieved *externally* by small municipalities. Water supply and sewage disposal, two public services for which substantial scale economies have been reasonably well established, can be purchased on long-term contract from large, efficient outside suppliers, such as the central city, the county, or private enterprise. Or many small municipalities might, through negotiation, jointly finance and operate an efficient-size plant. The new rationalization of the very small public economy goes beyond *potential* efficiency to argue that the presence of alternative sources of supply—a county incinerator, a privately owned dump, and the municipality's own devices—will *ensure* that the low costs of volume operations will be passed on to the small municipal buyers through competition.[13]

Economists might be excused for approaching this argument with caution; significant internal economies of scale are more substitutive for than complementary to competition. If the political subdivisions are many and small and if unit costs for some given public service fall only up to, say, one half or one third of the full metropolitan area market, then efficiency may be achieved short of areawide monopoly by the presence of two or three suppliers. But those who would link political fragmentation with productive efficiency are faced with *duopoly or oligopoly,* not competition. Product prices administered by two or three firms are usually quite like monopoly prices. But in all fairness, the big three may well compete in extra service or innovativeness.

But probably more important, the spatial dimension of efficiency in local pubic services, briefly mentioned above, has been glossed over by those who would rationalize political fragmentation. Many local public services resemble public utility services in that distance or area coverage is a factor in cost. Water supply and sewage disposal, for example, have high transportation costs so that a given output costs less if rendered near and/or over a contiguous area and more if the customers are scattered afar. If,

---

[13] See, for example, Vincent Ostrum, Charles M. Tiebout, and Robert Warren, "The Organization of Government in Metropolitan Areas: A Theoretical Inquiry," *The American Political Science Review,* December 1961; and Robert Warren, "A Municipal Services Market Model of Metropolitan Organization," *The Journal of the American Institute of Planning,* August 1964.

then, contiguity is critical, we are reduced to exclusive jurisdictions and spatial monopoly, even if internal economies of scale of production are limited. What do we gain from the *coexistence* of contiguous monopolies? And who will regulate the large quasi-monopolistic supplier that lies outside the municipal buyer's corporate limits? Would local autonomy—home rule—be served by creating another state regulatory body?

Is it merely a matter of taste?

We must take care not to overdo the criterion of technical efficiency—minimizing the unit cost of producing a standardized product. Perhaps allocative efficiency is more relevant—producing the best combinaton of public services for a heterogeneous population with very different tastes and income. In virtually every large metropolitan area, a wide variety of living arrangements is possible. One may choose the industrial enclave with almost indecently luxurious public services provided at low tax rates, courtesy of the local industrial taxpayers. The price to be paid there is reckoned in dirt, noise, and pollution, and for those who arrive after the factories, in higher land prices (part of the low tax rates having been capitalized and taken in capital gains by the early landowners).

Or one may select a low-density suburb of oversize lots and undersize public services, with fresh air dispelling in part the odors emanating from drainage ditches fouled by septic tanks. Again, urbane young adults and older empty-nest households may choose the exciting variety of the central city, within easy access of offices, stores, theaters, museums, skid-row derelicts, drug addicts, and muggers. Differentiation of environment, founded basically on differences in *private* capital and neighborhood life styles, is enhanced by adding on variations in *public* services.

The analogy between differentiated products in the marketplace and differentiated political subdivisions suggests the applicability of the concept of monopolistic competition to the large metropolitan area. Charles M. Tiebout was the first to apply, in a formal way, the theory of monopolistic competition to the politically fragmented large metropolitan area. In a highly imaginative, and to his critics heroic, attempt to rationalize political fragmentation, Tiebout saw the consumer-voter

picking that community which best satisfies his preference pattern for public goods. . . . The greater the number of communities and the greater the variety among them, the closer the consumer will come to fully realizing his preference position. . . . Moving or failing to move replaces the usual market test of willingness to buy a good and reveals the consumer-voter's demand for public goods. . . . Such studies as have been undertaken seem to indicate a surprising awareness of differing revenue and expenditure patterns. The general disdain with which proposals to integrate municipalities are met seems to reflect, in part, the fear that local revenue-expenditure patterns will be lost as communities are merged into a metropolitan area.[14]

---

[14] Charles M. Tiebout, "A Pure Theory of Local Expenditures," *The Journal of Political Economy*, October 1956, pp. 418, 420, 423.

Can we sort out those public services that are highly standardized and exhibit substantial economies of scale and consolidate them at the regional level, and still decentralize the high-style services to retain responsive small government?

Compare sewage disposal and storm drainage systems with neighborhood playgrounds. In sewage and drainage, internal economies of scale (through consolidation) are considerable, especially for those communities far from the river or other place of final disposal. But external *dis*economies of *small* scale are even more critical; one community's sewage can pollute another community and one's storm runoff can flood basements in another. With both efficiency and equity heavily favoring consolidation of sewage and drainage systems at the regional level, nuances of taste are trivial forces pulling toward localism. Sewage and drainage systems do not offer much latitude for distinctive personal expression, through community differentiation.

Neighborhood playgrounds fall at the other end of the spectrum—trivial economies of scale with substantial taste differences. Additional swings, tennis courts, and baseball diamonds are added at nearly constant unit costs. If anything, larger tracts of land are harder to locate in urbanized areas and will tend to come at higher prices per acre than smaller tracts. Finally, a modest element of product differentiation is evident in playgrounds. In densely populated central city neighborhoods, playgrounds would normally have swings and sandboxes in profusion, and these playgrounds would normally be both smaller and more frequent. Conversely, in suburban areas where private swingsets and sandboxes fit easily in large backyards and mobility is greater, fewer but larger areas capable of supporting football and kite-flying might be preferred.

Moreover, the playground is an extension of the home and school and reflects community values. Community recreation programs might stress fencing, model airplane building, or basketball, depending on local values, reflecting different educational and income levels. While differentiated recreational programs *could* come from a high central office, variation would more surely come out of local autonomy. Besides, the decentralization of neighborhood playground administration presents one of the all-too-scarce opportunities to achieve local government and fuller political participation with little if any sacrifice in efficiency.

Much more important than the latitude within which local public services can vary to produce choice is the actual variation and its impact on equality of opportunity. To repeat from *A Preface to Urban Economics:*

> But differentiating public services between the various political subdivisions of a large metropolitan area has some very subtle and pervasive social ramifications. Many local public services are critical to creating an environment of equal opportunity for the next generation (e.g., education, libraries, museums, recreation) and should perhaps not be allowed to vary too greatly because of differences in the education,

income or taste patterns of the parents. The invariable rejoinder to this position is that the general social welfare requires only that some basic minimum level of public services be provided to all. But the meaning of a "basic minimum" education as preparation for a life-and-death contest for relative position in the labor market is a very slippery concept. And how does this square with the professional judgment that slum area schools should be spending much more per student to give their students even a fighting chance in competition with the youth of suburbia? Critical social goals, such as equal opportunity, become expressed in urban public services, so we must take great care that some easy market analogies between the private and public sectors are as socially responsible as they are analytically intriguing. (pp. 282–83)

Equity in the financing of public services

As much as we have to gain in increased efficiency, the case for political consolidation in our metropolitan areas generally rests even more on equity. The very great differentials among the constituent political subdivisions in fiscal capacity (e.g., taxable real estate) on the one hand and public service needs (e.g., public assistance expenditures) on the other hand is well documented in the literature on urban problems and obvious on even casual observation. This now-classic dilemma of the divorce of means and needs arises quite naturally out of the centrifugal growth of urban areas, which implants the higher income families in the newer dwellings on the urban fringe, confining the core area to the older housing and, in general, the poorer households.

The central city's fiscal position is, moreover, usually further weakened by the fact that its old housing still has some useful life left. With little or no vacant land in hand and with demolition adding very little to the scarce supply of central city building sites, few new houses are erected to begin the process of blending some new dwellings with the old. If, moreover, there is substantial in-migration of the poor into the core area, old housing is kept in service longer than usual, and rebuilding is further slowed in the core area.

Finally, resistance in the suburbs to the construction of low-income (public) housing concentrates this kind of building in the central city, absorbing most of the small amount of land that is vacated.

Renewal and renovation of nonresidential property, especially in the central business district, may provide a partial offset to the aging and decline of the central city property base. But retail trade has always decentralized with urban growth, following the more affluent householders outward, and manufacturing has suburbanized at a remarkably rapid rate over the past two decades. With reverse commuting from the central city to the new suburban shopping centers and factories coming near to balancing the inward movement, the argument that the suburbanites as shoppers and workers create a commercial and industrial tax base in the central city is losing its force as the suburbs reap these land value gains, too. Besides, much of the recent central city construction is nontaxable—museums, universities, government offices.

Politics and policy

With all due respect for the great need to achieve efficiency in the production of urban public services and equity in their financing, surely the most serious ramification of political fragmentation in the large metropolitan area is that local government has lost the capacity to govern. Fragmented local government is becoming increasingly unable to resolve vital issues that divide various elements of the population: discrimination in housing and employment; unequal opportunity in education; new transportation facilities that distribute the benefits and costs so unevenly by income, age group, and place of residence. In planning and policymaking, difference of interest and opinion is inevitable, and confrontation is healthy, especially within a framework that can arrange the necessary trade-offs and compromises. Clearly, local government can mediate effectively only if it embraces the diverse parties to the issue.

But population mix differs so greatly between the central city and the suburbs, and among the many and diverse suburbs, in their proportions of rich and poor, old and young, white and black, educated and uneducated, that no effective political unit short of the state spans a substantial portion of the cross-section of population—none has jurisdiction over the issues of the day. Because the responsibility of government to mediate and adjudicate is clear and pressing, an act, explicit or implicit, to evade assuming this responsibility at one level of government, becomes, in effect, an implicit decision to delegate the power to act to some other (higher) level of government.

The state has the breadth of jurisdiction to bridge the heterogeneous population and join the issue, but the states have been unwilling or unable to pick up those functions in which local government has become delinquent. We have, in fact, seen a steady transfer of local responsibility over health, education, and welfare activities past the states to the federal government. The steady growth of federal poverty, manpower, and housing programs has been due only in part to the superior fiscal resources of the federal government; the division and debilitation of local government in politically fragmented areas is also a root cause.

To the degree that the nation moves to a system of tax-sharing in which the federal government rebates to the states and localities part of the swelling income tax receipts (the Heller-Pechman Plan), the fiscal crisis of the cities will be turned. Surely, though, it will be some time, if ever, before federal transfers become the dominant source of local public revenue, and a need will still remain for a structure of local government which brings together the contestants in matters of public policy, and one which can draw on the leadership talents of the full region. Because federal grants-in-aid to localities are almost certain to carry more strings where local government is divided and weak, the most basic and profound implication of political fragmentation in the metropolitan area is that it has quietly brought about a revolutionary change in the division of powers, and come near to converting local government from a reality to an illusion.

The principal current hope for the restoration of the vitality of local government rests on a social innovation: two-level government. Transportation, water, and sewer systems, and environmental protection would be centralized in some form of regional government, while some aspects of school policy and operation and some land-use planning would be decentralized to the community level. But the motivation to rationalize local government may well have to be prompted and reinforced with tied grants. There are many close students of government who will not buy massive tax-sharing until it carries the strings necessary to reform our federal system [15]—so that we can come to deal effectively with the economic base of urban problems.

---

[15] *Problems and Response in the Federalism Crisis,* a seminar sponsored by the John C. Lincoln Institute and the National Academy of Public Administration, Hartford, Conn., June 13-15, 1971 (Washington, D.C.: The National Academy of Public Administration, 1971), especially pp. 96-98.

2

Poverty in an Affluent Society

MARY JEAN BOWMAN
Professor of Economics and Education
University of Chicago

The association of poverty with progress is the great enigma of our times. It is the central fact from which spring industrial, social and political difficulties that perplex the world, and with which statesmanship and philanthropy and education grapple in vain.[1]

Poverty and education have become two of the most widely discussed problems over the past decade. Neither is new to the literature of economics, but both have enjoyed something of a renaissance in economics, both theoretical and applied. Paradoxically, this renewal has occurred in a situation in which poverty, which is presumably bad, is less than ever before, and education, which is presumably good, has grown to heretofore unimagined dimensions. In part, we may trace the contemporary high tide of concern with both poverty and education to the very affluence of our society, in part to the disruptive innovative energy that has brought us into that affluence. The principal foci of work among economists mainly concerned with poverty and those mainly concerned with education have been quite different, however.

During the 1960s, the emphasis in most economic discussions of education was on its value as an investment, its contributions to national income, and the seemingly limitless demands for highly qualified persons to man a progressive economy and raise the GNP still further. The considerable attention directed to study of relationships between schooling and

---

[1] Henry George, *Progress and Poverty,* 1879, chap. 1.

subsequent earnings has been linked into the human investment models in most cases. Even when economists interested mainly in economics of education have directed their attention to the so-called dropout problem or to head start or MDTA programs for unemployed workers, the tendency has been to cast the analysis in a productivity, benefit-cost framework. Efficiency is the criterion. Only in the last two or three years has "equity" or the distribution of opportunity come to occupy a major place in economic writings on education, analysis of racial discrimination aside.

By contrast, from the start the contemporary concern with poverty has been, in a much more direct and imminent way, primarily a concern with social justice. It is the more so because of both the political-social environment and the general affluence of the 1960's. I find very little evidence that today's minimum-family-budget estimators are consciously hanging their poverty line estimates on notions of the income needed to maintain working efficiency in the labor force, even though Marshall and others of earlier generations had propounded such concepts, and despite contemporary interest in not only education but also health as an investment. Instead, GNP comes into discussions of poverty primarily in terms of how much poverty we can afford to eliminate by transfer payments or, more importantly, how far the process of growth in GNP (in contrast to its level) may provide a labor market situation that minimizes poverty and thins out its discriminatory props.

Turning from economics to the politicosocial environment, it is no accident that many people today believe most of the poor, especially the urban poor, to be black, even though most are, in fact, white. Neither is it an accident that articulate grass roots leadership in the war on poverty and the political drive behind it has come preponderantly out of the civil rights movement and an increasingly aware and hence angry black America. This gives a special thrust to the meaning of poverty in our day and its identification by many as a broader deprivation that is at once social and economic, as much concerned with human dignity as with full stomachs. Probably what is most distinctive about the new poverty is not that it is "invisible," as Michael Harrington would have us believe; such invisibility is a long-time thing. The veil covering it has been lifted only when men who had known better days have been caught up in large numbers in the flaying fears of unemployment and inadequacy, as in the 1930s. Rather, what is distinctive about the new poverty is the voices through whom it speaks, and the distances they carry, both out of the past and, let us hope, into the future. It is only when we perceive today's poverty in this perspective that we can begin to sort it out, to encompass its variants, and to organize our thinking concerning this plural phenomenon—its incidence, its causes, and at least some of the implications for public policies.

The present chapter attempts a survey of poverty in the affluent society. It is an economist's chapter, and poverty is defined as inadequate command over economic resources; I shall not explore the endless morass of all the other poverties and deprivations men may suffer almost regardless of their economic means. But this does not get around the question of what is inadequate economically, nor does it imply that the most important roots of poverty or its most important effects on people can all be conceived in economic terms.

This chapter is divided into four main sections. (1) The first of these discusses meanings and measures of poverty. (2) The second is concerned with who is poor and why. It summarizes characteristics of families and individuals categorized as poor by current measures, and then turns this around to look at the incidence of poverty among certain categories of the population, asking who is most likely to be poor. A few more fundamental questions are raised and evidence is examined concerning factors determining the extent and incidence of poverty or of its elimination. (3) The third section of the chapter discusses some of the problems and issues that have arisen in connection with income transfers as the most direct attack on poverty. (4) Finally, attention is directed to some of the policies that attack poverty problems primarily through the labor market, whether on the demand or the human resource qualification and supply side.

I. The meaning and measurement of poverty

Poverty, like wealth, is unquestionably a matter of degree. Indeed, we might define poverty as distance along a continuum toward zero purchasing power, wealth as distance along that same continuum but in the opposite direction. It will help to set poverty measures in perspective if we look first at a straightforward picture of shifting income distributions without benefit of poverty lines or poverty definitions of any kind.

Shifts in family income distributions since 1948

Distributions of income among U.S. families are shown in Figure 2–1 for the years 1948, 1955, 1962, and 1966. All the distributions are in 1962 dollars, which eliminates inflation effects, and individuals living alone are excluded. However, the population covered remains diverse in all other respects—age, sex, race, size of family, urban or rural residence, and so on. Incomes are plotted in logarithmic form (the horizontal scale), while the vertical axis, which measures proportions with incomes below any designated income level, is ruled on a probit scale. On such a chart, a lognormal distribution would give a straight line, and the steeper the line, the more egalitarian the distribution.[2] If a particular family income level were

---

[2] Note that if all families had an income of, say, $4,000, this would appear as a vertical line at exactly $4,000. For a discussion and graphic presentation of various inequality measures and income structures, see my "A Graphical Analysis of Personal Income Distribution in the United States," *American Economic Review,* 35, 4 (September 1945) pp. 607–28. Reprinted in American Economic Association, *Readings in the Theory of Income Distribution,* Philadelphia, Blakiston, 1946.

established as a minimum, regardless of family characteristics, and if that minimum were ensured year in, year out by transfer payments, the curves would become vertical at the minimum income point. Such minima are illustrated at four distinct levels by the vertical lines pointing upward and bracketed as "Fuchs criteria" (to be explained later). If we follow a horizontal line across the chart at any given percentile level, it is possible to read off just how incomes of families at that position in the distribution in 1948 compare with incomes of families in the same relative position in the later years. Also, because the income scale is logarithmic it is possible to judge whether there has been any marked difference in the rate of increase of incomes at the median, as against rates of increase for those at lower or at higher relative positions. It is immediately obvious from the figure that there has been general movement up the income scale in all segments of the distribution, and also that the shapes of the distributions have remained very much the same. Rates of increase at the lowest quintile, for example, are very like those at the median.[3]

Poverty and inequality at the bottom

When the poor are taken by definition to be the lowest 10th or the lowest 5th, or the lowest 3d, we will, of course, arrive at the not very startling conclusion, "the poor we will always have with us." In fact, we could add that we will always have them in the same proportion. This is the arithmetic absurdity to which a colleague of mine referred when he remarked, "some people think there shouldn't be a lowest quartile." Evidently, it can be useful to consider what has changed in the composition and levels of the lowest x percent on an income distribution, but to talk of getting rid of the lowest 10 percent as a generalized goal of a war on poverty is sheer semantic nonsense. This does not mean, however, that poverty lines must, or even can, be absolute. Nor does it condemn outright the use of explicitly relative poverty measures. Thus far, I have seen such proposals in two main variants.

The first, which in my judgment has relatively little to be said for it as a tool in the poverty kit, focuses on the proportion of aggregate income accruing to the lowest fifth (it could be some other fraction) of the population. This is the Lorenz curve approach. Poverty is reduced, according to this view, only when the lowest fifth secure a rising proportion of aggregate income. By this criterion, there has been little or no change in the United States over the past two decades, but this says nothing about how poor is poor, either absolutely or relative to median levels of living. Indeed, by this

---

[3] Data that break down the distributions of income in the lower tail by family type and farm or nonfarm residence are available for 1965, and have been used to estimate components of the poverty gap, discussed later. But even such data are subject to the limitations (among others) that they provide inadequate clues with respect to the proportion of poor people who are only temporarily in that state, or to the extent to which those counted "poor" by annual money income measures have assets on which they can draw (including ownership of their homes).

application of Lorenz measures the indicated amount of poverty would be reduced merely by lopping off the top incomes without changing incomes around and below the median at all.

The second variant of overtly egalitarian relativism in assessing poverty and progress toward its removal is what I shall designate as the Fuchs-point.[4] Fuchs specifies what amounts to a moving poverty line at 50 percent of median incomes. For all years from 1947 through 1960, Fuchs found a fifth of U.S. families to have incomes less than half the median; variation in this proportion was only from 19.0 to 20.7 percent. I obtained similar estimates from like data for the years following 1960. (With close inspection, this can be read off Figure 2–1.)

Figure 2–1. Distributions of incomes of families in the United States; 1948, 1955, 1962, 1966

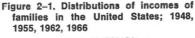

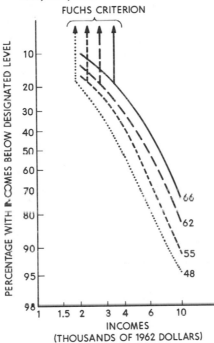

The Fuchs-point approach differs from the Lorenz-based measures in two important respects. (1) Whereas the Lorenz-type assessments take the

---

4 See Victor R. Fuchs, "Toward a Theory of Poverty," in *The Concept of Poverty,* a report of the Task Force on Economic Growth and Opportunity, Chamber of Commerce of the United States, Washington, D.C. 1965, pp. 69–92. A similar suggestion was made earlier by Allan M. Cartter in *The Redistribution of Income in Postwar Britain,* New Haven, Conn.; Yale University Press, 1955, pp. 77–78. Cartter has also suggested that an "ideal" distribution would limit top incomes to five times the median.

entire income distribution into account, the Fuchs-point depends on the shape of the distribution only among the lower half of the population, and focuses attention thereby on the magnitude of the gap between those who have least and the average, ordinary man.[5] This is an important characteristic of the Fuchs-point to which I will return. (2) The Fuchs-point for any given time can be used to set a specific absolute, if temporary, goal against which degrees of progress can be assessed and to which antipoverty programs might, in principle, be geared; by the same token, like any poverty line measure it can be used for analysis of the characteristics of the subpopulation that has been indicated as in poverty. Fuchs did this using the 1960 census data (referring to incomes as of 1959) with results that broadly match those obtained using the indiscriminate $3,000 per family chosen as a rough initial cutoff point by the Council of Economic Advisers.

Of more distinctive interest is Fuchs' test of the implications of his poverty measure in application within particular geographic regions or populations classified by types of residence. The upper section of Table 2–1 reproduces those findings. One of the most striking results is that areas or residence locations characterized by the most decided negative skews in the lower halves of their income distributions (the largest percentages below the Fuchs-point determined by their own median levels) had also the largest proportions below the Fuchs-point as derived from the national median. This applies to rural nonfarm populations across the country, to residents in all locations in the South, and—most dramatically —to the rural farm populations of the United States as a whole.

There is no a priori reason why proportions below the internal (within region or within rural-urban residence category) Fuchs-point should be associated with proportions of these subpopulations below the externally derived (national) Fuchs-point. This comes about only because the drag of the poor minorities (of any race) behind the average man is greatest in areas and populations within which the average man is relatively unfavored as compared with the average (median) in other areas or residence groups. In relative terms, the socioeconomic inheritance of the South, urban and rural, overshadowed the problem of relative poverty in urban ghettos elsewhere.[6] But if we look at the actual 1959 numbers, the urban poor were somewhat more numerous than the rural (4,855,000 against 4,214,000) even taken against the national Fuchs-point. They were, of course, much the more numerous (almost twice as many as the rural poor) when taken against their own Fuchs-point of $3,084.

---

[5] D. J. Aigner and A. J. Heins have contributed some fresh thinking to the literature on "inequality" in "A Social Welfare View of the Measurement of Income Equality," which considers these distances at the bottom as well as other aspects of the income distribution structure. *Review of Income and Wealth*, Series 13, Number 1 (March 1967), pp. 12–25.

[6] The development effects of the long lower tail in southern income distributions, as in other features of the southern economy, is discussed in my "Human Inequalities and Southern Underdvelopment," in James W. McKie, ed., *Education and the Southern Economy*, Chapel Hill, N.C., published as a supplement to the *Southern Economic Journal*, July 1965.

Table 2–1. Fuchs-point poverty by region and location in the United States, 1959 data and 1969 estimates

Location	Median Income	No. of Families (000)	Number of Families with Income		Percentage of Families with Income	
			Less than ½ Own Median (000)*	Less than ½ U.S. Median (000)	Less than ½ Own Median *	Less than ½ U.S. Median
1959 Data:						
U.S.	$ 5,660	45,128	9,011	9,011	20.0	20.0
Northeast	6,191	11,474	1,721	1,503	15.0	13.1
North Central	5,892	13,119	2,401	2,283	18.3	17.4
South	4,465	13,512	3,256	4,202	24.1	31.1
West	6,348	7,024	1,194	1,018	17.0	14.5
Urban	6,166	31,940	5,462	4,855	17.1	15.2
Rural nonfarm	4,750	9,856	2,208	2,681	22.4	27.2
Rural farm	3,228	3,332	856	1,533	25.7	46.0
Estimate for 1969:						
U.S.	9,433	51,239	9,755	9,755	19.0	19.0
North and West	10,020	35,467	5,958	5,497	16.8	15.5
South	8,104	15,772	3,233	4,258	20.5	27.0

* "Own median" is median within the particular regional or rural-urban residence category.

Sources: 1959 Victor R. Fuchs, "Toward a Theory of Poverty," in Chamber of Commerce of the United States, *The Concept of Poverty*, Washington, D.C., 1965, p. 77. 1969 Estimates by graphical analysis based on data from *Current Population Reports*, p. 23, No. 37, June 24, 1971, Special Studies: Social and Economic Characteristics of the Population in Metropolitan and Nonmetropolitan Areas.

Data that would permit a full comparison of 1969 with 1959 distributions as analyzed in Table 2–1 are not yet available. However, in the lower section of that table I have entered estimates for 1969 for the United States, the South and the non-South. Overall the picture is much as in 1959, but there is a significant drop in the proportions of southern families below either the national or their own Fuchs point. This clearly reflects both developments within the South and the migration of poverty from the South to other parts of the nation; that migration has been both white and black.

Earlier, I stressed the importance of the fact that the Fuchs approach focuses on the spread or gap between those at the bottom of the income scale and those in the middle. It asks how large a fraction of the population has half or less the income of the median family. To be in poverty by the Fuchs measure is to be more than that relative distance away from median levels of attainment. This lends itself to interpretation in terms of communication gaps, and the gulf over which those from disadvantaged backgrounds must travel to join the mainstream. Looking at poverty in this way can be very illuminating, from both political-social and economic points of view. It is as valid an approach as any other, provided—and this must be a universal proviso for any method or measure—we remember just what we have done and, hence, for what purposes the measure is or is not appropriate. Because this is an overtly relative measure, its absolute value is also constantly moving as median income moves, and it is quite capable of moving down as well as up. Indeed, it must do so in any major recession. But by the same token, it may be particularly useful in a socioeconomic analysis of what poverty means in particular segments of a society. To dwellers in urban ghettoes, the urban Fuchs-point is likely to have more meaning than a nationally derived poverty line.

Needs or requirements and the meaning of poverty

Whereas those who start from an explicitly relative definition of poverty come to consider needs only indirectly or implicitly if at all, most attempts to set up poverty measures have started with some attempt to identify needs or requirements. Common to all definitions of need must, of course, be provision for sheer survival as a precondition of anything else. But poverty in the United States today, visible or invisible, rarely hangs over the edge of starvation, and a poverty line concept that would be relevant in India, where per capita income is less than $100 per annum, would have little meaning in the United States. Indeed, as soon as we rise above the lowest hand-to-mouth level of existence the identification of needs or requirements raises problems of two kinds: (1) the philosophical identification of purposes or ends—needs or requirements for what?—and (2) the specification of just what realization of those ends would require in command over economic resources.

On the more philosophical side, I shall confine my remarks to the noting of a few conspicuous strands in the development of the "for what" of poverty lines—excluding the extreme versions of egalitarianism as having very little to do with anything most people would regard as poverty.

First and most rudimentary has been the humane but limited view that men, like dogs, should not suffer undue physical hardship: at a minimum, a man should not persistently go hungry. This, in fact, has been all that was possible for majorities of vast populations over most of human history. But there has also been a pervasive notion, remnants of which can be found even in the United States of 1972, that somehow large groups of the poor need less and/or that by nature they will spend any additional money unwisely. Understandably, since they would not buy it voluntarily, among the services provided in kind to the "lower orders" of 18th- and 19th century Britain was moral instruction. Beyond that, for the poor (if not for the rich) the "goods things in life" were free as the sky. And American Negroes were supposed to be capable of both filling their stomachs more cheaply and enjoying life on less.[7]

Branching out from this rudimentary humanism we may trace two main themes that have accompanied economic progress. One of these focuses on man as an end, but takes an ever wider view of what is relevant in the human condition; we might call it expanded humanism. From the bare minimum of elemental physical necessities, it extends to the mental and psychological, to human dignity, and finally to opportunity for all men to participate in the mainstreams of the ongoing national life. The last of these is politically manifest today In the poverty marches and in the struggles over community action and the "maximum feasible participation" components of OEO programs. But this more dramatic display is not the most important element in the socioeconomic participation theme. Backstage, poverty prevention and cure are seen increasingly as requiring, among other things, programs that will bridge cultural and communication gulfs. It is around these gulfs and these bridges that the arguments, the insights, and the pernicious fallacies of the culture of poverty debates are entwined. But the broader the perceptions of what constitutes relevant deprivation, and of what are the human conditions an antipoverty program would aim at, the more ambiguous the idea of escape from poverty becomes, and the more elusive is the link between the "for what" of the escape from poverty and the specification of economic levels that signal such escape.

The other branching-out from rudimentary humanism focuses on man as a productive resource, rather than treating men and their condition as

---

[7] It might be added that the idealizing of modest living was not confined to proscriptions for the poor alone. There was a theme running through popular songs of the late 19th century, recurring periodically in the first 40 years of the 20th, that bears this out. In some respects, the poor may be less poor today, but urban poverty gives less opportunity for escape into "the best things in life are free."

the end values. Most economists will hasten to add, and I will agree, that we are interested in human resource effectiveness for the sake, ultimately, of man himself. But there is still a distinct difference between concentrating on the interest of those who are currently poor, to enable them to lead more satisfying lives, and concentrating on what they must have in command over economic resources if they and their children are to be efficient contributors to the national product. The two views—that of expanded humanism and that of productive efficiency—converge, of course. They converge indirectly and in the longer run because of the circular causal linkage: having enough to maintain (or increase) one's productive efficiency and that of his children will provide the basis for earning the income that provides the economic requirements for realization of the more humanistically defined ends. Also, the humanist and efficiency views converge partially but more directly because human dignity is normally interpreted to require access to a "decent job at decent pay"—though, in practice, this is one of the most serious points of conflict between broader economic efficiency and humanistic criteria in the development of antipoverty policies.

That the establishment of a poverty line must always be relative to a particular societal context is clear enough even when the view taken is more of the efficiency than of the expanded humanist type. Nowhere have I seen this more clearly stated than in two excerpts, now half a century old, that were brought to my attention by Donald C. Taylor.[8] Writing in 1921, Gillin put it succinctly.[9]

Shall we not therefore define poverty as that condition of living in which a person, either because of inadequate income or unwise expenditure, cannot maintain a standard of living high enough to provide for the physical and mental efficiency of himself and to enable him and his natural dependents to function usefully according to the standards of the society of which he is a member.

It is interesting, incidentally, that Gillin included the phrase "or unwise expenditure" in this statement. Setting aside his connotations, it could carry some interesting meanings today. For example, limited schooling and experience, which means a poverty of human capital that escapes our direct income and wealth measurements, is the main reason that, all too often, the poor pay more. As will be noted shortly, unwise expenditure is allowed for implicitly in the way nutritional-adequacy bases have been used to derive broader based modern poverty lines.

---

[8] In an unpublished paper, "Some Economic Views about Poverty at the Turn of the Century," University of Chicago, Investment in Human Capital Series, Paper 64:02; June 22, 1964. There are several recent collections of citations from earlier treatments of poverty, usually published as part of a wider range of selections from poverty literature in the fashion of the 1960s. For a more intensive, scholarly study of this history of perceptions of poverty and of public policies and programs related thereto, the outstanding work is Samuel Mencher, *Poor Law to Poverty Program*, Pittsburgh, University of Pittsburgh Press, 1967. See also Gaston V. Rimlinger, *Welfare Policy and Industrialization in Europe, America and Russia*, New York, John Wiley and Sons Inc., 1971.

[9] J. L. Gillin, *Poverty and Dependency*, New York, Century Company, 1921, p. 23.

Alfred Marshall distinguished between a level of living that would merely sustain life (which he did not attempt to specify) and a more meaningful poverty line for his times, a minimum efficiency standard.[10]

... there is for each rank of industry, at any time and place a more or less clearly defined income which is necessary for merely sustaining its members; while there is another and larger income which is necessary for keeping it in full efficiency. ... But it will serve to give some definiteness to our ideas, if we consider here what are the necessaries for the efficiency of an ordinary agricultural or of an unskilled town laborer and his family in England in this generation. They may be said to consist of a well-drained dwelling with several rooms, warm clothing, with some changes of underclothing, pure water, a plentiful supply of cereal food, with a moderate allowance of meat and milk, and a little tea etc., some education and some recreation, and lastly, sufficient freedom for his wife from other work to enable her to perform her maternal and her household duties. If in any district unskilled labor is deprived of any of these things, its efficiency will suffer in the same way as that of a horse that is not properly tended, or a steam-engine that has an inadequate supply of coal.

Economy budgets and poverty lines

The estimation of minimal and economy budgets at various levels has a long history, both nationally and on more local levels. Among other purposes, these budgets have been put together as part of the construction of cost of living indexes and for use in the administration of welfare programs. The literature is extensive, and I have no intention of going into it here. The general basis for construction of the Social Security Administration's poverty lines, which are now being used in census publications, claims some attention, nevertheless.[11] They begin with identification of the costs of a "nutritionally adequate" diet for families of various sizes. Those are the costs at which some given percentage of families (apparently the favorite figure is 75 percent) have met specified standards of nutrition, or have reached a specified proportion of attainment of such standards. This is definitely and explicitly not the food expenditure level where nutritional standards *could* be met, which would be much lower. It allows for both ignorance in spending and a fairly high measure of preference in food tastes that are considerably less than maximally efficient as far as nutrition is concerned. Estimates are made separately for farm and for nonfarm families. Even though budget-based poverty lines are expressed in absolute terms and can be so treated for some purposes, their derivation is ultimately a relative matter; the budgets of 1962 are not those of 1935, and the poverty lines set for 1962 have been very substantially higher than those of 1935 in absolute terms. This is in addition to the fact that at any given time poverty line calculations have diverged widely. For example, accord-

---

[10] Alfred Marshall, *Principles of Economics,* New York, 1920, pp. 68–69.

[11] The methods and criteria are described by Mollie Orshansky in "Counting the Poor; Another Look at the Poverty Profile," *Social Security Bulletin,* 28, 1 (January 1965), pp. 3–29. For a critical appraisal of these criteria, see Rose D. Friedman, *Poverty, Definition and Perspective,* Washington, D.C., American Enterprise Institute for Policy Research, 1965.

ing to budget calculations carried out by Mollie Orshansky, a fifth of American families were below the poverty line in 1962. Estimates made independently by Rose Friedman and by Ruth Mack [12] came out with 10 percent below the poverty line in 1962 and in 1960, respectively. Proportions of families who were poor according to various contemporary definitions of subsistence levels or poverty lines—Ruth Mack, the Council of Economic Advisers and the Social Security Administration—are shown in Table 2–2 for the years 1935–70.

Table 2–2. Proportions of families in poverty, 1935–1970, according to poverty line definitions

Year	Contemporary Definitions (a)	1960 Mack Definitions (a)	Council of Economic Advisers: $3,000 (1959 (b)	Social Security Criterion (c)
1935	28	47	. . .	. . .
1941	17	31	. . .	. . .
1947	. . .	. . .	34	. . .
1950	13	26	33	. . .
1956	. . .	. . .	24	. . .
1960	10	10	22	18
1966	. . .	. . .	. . .	12
1970	. . .	. . .	. . .	10

Sources: (a) Herman P. Miller, "Measurements for Alternative Concepts of Poverty." Amer. Stat. Assoc., December, 1964 (b) Herman P. Miller, "Trends in the Income of Families and Persons in the U.S., 1947–1960" Technical Paper No. 8, Washington, U.S. Government Printing Office, pp. 36–44. (c) See footnotes to Table 2–3.

This table tells us less about poverty in the United States as a real phenomenon than about the wide scope for definition of what constitutes poverty at any given time and, again, the relative nature of poverty measures over time. Also, as a comparison between the first two columns of Table 2–2 illustrates, the poverty line drawn in minimum budget figures rises with rising average incomes, but not so rapidly as incomes in general go up.[13]

II. *Who is poor and why*

Who are the poor and why are they poor? Are most of them members of families whose heads are disabled or too old to work, or are large numbers

---

[12] I have seen Ruth Mack's figures only as they have been cited by Herman Miller (from her unpublished manuscript). She carried her estimates back to 1929. In using her figures, Miller urges caution because he did not reproduce the detailed analysis of their derivation or the qualifying conditions included in the original manuscript. For further comment see Herman P. Miller, "Changes in the Number and Composition of the Poor," in Margaret S. Gordon, ed., *Poverty in America,* Berkeley, Chandler Publishing Co., 1965, pp. 81–101.

[13] This pattern is as evident when we look at local variations in what is regarded as "poor" at any given time (including now) as when we look at historical sequences. As Margaret Reid has put it, furthermore, the only real poverty line in the United States behaviorally speaking is the local public assistance standard—and hence not one line but many.

of those judged to be poor members of families with male heads in the working ages? Are they disproportionately rural or urban? How far does the incidence of poverty appear to reflect racial discrimination? Are poor families and individuals clustered in tight geographic pockets, making up islands or communities of poverty set apart from other areas? Or are they widely scattered? How do they compare in educational background to the nonpoor?

These are all critical questions, whether for the understanding of what poverty is and means, for the identification of factors that determine the likelihood that a person or family will be poor, or for the development of strategies and tactics in a war on poverty. The answers will also depend, in part, on how conservatively we draw the poverty line. In general, the lower we draw that line in any given year, the lower will be the proportion of poor persons living in families with male heads in the active labor force, and the stronger will be the negative educational selectivity into poverty among the working population.

Looking at this in another way, for any given poverty line the proportions of families and individuals who are poor will be lower the lower the rate of unemployment, almost (though not quite) regardless of demographic and educational characteristics. But fuller employment will have much more effect in raising some categories of persons and families above the poverty line than others. In fact, just how far rising aggregate labor demand can raise even individuals and families with working-age heads above any given poverty line has been one of the most debated issues in writings on the economics of poverty. Before going into this matter, or to the problems of discrimination and of other disequilibrating and even perverse institutions and public programs, it will help to take our bearings with a few quantitative data concerning the demographic characteristics of the poor and of who is most likely to be poor.

Some demographic characteristics of the poor and the nonpoor

A recent publication of the U.S. Bureau of the Census enables us to compare 1970, 1966 and 1959 characteristics of families, persons, and children who fall below and above the poverty lines laid out by the Social Security Administration. These are the poverty lines as adjusted to distinguish needs by family size and by farm versus nonfarm residence. The poverty lines were adjusted for changes in price levels over the period covered, so that they have the same real-income implications in all three years. Some of the results are summarized in Table 2–3 and in Figure 2–2. The data are laid out in such a way as to facilitate taking a double view, to ask the two distinct questions: What are the characteristics of those below the Social Security Administration's poverty line, and what is the likelihood that an individual or a family with the designated characteristics will have been among those below the poverty line in the three years

Table 2–3. Summary of the incidence of poverty and the race and sex characteristics of persons and families below the poverty level, United States, 1959, 1966 and 1970

	Total Number (thousands)		Percent below Poverty Level			Percent of All Persons or Families below Poverty Level			Percent of All Persons or Families Not below Poverty Level		
	1959	1970	1959	1966	1970	1959	1966	1970	1959	1966	1970
All persons											
Total	176,479	202,534	22	15	12	100	100	100	100	100	100
White	156,869	177,429	18	12	10	72	68	69	94	92	90
Nonwhite	19,610	25,105	55	41	32	28	32	31	6	8	10
Families											
Total	45,025	51,239	18	12	10	100	100	100	100	100	100
Male Head	40,559	45,657	16	10	7						
White	37,273	41,838	13	8	6	60	54	50	88	86	85
Below age 65		36,274		6	5		36	32		76	75
Age 65 or more		5,564		20	16		18	18		10	10
Nonwhite	3,286	3,819	43	27	17	17	17	13	5	6	7
Below age 65		3,420		24	15		13	11		6	6
Age 65 or more		399		48	36		3	2		*	1
Female Head	4,493	5,582	43	35	32						
White	3,543	4,186	35	28	25	15	18	22	6	7	7
Nonwhite	950	1,396	71	60	53	8	12	15	1	1	1
Related children under 18											
Total	63,745	69,788	26	18	14	100	100	100	100	100	100
In families with male head	58,222	61,737	22	13	9	76	64	56	97	95	94
White	51,548	54,374	17	10	7	53	42	38	91	87	85
Nonwhite	6,674	7,363	58	39	24	23	22	18	6	8	9
In families with female head	5,523	8,015	73	61	54	24	35	44	3	5	6
White	3,469	4,668	67	48	45	14	16	21	2	4	5
Nonwhite	2,054	3,383	83	78	68	10	19	23	1	1	1

	Total Number (thousands)		Percent below Poverty Level			Percent of All Persons or Families below Poverty Level			Percent of All Persons or Families Not below Poverty Level		
	1959	1970	1959	1966	1970	1959	1966	1970	1959	1966	1970
Unrelated individuals											
Total	10,702	14,452	47	39	34	100	100	100	100	100	100
Male	4,216	5,441	37	28	25	31	27	29	47	43	42
White	3,424	4,473	34	26	23	23	21	22	40	37	35
Nonwhite	792	968	51	36	34	8	6	7	7	6	7
Female	6,484	9,011	54	45	39	69	73	71	53	57	58
White	5,729	8,000	52	43	36	59	62	60	49	53	55
Nonwhite	755	1,011	68	63	55	10	11	11	4	4	3

* Under 0.5 percent

Source: Compiled and computed from data provided in U.S. Bureau of the Census, Current Population Reports, Series P–60 No. 54 May 31, 1968, Tables B and C, pp. 3 and 5, and Series P23, No. 37, June 24, 1971, Tables B, E, 5 and 19. The poverty income cutoffs, adjusted to take into account such factors as family size, sex and age of family head, number of children, and farm or nonfarm residence, are specified in Current Population Reports, Series P 23, No. 28, "Revisions in Poverty Statistics, 1959 to 1968." Cutoff levels are updated every year to reflect changes in the Consumer Price Index.

studied? Even without going beyond these tables, we have evidence on several important questions.

1. How far is poverty associated with race? This one is clear enough. White persons below the poverty level are more than twice as numerous as nonwhites, but the likelihood that a nonwhite will be poor is nevertheless three times the likelihood that a white person will be among those below the poverty lines. Though the proportions of total persons in poverty dropped by 8 percent among the whites and by 23 percent among the nonwhites over the 1960s, there was no net relative gain of the nonwhites over the whites; in 1966 and in 1970 the nonwhites made up a slightly larger proportion of the total in poverty than in 1959. Interpretation of this fact is tricky, however. Given that to start with the nonwhite poor were the poorer, it would take a greater relative gain among the nonwhites to bring about the same relative rate of crossing to above the poverty line. This is one of many of the difficulties of interpretation that inhere in any artificial dichotomizing of the poor and the nonpoor. I shall come back to the question of schooling, skill, and labor market discrimination from another approach.[14]

2. How large a proportion of the poor were old, and what is the incidence of poverty among oldsters? Early estimates of proportions of the poor who were old gave very high figures, as much as a third or more, but these were based on use of poverty-line incomes that took no account of either family size or residence; those estimates were cut to less than a fifth with adjustments for family size. Over the period from 1959 to 1966, the proportion of older people among the poor seems to have changed very little. As of 1966, a fifth of the white and half of the nonwhite families with male heads over 65 years of age were below the poverty lines; together they made up a fifth of all poor families. Poverty rates in families with older male heads dropped considerably between 1966 and 1970, especially among nonwhites, but those rates still were high and in 1970 again such families accounted for a fifth of all families counted by the census as poor. By far the highest incidence of poverty among the elderly is among rural nonfarm residents.

3. How heavily does poverty bear on children? Consistently in all three years shown in Table 2–3 the proportions of children in poverty families exceeded the proportions of all persons below the poverty line, and children have constituted from 40 to 43 percent of all persons designated as below the poverty line. There has been little change in the share of children in the poverty population; the substantial reductions in proportions of fami-

---

[14] According to findings of the Current Population Survey conducted in March, 1971, the proportions of persons below the poverty line in 1970 were: Negroes, 34 percent; Mexican Americans, 24 percent, Puerto Ricans, 29 percent. For whites (inclusive of almost all persons of Spanish origin) the proportion of persons who were poor was 10 percent. (*Current Population Reports,* Series P-20 No. 224, October 1971, Table 6, p .8.)

lies with male heads that are poor has not been matched by comparable declines in poverty among families with female heads and there has been a marked increase in numbers of children in female-headed families. Nevertheless, many fewer children as well as adults are poor by the Social Security Administration's index today than a decade ago. The baffling and critical situation is in the compounded problems that encircle large numbers of those children who are in poverty families today. The proportions of poor children who were in families with male heads declined from 76 percent in 1959 to 56 percent in 1970; the proportions who were in families with female heads, conversely, have risen from 24 to 44 percent over the decade. Also, as we will see shortly, they are increasingly residents of the central cities of our huge metropolitan areas.

4. How important in fact is poverty among families with male heads in the active working ages? Very evidently it is highly important if we look at the proportions of poor families headed by males under 65. Taking white and nonwhite together, they were half of all poor families (36 percent plus 13 percent) in 1966 and two fifths of all poor families (32 percent plus 11 percent) in 1970. Even if we were willing to cross off both women and men over 65 so far as the labor force is concerned, a serious poverty problem remains for some two million men in the working years and their families. But it is by no means of the magnitude of the problems faced by poor families headed by females. Among other things, these families with male heads are not typically so far below the poverty line, and they can more easily move forward to a better economic situation. On the other hand, poverty and a sense of failure on the part of family men in the working years is undoubtedly a factor that contributes to the breaking up of families and the rise in numbers headed by females. Moreover, misguided welfare policies have aggravated these tendencies. One of the statistical results is the disappearance of some poor families headed by males, and the appearance in their place of poor families headed by females.

5. Poverty among families headed by females is one of the most serious and even pernicious of the poverty problems of the 1970s. The incidence of poverty among such families is high regardless of race, although again it is nonwhite families that are worst off. Among both whites and nonwhites there was a marked increase in the proportion of poor families that were headed by females over the period from 1959 to 1966 and then again from 1966 to 1970. As of 1959 these families made up 23 percent of all poor families; by 1966 they constituted 30 percent and by 1970 they were 37 percent. The dramatic increase in proportions of poor children who were in families headed by females has already been remarked. Demographic, social and economic factors are intertwined in these developments, with more female-headed families, more children in them, and a much slower

rate of progress out of poverty levels among women who are handicapped in the labor markets and burdened with sole responsibility for children at home. This brings us back to children again.

Poor children are particularly likely to be in big families, both because of differential birth rates that are negatively associated with parental schooling and income, and because a large number of children pushes a family below a poverty line that takes family size into account, even though earnings might support a small family well above poverty-line levels. This set of interrelationships is clearly revealed in Figure 2–2 which is of

Figure 2–2. Effects of number of chidren on incidence of poverty; families by race and sex of head, 1959 and 1966

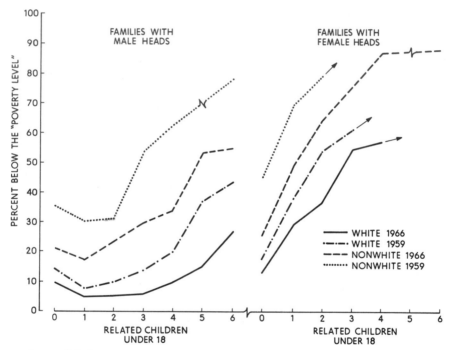

Source: U.S. Bureau of the Census, *Current Population,* Series P–60, No. 54, May 31, 1968 Table 5, pp. 18–20.

interest in several respects. That there is a slightly higher incidence of poverty among families with male heads but no children under 18 than in other families with male heads reflects age factors; in the no-child families with male heads, those heads tend to be over 65 or to be very young. Among whites with children, the proportions who are poor increase with the number of children very gradually until that number reaches four or more, when the increase becomes rapid, even in 1966. Among nonwhite families with male heads, the effect of numbers of children on proportions counted poor is sharper—though not nearly so sharp, even in 1966, as the impact of number of children on poverty in families headed by females—white or black.

The high poverty rates and steep increases in those rates from the first child on among families headed by females speaks very clearly to the problems faced by women who must both take care of their children and either earn enough to support them or apply for assistance. Since transfer payments are included in the income data before determining who is in poverty, we are looking at the situation after transfer payments. This is why Eugene Smolensky has referred to the incidence of poverty among the old and among families headed by females as primarily an indication of "political failure," poverty among families headed by able-bodied males as primarily an indication of "market failure." [15]

Poverty in countryside and metropole

What poverty means to people, both those who are poor and those who are not, depends in part on where they live. Over the past two decades there have been fundamental changes in this respect. Two quite distinct sorts of shifts claim our attention: migrations from farm to town and the movements of populations between central cities and outlying parts of metropolitan areas.

To what extent is poverty still a farm, to what extent a nonfarm problem? A partial answer to this question is provided by Table 2–4, which divides all persons, families and children into farm and nonfarm populations. According to the figures in the lower half of that table, a fifth to a sixth of all poor persons, families, and children lived on farms in 1959, but by 1966 this proportion had dropped to only 1 in 12. The pace of change in the location of poverty and its migration to the cities is dramatically evidenced in these figures. How far the migration of poverty off the farms has been accompanied by a reduction of the incidence of poverty among those remaining on farms is indicated in the upper half of the table. In 1959, 30 percent of all white farm families and 40 percent of all white farm children fell below the farm poverty line, but these proportions were cut in half over the seven year interval to 1966. Among nonwhites on farms, on the other hand, four fifths of the families and over nine tenths of the children were living in poverty in 1959, and three fourths of the children were still in that situation in 1966. This is the depth of poverty in the rural South, where it is compounded by a very high incidence of functional illiteracy (in fact, probably a rising incidence) among those who have not left the farms. However unqualified those who have left, they have never-

---

[15] See his "The Past and Present Poor," in *The Concept of Poverty,* pp. 35–68.

Table 2–4. Incidence and distribution of poverty by race and farm or nonfarm residence, United States 1959 and 1966

	Nonfarm		Farm		
	White	Nonwhite	White	Nonwhite	Total
Percentages below poverty level:					
Persons					
1959	17	50	34	88	22
1966	12	40	16	73	15
Families					
1959	14	46	30	82	18
1966	10	34	14	67	12
Children					
1959	18	58	41	93	26
1966	12	49	18	77	18
Percentage distributions of those in poverty:					
Persons					
1959	61	22	12	6	101
1966	63	29	5	3	100
Families					
1959	62	21	12	5	100
1966	66	26	6	2	100
Children					
1959	55	25	11	8	100
1966	54	37	5	4	100

Source: U.S. Bureau of the Census, *Current Population Report,* Series P–60, No. 54, May, 31, 1968, Table 2, p. 13.

theless been creamed off of the top of the Negro farming populations of the southern states.[16]

Remembering the dramatic shift from farm to nonfarm populations indicated for the period 1959 to 1966 in the lower half of Table 2–4, we may look back at the 1959 estimates made by Fuchs and shown above in Table 2–1. Taking the national 1959 Fuchs-point of $2,830 (half of the median family income of $5,660), we find 2,681,000 rural nonfarm families and 1,533,000 rural farm families to have been "in poverty" at that time. These account, respectively, for 30 and 17 percent of the 9 million families then below the Fuchs-point poverty line. This is the same 1959 farm representation that we get with the more refined Social Security Administration poverty criteria. It is indicative of the stubbornness of the poverty problem in the rural nonfarm populations that even in 1959, which followed a period of extremely high rates of migration to the cities, poverty was still of such

---

[16] On this, see my "Human Inequalities and Southern Underdevelopment," cited above. Also, Mary Jean Bowman and W. Warren Haynes, *Resources and People in East Kentucky,* Baltimore, Johns Hopkins University Press (for Resources for the Future, Inc.), 1963, chaps. 10 and 12.

magnitude among the populations that remained. This problem is very much bound up with that of lagging and depressed regions, whether in Appalachia, the cutover areas of the Upper Great Lakes, or elsewhere. Migration to the cities from these areas has continued, of course, as it has continued from the farms. But a hard-core problem is left behind, and for many of those who have moved as well as those who have stayed behind, migration to the city means not so much an escape from poverty as a change in its locale.

Meanwhile, urban poverty is closely locked into the central cities of metropolitan areas, where poverty rates are double the rates in suburbs. Furthermore, among the urban poor those in the central cities are the poorest and the most persistent in their experience of poverty year after year. They are also increasingly Negro, and this trend will certainly continue. It has been estimated that nonwhite residents of the central cities will almost double over the period 1960 to 1985, and already more than 60 percent of the poor children of the central cities are nonwhite.[17] A number of dimensions of these urban patterns are laid out in Table 2–5. Two main features of these patterns command special attention.

First of all it is evident that the relationships between residence and proportions in poverty are quite different for the white and nonwhite populations. This is easily seen in the first two rows of the table. Blacks living in outlying parts of metropolitan areas do not have the advantages over central city blacks that may be observed among most white suburbanites. But neither is there any clear difference in the incidence of poverty among white female-headed families in suburbs and central cities. Back of these figures are white social status selectivity in migration to suburbs and constraints on residence choices for Negroes.

Secondly, the increase in proportions of all families, poor and nonpoor, that are headed by females appears in every residence category and for both races, but most emphatically for nonwhites and among them especially in the central cities. Along with this has gone a very substantial increase in numbers as well as proportions of children who are in families with female heads. This phenomenon too can be observed across all residence categories, but is most extreme among nonwhites in the central cities and among whites in the suburbs. Taking metropolitan residents in central city and suburb together, between 1960 and 1970 there was a 99 percent increase in the number of nonwhite and a 57 percent increase in the number of white children in families headed by females. By contrast, the rates of increase of metropolitan-area children in families headed by males were 26 percent among the nonwhites and 7 percent among the whites. The national overall increase between 1960 and 1970 in numbers of children in families headed by males was 3.1 million (a net 5 percent gain) while the overall increase in children in families headed by females

---

[17] See Anthony Downs, *Poverty in U.S. Metropolitan Areas,* Washington and Chicago, Sysmetrics, July 1968 (mimeo).

Table 2–5. Family patterns and poverty by race and residence, 1959 and 1969

	Metropolitan				Non-metropolitan	
	Central Cities		Outside Central Cities			
	White	Black	White	Black	White	Black
Percentages below poverty line:						
Persons						
1959	14	41	10	51	28	78
1969	10	25	5	23	13	52
Families with male heads						
1959	9	28	7	40	23	71
1969	5	10	3	12	10	37
Families with female heads						
1959	23	57	26	61	40	82
1969	24	47	21	46	31	70
Children in families with male heads						
1959	12	43	9	57	29	83
1969	7	14	3	18	11	47
Children in families with female heads						
1959	46	77	45	80	56	89
1969	46	63	37	65	51	81
Percentages of all families that have female heads:						
1960	10	23	6	18	8	21
1970	12	32	8	22	8	28
Numbers of children in all families (thousands):						
Children in families with male heads						
1960	13,390	2,704	18,441	843	20,132	2,310
1970	11,264	3,295	22,890	1,188	20,219	2,050
Children in families with female heads						
1960	1,108	996	900	173	1,313	638
1970	1,476	1,942	1,608	380	1,585	960
Percentages of all poor children who were in designated residence–race–family categories, 1959 and 1969:						
1959 in families with						
Male heads	10	8	8	3	38	12
Female heads	3	5	3	1	5	4
1969 in families with						
Male heads	7	10	5	2	10	8
Female heads	9	16	8	3	11	10

was 2.8 million (a whopping 55 percent net gain). What has happened to distributions of the children of poverty across residence categories, family structures and races is laid out clearly enough at the bottom of the table. No matter how one looks at it, the information presented in this table spells economic, social and political problems, focussed increasingly on children of the central cities, and the dilemmas of women who are overloaded with responsibilities they are ill-prepared to carry. Human beings have always spent a large proportion of their adult lives raising the younger generation, but normally the major part of these activities has been carried out informally in the home or extended family and neighborhood; usually it has not been included in economic assessments, let alone in the national accounts. But we have slid into modes of life and institutions that have caught us unawares; urban black protest, Women's Lib and the pressures for subsidized child care have not grown by accident. In particular, no previous generations have seen anything comparable to the societal problems of child rearing that face us today and in the future. This is not a poverty problem alone, but it is very much entangled with the economics and politics of urban poverty, nontheless.

Poverty and unemployment

A few years ago, a goodly number of economists were concerned with unemployment of the able-bodied as a long-term problem in an automating, cybernating economy. At the extreme, Theobald,[18] for example, argued that no matter what progress might be made in the diffusion of education and skills among the members of the population of this country, technological advance would be such that we are destined to a future in which, *for virtually everyone,* leisure would be in surplus, national income ample to maintain a leisurely life, the opportunity to work a scarce and highly desired "good."

Few of those arguing the structural unemployment case went so far as that, however, even when they argued that automation had produced a situation in which increasing numbers of our population had become unemployable, and that this problem would grow worse in the future. To the more moderate structuralists, an increase in aggregate demand for labor would run into bottlenecks in the skilled ranks long before it soaked up the less skilled. Those accepting this argument supported upgrading programs not only from humanitarian and labor-quality, economic-efficiency considerations, but also as a way of reducing aggregate unemployment.

In opposition to this structuralist emphasis has been the argument that as concerns overall levels of employment, and with them both low-wage

---

[18] Robert Theobald, *Free Men and Free Markets, New York,* Potter, 1963. For a short popular statement, see his "Cybernation: Immediate Threat and Future Promise," and discussions by others of his position in *Poverty: Four Approaches; Four Solutions,* published by the Associated Students of the University of Oregon, Eugene, Oregon, 1966.

and unemployment-linked poverty, the important thing was to pursue monetary and fiscal policies that would stimulate and sustain high aggregate demand for labor. Among those who argued this deficiency-of-aggregate-demand position, the tax cut of 1964 was heralded as the most important and effective weapon in the antipoverty arsenal.[19]

Whatever one's interpretation of causes of unemployment and of future longterm prospects, there can be no question that lack of employment (or irregular employment) and poverty are empirically related. A crude overall indication of the degree of the relationship between unemployment and poverty is provided in Table 2–6 for 1966. In the main, that table speaks for itself,[20] though it fails to distinguish one group among whom unemployment rates, while reduced, have remained comparatively high—the very young.

Qualifications and discrimination

The word "discrimination" is a much misused term. It is often applied when it is quite unsuitable, as though it were synonymous with inequality.[21] On the other hand, it is often not used when it would be the appropriate way of describing the situation. Discrimination selects out certain categories of people for unfavorable treatment on grounds that are irrelevant to the task at hand. That "task" may be the formation of skills, whether in school or on the job; that is, the discrimination may operate to prevent acquisition of higher productive capacities among those against whom it is directed. Such discrimination has unquestionably operated against nonwhites and against women, and not only or primarily with respect to schooling; indeed, much more important may be discrimination that excludes nonwhites and women from opportunities for learning and training on the job.[22]

---

[19] Harry Johnson and R. J. Lampman have been among the considerable number of economists who have underlined this position, but without suggesting that full employment is enough. See, for examples of their positions, Harry G. Johnson, "Unemployment and Poverty," and Robert J. Lampman, "Ends and Means in the War on Poverty," both in Leo Fishman, ed. *Poverty amid Affluence,* New Haven, Conn. and London, Yale University Press, 1965. A stronger position on this matter is taken by Lowell Galloway in "The Foundations of the 'War on Poverty.' " *American Economic Review,* 55, 1 (March 1965), pp. 122–31. A much less sanguine view of how much full employment can do or has done to reduce poverty is presented by W. H. Locke Anderson, "Trickling Down: the Relationship between Economic Growth and the Extent of Poverty among American Families," *Quarterly Journal of Economics,* 78, 4 (November 1964), pp. 511–24.

[20] More detailed data from the same source show that among those who worked part of the year, whether poor or nonpoor, the proportions reporting some unemployment were substantially higher for the nonwhite than for the white men.

[21] For an analytically sharp treatment of these concepts and a critique of their use, see C. Arnold Anderson and Philip Foster, "Discrimination and Inequality in Education," *Sociology of Education,* 38, 1 (Fall 1964), pp. 1–18.

[22] I have written about this on several occasions. For a recent, brief statement, see my "The Assessment of Human Investments as Growth Strategy," in *Federal Programs for the Development of Human Resources,* Washington, D.C., Joint Economic Committee of the Congress of the United States, 90th Cong. 2d sess., 1968, pp. 84–99.

Table 2-6. Employment history and incidence of poverty by family type and race, 1966

	Total		Head Worked Full Year	Head Worked Part Year	Head Did Not Work	In Armed Forces
	Number (thousands)	Percent				
Families with male heads:						
All ages						
White: Total	40,007	100	73	14	11	2
Above poverty level	36,733	100	76	14	8	2
Below poverty level	3,264	100	35	25	38	2
Nonwhite: Total	3,743	100	64	23	11	2
Above poverty level	2,731	101	72	20	7	2
Below poverty level	1,012	100	45	30	24	1
Age 25-64						
White: Total	32,117	100	82	13	3	2
Above poverty level	30,228	100	84	12	2	2
Below poverty level	1,889	100	51	28	19	2
Nonwhite: Total	3,066	100	70	23	5	2
Above poverty level	2,330	99	75	20	2	2
Below poverty level	736	100	53	32	14	1
Families with female heads:						
All ages						
White						
Above poverty level	2,899	100	44	19	37	...
Below poverty level	1,111	99	15	27	57	...
Nonwhite						
Above poverty level	462	100	50	23	27	...
Below poverty level	699	100	24	31	45	...

Source: U.S. Bureau of the Census Current Population Reports, Series P-60 No. 54, May 31, 1968, Tables 12, 13, and 14, pp. 29-31.

It is difficult, in practice, to separate out those aspects of discrimination in labor markets that block access to the better jobs (and aggravate unemployment among the victims of discrimination) from those that block opportunities to accumulate skill through experience. It is also difficult, in practice, to determine how far employers' prejudgments about the less educated or the older man, even when he is white, may screen him out of jobs that he could perform very well. Whether one considers this as a problem in the costs of information or as discrimination, it undoubtedly increases the incidence of poverty among both school dropouts in the younger age brackets and men who have passed age 65. These are issues about which economists, sociologists and publicists have been writing extensively, and about which they will continue to write—sometimes on the basis of research and sometimes in more visceral mood. I shall therefore limit myself to two points.

My first point relates to analyses of racial discrimination as reflected in incomes of whites versus nonwhites after controlling for education. There are many ways of trying to break up racial income differentials to explain them statistically, and there can be no definitive answer. We can go around endless circles doing this. Suppose a statistician should come up with evidence that some large percent of the difference between earnings of whites and blacks with the "same schooling" is attributable to differences in achievement levels attained (differences in "quality" of these resources), arguing that "only the rest of the difference" is discrimination. Those who want to lay stress on discrimination can argue, and rightly, that he isn't taking account of discrimination that has its effects earlier, in the schools —or that had its effects in past history and carries its long shadow down into the present. In fact, we already know that some decidedly significant, but unmeasured, percentage of the difference between white and nonwhite earnings of men with the same number of years of schooling could be attributed to differences in what they have learned by the time they leave school. This is a problem of rising political dimensions in our cities. But we also know that a large measure of sheer labor market discrimination remains, and that this makes the poverty problems of the black urban ghettos of today something quite different, and probably more destructive, than the greater absolute poverty of white immigrant residents of inner cities a generation and more ago.

My second main comment in connection with qualifications and discrimination is one already made, but warranting reiteration. I refer to the compounding effects of discrimination on the development of skills and productive potential among the victims of discrimination—mainly women (regardless of race) and black men. The problem is not just what happens, and does not happen, in the schools or in formal apprenticeship programs. It ramifies through the whole sequence of experiences that make up a

man's life at work, that make him what he is and open or close opportunities for what he (or she) can become.

Effects of schooling, race, and region of residence on the distribution of
income among males aged 45 to 54 are shown for 1959 in Figure 2–3. The
patterns for men age 25 to 34 are very similar in their relationships, except
that among the younger white men with college education we do not yet
see the tailing out at the top that characterizes the grade 16+ curves of
Figure 2–3. One of the great advantages in looking at relationships in this

Figure 2–3. Distributions of personal incomes of males, age 45–54; region, race, and
selected school completion categories, 1959

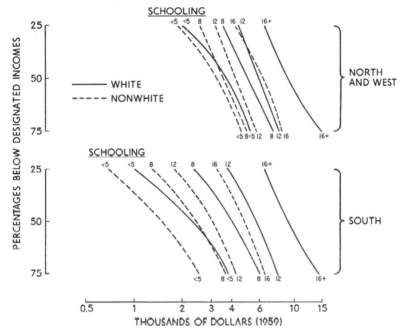

way is that we can see the patterns that lie back of more summary statistics.
Be he white or nonwhite, a man's schooling obviously makes much more
difference in the South than in the North and West; so does his race. But
even in the non-South, a white man with eight years of education had
higher earnings than a nonwhite high school graduate, and the white high
school graduate did almost as well as the nonwhite college man.

Controlling for education, black-white differences in incomes are much
less for women than for men. Indeed, they are generally quite small, and
in 1968 the mean incomes of black female college graduates actually
exceeded the mean incomes of their white counterparts by 18 percent.

Comparisons for women are complicated, however, by the fact that the white college women are decidedly the more likely to work only part time. The effects of this fact are easily seen in a comparison of entire income distributions (not reproduced here). Ranking college women of each race according to their 1968 incomes, at the lowest quintile the black college graduates had annual earnings almost three times those of white college graduates, and black exceeded white incomes of college women up to the high 80th percentile. The top fifth of white college women had higher incomes than the top fifth of their black sisters, but even at the 90th percentile the white advantage was only 10 percent. Among high school graduates the black and white distributions for women cross just below their medians, but they run very close together above median levels. The least educated of black women generally earn a little less than white women, but the differences in both absolute and relative terms are small. This brings us back to the fact that families headed by females are commonly poor, regardless of race; they are extremely poor when the women have little education and no private source of income other than their own earnings.

Whether educational and job opportunities for black relative to white people have improved or deteriorated over the past decade, and in what respects, is a much debated topic, important in its own right. That black college men have gained substantially can be clearly documented. But lower down the scale the picture is not so clear. In a new unpublished research paper, Finis Welch has argued cogently that returns to education for black men have risen substantially and are much higher for the more recent "vintages" than they have been for those who went through school earlier; he attributes this change to improvements in the quality of education for blacks relative to whites, presenting empirical evidence to support that position. Others have argued that the main change has been in the labor markets for college men. Unfortunately, however, there is as yet little justification for supposing that the position of noncollege black men has improved significantly in relative opportunities for employment in situations that provide substantial learning and promise of progress in earnings and job status with experience. Lack of opportunity to move up internal job ladders with experience and lack of commitment on the part of the individual are mutually reinforcing. One result is a relatively large fraction of black men and their families hovering in the vicinity of the poverty line even when counted above it.

The costs of being poor

In addition to discrimination against broad categories of the population, such as nonwhites, females, older people, and those lacking formal certification, many of the institutions of our society and our public policies discriminate against the poor by virtue of their poverty. We block progress out of poverty and maintain barriers that keep the poor poor. They pay more for the same things or for goods of poorer quality. They receive inferior services from government and often they pay indirectly, but heavily, for services provided to the more fortunate. They are weak bargainers in the arenas where government favors are dispensed. It is expensive to be poor. The variety and magnitude of these costs of being poor are still little appreciated by most middle-class people. Here, I can only suggest something of what this means by a few examples of the costs of being poor and the perversities of institutions and actions that impede the journey out of poverty.

1. **The poor are charged more for inferior goods and services.** This fact has been well documented, and it extends across a wide range of expenditures, especially among urban dwellers. The poor pay more to start with because they buy from small local shops instead of big supermarkets. But more important, the poor are exploited by unscrupulous merchants. Because they have low credit ratings, they pay extortionate prices for goods purchased on an installment basis; usury laws are evaded by a pricing system that is, in fact, highly usurious. If a well-heeled purchaser does not meet his payments on time, he has little to fear, but the poor man may find his wages garnisheed before he knows what is happening—or he may lose what little he possesses because of the fine print on a contract.[23]

High housing costs relative to quality are particularly burdensome for the urban poor. Those costs are high for a number of reasons. For one, the poor person, again, is a poor risk financially, and rentals are set at levels to cover the costs to landlords of irregular rental payments. This is part of the whole vicious circle by which rental costs are pushed up: payments become more difficult to meet; because some of them are not met, rents are raised; and so on. Even the individual resident of the ghetto who meets his rental bills regularly pays on account of those who do not. And if he tries to buy a house, he is likely to find credit difficult or impossible to obtain simply because of the condition of the neighborhood where he lives—or because it is black.

Discrimination crowds Negroes into congested areas, and the consequent shortage of housing both raises rents and contributes to deterioration in levels of maintenance. Black or white, poor families often pay heavily for urban renewal. Those who gain are the real estate developer and builder and the new comfortably situated occupant; meanwhile, the original residents of the area are displaced and must look for a place to live elsewhere. Typically, the clearing of one slum crowds more people into the

---

[23] In the Kentucky mountains, contracts written 50 years ago, when mining technology was not at all what it has become today, have allowed purchasers of subsoil rights to totally destroy the farmer's land and home, and that of his neighbors down the hill. Only recently have lawyers acting on behalf of the little man succeeded in blocking some small fraction of this ruthless exploitation of fine print provisions of the past—and in at least one place this was accomplished only after the mountain people organized lie-downs in front of bulldozers.

slums that remain and raises the rents they pay there. Rarely are the displaced adequately compensated for the costs thus imposed on them, and never is such compensation forthcoming for the families whose rents are raised because the displaced move into their neighborhoods.

2. **Urban transportation systems penalize the poor.** This again is a problem with many facets. For one, suburban automobile owners are heavily subsidized by our investments in the urban highway system. For their convenience, cities go into debt and public transportation facilities are allowed to deteriorate. With the reduction of public transportation services and the deterioration of those that remain, the pressure to build yet more highways and subsidize the suburban commuter still more heavily continues the cycle. Meanwhile, the new jobs created are in outlying areas, distant from the ghettos, especially the Negro neighborhoods. And to top all this, the new urban highways are frequently built deliberately in and across the areas where there are the greatest concentrations of poor families. Their neighborhoods are broken up, their accessibility in all directions is reduced rather than improved, and housing becomes still shorter and more congested. Again, the displacements that follow from construction of these highways (and the outward shift of jobs that they encourage), impose heavy costs, costs that are paid by poor people. And so another spiral builds up to choke the poor of the central cities for the immediate (though not the ultimate) benefit of the middle and higher income groups.

3. **"To him that hath shall be given."** This is all too applicable to many of our programs, including some of those that have been justified at one time or another on grounds of distributive justice or special need.

Poor areas, both rural and urban, have the lowest quality schools, with respect both to buildings and equipment and to quality of teachers. They have the poorest city services, even lacking in many instances services adequate to maintain minimum sanitary conditions. Yet, these services are presumably public because, among other things, we believe that they should be made available to all, regardless of ability to pay. This goes beyond local government to federal grants, which frequently subsidize suburban sewer and water developments while bypassing the central cities. More police are, indeed, usually assigned to poorer districts in the city, but police protection is nevertheless less effective there. That this reflects behavior of many slum dwellers does not help the honest poor, or the children who were so unfortunate as to have been born or transported into urban poverty.

The most obvious case of perversion of a presumptively poverty-oriented urban program is probably urban renewal as it has developed in practice. But far surpassing that as the villain of the piece is agricultural price supports. An estimated two thirds of all subsidies for this purpose now go to farm households with incomes of $20,000 a year or more, while the poorest farmers are helped not at all. T. W. Schultz concluded a statement concerning poverty in agriculture and the neglect of investment in human capital among the farming population (as against subsidy to non-human capital) In these words: [24]

It should also be said that the vast expenditures by the federal government on behalf of agriculture have not been used to raise the levels of these skills [of members of the farm labor force]; on the contrary, they have been used in ways that enhance the income from other classes of property and that worsen the personal distribution of income among farm families.

4. **Treating the poor as men of very little worth is a frequent, if not a pervasive practice.** In all its ramifications, this sort of treatment aggravates poverty and discourages escape out of poverty. In one sense, almost everything noted under the three preceding headings, but especially under the second and third, might also be classed here. However, I have in mind something more explicit—treatment of poor people by public and quasi-public personnel (and agencies) who come into direct contact with them as individuals. Examples are many. Poor youth acquire police records for acts that would never be recorded were they the sons of better placed families, but those records then sharply reduce their education and job opportunities, sometimes with cumulative effects. In Sweden, bail is set for any given offense according to a man's ability to pay, but in the United States the poor man who runs afoul of the law may spend months in jail (even when he is innocent), simply because he could not raise bail. His time, it seems, is not worth much—and neither, at this point, are his career chances. Personnel of the U.S. Employment Services discriminate against the poorer applicants, creaming their clientele to give most attention to exactly those men who are most easily placed and would have the best chances without their help, and they scarcely serve the rural poor at all.

Meanwhile, our public assistance programs are little calculated to reassure a man of his human worth, to give him self-confidence, or to encourage him to earn or learn what he can. Even their schoolteachers often make very clear to poor children that they are worth very little. It is all too easy to carry conviction in this respect when the child comes from a home where there are no books, no magazines, and scarcely a consecutive conversation—a home where there is no father, or only a father who feels himself to be and is regarded by others as a failure. That youth from such an environment see themselves, others, and the system in ways quite unlike the perceptions of more fortunate, usually suburban, Americans should hardly give cause for surprise. But neither is this a measure of their potential—or of their human worth.

5. **Finally, it is costly to migrate and it is costly to be one of those who are left behind in the migrations from rural places to the cities.** The two

---

[24] T. W. Schultz, "Investing in Poor People; an Economist's View" in *American Economic Review,* 55, 2 (May 1965), p .519.

sides of the rural-urban migration process are little appreciated by most urban Americans, but they are very vivid realities to rural people. The Commission on Rural Poverty put it this way.[25]

The total number of rural poor would be even larger than 14 million had not so many of them moved to the city. They made the move because they wanted a job and a decent place to live. Some have found them. Many have not. Many merely exchanged life in a rural slum for life in an urban slum, at exorbitant cost to themselves, to the cities, and to rural America as well.

Though the problem of those who are left behind is by no means confined to the coal regions, it has taken especially dramatic form and has been most loudly voiced there.[26] Generally, those leaving poor rural areas are the youth and young adults most able (or, more correctly, least unable) to cope with a new environment, and with the best chances of finding regular jobs. Those who remain are disproportionately the functionally illiterate, the old, and sometimes the very young (including children of some of the migrants).

It is in rural nonfarm areas that rates of poverty among the elderly are greatest, for white and nonwhites alike—but especially, relative to their poverty rates elsewhere, among whites. And large proportions of rural nonfarm poor are elderly despite propensities of rural people to have many children. With the draining out of the least disadvantaged educationally and those best able to do productive work, the base on which community services must rest is severely eroded, and local governments cannot cope with local needs. In some of the poorer areas, basic services deteriorate substantially, and on an absolute, not merely a relative, scale. Generally, the magnitude and selectivity of out-migration aggravates the problem of communication gaps between the remaining rural poor and the rest of a rapidly moving, technological society.

Is there a culture of poverty?

Sometimes, the verbal duels concerning the culture of poverty that have dotted the literature recently seem a sort of shadow play in a fantasy world. Sometimes, they seem all too real, even when as old as the Poor Law of

[25] *The People Left Behind.* Report of the President's National Advisory Commission on Rural Poverty, Washington, D.C., September 1967, p. ix.

[26] The set of attitudes that Dudley Plunkett and I have designated the "anti-migration syndrome" has been particularly pervasive in the Kentucky mountains, with decided political ramifications and impact on policy making at both state and national levels. Though it is less pervasive today than it was 10 or more years ago, a large minority of the Kentucky mountain elites still cling passionately to this attitude syndrome, which includes the notion that men should be provided, as a matter of right, with the opportunity to get a job both wherever they most want to live and at "national standards of living." (A brief discussion of this attitude complex is included in Bowman and Haynes, *Rsources and People in East Kentucky,* but the only systematic study of this and related attitudes, who holds them, and with what these attitudes are associated, is in Dudley H. Plunkett and Mary Jean Bowman, *Elites and Change in the Kentucky Mountains,* Lexington, Ky., University Press of Kentucky, 1973.

1834. This is one of those tell-it-like-it-is situations in which, in fact, communications are most likely to break down. But perhaps some of the facts of life and some of the genuine issues can be pulled out of the semantic debris.

We may begin by asking: Why does it matter whether or not there is such a thing as a culture of poverty? This leads us to ask what the phrase means, and why "it" has been an issue. There are three main reason: (1) associated with today's mood of dissent we sometimes find a romantic misidentification of rural or ethnic cultural traits as a culture of poverty; (2) more objectively, there is concern with communication gaps between the supposed hard-core poor among the able-bodied and the middle-class American; (3) most important, there are disputes over why people are poor —particular people—and how far the poor would respond to opportunity, even if it came their way.

(1) Although the romantics of dissent having something important to say, we can set aside the notion that the poor *per se* (i.e., by virtue of the fact that they are poor) have a distinctive culture of special value that should be preserved. It is one thing to argue that mountain people take a more personal approach to human relationships that rejects the segmentalizing of men so common in human relationships in the cities, or to argue that rural people generally are more generous in helping each other, or that black men (or Poles, or Irishmen to go back a generation) have distinctive cultural attributes that should be respected. It is something else to call any of these a culture of poverty. Rurality or affiliation with an ethnic group that has a high incidence of poverty is not the same as being poor or, more poignantly, being one of the poor. But in dismissing the misidentification of a culture of poverty, it is important to remember, nevertheless, that romanticizing of the poor by people who have never known poverty is part of a syndrome whose core is indignation at the insufferable intolerance and bigotry sometimes displayed vis-à-vis poor people. This brings us to the communication problem.

(2) The second reason the culture of poverty theme has developed and persisted derives from the communication gap that unquestionably divides large segments of the poor—those who have known little but poverty— from the rest of the American society. Again, it is important to distinguish attributes of particular groups who happen also to be disproportionately poor for other reasons (including discrimination) from *(a)* attributes that inherently make men poverty-prone and *(b)* the "culture" that develops as a way of adjusting to poverty, both physically and psychologically—including ways of protecting oneself against the indignities that those long in poverty suffer. Where these adjustment mechanisms inhibit movement into the worlds of the nonpoor, we do, indeed, have a vicious cycle of poverty in which malnutrition, lack of education, and psychological adjustments are mutually reinforcing. But this is certainly not the culture of poverty of

the romantic; neither is it the "culture" attributed to the poor by a long outdated variety of self-righteousness. Unquestionably, there is need for much more careful and more adequately sensitized consideration of the problems of communication and mutual understanding that this cultural impact of persisting poverty entails.

(3) Finally, the culture of poverty theme has become a battleground between those who regard the able-bodied poor as lazy riffraff, who would rather be on the dole than do a good day's work for pay, and those who argue that on the contrary the poor would take jobs if (decent?) jobs were available to them. Two facts seem to slip by in the polarizations of the argument. One is the gross oversimplification in speaking of the poor as if they were a homogeneous population, identical with particular groups who, in fact, make up only one or another segment of those who are poor by our income measures. In fact, men who are poor may be as diverse as those who are rich, or in a middle income range, as far as their responses to visible economic and job opportunities are concerned.

They are diverse also in the range of opportunities they may have to escape from poverty. For some those opportunities are very slim indeed, and perceptions of opportunity may be narrower still. Such perceptions, after all, must be a function of prior experience. If hustling looks like the best economic bet to a son of the ghetto, and he chooses that path rather than one his experience suggests is the dead end of "an honest day's work," he may not be so very different after all. Neither is his cousin who breaks away from his background to make the other, socially approved choice. And neither, as a rational economic decision maker and a man who cares for his family, is the welfare recipient who will not risk taking a temporary job because he is afraid that when (not if) he loses it his family will go hungry while waiting to be requalified for public assistance. We will get further by examining the objective and visible incentives, and responses to them, than by arguing the culture of poverty position on the question of willingness to work. This has been done in what is probably the biggest deliberate social experiment of all time—a $5 million negative income tax experiment in New Jersey.

R. J. Lampman, an outstanding student of poverty problems, has challenged the derogatory "culture of poverty" notion.[27]

People seem to believe that the poor have an entirely separate set of attitudes, goals, and purposes. A number of studies are in conflict with this. Measurement of attitudes of poor children show that they have a lot of ambitions, fantasies, and dreams not too different from those of middle class children. More persuasive to me is that there is a dynamic element that when given an opportunity causes this apparent culture of poverty to melt away like an iceberg in the sun.

Lampman's point of view is one with which I am fully in accord, provided we interpret it to say *(a)* that a large proportion of those able-bodied adults

---

[27] "An Economist Looks at Poverty," in *Poverty: Four Approaches; Four Solutions*, p. 35.

who are classified as poor by our income definitions would respond to the chance for a regular job, and *(b)* that until poverty and the conditions of life associated with living in poverty has beaten them down, children of even the poorest of the poor will respond to opportunities to learn and to work, now and in the future, just as children born into other strata of our society.

But to speak of an "apparent culture of poverty" and dismiss it with that is, in my judgment, to pass too easily over something that is very real and very important in the cycle of poverty causation. It is to estimate too lightly the burden of poverty on its children. There is no denying that children born and brought up in poverty experience life in ways that make the journey out of poverty a difficult one from almost every point of view; this is what persistent hard-core poverty is all about. The key phrase in Lampman's statement is "when given an opportunity"—and both the when of this opportunity and its visibility are important. The light and warmth of Lampman's sun may have to break through a heavy cloud cover to reach those longest and deepest in poverty.

What it comes down to is that among those who have long lived in poverty without hope, where poverty has meant persistent failure and human indignities, family life is eroded, expectations of failure are cumulatively reinforced, and men react both by devaluing and by protecting themselves. So do children. Only literary language can convey the meaning of this culture, for in a real sense it is indeed a culture of poverty, so that the feet of the would-be traveler sink in it. But this is not a culture common to all those who are poor. It is the product not so much of poverty as such; rather, it is a product of repeated failure, a residue of hopelessness.

There is a reason poverty in our cities today seems in some ways worse than it ever was before—even when living conditions were far worse than those of the rural and urban slums of today. White or black, the modern slum dweller, unlike the immigrants of yesteryear, has had repeated experience of failure here in the United States, and men of the black ghettoes face a degree of discrimination that was unknown to those who preceded them in such areas. But the passive, fatalistic culture of poverty that negates success has by no means taken over. On the contrary, we are seeing today an angry, more positive reaction that denies the hold of a culture of poverty and insists on opportunity to break out of its clutches. It is no accident that the leadership of this movement comes from young men who perceive their situation not as failure in themselves, or even as the fault of the system, but, rather, as the injustices wrought by a discriminatory society. This reaction out of poverty is shaking America today.

III. Transfer payments as antipoverty instruments

There have been various estimates of what it would require to "eliminate poverty" if we were simply to tax those who have and pay over to those who have not. Taking the Social Security Administration's poverty line for 1962 and adjusting it to each year's price level, the total estimated gap has narrowed considerably. It is estimated to have been close to $14 billion as of 1959; by 1965 it was down to $11 billion (in 1965 prices), and more recent estimates put it at $10 billion for 1969 (at 1969 prices). This 1969 figure is in fact only 54 percent of the aggregate deficit for 1959 when the 1959 values also are in 1969 prices.[28] Today the deficit is substantially less than 2 percent of gross national product, and poverty could have been wiped out in our arithmetic for 1966 and the years thereafter if we had merely added to present transfer payments an annual amount equal to less than half of one year's *increase* in GNP—provided, that is, the transfer payments were systematically directed to those most in need, and in order of their need. If we let the poverty line stay at the same absolute level, we would quickly reach a point where we could wipe it out. Why, then, don't we do this? There are at least three important reasons why we don't.

One reason is that poverty is not just a lack of money, and we may prefer to help those who are poor to help themselves out of poverty by policies that enable and encourage them to become self-supporting. Herman Miller puts this succinctly: "The generic term 'poverty' hides more than it reveals. There are, in fact, many different types of poverty which have different causes and, of course, require different solutions." But in the short run, this is more expensive, and it calls for quite other sorts of expenditures.

A second reason we don't wave this transfer wand is that we would not get quite the results the arithmetic suggests, since any program of transfer payments alters incentives with respect both to work and to household composition. The devising of practical policies to wipe out poverty by direct transfer payments is a more complex matter than it seems on first thought.

But equally important is a third factor. Poor people are a minority, and the voting majority are not really so committed to helping the poor as the oratory on this subject might sometimes suggest. Most voters will be considerably more enthusiastic in support of a measure that gives something to everyone, including themselves, over a program that unambiguously takes money from the pockets of most of us to pay it to the poor. This fact is indisputable, whatever position we may take in arguments concerning what social welfare programs should be, or on whether minimum wage legislation for example, should be viewed as poverty-inducing or poverty-reducing.[29] And today it is compounded by the pressures to do something

---

[28] The reduction is much less in the central cities; among Negroes in central cities in particular the 1969 aggregate deficit is 73 percent of the 1959 figure (in 1969 dollars).

[29] This long-standing debate has been revived with renewed intensity in the past few years. The best-known protagonists are probably Milton Friedman and Leon Keyserling. Friedman opened a short, sharp attack on minimum-wage legislation with the remark: "Minimum wage laws are about as clear a case as one can find of a measure the effects

for poor regions, just as some 30 years ago farm parity programs were argued on grounds of the relative poverty of farm versus nonfarm populations.

The poverty gaps and income maintenance payments in the United States in 1965–66

One of the first things needed if we are to attain some measure of objectivity in arguments concerning the potential and the actual antipoverty roles of public transfer payments is to take a look at what we now have and how it operates. Some data relevant to this question are summarized in Tables 2–7 and 2–8. I have already made reference to the figures for the total poverty gap as of 1959 and 1965, shown in the last two entries in the first row of Table 2–7. That table speaks for itself with respect to the distribution of that gap by type of household, by old and young, by families with and without children, and I therefore omit comment on it, though there will be occasion to turn back later to these facts. Table 2–8 requires some explanation. Miss Orshansky's analysis is based on a special current population survey taken by the Bureau of the Census in March, 1966. Family characteristics relate to the time of the interview, but data on income received under public income maintenance programs refer to calendar 1965, when members of the March, 1966, household of related persons may have had other living arrangements; for example, an older person or couple may have been living by themselves in 1965 but may have been taken into a son's or daughter's home (or vice versa) between 1965 and the spring of 1966.

Another complication is that respondents may have been poor during part of 1965 but not during another part of that year, changes in household composition quite aside. This is a partial explanation [30] of the fact that even among the recipients of public assistance large minorities of families with male heads were classified as "not poor" on an annual income basis even before receipt of the public assistance payments (48 percent of those with no children and 39 percent of those with children); similarly, 39 percent of the no-child families with female heads that received public assistance at some time in 1965 were classed as nonpoor on the basis of total income for that year without public assistance. These figures are indicative of the substantial fraction of transitory or temporary poor, even among recipients of public assistance, provided they are families headed by able-bodied males, or females without children. The story is very different for

---

of which are precisely the opposite of those intended by the men of good will who support it." (*Capitalism and Freedom,* Chicago, University of Chicago Press, 1962). Leon Keyserling has, of course, taken quite the opposite view. I shall come back to this subject below, though not, I hasten to add, in the expectation of resolving the argument.

[30] Also, some states and localities make assistance payments up to levels exceeding the national poverty line on the Social Security Administration's criteria.

Table 2–7. The poverty gap: 1959 and 1965, difference between actual and poverty-line income

Type of Household	Number of Households (millions)		Aggregate Dollar Deficit (billions)	
	1959	1965	1959	1965
Total	13.4	11.2	$13.7	$11.0
Unrelated individuals				
Men	1.6	1.3	1.2	.9
Women	3.5	3.5	2.8	2.5
Families				
All				
no children under 18	2.9	2.2	2.3	1.7
with children under 18	5.4	4.2	7.4	6.0
Male head				
no children under 18	2.5	1.8	2.0	1.4
with children under 18	3.8	2.8	5.0	3.8
Female head				
no children under 18	.4	.4	.3	.3
with children under 18	1.6	1.5	2.4	2.3
Race				
White				
Unrelated individuals	4.2	3.9	3.2	2.8
Families	6.2	4.6	6.6	5.2
Nonwhite				
Unrelated individuals	.9	.8	.8	.6
Families	2.1	1.9	3.1	2.6
Age of head				
Under 25				
Unrelated individuals	.5	.5	.5	.5
Families	.6	.6	.7	.7
25–64				
Unrelated individuals	2.1	1.7	1.8	1.4
Families	5.8	4.4	7.4	5.9
65 and over				
Unrelated individuals	2.5	2.6	1.7	1.5
Families	1.9	1.5	1.6	1.1

Source: Mollie Orshansky, "The Shape of Poverty in 1966," in *Social Security Bulletin 31,* 3 (March 1968), p. 23.

families headed by females with children, and for unrelated individuals who receive public assistance, whatever their ages. Indeed, even after public assistance, 80 percent or more of these recipients remained below the Social Security Administration's poverty line.

Table 2-8. Poverty status of households receiving public income payments in 1965

	All House-holds	Characteristics of Households								
		Under Age 65					Age 65 and Over			
		Unrelated Individ-uals	Male Heads		Female Heads		Unrelated Individuals		Families	
			No Children	With Children	No Children	With Children	Male	Female	Male Head	Female Head
Total number of households (000)	60,410	7,460	12,740	24,780	1,180	2,690	1,280	3,400	5,770	1,130
Number of households receiving public income payments										
Any program	19,510	1,530	2,670	3,740	520	1,310	1,110	2,830	5,030	960
Social security	12,990	620	1,280	1,060	370	570	1,000	2,530	4,740	820
Public assistance	2,910	250	200	520	100	700	140	440	350	220
Other programs	6,740	600	1,450	2,530	120	280	190	330	1,060	180
Percentages poor before payment										
Any program	55	68	22	24	35	79	84	88	63	51
Social security *	59	82	26	26	29	68	81	85	59	46
Public assistance *	81	95	52	61	61	93	98	99	81	66
Other programs	29	45	14	16	29	46	78	73	40	41
Percentages poor after payment										
Any program	31	47	12	15	22	58	47	62	21	30
Social security	32	58	15	15	18	35	45	60	20	26
Public assistance	67	79	42	48	42	84	84	86	56	45
Other programs	12	24	6	9	13	30	18	29	11	20

* Before payment from this program, but after payment from any other program.
Source: Mollie Orshansky, "The Shape of Poverty in 1966," Social Security Bulletin 31, 3 (March 1967), p. 28.

The numbers of families and individuals counted in Table 2–8 as recipients of social security payments include only recipients of old-age, survivors, disability, and health insurance payments (OASDHI). Apparently, unemployment insurance was included with "other programs," which also include various special provisions for veterans along with miscellaneous other forms of assistance that are neither categorized as "insurance" nor tied to a means test. (Payments received under the programs for aid to dependent children, whether federal or state or local, were included with "public assistance.") Again, among unrelated individuals of any age who received such payments, very high proportions would have been classified as poor without them; the proportions in these groups who crossed over the poverty line with the help of such payments was substantially greater than among those who were recipients of public assistance, however. This was especially the case among those over 65 and, most dramatically, among families headed by females with children (a cut from 68 percent who would have been poor without OASDHI to 35 percent poor after receiving payments under those programs). Among recipients of OASDHI payments who were normally members of the labor force (male heads of families under age 65 and females heads under 65 without children), or who resided in such families, the situation is strikingly different. Less than 30 percent of these families would have been poor without the social security money, and 15 percent were still classified as poor with it (slightly more for the female family heads without children).

What does all this say with respect to OASDHI as a poverty-reducing transfer program? The question is an important one because OASDHI is a big program and has rapidly been growing bigger as its coverage and pay-may levels have been extended. From $4.4 billion in fiscal 1959–60, it had jumped to $20.3 billion in 1965–66 and in 1967–68 it reached $28.7 billion. In fact, in 1967–68 it accounted for half of the total federal outlays on *all* welfare programs, including education and housing, and it is now approximately twice the sum of all state and local expenditures on social insurance, public assistance, and health and medical care.[31]

As concerns OASDHI payments accruing to families whose heads are normally in the active labor force, it gives substantially more to those who would not be poor anyway than to those who are poor; even among recipients in families headed by men or women over 65, two fifths to over half of the recipients would not have been classified "poor" without their retirement benefits. Furthermore, since the amounts received in retirement benefits are positively related to previous levels of earnings, those recipients of such benefits who "needed" them least typically received the most. Evidently this is not the most efficient possible system if we conceive its main

---

[31] For data on this and other welfare expenditures over a 20-year period, see Ida C. Merriam, Alfred M. Skolnik, and Sophie R. Dales, "Social Welfare Expenditures, **1967–68**," *Social Security Bulletin,* 31, 12 (December 1968), pp. 14–27.

purpose to be transfer of cash to those with the lowest incomes—even if we ignore the fact that it does not reach some major categories of poor people at all. On the other hand, it does very sharply reduce the incidence and the severity of poverty among half of the families headed by older men and women and among four fifths of elderly people living by themselves, and it does this in a way that preserves their dignity and self-respect. It does the same thing for oldsters living with relatives, as for younger disabled men and women.

Indeed, one of the strengths of OASDHI is precisely that it is *not* a program "for the poor," that it is much simpler to administer, and entails no means test and no probing into the lives of recipients. But for the same reason, it cannot eliminate poverty among beneficiaries with no other source of income.[32] Somewhat similar considerations are involved in assessing the other income maintenance programs, which, as Table 2–8 shows, are much broader in their reach to families that would not have been poor in any case; but those programs do not compare in magnitude with the OASDHI outlays.[33]

Let us grant, then, that OASDHI is to be judged not just as a program for transferring cash to the poor but as a program that aims at, though it does not yet reach, every American who suffers disabilities along the way and every American when he reaches retirement age. And let us agree, further, that it plays a substantial role in the alleviation of poverty. (I am not so concerned with how many cross any particular, always arbitrary, poverty line as in the fact that, whether they cross it or not, poor recipients are much better off than they could be otherwise.) Does it follow that if a little OASDHI is good, more is better, and still more is better still?

Poverty policies and majority politics

In the December, 1968, issue of the *Social Security Bulletin,* Wilbur J. Cohen (then Secretary of Health, Education, and Welfare) laid out "A Ten-Point Program to Abolish Poverty."[34] One of those 10 points was: "The social security system should be improved." Secretary Cohen recommended a number of revisions in the system, none of which would extend

---

[32] Eveline Burns summed up this problem in 1956, when she posed the question to what extent could the OASI system be used "both to provide an adequate floor or security for those most in need of assurance and to preserve substantial differentials above the minimum subsistence benefit without allocating to old age security purposes an unduly large proportion of current incomes." (In John J. Corson and John W. McConnell, *Economic Needs of Older People,* New York, Twentieth Century Fund, 1965, p. 506.)

[33] For an international perspective with regard to income maintenance and welfare policies, and how these compare and contrast with provisions in the United States, see Margaret S. Gordon, *The Economics of Welfare Policies,* New York and London, Columbia University Press, 1963. More details for the United States are provided by the contributors to the book edited by Otto Eckstein, *Studies in the Economics of Income Maintenance,* Washington, D.C., Brookings Institution, 1967. See, also, Sar Levitan, *Programs in Aid of the Poor,* Kalamazoo, W. E. Upjohn Institute, 1965.

[34] *Social Security Bulletin,* 31, 12 (December 1958), pp. 3–13.

its population coverage, but all of which would increase its scale, requiring either higher tax rates on employees and employers or more general revenue financing. In this connection, he remarked that in order to avoid an increased burden of the higher rates on employees with low earnings we might want "to amend the income-tax laws so that, for low-income people, a part of the social security contribution would be treated as a credit against their income tax or, if no tax were due, could be refunded."

However, I find no indication otherwise that the Secretary was seeking out those features and possible adaptations of the social security system that would maximize its impact in reducing poverty. In fact, one of his recommendations for "improvement" of the system was legislation that would embody: [35] *"a way to make the program more effective as the basic system of economic security for those who earn somewhat above the average, as well as for average and below-average earners."* (Italics are Cohen's.) Following this recommendation, he went on to state explicitly that "The social security program should be kept meaningful for workers at all earnings levels, not just for low earners." Perhaps it should, but how much of the added benefits would go to the poorest people? Does such a suggestion belong in a "ten-point program to abolish poverty," or does it illustrate what happens so often—that large spending programs grow almost of their own momentum, but always in the direction of providing more for those who have more or who are the majority?

Another of the Secretary's comments in this connection was: [36]

Important as private pensions are, it is clear that the job of providing protection against loss of earnings suffered by those who have had even above-average earnings should be done substantially through the social security program and not left largely to private arrangements.

I'm not sure about its intent, but this seems to state both *(a)* that men must be forced to save for their old age, *and to do it in a government scheme,* and *(b)* that they must be forced to do this not only to provide a minimum sufficient to ensure independence in old age but also in accordance with their incomes beyond that. However, let us set aside the questions of forced saving, choice in how to save, and the place of public versus private schemes. It is true enough, as Mr. Cohen has said, that the original social security act was directed to the large majority of workers, and was intended to tax and pay benefits in relation to their full earnings—which is what he wants to bring back by raising ceilings to match the increases that have taken place in real incomes (as well as to allow for inflation). But is providing more in their old age for those who have had more up to that time the most reasonable way to help the poor?

The scale of these programs is large even when viewed in the perspec-

---

[35] Ibid., p. 7.
[36] Ibid., p. 8.

tive of the total GNP. Affluent though we may be, we should exercise every caution to see that we do not use up our margin for maneuver by handing out "something for everyone" instead of focusing on the problems that face our cities, the alleviation of genuine poverty, and the breaking of its lockstep.[37]

Family allowances and Aid to Dependent Children

In a very thoughtful and inquiring essay, Herman Miller has asked.[38]

Would it help or hurt matters to appreciably increase AFDC payments so as to provide the wherewithall to raise the children in these families properly? Boulding cautions that attempts to make per capita incomes among families a little more equal by such devices as family allowances and aid to dependent children—may have deplorable dynamic consequences. The elasticity of supply of children may be large, and an undertaking to support them may produce them.

I infer that Miller is disturbed by Boulding's suggestion, and certainly such a possibility cannot be set aside a priori. On the other hand, neither is there necessarily a strong presumption that these elasticities would turn out to be positive rather than negative within the modest income range over which family allowances would extend. In family planning, the immediate outlays are for birth control, whereas costs of having children and raising them come later; there is some evidence, at least, that birth control expenditures may be associated positively with income in the lower income ranges.

Miller was speaking specifically of AFDC, not child allowances that would be passed out to everyone regardless of income. However, that family allowances are widespread in Europe whereas we do not have them in the United States has led some would-be imitators to argue that we should have them here. The Social Security Administration prepared estimates of the cost and antipoverty effects of family allowances for all children under age 18. The most generous of several alternatives presented would have paid $50 per child per month—just at the exemption level on income taxes.[39] Applied in 1965, this would have cost gross $41.2 billion,

---

[37] The using up of room for manoeuvre is in part economic; however wealthy this nation, we cannot do indefinite amounts of everything at once. But the problem may be equally that of using up political capital and the scarcity of sheer promotive energy. T. W. Schultz pointed to a clear example in the case of farm people. First, he outlined the story of the disinterest that farm leaders have displayed in the past as concerns extension of social services to rural people, despite the early and active role of farmers in the creation of a welfare state. He concludes by saying: "This brings us to the principal reason for the neglect by government of the welfare of farm people. These price supports, acreage restrictions, and subsidies hold top priority in the United States farm policy. Virtually all of the time and thought of the United States Department of Agriculture, the agricultural committees of Congress, and the farm organizations is spent on them. They exhaust the political influence of farm people." ("Our Welfare State and the Welfare of Farm People," *The Social Service Review*, June 1964, pp. 123–29.)

[38] Herman P. Miller, "Major Elements of a Research Program for the Study of Poverty," in *The Concept of Poverty*, p. 131.

[39] The alternatives examined and their effects are reported by Mollie Orshansky in "The Shape of Poverty in 1966," *Social Security Bulletin*, 31, 3 (March 1968), pp. 3–32.

of which $6.5 could have been recovered on the income tax by elimination of the tax exemption, and another $6.2 could have been recovered by taxing the allowances; the net cost if both of these offsets were used would have been $28.5 billion. Out of that $28.5 billion, payments of $8.4 billion would have reached poor families, probably raising a large proportion of them (especially of those with male heads) above poverty lines, but nevertheless leaving some below criterion levels. Even the $8.4 billion exceeds the poverty gap for all families with children under 18, which was $6 billion in 1965 (see Table 2–7). This, again, is an expensive and inefficient way to proceed to get rid of poverty. Evidently, raising AFDC assistance would be a more effective way of getting income to those who need it.

When aid to families of dependent children has been predicated on a means test, concern has been voiced over its possible diversion to other purposes. This is one reason the program at first admitted as eligible only families in which no adult male was present; but this provision created an incentive to the breaking up of families or the concealment of the male. Subsequent extension of the program to include families in which there was an unemployed male head then raised a problem that had caused little concern when only mothers were involved: What of the effects of the aid on incentives to look for or accept work? This question is a recurring one, in fact, in all programs designed to relieve poverty. It was raised by Secretary Cohen in another of his suggestions for improving social security, when he specified that new legislation should embody provisions that would "improve work incentives by liberalizing the provision under which a beneficiary's earnings reduce the benefit he receives." [40] It is a question that men have tussled with since the days of the Elizabethan Poor Laws, however much perceptions of the poor and poverty levels of living may have changed over three and a half centuries. It is one of the questions that takes a central place in discussions of the "negative income tax" and guaranteed income approaches to the removal or reduction of poverty.

Guaranteed incomes: Social-dividend schemes

There is a very strong appeal in the idea of providing for everyone a guaranteed minimum income, this income to be assured on a national basis and by impersonal, standardized rules, and so structured that men will not be penalized too heavily (if at all) by the cutting of allowances when they take jobs or increase their earnings. Such plans are not guarantees that public assistance will fill the income gap up to some minimum, but rather that such a minimum, at least, will be provided in other, less demeaning ways. Schemes that have been proposed for accomplishing this have been of two-broad types: social-dividend plans and negative income taxes.

---

[40] *Social Security Bulletin*, 31, 12, p. 8.

The social-dividend plans would pay out a guaranteed allowance to every man, woman, and child, rich and poor alike, without consideration of need (except that payments might be differentiated by age and sex). They are thus very like family allowance systems that impose no means tests, except that payments are extended to everyone. The Townsend proposals for such unconditional payments to older people, which had a considerable political following in the 1930s, could similarly be regarded as forerunners of the social-dividend proposals. But the first generalization of this scheme should probably be credited to Lady Rhys-Williams, who argued in 1943 that the entire British state welfare system should be supplanted by a minimum allowance to everyone.[41] Her proposal stemmed, in part, from dissatisfaction with the work disincentive effects of the unemployment insurance system in Britain at that time. In her words: "The lion in the path of curing want by means of insurance is that if the standard of unemployment pay is raised to a level at which real want is banished, . . . then the advantages of working for wages largely disappear."

In this view, the disincentive problem is not that men who have enough to live on will not work, but that work is discouraged when earnings are offset by reductions in social benefit payments. She provided for idlers, however, by stipulating that the allowance should be cut off when ablebodied unemployed men refused to accept jobs offered them. The extension of the allowance to rich and poor alike was regarded by Lady Rhys-Williams as a provision more just or equitable than limiting payments to the poor and the sick. Thus, in her view, a social-dividend scheme rests on "the democratic principle that the state owes precisely the same benefits to every one of its citizens." The payments would have been financed by a proportional tax on all incomes. Christopher Green has estimated that this would have necessitated a rate close to 40 percent, given the proposed allowance levels for the guaranteed income and the level of national income in Britain at that time.[42]

Understandably, this plan has had little impact in practice, although its basic simplicity has appealed to a few academicians and modern political-utopians, who have suggested minor variants of essentially the same scheme proposed by Lady Rhys-Williams. Probably the strongest case that has been made for it is Robert Theobald's argument, which looks to a future in which cybernetics will make for a degree of affluence and a scarcity of jobs that, were it to eventuate, would make this quite another world.[43]

---

[41] *Something to Look Forward To,* London, MacDonald, 1943; and *Taxation and Incentive,* New York, Oxford University Press, pp. 121–37. The following quote is from *Taxation and Incentive,* p. 121.

[42] Christopher Green, *Negative Taxes and the Poverty Problem,* Washington, D.C., Brookings Institution, 1967, p. 53. Green summarizes briefly most of the more recent variants of social-dividend proposals and analyzes their economic implications, which he compares with negative income tax alternatives.

[43] See *Free Men and Free Markets.*

Negative income taxes

Proposals for the use of a negative income tax system as the backbone of an attack on poverty have proliferated recently, following the case made for this approach by Milton Friedman.[44]

This suggestion, too, has an earlier history, going back to World War II, although, so far as I am aware, nothing was published on it at that time. Walter Heller, William Vickrey, and others, then in the Division of Tax Research in The Treasury Department, were discussing such a possibility in the early 1940s. I happened to be at Iowa State College in 1941–42 when Albert Hart stirred up the economics faculty there with a proposal that the income tax should be revised to carry through the logic of exemptions that eliminated taxes on the first few hundred dollars of income per person; the argument was that if we took these exemptions as representing a minimum (or subminimum) amount that everyone must have, wherever he lived and whatever his circumstances, then it must follow that incomes lower than this should automatically be supplemented by payments from the government. However, Hart did not pretend that this was a program that could take over the task of subduing poverty in American society, and he never suggested that it should be central in anything like a war on poverty. The levels implied in meeting minimum exemptions were too low to accomplish such a purpose, other problems aside.

As Christopher Green has pointed out in his excellent book on *Negative Taxes and the Poverty Problem,* all the versions of these plans have at least three variables in common, and by which they are distinguished: *(a)* a minimum level of income; *(b)* a positive "tax" rate at which government allowances are reduced for each dollar of increase in private income; and *(c)* a break-even level of income at which the allowance is reduced to zero.[45] In setting up such schedules, a major difficulty is that if the absolute minimum is set high enough to really take care of those with no other sources of support, and if the requirement that work incentives be maintained is met, the break-even points may be pushed to intolerably high levels, eating into the tax base and subsidizing many who are, in fact, quite well off.

A considerable variety of schedules has been suggested. I select for illustration here the schedules used in the OEO "graduated work incentive" experiments initiated in 1968. That study was confined to families

---

[44] See chap. 7, "The Alleviation of Poverty," in *Capitalism and Freedom.* In support of the negative income tax, Friedman writes (p. 192): "The advantages of this arrangment are clear. It is directed specifically at the problem of poverty. It gives help in the form most useful to the individual, namely cash. It is general and could be substituted for the host of special measures now in effect. It makes explicit the cost borne by society. It operates outside the market. Like any other measure to alleviate poverty, it reduces the incentives of those helped to help themselves, but it does not eliminate that incentive entirely, as a system of supplementing income up to some fixed minimum would."

[45] Christopher Green, p. 11.

headed by able-bodied men in the working force ages; it excluded un-attached persons, families headed by females or by aged individuals, and rural populations.[46]

Starting with a "basic income guarantee" that is varied by size of household, nine alternative benefit schemes were tested. These were built up by applying alternative multipliers, g, to the basic income guarantee and by using different tax rates r. Designating the basic income guarantee for household size n as $G(n)$, the actual guarantee for such a household will be $g \cdot G(n)$. This is what the household will receive in negative tax payments if it has no other income at all. The household's net benefit is the difference between the maximum benefit $g \cdot G(n)$ and the product of the negative tax rate and pretax income. The break-even point at which no payments are received, is accordingly when pretax incomes equals $\frac{g}{r} \cdot G(n)$. The basic guarantee sums for families from two to eight or more members is as follows.

n	$G(n)$	n	$G(n)$
2	$2,000	6	$4,050
3	2,750	7	4,350
4	3,300	8 or	4,600
5	3,700	more	

The combinations of r and g used in the experiments are shown in Table 2–9, along with the net benefits to a family of four with various levels of earnings. A family's total income after receipt of these benefits is, of course, the sum of the net benefits shown in a column and the earned income figure at the head of that column. (I selected earnings levels to give exact breakeven points for five of the nine schedules.)

The minimum income guarantees under these various schedules can be read directly from the first net-benefit column for families with no pre-tax income. In the first two schedules, this was below the existing exemption level on positive taxes, which would have been $2,100 for a family of 4, and the minimums on the first five schedules are all below the social security poverty line. Schedules VI and VII guarantee minimum incomes at that line, and the last two schedules are set with minimums somewhat higher. The tax rates on earnings, variously 30, 50, and 70 percent, determine the pace at which net benefits drop off when other income rises. Schedule II is, of course, the least favorable to the recipients.

[46] This experiment is popularly known as "the New Jersey experiment." Other OEO and HEW income maintenance experiments, with other focal questions, were initiated in 1969 and are under way in Seattle, Washington; in Gary, Indiana; and in rural counties in North Carolina and Iowa.

Table 2–9. Parameters of experimental negative income tax schedules, with associated net benefit payments to a family of four at five pretax income levels

Schedule Type	r	g	g/r	Pretax Income None	$1,650	$3,300	$4,950	$6,600	$8,250
I	.3	.50	1.67	1,650	1,355	660	165	*	*
II	.5	.50	1.00	1,650	825	zero	*	*	*
III	.3	.75	2.50	2,475	2,180	1,485	990	495	zero
IV	.5	.75	1.50	2,475	1,650	825	zero	*	*
V	.7	.75	1.07	2,475	1,320	165	*	*	*
VI	.5	1.00	2.00	3,300	2,475	1,650	825	zero	*
VII	.7	1.00	1.43	3,300	2,145	990	*	*	*
VIII	.5	1.25	2.50	4,125	3,300	2,475	1,650	825	zero
IX	.7	1.25	1.79	4,125	2,970	1,815	660	*	*

* Beyond the break-even point.

Three schedules, III, VI, and VIII, would still be paying out money to families whose incomes were above $6,000, and two continue paying out something up to an income of $8,250—Considerably above median income at the present time. Clearly, any attempt to put schedule IX or even schedules III and VI into effect would dig deeply into revenue from the present federal income tax. Taking schedule III as an example, a family of 4 with an income of $6,600 would be receiving payments of $495 (bringing total income to $7,095) instead of paying approximately $750 into the federal treasury. Yet, the minimum guaranteed by that schedule is only $2,475. The reason is, of course, the low tax rate applied to earnings up to the break-even point in making adjustments of allowances; this (like schedule I) maximizes incentives to work, but as a trade-off against a lower minimum guaranteed income level. Schedule VII, on the other hand, raises the minimum to $3,300 but heavily penalizes earnings, taking 70 percent of earnings out of the payments. These patterns clearly illustrate the problem of attempting to eliminate poverty by transfer payments (whether as negative tax paymens or in the form of public assistance) while at the same time retaining work incentives or, more correctly, avoiding the injection of strong disincentives to work. Neither horn of the dilemma is satisfactory. A low guaranteed minimum strips the negative income tax of its appeal as a simple solution with respect to those at the bottom, since it would have to be supplemented from other sources. But if we raise the minimum *and* maintain work incentives, the system quickly gets out of hand and we are soon in a fiscal position not unlike that under a social-dividend scheme.

The problem of maintaining work incentives may be somewhat less important than has often been assumed. There was indeed some effect of income supplements on hours worked according to preliminary reports of the New Jersey experiment: families receiving supplements averaged 12 percent fewer hours worked by all family members combined than corresponding families in the control group. However, most of the differential was attributed to wives and adults in the family other than male heads, and there were no significant differences associated with the use of a schedule with high or low built-in work incentive or disincentive components (tax rates). Similar results were obtained in an important new study sponsored by the Upjohn Institute using data tapes from the second Survey of Economic Opportunity (conducted by the Bureau of the Census in the spring of 1967.[47] This study analyzed income and substitution effects on hours worked by making use of data on "nonemployment income" (NEY), actual wages, and estimates of potential wage rates. They found strong negative effects of NEY on hours worked by female household heads, with an NEY/hours elasticity of −.69 for women with actual or potential wage rates under $3.00. For male household heads also, higher NEY reduced hours worked, but the effects were very small except for very large changes in NEY. Taking earnings or potential earnings of husbands and wives jointly into account and varying NEY gave NEY/hours elasticities of −.16 for husbands and of −.31 for wives where both had potential (or actual) wages under $3.00. Separate calculations showed hours worked by female heads of households to be highly sensitive to estimated implicit tax rates on earnings, with estimated elasticities of substitution between market and non-market activities of .89 to 1.14; among men analogous figures were only .16 to .18. The importance of productive activities in the home, definitely including among those activities child care, is clearly indicated in all of these findings. Tella, Tella and Green, authors of the Upjohn study, went on to analyze effects of alternative negative income tax plans applying the coefficients from their analysis of the Survey of Economic Opportunity data. Their concluding paragraphs are worth quoting: [48]

Under all the plans the income distribution of families below the break-even point is compressed from the top as well as from the bottom. For some families the loss in income from reduction in labor supply exceeds their initial supplement, and income goes down. In the case of male family heads for whom substitution effects are fairly moderate, only the incomes of families very close to the break-even point go down, and they do not decline very much. In the case of female family heads for whom the substitution effects under all three plans are large, incomes well below the break-even point go down, and those near the break-even point decline substantially.

For male household heads with the characteristics of those in our sample, the reduction in labor supply in response to a negative income tax with a tax rate no greater than 50 percent, such as Plan A, would consist entirely of a reduction in moonlighting or overtime, leaving average annual hours still at a normal full-time full-year level.

While work incentive effects have been the most widely discussed issue in connection with income transfer programs ranging all the way from the

---

[47] Alfred Tella, Dorothy Tella and Christopher Green, *The Hours of Work and Family Income Response to Negative Income Tax Plans,* Kalamazoo, Michigan, the W. E. Upjohn Institute for Employment Research, December 1971.
[48] Ibid., pp. 29–30.

present mix of welfare programs through negative income taxes to the guaranteed minimum income extreme, effects on hours worked for pay are by no means the only relevant concern. Negative income tax plans, like all alternatives, may have many other sorts of impacts on behavior and on the society. What, for example, about incentives to combine or split households? What is to be done about the fact that incomes, especially in the lower ranges, may be very irregular over the year, especially when they rise in the second half of the year? And how would a negative income tax plan be adapted to take account of the different situations of farm and nonfarm families, or the very different costs of living in New York City, for example, as compared with either urban or rural areas in the Southeast? [49] Is a national minimum standard, whether implemented by a negative income tax scheme or in some other way, appropriate across a country as large and diverse as the United States in any case? Would it discourage migration from poor areas, for example? This is an incentive question of major importance, and unfortunately it is one on which the New Jersey experiment can shed no light.[50] It brings us back to the indubitable fact that poverty is not one thing but many, and that prevention and amelioration of poverty, though interconnected in some respects, may call in the main for very different policies.

IV.   *Poor people, public policies, and labor markets*

Except for the totally dependent poor—those who are too old, too young, too sick, too disabled to help themselves—programs to relieve poverty should provide people with the help and opportunities to move out of poverty and become productive citizens, instead of relief payments to guarantee them minimum income.[51]

This is a large task, whether we look at the job market end or the development of the human resource potentials of adults who may need special help, and of their children. But this simple statement nevertheless puts the spotlight on the key requirements for an antipoverty program that would go to the roots of the most serious aspects of poverty; it puts human beings in the central place where they belong.

In treating this subject, I shall be highly selective. The reader who wants a summing up of the Economic Opportunity Act and its history, for example, will have to look elsewhere. Neither do I intend to go into the arguments over provision of housing, or even, except incidentally, on the pro-

---

[49] Milton Friedman has suggested (in informal discussion) a national negative income tax at a minimal standard suitable, for example, to rural Mississippi, to be supplemented by state and, where needed, city negative taxes in high-cost areas.

[50] For a fuller discussion of some of the practical problems that arise in attempting to implement the negative income tax idea, see Christopher Green, *Negative Taxes and the Poverty Problem.*

[51] This is one of the recommendations underlined by the Task Force on Economic Growth and Opportunity of the U.S. Chamber of Commerce in *The Concept of Poverty,* Washington, D.C., 1965. The quotation is from p. 13.

vision of medical care as an investment in people. Instead, I shall focus, first, on the problem of job creation and job guarantees, giving special attention to issues in the location of jobs. I go on from this to a discussion of the impact of minimum wage legislation, with some related remarks about payroll taxes and wage subsidies (versus other subsidies to enterprise). Finally, I shall raise a couple of irascible and rebellious questions about the directions in which recent policies relating to education and training are heading.

Job creation and Job guarantees

No one will challenge the assertion that the best route out of poverty, for the able-bodied male, at least, is to earn his way out in a "decent" job (though the definition of "decent" remains ambiguous). Probably everyone would agree that whether it proves sufficient or not a *first requirement in pursuit of this goal must be a monetary and fiscal policy favorable to full employment.* I have said something about this earlier, but the main point bears repeating. A full-employment economy is the first condition for the enlargement of job opportunities and the breaking down of other barriers to the progress of human beings into dignity and freedom. Full employment is the foundation on which we must build not just a system that ensures that none shall suffer from dire economic want, but a society that provides opportunity for all to play a part that has meaning. When this is not possible, progress out of poverty becomes a snare and a delusion.

But even waiving aside the arguments over how "full" employment must be to qualify as "full employment," monetary and fiscal policy may not quite bring us up to the mark. Neither can it go all the way toward assuring that available jobs will be at levels of pay that are high enough to support a family (or even, in some cases, a single individual) at a level we would today consider high enough to preclude poverty. Are we then to turn back to relief for able-bodied men, or should we take action to create jobs in other ways? Should we be doing that anyway? And should we guarantee jobs, with government filling the gap directly when other means fail?

Today, both job creation and job guarantee recommendations appear and reappear in reports of commissions and task forces of various kinds, and in books and articles written by individuals concerned with anti-poverty policy. Sometimes, these recommendations are linked with discussions of the problem of work-disincentive effects of transfer payments. Thus, Victor Fuchs has remarked: [52] "If one of the major objections to a policy of guaranteed incomes is that people would collect money without

---

[52] Ibid., pp. 87–88. (This is part of his essay, "Toward a Theory of Poverty," cited earlier, which, with several others, is appended to the summary and recommendations of the Task Force as a collective group.)

working, the government could propose, as an alternative, a program of guaranteed jobs." It may well be that the Swedish system should be enlisting more attention in this country. The unemployed man in Sweden is normally required to take an upgrading course, and the government pays the costs when he must migrate to a job. But this in itself is not a job guarantee.

Most of the neatly underlined proposals that jobs be created or guaranteed, by the government if need be, pursue the problem no further. A few do go on, however, to be more specific. It is then that issues begin to be clarified, and it turns out that most of them head up in arguments over special policies (other than monetary and fiscal) to induce private provision of jobs versus direct creation of jobs by government, over which measures are most appropriate in the stimulation of job creation in the private sphere, and over where the jobs should be—whatever the ways they are brought into being. And running through all this, sometimes in a subterranean flow, sometimes quite visibly on the surface, is the related debate over what is a "decent job at decent pay" and how far government policy should be directed to the ensurance not only of jobs but of jobs at "decent" or "adequate" pay levels—and of what policies will, in fact, contribute to realization of such goals.

If we are to make some sort of order out of this maze of suggestions and countersuggestions, even looking at them selectively, we must first go back to review who of the able-bodied remain poor even as we have approached moderately full employment, why they are still poor, where they are and what impedes their mobility (whether geographic or of other kinds). To whom, in other words, should our job creation (with or without job guarantee) program be directed, and what are some of the conditions of its success?

(1) Evidently, no feasible job creation or job guarantee program could eliminate inadequacy of earnings among men of modest earning potentials when they have very large families. This is a problem that cannot be resolved in the labor markets.

(2) A large proportion of the poor among able-bodied adults are ill-equipped to undertake work productive enough to raise them out of poverty, and their children often follow in their footsteps, even when families are of modest size. Every job-creation and job-opportunity endeavor runs into this snag, which requires a complementary concern with human resource development—among both today's adults and the children of poverty and ignorance.

(3) Minimum wage legislation, though it is intended to ensure that pay will be high enough to prevent or at least alleviate poverty among employel workers, aggravates the difficulties of the poorest of the poor. If we are to have minimum-wage laws (and it is a political fact that we will continue to have them), some compensating policy would seem to be called for. I shall

come back to this, with a few comments on the case for as well as against such minimum-wage legislation in a war against poverty.

(4) It has often been asserted that one of the stumbling blocks in the provision of job opportunities is that they are created in the wrong places. This is argued both with respect to megalopolis and its cumulating problems and with respect to depressed or laggard rural areas. The important kernel of truth in these locational disputes is the very real costs, economic and psychological, of mobility, and the ignorance and failures of communication that impede adjustment processes. But meanwhile, as I have noted previously, there has been a growing confusion of antipoverty policies with regional rehabilitation and development programs that can easily divert effort and resources into both diseconomic public activities and programs that end up carrying perverse distributive impact.

(5) Discrimination (with respect to race, sex, and age) shunts some groups into jobs and occupations that provide neither adequate current pay nor opportunities to advance in the future. This creates poverty because of its cumulative impact in certain groups; it is not merely a matter of randomly dividing up a fixed amount of transitory poverty, but rather a repeated dealing out of poverty to certain categories of people. I have said something about discrimination earlier in this chapter. I shall go no further with its explication here except with respect to policies to reduce or eliminate racial discrimination. These may well go beyond the universalization of job-opportunity policies to compensatory policies affecting urban job locations and accessibility and to compensatory efforts in human resources development.

Jobs in the ghettos

I have given this topic its own heading to signal its importance, but I shall say very little about it, beyond referring back to my earlier remarks concerning the perversity of recent urban developments in their effects on accessibility of jobs to the urban and especially the Negro poor. Instead of pursuing compensatory policies that would favor development of job opportunities for black Americans, to help them catch up and overcome the dragging effect of a long history of discrimination in the past, we are failing even to prevent or neutralize those newer features of urban development that operate, however indirectly, to narrow the range of job opportunities open to dwellers in the black ghettos and to raise the costs they must incur in getting to and from work. The problem, I suspect, is not just, or even primarily, a matter of jobs in the ghetto, however. It is at least equally one of bringing the people out of those ghettos, both physically and psychologically.[53] How far jobs located in the ghettos can build com-

---

[53] The Kerner Commission made this very clear. The crucial importance of opening up suburbia, and the role that big industry could very easily play—and must play—in bringing

munication bridges across which ghetto dwellers will walk with greater ease remains an open question.

Jobs wherever men are?

All too often, proposals that the federal government should take the responsibility of creating or guaranteeing jobs take on such a sweeping character as to sacrifice all pragmatic impact or, if they have an effect, to encourage an indiscriminate expansion of activities along so many fronts that policy loses its thrust and we are swept away in an amorphous ocean of undirected activism. Unfortunately, the Commission on Rural Poverty fell into this quagmire in its report on *The People Left Behind.* Thus, for example, the Commission included as one of its many recommendations.[54]

> . . . the United States adopt and put into effect immediately a national policy designed to give residents of rural America equal opportunity with all other citizens. This must include access to jobs, medical care, housing, education, welfare, and all other public services, without regard to race, religion, *or place of residence.* [Italics mine.]

One might read most of this as a straightforward plank attacking discrimination, but the inclusion of the last phrase, *"or place of residence,"* could turn it into a prescription for national disaster. This sally into what can only be termed "ruralistic diseconomics" is the more unfortunate in that there is so much that is worthwhile in the Commission's report, and that there are genuine and serious problems for rural people in the costs and difficulties of adjustment to the pulls and pushes of a dynamic, technological, and continuously urbanizing economy.[55]

Minimum wage legislation, wage subsidy, and negative taxes once again

If there were no minimum-wage legislation, some people's wages would almost certainly be lower than the wages they are now receiving. Indeed, if they would be receiving just as much without the mininum wage legis-

---

this about is cogently argued by Jeanne R. Lowe in "Race, Jobs and Cities: What Can Business Do?" *Saturday Review,* January 11, 1969. That article is well worth reading, not only for the effectiveness with which its main theme is argued but also for the realism and insight with which the whole gamut of demographic, residential, and industrial trends in Metropolitan areas is brought together and assessed. One of her minor themes concerns the importance of encouraging Black Capitalism not just in the ghettos, where risks are highest and consumer incomes lowest, but where the economic thrust is greatest and opportunity is more open-ended.

[54] P. xi.

[55] A very well argued presentation of the case for development of strategies to encourage location of industry in smaller urban places, both as staging points in the rural-urban migration process and as a counteractive to the growing external diseconomies of metropolitis has been developed by Gordon C. Cameron, in his "The Regional Problem in the United States and the Role of the Economic Development Administration" (typescript of a paper delivered at the meetings of the Southern Economic Association in Washington, D.C., November 8, 1968). The approach argued by Mr. Cameron is related to but not identical with the emphasis on growth points that was pushed by Charles Schultze, Director, Bureau of the Budget, in the rewriting of legislation for aid to depressed areas during the Johnson administration.

lation as with it, the legislation could just be forgotten; if it is having an effect, we are forced to conclude not only that it is raising wages for some but also that it is forcing wages down for those who are shunted into uncovered jobs, or who are pushed out of the labor market altogether.[56] And In this process resources are being malallocated; we are putting people into producing less valued services when they might be adding more to the GNP by working in the industries covered by minimum-wage legislation (or union wage contracts), even though what they would add there is less than the fixed wage.

All this is undeniable. But the important question is how big is the effect on the employment mix, at what differentials of minimum wages above the rates of pay that would prevail otherwise? Is minimum wage legislation raising the wages of 95 poor men above the poverty level, while forcing 5 poor men into considerably worse positions? Or is it raising 40 men's wages to "adequate" levels, while pushing 60 further still into poverty? In other words, what is the elasticity of demand for the kinds of labor offered by men who are most affected by the minimum wage legislation? There is no general answer to this question. "It all depends . . ." But it is equally clear that whatever the answer may be, It Is most important for the South generally and, in the North, for the sons and daughters of the ghettos.

I have indicated that there are two disinct issues in connection with the effects of minimum wage legislation: an allocation effect and an income distribution (poverty and antipoverty) effect. In an ingenious note written in 1960, James Buchanan and J. E. Moes showed how a low-income region could neutralize the distortions of resource allocation that would arise when a minimum wage conforming to conditions in the economically more advanced areas was imposed on all alike. In effect, they would tax away the excess of the legal minimum over the equilibrium wage received by covered workers in the low-income region and pay it back to their employers as a wage subsidy.[57] Administrative costs aside, this would also bring about the income distribution that would have prevailed in the absence of the minimum-wage law. Commenting on the Buchanan-Moes paper, Laird and Rinehart went on to remark that "Subsidies can be used to circumvent such man-made impediments to economic development and to 'buy jobs' for labor surplus regions." [58] If we grant that definitions of poverty are always in considerable degree relative, as we must, it is only a small step to go on to suggest that the appropriate poverty line from a regional point of view is related to overall regional levels of living. In fact, It Is the internal

---

[56] In special situations of monopsonistic hiring of labor it is possible that introduction of a legal minimum wage could simply transfer income from profits to payrolls, but even in such markets to *raise* the legal wage will normally act as a damper on covered employment.

[57] J. M. Buchanan and J. E. Moes, "A Regional Countermeasure to National Wage Standardization," *American Economic Review,* 50, 3 (June 1960), pp. 434–38.

[58] William E. Laird and James R. Rinehart, "Neglected Aspects of Industrial Subsidy," *Land Economics,* 43, 1 (February 1967), p. 25.

standards that are immediately visible to local residents and that determine, in practice, local abilities to counter poverty by local efforts. A Buchanan-Moes scheme might then maintain a larger proportion of Southerners, let us say, above a *South*-related poverty line, preventing the downward push that minimum-wage legislation based on northern conditions would exert on employment in the South and on the wages of Southerners in uncovered activities.

But what if we regard the southern equilibrium wage level for unskilled labor as implying an intolerably low level of living? Should we then (a) reduce the legal wage minimum to match the southern conditions but use transfer payments to bring southern incomes up to minimum national norms, or *(b)* set a relatively high, national minimum wage and accept high levels of persistent unemployment (and of menial, uncovered employment) in the South, filling in the gap by public assistance from national coffers (or chiding the southern states that they do not do so), or might we *(c)* provide national funds to subsidize the national minimum wage in the South? None of these is a very satisfactory solution. All run into the inexorable fact that any attempt to approximate a guaranteed income in the South matching levels that might be regarded as acceptable in higher income (and higher cost) areas is inherently incompatible with sound long-term adjustments, and would tend to produce a situation in which the South would be permanently subsidized by the rest of the country.

The first and third alternatives, *(a)* and *(c)*, have one major advantage over *(b);* they would foster more efficient allocation of *any given* southern labor resources within the South.[59] But they would also discourage movement of labor from areas where it was less to those where it was more productive. National malallocations would persist and grow cumulatively larger at an imposing rate under these or any other subsidy or transfer systems that brought minimum wages or guaranteed incomes in the deep South to anywhere within shooting distance of equilibrium wage levels for unskilled and semiskilled workers in northern and western states. Under *(c)*, those malallocations would be of a magnitude that would make the work-disincentive effects of public assistance programs in their present, locally differentiated, form seem microscopic.

The important point in this damaging prognosis was, of course, the disincentive effects with respect to mobility of younger adults and oncoming additions to the labor force in southern (or other economically lagging) areas. But many who are left behind have no mobility potential, they simply could not make it in the city and are better off where they are, even on public assistance. Yet, minimum-wage legislation has inhibited the develop-

---

[59] If labor were immobile, the method of financing the subsidies suggested by Buchanan and Moes would not matter as far as their favorable allocative effect is concerned. This was pointed out by Ralph Gray in his "Industrial Development Subsidies and Efficiency in Resource Allocation," *National Tax Journal,* June 1964, p. 170.

ment of local low-wage enterprises that might employ these men; or when such attempts have been made they have foundered on the minimum-wage rock. Because I have seen this happen in eastern Kentucky, and have some knowledge of what it means to all too many mountain families, I have been giving a good deal of thought to the question: Is there a way of bringing jobs to these men, so that they may take home pay enough to support their families, however modestly, instead of going to the local welfare office for a dole? And can't this be done in a way that would avoid major economic maladjustments or open up a political grabbag?

If we suppose, as is probably the case, that minimum-wage legislation is here to stay, there may be a case for payroll subsidies to support such wage payments under certain highly restrictive conditions. Those conditions, I suggest, would specify the basic immobility characteristics of employees for whom payroll subsidies should be granted—whether their immobility is between places, between jobs, or both. Given the relatively high incidence of poverty among the least educated men (and women) and the difficulties faced by workers over 40 or 45 in adjusting to technological or other changes in the labor markets, it seems to me that there is a strong case for a program of subsidy grants to firms employing such people in proportion to the numbers they employ. The age should be set high enough and the schooling stipulations low enough to keep total national expenditures modest and to avoid creating a false perspective among youth and young adults concerning what schooling means for job chances, as well as to ensure that this is, indeed, a category of workers with very low potential for finding regular employment at unsubsidized legal wage minimums— and a group for most of whom programs for upgrading could offer little help.[60] However, given the other characteristics I just stipulated, there would be no need to fuss around with distinctions between new or additional versus prior employees or to select out those who are poor. Those over 40 with little schooling are a category of men with a very high incidence of poverty. Also, although such a program could be given a national scope geographically, it could equally well be applied under locational constraints that would confine eligibility for the payroll subsidy paymens to establishments (new or old) in designated depressed areas, rural or urban. The usual criticisms of special area constraints would have far less weight here because of the initial proviso that regardless of location the subsidy payments would be made only when certain categories of workers, who are highly immobile, are employed. Subsidies clearly should

---

[60] This sort of restricted wage subsidy program must presuppose improvements in employment information services and probably assistance in meeting the costs of migration. But the argument for policies to aid in job search and relocation is a general one, regardless of anything that might be done to help the immobile, or those least able to move, to find useful work at home. It does not carry any special implications with respect to the role of government in providing or in encouraging private enterprise to provide expanded programs for upgrading or on-the-job training of men (or women) who have been displaced or left behind by the rapid pace of economic change.

not depend on wages the firm is paying; they would be a flat rate per eligible employee. Assuming that there is a minimum-wage law and that employers will receive the subsidy only as they hire workers who are clearly poverty-prone (the least educated of men over 40 years of age, let us say), there is no cause for concern that the subsidy would become excessively expensive and that more than a very small fraction of what was paid out would find its way to the nonpoor. This is very different, therefore, from an arrangement whereby the government would pay employers a subsidy applicable to all workers. The reason for limiting proposed subsidies to some fraction of the difference (wage gap) between what the employer pays and some set amount, such as $2 per hour, is removed under the conditions I have stipulated.

There seems to be considerable confusion about wage subsidy effects because of a failure (a) to distinguish wage subsidies that are linked to wage gaps when the upper limit exceeds legal minimum wages, or in the absence of such legal minimums, from those that would take the legal minimum as the upper limit, and (b) to distinguish effects of wage subsidies on total take-home pay from their effects on the net (postsubsidy) payroll costs of the enterprise. There can be no question but that, given minimum-wage legislation, for labor-surplus workers a wage subsidy tends to reduce the net out-of-pocket expense of the employer; that, indeed, is the intent of both the Buchanan-Moes proposal and the one I put forward here. On the other hand, a wage subsidy has the effect of increasing not only employment but also worker take-home pay unless, as in the Buchanan-Moes scheme, the subsidy is paid out of a matched tax on payrolls.[61]

In the limited-eligibility type of wage subsidy that I have suggested, I stipulated that the subsidy should not be tied to the wages paid by the firm, because I would like to see a program as simple as possible, one that maximized incentives to hire those persons who are otherwise most likely to be persistently unemployed, or to be pushed out into irregular and low-wage employments, and a program such that incentives, if any, to cut payroll outlays in order to get bigger subsidy payments would be minimized. In the plan I suggest, the subsidy payments would not be conditioned by wage rates at all. The catch (there is always a catch) is, of course, that in favoring the hiring of the least capable workers their bargaining power would be raised relative to others. But this is, after all, a redistribution policy with only second-best allocative and GNP effects, under legal minimum wage constraints.

Before leaving this subject, it may be worthwhile to point out that one possibility would, of course, be to abolish national minimum-wage legislation altogether, and then to put in its place a negative income tax scheme

---

[61] This is clearly stated in Federal Poverty Programs, Report R-166 of the Institute for Defense Analysis, January 1966 (Richard Muth, project leader).

with a low minimum guarantee, but also a low tax rate—as in Schedule I of Table 2–9, for example. The man heading a family of four would still have to be helped after receipt of his negative tax payment if he had no earnings. On the other hand, if he earned as much as $2,500 the negative tax payment (of $900 in that case) would bring him up to $3,400 and humble but dignified independence. Yet, he has not been singled out in any way. He (or she) may be of any age and have had any prior amount of schooling. Neither would his sort of scheme pull southern minimums up to northern minimum standards. Undeniably, however, it would have disincentive effects on migration out of the South.

Are we getting education the wrong way round?

We have been hearing in recent years about a variety of training and rehabilitation programs for adults and out-of-school youth, and about "early childhood education." Under the Johnson administration these included the MDT programs (manpower development and training, or upgrading), Job Corps, Neighborhood Youth, and Head Start. Every one of these or their offshoots may be applauded in general despite particular flaws, some of them serious. But as yet these programs have been very small indeed. Moreover "Head Start," which was supposed to help ready disadvantaged children to enter school more nearly on a par with those from more advantaged backgrounds, has probably done more to set off an expansion of preschool education among the more advantaged sectors of the society than among the disadvantaged. And even as we talk about high school dropouts we are spending ever-increasing sums on free access colleges. I have increasing misgivings about this mad rush into more and more conventional schooling for everyone, regardless either of quality or of those left further and further behind. Certification bias is meanwhile receiving a big boost, which is not conducive to eradication of poverty among ablebodied men.

We say we want youth to be responsible, but do we? If so, why do we postpone for so long the time when most of them will be counted men? Perhaps we should be encouraging them to get out to work for a while, but the perverse interdependence between educational policies and labor markets for young people make this increasingly difficult. Why should education be in one unbroken lump? [62] And why must postsecondary voca-

---

[62] I am perfectly aware of the argument that the earlier a man receives his education or training, the longer the period in which he can realize returns from it (and the less his foregone earnings while studying). However, this argument totally disregards obsolescence, individual differences in motivation to learn in alternative circumstances, and the related questions of how men best learn what sorts of things, in what sequences. The presumption in favor of uninterrupted schooling as a full-time learning process before labor market entry, with gradually declining investments in learning at work (formal or informal) may be valid for a majority, but this does not justify its unqualified universalization as a decision rule for all people. (A highly technical, and important, literature on this subject has been growing

tional education be pulled continuously into the junior college and route-to-four-year-college mold, despite experimental efforts leading in the other direction? We talk of the defects in our lower and secondary schools, of their failure to adapt to pupil needs, and of how little the disadvantaged pupils coming out of some of those schools have learned. And we say this especially with respect to the schools in which black Americans have spent their formative years. But instead of devoting resources to improving those schools, seeking ways to reach children who have not been adequately reached before, we are piling additional years on top.

We talk about the need for special qualifications to teach in ghetto schools, and the special trials that teachers who work there must face, but we do not pay them more or offer them special training to cope with those problems. In fact, they are negatively selected. To make matters worse, we measure the so-called quality of a school either by teacher salaries or by achievement tests, but not by how much the school has done for its children. The result is that we often end up assessing the quality of a *school* by how much education is accomplished in the children's *homes.* And we talk about equality of opportunity for an education as though children were free to choose their parents: it seems that some just made poor choices of parents so far as human capital development is concerned.

Even when it comes to the talk about dropouts, I'm not at all sure we don't have things the wrong way around.[63] We treat "dropout" as if it were a cause, when it is more a symptom; but that is not all. Why shouldn't some people find more satisfaction and learn more effectively in a setting that is close to the job? If we add that for most dropouts schools have been the locus and have become the symbol of past failures and frustrations, this is all the more evident. Nevertheless, it is only in a few special programs that we are breaking through the barriers that have excluded those already most disadvantaged from access to learning outside school and at work.

The truth of the matter is that we have solved most of the easier practical problems as far as education and human development are concerned. We have built a system of education (both in schools and at work) that, in tandem with other investments and innovative endeavors, has carried us to levels of productivity heretofore unimagined. That system has served the vast majority of the American population, not just the elites. It has been geared to these majorities. But what we are asking today is that it should serve also the needs and problems of a minority (both rural and urban, and

out of what I have elsewhere described as "The Human Investment Revolution in Economic Thought," *Sociology of Education,* 39, 2, pp. 111–37. But this is an essay on poverty, not on economics of education.)

[63] I have argued this point somewhat more systematically elsewhere. See my "Decisions for Vocational Education: An Economist's View" in Carl J. Schaefer and Jacob J. Kaufman (eds.), *Vocational Education: Social and Behavioral Perspectives,* Lexington, Mass.: Heath Lexington Books, 1971.

of all races) who have been isolated from the mainstream or left behind in this kaleidoscopic world of change. Meanwhile, residential segregation in central cities and rural fragmentation and politicizing of social services are imposing almost insurmountable barriers to realization of these ends.

We know all too little about compensation for poverty of learning in the home in the best of circumstances, and what we do know how to do is apt to be extremely costly per child (or per adult) brought into a fuller participation in the life of this society.[64] Success is much more difficult of attainment among children who are clustered in communities of poverty and ignorance. Indeed, the distance that the majority of Americans have traveled changes the very nature of the educational task with the children of poverty and isolation. And because these endeavors are so often costly, they rarely pass normal benefit-cost tests of their worth be those tests formal or informal. Or to put it more precisely, they do not pass tests that start from a GNP vantage point within the constraints of existing residence patterns and labor market practices. Only the short-term adult upgrading programs seem to qualify on standard benefit–cost criteria.[65] Head Start is proving to be effective only when it is followed up with continuing special efforts. Moreover, special programs for schoolchildren in the slums, like Head Start, yield their economic benefits (whatever those benefits may be) in a future that is too far away to carry full weight in economic evaluations of social projects.

Although there can be no doubt that compensatory endeavors with slum children (rural or urban) can make some contribution to higher national income in the future, if such additions to GNP instead of more direct human values are taken as the criterion, compensatory education for children

---

[64] Educational psychologists have been concentrating increasing attention on this problem, nevertheless—especially among younger children. At the same time, experimental efforts under Office of Economic Opportunity programs have provided at least a minimal basis from which to make better judgments concerning the scope and nature of problems encountered in attempting to help disadvantaged youth. It is not my intention to downgrade the excellent research of some of those involved, but rather to suggest that we may need more of it.

Outstanding in the work by educational psychologists and social anthropologists along these lines are: Benjamin S. Bloom, *Stability and Change in Human Characteristics*, New York, John Wiley & Sons, 1964; and Benjamin S. Bloom, Allison Davis, and Robert Hess, *Compensatory Education for Cultural Deprivation*, Chicago, Holt, Rinehart and Winston, 1965.

[65] Economic assessments of these projects are multiplying, both in print and in preparation. Two musts for anyone interested in economic analysis of compensatory educational policies for children and of adult upgrading and training programs are: Thomas I. Ribich, *Education and Poverty*, Washington, D.C.: Brookings Institution, 1968, and Einar Hardin and Michael E. Borus, *The Economic Benefits and Costs of Retraining*, Lexington, Mass.: Heath Lexington Books, 1971. Ribich's book is interesting both for its conceptualizations of the problem and its careful methodology, empirical findings aside. But it is also important in bringing together such empirical evidence as was available when the book was being written. Drawing on work done by others, along with his own assessments and reassessments, Ribich found negative economic payoffs to compensatory programs in almost all cases except short adult vocational training programs. Economically, Head Start ranks very low, with benefits (discounted at 5 percent) falling decidedly short of costs. Hardin and Borus demonstrated that the economic payoff in programs with adults is from the short training sequences, not from the longer ones; but the longer programs included in that study were still in fact short term and quite narrowly vocationalized.

and hard-core youth will get only the crumbs from the table. And so our ignorance of how to grapple with some of these problems, the constraints within which we are currently working, and our habit of judging national success by national economic growth all drag against investments that might help compensate children born to the slums for the misfortunes of their birth. It is only when we are ready to give a high social and political priority to the raising of poverty's people out of poverty and ignorance to independence and fulfillment, *even when or if it should cost us a lesser rate of growth in GNP,* that we will concentrate any major effort on experimentation with ways that such an end can be brought about. But we will have taken a seven-league stride toward that goal, and rising GNP, too, when we break the back of racial discrimination in residence and job markets.

V.   Concerning a war on poverty; a concluding comment

Adding it all up, just what does or can a war on poverty mean? Evidently, the answer must depend in the first instance on whether we are talking about poverty of the majority of a people or of a minority, and at a level of sheer hunger or something less stark than that—at least biologically.

In the United States today, we are talking about poverty among a minority—wherever we put the poverty line. In this affluent society, there can be no question of our ability to eliminate the dire poverty of hunger, and no excuse for failure to do so. Given a few elementary cautions, it is not at the level of dire want that we need worry about the creation of a subpopulation of permanent mendicants living on the public purse. If to eliminate hunger were to win the war on poverty, there could be no excuse for a failure to bring the war to a successful conclusion. In fact, however, we have continuously raised the level below which we consider men to be poor, and we will continue to do so. In this sense, poverty will never be ended, for with each success we will raise our sights.

Taking any reasonable poverty measure, there are few major problems as concerns provision for the old and the disabled. Despite the many complications that turn up even in programs to reduce or eliminate poverty among these segments of the poor, there is no difficulty so serious that it cannot be satisfactorily resolved. The tougher and the more critical questions are of another order.

For today, the core of the war on poverty must be, above all, to extend opportunity and to break the bonds that lock men in. That war has two interconnected parts. It is a war to help men of this generation to raise themselves out of failure and social isolation into self-respect and a fuller participation in the national life. And it is a war to prevent poverty from perpetuating itself among the children of poverty and ignorance. In this sort of war, neither transfer payments to the poor nor the minor skirmishes that help to their feet those of the poor who are least disadvantaged are enough. Nor can such a war be conducted by the expansion of income-maintenance programs that shore up the average man in the name of poverty prevention. It calls for a full-employment monetary and fiscal policy that serves us all in a very direct way, to be sure. This can raise no argument. But today's war on poverty calls for more fundamental measures as well. It requires a concentration of effort on the removal of the root conditions that maintain and create communities of poverty in our midst, even as we simultaneously strengthen and enlarge compensatory measures among those, child or adult, for whom the time is already late.

3

Economic Issues in Health Services

HERMAN M. SOMERS

Professor of Politics and Public Affairs
Princeton University

B y any available measure, the health services industry has become one of the largest and most significant in the United States—in terms of total costs, persons employed, government expenditures, and in the growth rates of all of these. Simultaneously, it has become the subject of major wide-ranging public policy controversy.

Total expenditures for health and medical care in fiscal year 1970–71 reached $75.0 billion, or 7.4 percent of gross national product. Only six years earlier, the figure had been $38.9 billion and 5.9 percent of GNP. In fiscal year 1950, expenditures had been 4.6 percent of GNP. In 21 years, the health care share of GNP had been enlarged by more than 60 percent. It appears likely that costs will at least approach and perhaps exceed 10 percent of GNP by the end of the current decade.[1] (See Table 3–1.)

Many factors have contributed to this spectacular growth, including: a continuous enlargement of demand for health services, augmented by sharp advancement in government financing; new methods of financing, in-

---

[1] Some predictions are far more extreme. One report states, ". . . some experts have predicted an increase from the present 6 to 25 percent of the GNP for health services." Time not specified. *Report of the National Advisory Commission on Health Manpower,* G.P.O., November 1967, Vol. II, p. 182.

Table 3–1. Expenditures for health and medical care, selected years 1928–29 through 1970–71 (amounts in millions)

Type of Expenditure	1928–29	1949–50	1959–60	1966–67	1967–68	1968–69	1969–70	1970–71*
Total (dollars)	3,589.1	12,027.3	25,855.2	47,859.6	53,562.4	59,938.1	67,770.0	75,011.1*
Private expenditures	3,112.0	8,962.0	19,460.0	32,037.0	33,523.0	37,004.0	42,738.0	46,548.0
Health and medical services	3,010.0	8,710.0	18,815.0	30,652.0	32,017.0	35,257.0	40,140.0	43,873.0
Medical research	—	37.0	121.0	177.0	185.0	190.0	195.0	200.0
Medical facilities construction	102.0	215.0	524.0	1,208.0	1,321.0	1,557.0	2,403.0	2,475.0
Public expenditures	477.1	3,065.3	6,395.2	15,822.6	20,039.4	22,934.1	25,032.0	28,463.1
Health and medical services	372.5	2,470.2	5,346.3	13,672.0	17,581.1	20,391.5	22,376.3	25,604.9
Medical research	—	72.9	471.2	1,428.7	1,615.5	1,599.7	1,652.8	1,819.3
Medical facilities construction	104.7	522.3	577.7	721.8	842.8	942.9	1,003.0	1.038.9
Total expenditures as a percent of gross national product	3.6	4.6	5.2	6.2	6.5	6.7	7.1	7.4
Public expenditures as a percent of total expenditures	13.3	25.5	24.7	33.1	37.4	38.3	36.9	37.9
Personal care expenditures †	3,272.2	10,400.4	22,727.7	41,323.9	46,323.3	52,020.3	58,751.5	65,132.3
Private expenditures	2,990.0	8,298.0	17,798.0	28,863.0	30,118.0	33,309.0	38,225.0	41,841.0
Public expenditures	282.2	2,102.4	4,929.7	12,460.9	16,205.3	18,711.3	20,526.5	23,291.3
Percent from:								
Private expenditures	91.4	79.8	78.3	69.8	65.0	64.0	65.1	64.2
Direct payments	88.6	68.3	55.3	45.4	40.8	39.0	39.0	37.2
Insurance benefits	—	8.5	20.7	22.6	22.5	23.5	24.5	25.5
Public expenditures	8.6	20.2	21.7	30.2	35.0	36.0	34.9	35.8

* Preliminary estimates.
† Excludes: facilities construction; medical research; administrative and other expenses of public programs, private insurance, and philanthropy.
Source: Social Security Administration, U.S. Department of Health, Education, and Welfare.

cluding the steady growth of insurance; and extraordinarily large and persistent increases in health care prices.

From the close of World War II to 1966 government outlays for health care had steadily hovered around one fourth of the total. Expenditures of both the public and private sectors were increasing rapidly, but at about the same rate. Within the public sector, state and local governments were spending more than the federal government. The inauguration of several major health programs during 1966, particularly Medicare and Medicaid,[2]

Figure 3–1. National health expenditures and percent of gross national product, selected fiscal years 1950–71 (in billions)

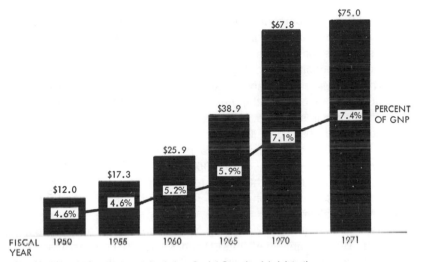

Source: Office of Research and Statistics, Social Security Administration.

altered these relationships. Public expenditures reached $28.5 billion in fiscal year (FY) 1971 and represented 38 percent of the total. Of this amount about two thirds was federal and one third state and local, in both cases representing substantial portions of public budgets.

Government spending for medical care has increased 163 percent in the five years ending 1971, an average of 21 percent each year. Private spending went up 49 percent in the same period, an average of 8 percent a year.

Government spending does not appear to have inhibited the growth of private health insurance; the reverse may be true. Private health insurance was a $1.3 billion annual business in 1950. In 1970 its premium income

---

[2] These programs were incorporated in the Social Security Amendments of 1965. Medicare combines two programs of health insurance for persons aged 65 and over, administered by the federal government. Medicaid is a federal grant-in-aid public assistance program for medical care, which is administered by the individual states.

totaled $17.2 billion, of which some $15.7 billion was paid out for health care, the remainder going for administration and overhead.[3] The recent growth of private health insurance benefits has paralleled the growth of Medicare payments. From fiscal year (FY) 1968 to 1971, the former have increased at a faster pace than Medicare payments, 59 percent versus 47 percent. As a result, the proportion of total personal care expenditures (excluding facilities construction, research, and administration) met through private insurance has risen from 22 percent in 1968 to 26 percent in 1971. When private health insurance benefits and government outlays are combined with other third-party payments, the proportion of the nation's health care bill left for the consumer to meet directly out-of-pocket is now only 37 percent.

About 3.9 million persons were employed in the health services industry (exclusive of those engaged in pharmaceutical manufacturing) in 1969 [4]—in hospitals, clinics, physicians' offices, and laboratories. About two thirds of these were in hospitals. Employment in this industry doubled in one decade. The U.S. Bureau of Labor Statistics has estimated that there may be 5.4 million persons employed in health services in 1975, another striking 38 percent increase in six years. Physicians active in medicine and osteopathy numbered about 305,000 in 1969. Between 1900 and 1969 they increased numerically 2½ times. However, as a proportion of the aggregate health manpower force they declined from 35 to 8 percent. This shift from a time when one health worker in three was a physician to a situation of only one in twelve symbolizes the changing character of health services and its rapid institutionalization.

Perhaps any industry evidencing such booming growth would have difficulties. But the universal importance of health and medical care, its special place of concern in the lives of people, the idiosyncratic character of the health care economy, the heady spiraling of prices and costs, and the growing governmental outlays have stirred wide anxiety and inevitably brought the problems into heated public policy debate. Accelerating costs have called into question the effectiveness of the entire structure for organization and financing of health care. Indicative of the public policy tensions, on July 10, 1969, the President of the United States forecast over national television a "massive crisis" in health care within the next two or three years unless immediate concerted action were taken by government and the private sector. The need for change is now very widely acknowledged, but there is relatively little agreement on specifically what changes are required or how they might be achieved.

---

[3] M. S. Mueller, "Private Health Insurance in 1970," *Social Security Bulletin,* February 1972, Table 17.

[4] *Health Resources Statistics, 1970,* Public Health Service Publication No. 1509, 1970 Edition, U.S. Department of Health, Education and Welfare, February 1971, p. 1.

Elements of cost

The major components in the large rise of national health expenditures can be classified as growth of population, rising prices per unit of service, increased per capita utilization of services and supplies and advancing level and scope of services because of new techniques and improved treatment procedures.

The population growth influence can be readily eliminated by presenting expenditures on a per capita basis. Between FY 1950 and 1971, per capita expenditures grew from $78 to 4½ times that figure, $358—the rise averaging 7.4 percent a year. For the most recent five year period, the increase averaged 11.1 percent a year.

Changing prices can also be eliminated by converting per capita expenditures to constant FY 1971 dollars by means of the medical care component of the consumer price index. Per capita constant dollars increased by $174 between FY 1950 and 1971, a growth of 94 percent. In the last five years the increase was 23 percent.

This increase represents in the main a growth in per capita utilization of health services. A portion of it indicates higher quality of care, but this factor is probably partially reflected in the price level which has already been accounted for. Thus per capita utilization appears to have grown at an average of 3.2 percent per year since 1950 and a remarkable 4.3 percent since 1966, both impressive compounded rates.

The reasons for increased demand despite escalating price levels are multiple. Larger incomes is one factor, but the demand has grown far greater than income alone could explain. Other contributing factors include: changing demographic composition, such as the relative increase of women in the population, especially at older ages; higher educational levels and resulting greater health consciousness; urbanization; a shift in morbidity patterns from predominance of acute episodic illness to chronic long-term ailments; increased public support of health care for the poor; and growth of insurance and other third-party payments. Perhaps the single largest element has been the spectacular advance in medical technology, which within this century has steadily altered medical care from a service of generally dubious efficacy to one regarded as a life-saving and life-enhancing essential.

Whatever the relative weights of these and other factors, Americans are conspicuously expressing their desire for more and improved health services, pressing a supply which, despite its own significant growth, appears to have fallen relatively far behind in quantity or structural capacity to meet the demand. Prominent among the frustrations that have accompanied the growing demand and rising expectations is spiraling prices. As we have indicated, much of the large increase in per capita expenditures was washed away by price inflation.

Despite significant increase in individual use of services and population growth, price rise has been a far greater factor in increasing costs. Rice and Cooper have calculated the proportion of the increase in personal health expenditures [5] produced by each of the major components. About 47 percent of the increase between FY 1950 and 1971 was due to rise in prices, 17 percent resulted from population growth, and the remaining 36 percent was attributable to greater utilization of services and the introduction of new medical techniques.[6]

Factor	Aggregate Increase (in $ billions)	Percentage Distribution
Total	54.7	100.0
Price	25.8	47.2
Population	9.2	16.8
Other	19.7	36.0

In the most detailed available study, made by Klarman, Rice, and associates in 1969, the three major categories of expenditure—short-term hospital care, physicians' services, and dental services—were examined. They show that over the long period 1929–68, prices contributed one half of the increase in expenditures, population growth about one sixth, and rising per capita use (which includes quality of services) about one-third. The picture varies among the three services and over time. During the most recent three-year period studied, 1965–68, population accounted for 9 percent of growth in total expenditures, per capita use for 17 percent, while increased prices were responsible for 74 percent. In that same period the increase in prices accounted for 82 percent of the growth of expenditures in short-term hospitals; between 50 and 75 percent of the increased expenditures for physicians' services; and 54 percent of the larger costs for dental services.[7]

Price movements

Of course, prices have been going up everywhere. But the differential between general prices and medical price increase since the end of

---

[5] Personal health care expenditures represent all expenditures for health services and supplies except expenses for prepayment (insurance) and administration, government public health activities, amounts spent by private voluntary agencies for fund-raising and administration, medical facilities, and research.

[6] D. P. Rice and B. S. Cooper, "National Health Expenditures, 1929–71," *Social Security Bulletin,* January 1972, p. 9.

[7] H. Klarman, D. P. Rice, B. S. Cooper, H. L. Stetler, *Sources of Increases in Expenditures for Selected Health Services, 1929–68,* paper presented at 97th Annual Meeting of the American Public Health Association, November 11, 1969 (mimeo).

World War II has been pronounced and persistent. From 1946 to 1971 medical care prices advanced 189 percent while the index of all prices advanced 107 percent, an average annual increase of 4.3 percent versus 3.0 percent. More pertinently, prices of medical care *services* rose 232 percent while all services rose 161 percent, an average annual increase of 4.9 percent versus 3.9 percent. By far the major influence was hospital daily service charges which increased 769 percent, more than seven times as much as all prices and almost five times that of all services in the Consumer Price Index.[8]

For years it was optimistically argued that this was in large measure a catching-up process, since medical prices had fallen behind other prices during the Great Depression and hospital wages were making up a notorious lag behind other wage scales. After a reasonable period, the argument ran, we could expect a levelling out, and medical price increases would then be generally consistent with other price movements. The prediction has proved conspicuously invalid. The large differential has gone on uninterruptedly for 25 years. For a brief period, between 1960–65, some observers were encouraged by an absolute decline in the rate of medical price increases. They apparently overlooked that even during that period of slowdown in general inflation, the relative rate of increase in medical services compared to other prices was actually accelerating. (See Table 3–2).

After 1965, medical prices shot up more sharply than ever. The infusions of the large Medicare and Medicaid programs undoubtedly were partially responsible, but it is equally clear that they were only aggravating influences. The forces of inflationary momentum in the health services economy are more basic and wide ranging, and they long preceded the advent of the new programs.

It has also been argued in some quarters that the unit for measuring medical care prices may overstate the real cost of health services. For example, one argument runs, while daily costs in hospitals have been rising, the average length of stay has been declining; if these factors balance out, the cost of an illness may have remained relatively stable. The facts do not fit the assumption. Average length of stay did decline during the decade of the Fifties, but it began to increase in the Sixties and by 1970 the figure was approximately the same as in 1950. Thus, from 1950 to 1970, while per diem costs rose 372 percent according to the American Hospital Association, the average cost per patient stay increased even more, by 380 percent, reaching $605.[9] By the end of 1971, the AHA reported that

---

[8] Ideally, in all these comparisons we should relate to the index of "all prices less medical care" and to the index of "all services less medical services." Unfortunately, these figures are not available for 1946. If those figures were used, the differentials indicated would be even more extreme.

[9] Calculated from data on "Non-Federal Short-Term General and Other Special . . . Community Hospitals" in *Hospitals,* August 1, 1971, Part Two (Guide Issue), p. 462.

Table 3–2. Consumer price index and selected medical components, selected years, 1946–71; average annual indexes and percentage changes. (1967 = 100)

	Price Index					Average Annual Percentage Change			
	1946	1960	1965	1970	1971	1946–60	1960–65	1965–70	1970–71
CPI, all items	58.5	88.7	94.2	116.3	121.3	3.0	1.2	4.3	4.3
Less medical care	*	89.4	94.8	116.1	120.9	*	1.2	4.1	4.1
CPI, all services	49.1	83.5	93.1	121.6	128.4	3.9	2.2	5.5	5.6
Less medical services	*	85.2	93.2	121.3	127.7	*	1.8	5.4	5.3
Medical care, total	44.4	79.1	89.5	120.6	128.4	4.2	2.5	6.1	6.5
Medical care services, total	40.1	74.9	87.1	124.2	133.3	4.6	3.1	7.3	7.3
Daily hospital service charges	18.5	56.3	76.6	143.9	160.8	8.3	6.3	13.4	11.7
Physicians' fees	48.3	77.0	88.2	121.4	129.8	3.4	2.8	6.6	6.9
Dentists' fees	52.5	82.1	92.2	119.4	127.0	3.2	2.4	5.3	6.4
Drugs and prescriptions	76.2	104.5	100.2	103.6	105.4	2.3	−.8	.7	1.7

* not available.
Source: Consumer Price Index, U.S. Bureau of Labor Statistics.

average cost in the nation's community hospitals was exceeding $100 per day.

In a related type of inquiry, economist Anne Scitovsky undertook extensive research to test a frequent criticism that the consumer price index overstates the true price increase because of inability to take account of improved effectiveness of a physician visit or a day in hospital, and that a more valid measure could be obtained by calculating changes in the total cost of treating specified episodes of illness. By measuring medical cost changes in terms of the average cost of treatment of five fairly common conditions—acute appendicitis, maternity care, otitis media in children, cancer of the breast, and fracture of the forearm in children—over a 14-year period, 1951–65, she found that the cost of treatment, with one minor exception, had increased considerably more than the medical care price index. The price index had risen 57 percent, while the median increase in the cost of treatment of the five illnesses was 87 percent, ranging from 55 to 315 percent.[10] Certainly no evidence here to suggest an upward bias in the price index.[11]

Cost measurement and price indexes in the health field are far from precision instruments, but the magnitude and persistency of the rises shown by every available measure are so consistent that they cannot be explained away by statistical shortcomings, and there can be little doubt about the validity of the general trends indicated.

Health effects

Despite the undisputed advances in the technology and quality of medical care, questions are being raised increasingly about the contributions these increased prices and expenditures are making towards better health. The objective is presumably *health,* not *health services* as such. Measures of health status are notoriously inadequate, but such rough gauges as are available indicate that the results of the enormous outpouring of additional billions of dollars in recent years are not encouraging. The long-term trend, since the turn of the century, is markedly favorable, but about two decades ago we arrived at a plateau which has not been significantly raised by the massive increased expenditures which followed. The health of the American people, as measured by basic mortality and morbidity figures, has apparently not improved in recent years.

Life expectancy at birth (about 70.2 years) has remained virtually constant for over a decade. While there has been improvement in infant

10 Anne A. Scitovsky, "Changes in Cost of Treatment of Selected Illnesses, 1951–65," *American Economic Review,* December 1967, pp. 1182–95.

11 The American Hospital Association annually surveys all hospitals to obtain average hospital expense per patient day. The percentage increases in these figures have been consistently greater than the index of hospital daily service charges, the largest component of medical care in the consumer price index.

mortality and length of life for females, and in the control of some remaining infectious diseases such as measles, these gains are offset by the near epidemics of heart disease, lung cancer, drug addiction, venereal disease, motor vehicle accidents, and a number of other conditions, especially among men. During the most recent five-year period for which data are presently available, 1964–68, there are increasingly disturbing elements within the over-all stationary rates. Mortality rates rose in all age groups between 15 and 74. Improvement was registered only for the very young and the very old. For those between 5–14 years of age, there was no change.[12]

Death rates of young and middle-aged American males are rising sharply. Between 1963 and 1968, mortality for white men, aged 15–19, rose 21 percent. For nonwhites, the rise was a shocking 35 percent. These figures do not include battle deaths. Mortality increases, smaller but still significant, applied to all white males under 45 and to all nonwhites under 65.[13] The leading factors in the upturn for young men, 15–24 years, were motor vehicle accidents, suicide, and homicide; for men, 45–64, there were substantial increases due to lung cancer, emphysema, diseases of the heart and circulatory system, cirrhosis, and bronchitis.[14]

Death is, of course, the ultimate in poor health. Disablement and morbidity are not as well reported. But it can be readily inferred that increased death rates are accompanied by similar or larger morbidity and disability changes from the same causes.

Comparisons with other nations are also not reassuring. For example, in the keynote address at the 1967 National Conference on Medical Costs, a leading economist in this field said: [15]

Although we spend much more per person for medical care than any other country, the blunt truth is that we do not enjoy the highest health levels. On the contrary, many European countries have age-specific death rates considerably below our own. The relatively high infant mortality rate in this country is disturbing, and difficult to explain. The disparity in death rates for middle-aged males is even more shocking, and has more serious economic implications. In the United States, of every 100 males who reach the age of 45, only 90 will reach 55; in Sweden the comparable rate is 95. During this critical decade when most men are at the peak of their earning power, the U.S. death rate is double the Swedish rate, and higher than that of almost every Western nation. It certainly seems legitimate to ask why. This is not necessarily with a view to spending less for medical care—I doubt if anyone can foresee a decline—

---

[12] *Statistical Abstract of the United States, 1968,* p. 55; *Statistical Abstract of the United States, 1971,* p. 55.

[13] *Leading Components of Upturn in Mortality for Men,* Public Health Service, U.S. Department of Health, Education, and Welfare, HEW Publication No. (HSM) 72-1008, Sept. 1971, p. 2.

[14] Such data help explain the rising differential in life expectancy advantage of females, now over seven years. In 1910, there were 106 males for every 100 females in the U.S., in 1970, there were only 95.

[15] Victor R. Fuchs, "The Basic Forces Influencing Costs of Medical Care" in *Report of the National Conference on Medical Costs,* U.S. Department of Health, Education, and Welfare, 1968, pp. 16–31.

but with a view to developing more effective use of resources that we are now devoting to health.

Such data do not necessarily reflect upon the quality of our health personnel or institutions. They do raise proper questions about the allocation and distribution of resources, about the cost-effectiveness of additional inputs for the system, and about the need for selectivity in respect to such additional inputs. There is reason to believe that we may have reached a stage of development where larger additional outlays for traditional forms of medical care are unlikely to have any commensurate effect upon health.

The mortality data show a preponderant incidence of preventable causes, but not of the kind that lend themselves to "cure." They reflect primarily the consequences of life style and portray circumstances wherein conventional medical intervention is too late. It has been pointed out by observers that the differential health status between Sweden and the United States, cited by Dr. Fuchs above, is not due to differences in health services as much as to life style.

The Council of Economic Advisers, in a recent annual report, noted that "good health is related to many factors in addition to medical care. Some of these are subject to an individual's control: diet, exercise, smoking, and consumption of alcohol. Other conditions such as the amount of pollution in the air and water, depend rather on the actions of society as a whole. . . . The importance of life styles and environment to health has become much more apparent in recent years." The Council concluded that such "considerations suggest that much is still to be learned about the complex 'technology' of producing health" and that "there is a clear need for developing tests for the effectiveness of medical care. . . ." [16]

Medical science has in recent years developed dramatic new procedures, such as implantation of vital organs, that are modern miracles. But they are in the main exotic affairs that do not touch the problems of the vast majority of people. There is increasing awareness of the relatively diminishing importance of traditional therapy in advanced societies, that the greatest potential for improving health of the American people is probably not to be found in increasing the number of physicians or hospital beds but rather in what people can be taught and motivated to do for themselves, and in improving their environment. Dr. René Dubos, one of the world's most respected health authorities, said several years ago, "Therapeutic medicine is probably now entering a phase of medically diminishing returns." [17]

Clearly, society has come to a point where it cannot assume that just any additional investment in health services is necessarily an investment

---

[16] *Economic Report of the President, January 1972,* GPO, 1972, pp. 136–38.

[17] René Dubos, *Man, Medicine, and Environment,* New American Library, 1968, p. 119.

in better health and those engaged in health services must reexamine the basic strategy, tactics, and organization of their mission. Unhappily, there is as yet no adequate measure of the effectiveness and productivity of medical care against which to weigh costs.

The poor

Despite frequent pronouncements declaring health care to be a "civic right," to which all people are entitled regardless of economic position, and despite great amplifications of government programs for low-income families, the poor are conspicuously disadvantaged in the quality and quantity of care they receive. The administration has reported:

> On nearly every index that we have, the poor and the racial minorities fare worse than their opposites. Their lives are shorter; they have more chronic and debilitating illnesses; their infant and maternal death rates are higher; their protection, through immunization against infectious diseases, is far lower. They also have far less access to health services—and this is particularly true of poor and nonwhite children, millions of whom receive little or no dental or pediatric care.[18]

Whatever the merits of the old maxim, "the sick get poorer and the poor get sicker," there is an undisputable statistical association of increased morbidity and mortality with poverty.[19] Among persons with family incomes of less than $2000, about 29 percent have chronic conditions which limit their activity as contrasted with less than 7.5 percent in families with incomes of $7000 or more. In the age group 45–64, the poor are affected 5–½ times the rate of the non-poor. Males in the lower income category of this working-age category have 3–½ times as many disability days as those in the higher income class. High differentials in nonwhite versus white mortality are found for tuberculosis, influenza and pneumonia, and vascular lesions affecting the nervous system. For each of these, the ratio is greater than two to one.

Government has increased its programs and expenditures for the poor at a rapid rate during the past decade. If money alone were the answer, there should be significant impact. In FY 1971, public expenditures for health care were $28.5 billion, most of it for the poor. This was three times the amount spent in 1965. It should, however, not be assumed that the poor can be provided the medical care they need if only government stands ready to pay their bills. There is a formidable array of other barriers to care confronting the poor, which includes, in addition to inability to pay, such factors as the paucity of good facilities and quali-

---

[18] *Towards A Comprehensive Health Policy for the 1970's—A White Paper,* U.S. Department of Health, Education, and Welfare, May 1971, p. 2.

[19] Some of the most useful data are assembled in R. Covell and R. N. Grosse, *Human Investment Programs: Delivery of Health Services for the Poor,* U.S. Department of Health, Education, and Welfare, Office of the Assistant Secretary for Policy and Evaluation, 1967. See also, J. Kosa, A. Antonovsky, I. Zola, eds., *Poverty and Health,* Harvard University Press, 1969.

fied professionals in ghettos and rural areas, racial discrimination in provision of services, attitudes of health personnel and institutions toward charity cases, and the inhibited, fearful, and uninformed attitudes of the poor themselves toward medical care. Especially important is the fragmented system of delivery of services which prevails for most of the health economy, but which negatively affects the poor particularly.[20]

Moreover, the general theme of the previous section, regarding the role of life style, is especially pertinent here. The most urgent health problems of the poor and their disadvantaged health status are not primarily attributable to lack of health services. They are rooted in their total living conditions: poor nutrition, depressed and crowded housing, unhealthful occupations, unsanitary environment, and lack of health knowledge.[21]

Health insurance

Significant steps have been taken to spread the risks and thus reduce the individual burdens of high costs, particularly through the development of health insurance and government programs. Private health insurance is mainly a post-World War II development, given considerable impetus by the threat of President Truman's proposal for compulsory national health insurance. Its growth was spectacular during the fifties. Currently, about four fifths of the population has some form of private health insurance, although with widely varying degrees of protection.[22]

The Medicare program relieved insurance carriers of the almost prohibitive task of adequately insuring the aged, a high-cost low-income population. The apparent inability of the insurance industry to reach remaining portions of the low-income population continues to be an important unresolved problem. About 38 million Americans were still wholly unprotected in 1970. A disproportionate number were among the poor and among children.

The proportion of people protected varies directly with income class and, except at higher income levels, with age. Ninety-two percent of persons in families with incomes of $10,000 or more had some insurance in 1968, but only 36 percent of those in families with income under $3000,

---

[20] A recent detailed survey by two physicians concludes: "The poor in the United States receive a disproportionately low share of health services. The barrier of direct cost is not sufficient to explain this underuse. . . ." Lawrence Bergner, M.D. and Alonzo S. Yerby, M.D., "Low Income Barriers to Use of Health Services," *New England Journal of Medicine,* March 7, 1968, p. 545.

[21] In a recent New York State survey to discover how communities of disadvantaged persons perceived their own health needs, the poor showed a clear understanding of their problems. When asked to identify the "three greatest health problems," "socio-environmental limitations" was selected more frequently than any other—almost twice as often as "inadequate facilities or service" and six times as often as "medical disease." *Health Needs of the Disadvantaged in New York State,* N.Y. State Health Planning Commission, February 1971, p. 4.

[22] M. S. Mueller, "Private Health Insurance in 1970," pp. 3–5.

and 57 percent in families with incomes between $3000 and $5000. Only 75 percent of all children under age 17 were covered by some insurance. In families with less than $3000 income only 23 percent of the children had coverage; in families with $3000 to $5000 income it was 49 percent.

The relatively high numbers of persons with some insurance can be misleading. The protection for most people has been improving, but is still relatively meager. The rise in third-party payments (and reduction of consumer out-of-pocket payments) for personal health care has resulted mainly from increased government expenditures. Government payments grew from 22 percent in FY 1966 to 36 percent in 1971. The portion paid by private health insurance moved slightly from 25 percent to 26. Direct consumer payments represented 37 percent of the total in 1971.[23]

Probably a more useful comparison is the relative role of insurance in consumer expenditures for personal health care, that is, omitting government outlays. Insurance met 32 percent of consumer expenses in 1966 and 41 percent in 1971.[24] Thus out-of-pocket payments were still producing about three fifths of consumer expenditures. Insurance payments are heavily weighted towards hospital care. They met 73 percent of consumer expenditures for hospital care in 1971, 48 percent of those for physicians' services (much of that for care within a hospital), and a mere 5 percent for all other health services.[25]

Insurance has greatly improved access to medical care, especially for employed workers and their families, since the large majority of protection is bought through employee-benefit group insurance plans. By increasing the total volume of money available as well as spreading payments over a larger population and a sharing of costs by employers, health insurance has brought the benefits of modern medicine to a far greater number of people than would otherwise have been possible. It has also improved the income of hospitals and doctors.

But health insurance's achievements have, with the passage of time and changing conditions, also developed a host of serious difficulties. Its own successes contributed to rising expectations which it is now having difficulty meeting. The cost crisis it helped stave off in the past appears to be catching up with it. To meet public expectations and avoid greater governmental interventions, the insurance industry will have to find means to enroll a larger proportion of the population, particularly to reach low-income classes more effectively. It has become clear that the Medicaid type of welfare program requires encompassing too large a segment of

---

[23] The remaining 1 percent is attributable to philanthropy.

[24] Some expenditures for health care probably should not be covered by insurance, such as nonprescribed drugs and additional cost for private room accommodations in hospital when not medically necessary. It has been estimated that if such items were deducted from consumer health expenditures, the proportion of the remainder then met by insurance would be three or four percentage points higher.

[25] D. F. Rice and B. S. Cooper, "National Health Expenditures, 1929–71," p. 16, Table 6.

the population to permit administrative effectiveness or public acceptance. Medical indigence [26] has proved to be far more widespread than was assumed a few years ago.

Probably the most serious challenge to health insurance is the need for more comprehensive benefits, covering a larger proportion of family medical costs. For a long time health insurance has been accused of aggravating cost inflation by its imbalance in benefit coverage, which was originally concentrated almost entirely on hospital care and contributed to inappropriate and expensive patterns of utilization. Since people were covered for expenses incurred in a hospital, but not for care outside, a strong tendency developed for use of hospitals even when care of a less expensive kind was equally or more appropriate. Despite recent progress in development of policies designed to render broader protection, the major emphasis still remains on services provided in a hospital, and ambulatory care remains relatively uncovered. While no definitive data are available, it is probable that about 80 percent of all insurance benefits are paid for hospital-related care.

Not only does the lack of comprehensive coverage cause unbalanced and expensive patterns of utilization, but it makes infeasible an adequate level of over-all protection. Large classes of personal health care costs are now in generally uncovered categories. As indicated earlier, private health insurance meets only 5 percent of consumer expenditures for all health services other than those for hospital care and physicians' services. The physicians' services included in most policies do not cover office or home visits.

Although consumers have been rapidly increasing their expenditures for health insurance, the portion of consumer expense met by insurance has advanced at a slow pace. The pace has increased during the past five years, but even then averaged only 1–½ percentage points a year. As we have already noted, the 1971 figure comes to only two fifths of consumer expenditures. At that rate, it would require another seventeen years before some two thirds of consumer expenditures would be covered, a goal that most experts regard as reasonable. The benefits available to Medicare beneficiaries are far more extensive than those currently available to most people with private insurance. The inadequacy of the typical insurance policy has thus become more conspicuous and vulnerable.

Several high-level commissions have recommended legislative action, either state or federal, to require a minimum range of benefits in all health insurance sold.[27] Some leaders of the industry have recognized the seriousness of the problem and have strongly urged insurers to make

---

[26] This is the term applied to people who can manage to meet the normal expenses of living but who require welfare assistance to meet medical expenses.

[27] See, for example, Secretary's Advisory Committee on Hospital Effectiveness, *Report,* U.S. Department of Health, Education, and Welfare, 1968.

policies more comprehensive, to place more emphasis in their coverage on ambulatory care, and to relate their coverages to the encouragement of preventive services.[28]

However, insurance is also a victim of medical price inflation. If carriers are to broaden the range of benefits, they must raise premiums. If, to meet rising prices, premiums must be raised 10 percent or more each year just to finance the same package of benefits (the services that most insurance covers have been experiencing the greatest degree of price inflation), it obviously becomes that much more difficult to tack on still higher premiums for enlarged benefits.[29] Nonetheless there is considerable evidence that when consumers are given a choice, they will select broader coverage. This is particularly true when an employer shares the cost.

Strengthening insurance

There are a number of steps, short of some form of government subsidy, that the industry could take to reduce the cost of insurance and enhance the chances of expanding enrollments and benefits. Of the gross total enrollment in health insurance (the gross includes a substantial number of duplicating policies held by the same persons) about 20 percent held individual policies (as opposed to group policies) sold by insurance companies (as distinguished from Blue Cross and Blue Shield and independent plans). Premiums paid by those who held such policies represented some 23 percent of the premiums of insurance companies. Characteristically such policies are relatively expensive and their protection meager. Under their group business in 1970, insurance companies returned 90 percent of premium income in benefit payments (slightly less than Blue Cross and Blue Shield) but on individual policies, the companies used only 58 percent of premium income for benefits, and that was better than they had done in previous years. About 42 cents of every premium dollar was never translated into health care payments, even though the companies sustained a net underwriting loss.[30]

More effort can be made to convert much of this unfortunate portion of the business into group policies and at the same time enable persons now ineligible for group purchases, and those who hold no policies at all, to join groups at more attractive rates and benefits. For example, it would appear entirely possible to permit the self-employed to enjoy group rates by contriving viable and appropriate groupings by use of associations,

---

[28] See, *Health Care Delivery in the 1970's,* Report, Findings, and Recommendations of the Subcommittee on Health Care Delivery, Committee on Medical Economics, as accepted by Board of Directors, Health Insurance Association of America, October 28, 1969.

[29] Between 1966 and 1971, benefit payments by insurance increased by an average of about 13 percent a year, but most of it was absorbed by inflation.

[30] M. S. Mueller, "Private Health Insurance in 1970," p. 13, Table 13.

geographical, or other bases. Similarly, it would be advantageous if carriers did not experience-rate [31] very small groups, wherein one catastrophic illness can make the group rates impractical to sustain. The experience of small groups could be pooled until an account could stand reasonably on its total experience, thus making the small groups less vulnerable.

Employee-benefit plans could be required to cover employees over layoff periods, for at least 90 days, as members of the employed group. This would simply be extending a fringe benefit to conform in part with what is already accepted in principle on basic pay through unemployment compensation.

It is generally believed that a considerable share of all insurance company individual policies are supplementary to other coverages. If the range and adequacy of basic policies were enlarged, as previously suggested, this would reduce the need for purchase of expensive and socially undesirable individual policies.

In short, it appears that the possibilities of private health insurance have not yet been sufficiently exploited, and time is now a critical factor. The industry may not find it possible to move effectively in such directions without some limitation being imposed upon the number and character of companies operating in this field—elimination of dubious mail order houses, for example. It will probably require that Congress reclaim from the states, at least in part, jurisdiction over insurance regulation, as the Nixon administration has already suggested. The future of the public-private mix in our pluralistic health economy, indeed whether the financing system remains pluralistic at all, may largely be determined by developments in this area in the near future.

Employers and labor

The stakes of employers and labor are also great. It is estimated that 85 cents of every dollar of benefit payments of all private health insurance comes from employee-benefit plans. By 1970 employer and employee contributions to such plans reached almost $14 billion and represented about two fifths of total contributions towards all "fringe benefits." [32] Employers are gradually assuming a greater proportion of these premiums, and in the larger industries, like automobiles and steel, they are paying 100 percent. A major portion of all health insurance now appears on the books of

---

[31] Experience rating refers to the practice of setting premium rates for each group contract in accordance with the claims experience of the particular group—as distinguished from community rating whereby all groups are charged at the same rates in accordance with the claims experience of the broader community.

[32] W. W. Kolodrubetz, "Two Decades of Employee-Benefit Plans, 1950–1970" *Social Security Bulletin,* April 1972, pp. 13, 15.

American industry as a cost of labor.[33] Labor feels that it is paying for the insurance, either directly or indirectly, because it assumes that the payments made by the employer are in lieu of wages. There are tax advantages in this method.

The frustrations are great for both sides. Labor feels it is on a treadmill in its attempts to gain improved protection. One writer informs us that labor estimates that of benefits received from 1954 to 1962, "about one-fourth of the increase in aggregate hospital payments and two-fifths of the increase in medical payments represent net additional services to individuals that are an improvement in the scope and adequacy of benefits." [34] On the other hand, employers face progressive escalation in costs without commensurate benefits or satisfactions to workers. Both are assuming activist roles in attempts to control the problem.

Government's stake

Government at all levels spent over $28 billion on health in FY 1971, about $23 billion of it for personal health services, most of which was provided by the federal government. The rise in the portion of the health bill paid by government to 38 percent reflects the fact that government spending for medical care increased 163 percent in the past five years—an average of 21 percent per year—while private spending went up 49 percent in the same period, 8 percent a year. Obviously, neither in terms of political, fiscal, nor ethical responsibility can government pour out such tremendous, steadily increasing, sums and yet assume a neutral posture in regard to the price and quality of what it is purchasing, as well as the influence its activities are having on other purchasers of care.

Cost infllation has been severely felt by government programs. Medicare and Medicaid are far exceeding anticipated costs because of greater price rises than seemed reasonable to allow for in original estimates. For the hospital insurance part of Medicare, Congress very early had to raise the projected long-term tax rate. The deductible and copayment charged to the patient have been substantially increased several times in the brief history of the program. Premiums for the supplementary medical insurance part of the program have almost doubled. Medicaid benefits have been cut back in many states, and Congress introduced restrictive limits on income levels for eligibility the year after the program went into effect. The legislated goal of reaching all medically indigent by 1975 had to be

---

[33] The Social Security Administration estimates that about 80 percent of the premiums for employer-employee group health insurance was paid for by employers in FY 1971, and that employer contributions represented more than 50 percent of total private health insurance premiums in the U.S., D. P. Rice and B. S. Cooper, "National Health Expenditures, 1929–70," p. 12.

[34] Raymond Munts, *Bargaining for Health: Labor Unions, Health Insurance, and Medical Care,* University of Wisconsin Press, 1967, p. 98.

abandoned. In both programs, the administration has cut back on its payment formulas to providers of care, and the latter have accused the government of welshing on its obligations.

More important, government finds that great additional expenditures have not only failed to produce equitable distribution and utilization of health care resources but that there has been relatively small net gain. Government reports make clear that, despite its generous intentions, its programs have failed to supply the medical needs of the poor and the black community. Public programs reach only a minority of the 40 million poor and near-poor, as officially defined, and there is considerable question about the extent of the need met even among those who are reached. Medicare is aimed at the aged and therefore does reach a group in which there is heavy concentration of poor and near-poor. Medicaid reached slightly more than 8 million people in 1969, about one fifth of the poor and near-poor. But of the total Medicaid budget, about 46 percent goes to the elderly, although they represent only about one third of the recipients, presumably to cover gaps arising from the fact that Medicare pays for an average of only 45 percent of health care expenditures of the aged. Other public programs for the poor—such as Office of Economic Opportunity programs and the maternal and child health program—are relatively small. If the 2 million children who received services under Medicaid are added to the 400,000 under maternal and child health programs (disregarding overlaps) we find about 2–½ million children being aided compared to the 19 or 20 million children among the poor and near poor, about one child out of eight.[35]

All of this has resulted in dismay and substantial soul searching in government, as it has in the insurance industry and among providers of care. There is grave doubt being cast upon the allocation of government resources for health; doubt, for example, about whether it is equitable or wise that almost one half of all government payments for personal health care is spent for the aged; [36] and reservations about the division of expenditures between purchase of services versus building adequate supply capacity. More fundamentally, it is now widely agreed that further progress will not be made simply by enlarged spending. Government must direct its attention to the shortcomings and inefficiencies in the basic organization of financing and delivery of health services.

There is widespread agreement among all interests that new governmental interventions are called for, but very little agreement about just what needs to be done or how to do it. A brilliant study by The Brookings Institution concludes that the failure of the highly motivated array of socioeconomic reform programs initiated during the optimistic sixties was

---

[35] For an authoritative review of this problem, see, *Report of the Task Force on Medicaid and Related Programs,* U.S. Department of Health, Education, and Welfare, 1970.

[36] Less than one eighth of government payments are for children under 15.

not due to lack of willingness to spend dollars. (In ten years federal social spending soared from $30 billion to $110 billion and Great Society programs alone jumped from $1.7 billion to $35.7 billion.) The underlying shortage, the Brookings analysis contends, has been knowledge; in the last ten years, the government has been called on increasingly to do things we do not yet know how to do.[37]

Like all generalizations, this explanation tends to oversimplify some multidimensional difficulties. It does, however, basically jibe with our experience in health care, that good will and money are themselves not sufficient to furnish solutions. The search for solutions is continuing vigorously, as it must, and there is no scarcity of plans for what to do now, but the frame of reference has changed. We will return later to a review of some leading proposals.

Factors in price rise

Explanations of the extraordinary price inflation are controversial. Different sectors of health care operate differently and are subject to different influences. Also, as we have seen, the price behavior of the several sectors varies. We will concentrate largely on hospitals and secondarily on physicians' services. The reasons should be noted:

1. Hospital care constitutes the largest single item of both public and private health expenditures, almost 40 percent in 1971. If construction and research costs were included the figure would be considerably higher. The second largest item is physicians' services and that lags far behind, amounting to 19 percent. The hospital component is steadily rising relative to all other aspects of health care, having moved up from 30 percent in 1950.

2. "Unit prices" for hospital care are rising far more rapidly than any other component of medical care, over twice as fast as medical care services as a whole.

3. If one were to add to hospital care the expenditures for medical services received in the hospital, which are affected by hospital practices but are paid to other categories of service, the hospital care portion of health expenditures would undoubtedly well exceed 50 percent. An increasing proportion of physicians' fees is derived from services rendered in and through the hospital.

4. As the modern hospital has become the hub of the medical care world, both financially and professionally, its influence on other elements of medical care and their costs is increasing. Already almost two-thirds of the nation's health personnel, about 2.9 million, are employed directly by hospitals.

---

[37] Charles L. Schultze and associates, *Setting National Priorities: The 1973 Budget,* The Brookings Institution, 1972.

Prominent among the more frequent justifications advanced for accelerated hospital costs are:

1. Medical and hospital technology have been advancing at a phenomenal pace with commensurate demands on facilities, equipment, personnel, and services. Per capita, patients use more services, such as diagnostic and therapeutic X-ray procedures, drugs, and laboratory services. There has been a growth in the range of services made available. For example, between 1963 and 1968 the proportion of community hospitals with intensive care services (including coronary care services) jumped from 18 percent to 42 percent. The equipment for all such services grows more elaborate and costly, and its rate of obsolescense more rapid.

2. The rise in labor costs is conspicuous. A by-product of advancing technology has been additional and more specialized personnel. Also, hospitals have been gradually catching up with long overdue improvements in wages and working conditions. Reduction in hours of work has caught up with other industries. Many hospital officials assert that when wage levels catch up, hospital prices will stabilize in relation to other prices.[38]

It should be noted, however that the common view that payroll has been advancing more rapidly than other hospital costs is inaccurate. From 1960 to 1970, despite a 29 percent increase in personnel per hundred patients, total expense per patient day rose more rapidly than payroll per patient day, 248 percent against 226 percent, and payroll as a proportion of total expenses declined from 62 percent to 58 percent.[39]

3. Hospitals have assumed increased functions in addition to direct patient care. Important among these is education. Despite the decline in hospital-based schools of nursing, they still account for about 80 percent of RN graduates. With federal subsidies for nurse education and the trend toward academic settings for such education, this burden should decline, but slowly. Also, many hospitals have been adding fulltime directors of medical education, an additional, although modest, factor in costs.

4. Hospital financing is increasingly coming from commercial borrowing, rather rare in the past. Interest charges, still a small part of total operating expenses, are nonetheless adding a new factor to hospital costs.

5. The common measure of hospital prices, the average per diem expense, is misleading. The factors in the numerator—total operating costs—have less and less relationship to the denominator—inpatient days. Hospitals increasingly engage in a variety of other services and activities, particularly there has been a rapid increase in outpatient services. The

---

[38] In respect to the validity of the "catch-up" argument, see, Martin S. Feldstein, *The Rising Cost of Hospital Care,* Information Resources Press, 1971, chap. 5.

[39] *Hospitals,* Guide Issue, August 1, 1971, Part Two, p. 462.

American Hospital Association has, therefore, recently developed a different denominator. It takes into account outpatient services by converting them into inpatient day equivalents, and deriving an "adjusted patient day" figure. This, of course, reduces the average per diem figure. However, when this adjustment is carried back in time the result has no significant effect upon hospital price *trends*.

6. Another factor, perhaps overlapping point 1 above, is the changing mix of patients. Patients with relatively serious illness requiring the more complex and expensive procedures represent an increasing proportion of the hospital population.

There are other factors that could be identified, but most of them could be readily subsumed under the enumerated points. It should be noted that the balance of supply and demand is not a frequently advanced explanation. It does not play the familiar role that students might assume.[40] In the main, hospitals are nonprofit institutions whose overall price structure generally reflects actual expenses. While the experience varies from place to place, there is generally no shortage of hospital beds. Occupancy rates of beds rose slowly during the sixties but appear to have stabilized around 78 percent, still relatively low. A rising level of occupancy should normally result in lower average expense per bed.

Critics of hospital costs do not find the explanations satisfying. As statements of fact, they are generally true. But they do not enlighten one on the extent of the price rise which each, or their aggregate, may explain. Nor do they indicate to what extent the factual developments are justifiable or necessary.

Without unit cost definitions and some acceptable measure of productivity, no precise answers are attainable. This is a field notoriously lacking in both. Thus far the problem of identifying the hospital's unit of production or service for purposes of measuring unit costs or output has proved elusive for the technicians. There may be a hen and egg quandary here: lack of clear concepts has probably delayed collection of usable data, and lack of data has undoubtedly deterred the analytical work to develop realistic concepts.

The common measure of hospital unit costs is the average expense per

---

[40] Among the reasons are the following: 1) Hospital prices are generally set in accordance with actual expenses incurred for the service, irrespective of demand. The effect of demand is only indirect in that a fully occupied hospital is likely to enjoy lower unit costs than is a similar less-occupied hospital. 2) Because of its nonprofit character, supply may be expanded to meet social satisfactions of sponsoring groups even in the absence of demand, or supply may be sluggish in response to increased demand. 3) Demand is relatively inelastic in relation to price either in micro or macro terms. First, most hospital bills are now paid by insurance carriers or government rather than the consumers. Second, if a physician says a patient requires hospitalization, the patient generally accepts the judgment without bargaining. Third, the patient generally makes no choice among individual hospitals; he enters the one with which his physician is affiliated or recommends. 4) Demand is elastic in relation to availability of beds. For such reasons, it is generally accepted that the supply-demand relatonship is a minor factor in hospital pricing.

patient day. It has the virtue of simplicity: total operating expenditures divided by total inpatient days for the year. But it is increasingly recognized as a faulty and often misleading measure. Patient days are a measure of input rather than output. Critics say the hospital is presumably engaged in producing "health" and that is what should be measured. Without a definition of such a health "product" it is futile to talk of "productivity." For example, it is known that on average New England hospitals tend to keep obstetrical cases in hospitals a few days longer than West Coast hospitals. Apparent health results do not differ. But in respect to any given number of patients the New England hospitals are "producing" more patient days!

In any case, there is now no index of health that can be specifically attributed to hospital services. In the meantime, measurements do have to be made, and the only practical approach appears to be one that concentrates on units of service, of which the inpatient day is the most identifiable in terms of cost and revenue. But as per diem is now calculated, the factors in the numerator—total operating expenses—often bear little, and quite inconsistent, relationship to the denominator. Hospitals are increasingly engaged in a growing variety of other services and activities, some of which have no direct bearing on inpatient services.

It is thus understandable that explanations of hospital prices tend to be general and imprecise and usually stated in nonmeasurable terms. Nonetheless, there are a considerable number of factors in the picture, which must be stated in equally imprecise terms, that suggest that at least part of the explanation for the steep increases lies in less justifiable causes than those listed.

In the first place, the growth of health insurance and other third-party financing programs has not only affected utilization but unit costs as well. The average consumer pays only a small portion of his hospital bill out-of-pocket; he is now less interested in the size of his hospital bill than in his insurance premium rates. And to the extent that these premiums are paid for him by his employer or through a group plan, the relationship to his own, or other people's, hospital bills becomes in his view more and more tenuous. Individual consumer resistance to rising hospital prices—on which a normal market situation would place considerable dependence—has almost disappeared. Similarly, the physician's inhibitions to additional laboratory procedures or prescribing another day in the hospital have been reduced. The result is the widely recognized "cost-pass-through." Some of the insurance programs and health and welfare plans have attempted to exercise resistance but without conspicuous success.

Do such factors explain why there has been little serious attempt to measure the relative value to health care represented by new equipment and added services, or are "improved models" bought without such criteria because hospitals now have a virtual guarantee of repayment of all their costs from third-party payors? Why has there been little progress towards developing measures of cost-benefit relationships? [41]

The hospitals are accused of an insatiable capacity for absorbing more manpower, the only restraint being their availability. They had an alleged manpower crisis in 1950 when hospitals were employing 178 persons per 100 inpatients; now there are 292 employees per 100 inpatients—a striking increase of 64 percent which cannot be fully explained by the growth of outpatient services—and a manpower crisis is even more loudly proclaimed. In the last five-year period alone, 1965–1970, the number of employees per 100 *adjusted* patient days increased 18 percent. There are wide variations in the personnel-patient ratios among states, but there are no indications of any correlation with quality of care received or health results.

A major factor is the hospital's failure or inability to employ new technology for net productivity increases, which has characterized the rest of the economy. Increased wages in hospitals have not been matched by greater productivity, at least as this is now measured, and introduction of new equipment and procedures has been accompanied by more rather than less personnel.

Such data do not prove anything definitively because quality—one element in productivity—has undoubtedly risen. But there is basis for a strong presumption that net productivity is falling or, at best, static. One may concede that a labor-intensive personal-service industry, such as hospitals, will have more difficulty improving productivity than manufacturing firms, but it is another matter to conclude that productivity in hospitals cannot be raised. While precise parallels are never available, some other service industries—for example, banking—have demonstrated that very significant gains can be made. Perhaps it is the eleemosynary tradition, or perhaps the persistent myths built around the special character of personalized services—as is true in education as well—that fosters the widely-held notion that efficiency and concern for productivity are enemies of quality. The contrary is true. Effective quality control is one of the important means to cost control, and vice versa.

It is increasingly accepted that only by grappling with the basic structural anomalies, of which the price aberrations are one important symptom, will it be possible to cope with the myriad of related issues: for example, is it impossible for most hospitals to do what some have done,

---

[41] Professor Richard Nelson, one of the country's leading authorities on the economics of technological change has said, "In both defense and health there has been a lot of R and D, and technical change has been extremely rapid; but it also has been extremely expensive and poorly screened. . . . In health one has the strong impression that one of the reasons for rising health costs has been the proclivity of doctors and hospitals to adopt almost any plausible new thing—drugs, surgical methods, equipment—that increases capability in any dimension (and some for which even that isn't clear) without regard to cost." Cited in V. R. Fuchs, "Health Care in the United States Economic System," *Milbank Memorial Fund Quarterly,* April 1972, p. 232.

introduce economies of scale and new organizational techniques as they enlarge and introduce new equipment and services? Must they follow caste-like personnel policies that offer no opportunity for vertical or horizontal mobility? Is it not possible to undertake organizational changes so that costly low occupancy rates are not promoted by the segregations that cause one service to be half empty while others turn people away? Must neighboring hospitals duplicate expensive, infrequently used equipment and each offer the same full range of services? Must a community tolerate a number of small, inefficient, independent hospitals which could be effectively integrated or combined or placed under joint management? Must we continue to add beds or expand facilities according to the aspirations of individual hospitals without regard to the needs of, and ultimate cost to, the community as a whole?

The partial successes achieved in some places by the progressive vanguard in the health field sustains the view that all these questions can be answered in the negative and that in these and similar areas lies a great unfathomed productive potential for mitigating cost advances and confining them to those justified by increases in amount and quality of care.

The payment dilemma: hospitals

Third-party payments, by government and health insurance, now account for 87 percent of hospital revenue for patient care. Most such payment is based on reimbursement of actual costs. The particular formulas are, of course, always in controversy but both sides have accepted the principle of payments for costs. However, the principle has now fallen into general disrepute as inherently inflationary and as a failure of the payors to meet their fiscal responsibility. The heavy infusion of Medicare and Medicaid money dramatized a problem which had been in operation on a smaller scale for a long time.

The method is accused of generating disincentives for efficiency or economy and in some quarters has been blamed for a large part of the price acceleration. If a hospital has a virtual guarantee of repayment of its costs, where is the motivation to drive for more economical procedures, to resist staff demands for more expensive equipment, or to abstain from adding personnel? Almost everybody now expresses discontent; the philosophy of open-ended retroactive cost reimbursement is no longer defended. But what should be substituted? Here the agreement breaks down; in fact, there are very few viable ideas in circulation on this knotty problem.

In 1967 the Congress authorized Medicare experimentation with different methods of payment to institutions. A small number have been started but results will not be available for some time. However, there is only small optimism about their prospects. Most are built around some version of "incentive payments;" an institution that experiences cost saving as measured against a preset target cost, or against some general average of comparable hospitals, is permitted to share in the savings by being paid something more than actual costs. There is some question about the effectiveness of this type of incentive in relation to nonprofit voluntary institutions which cannot distribute dividends from such "profits." They can be used for additional perquisites for staff or for capital investment, but this raises questions about long-term effects because such expenditures drive up costs in future years.

"Ceiling rates" are employed in some areas for Blue Cross payments (in New Jersey, for example, where they are set by the State Commissioner of Banking and Insurance) but the arbitrariness of such lines can be destructive and can unwittingly penalize the wrong institutions. Among the more prominent proposals are various versions of prior budget review and advance negotiated rates. While it seems likely that rates negotiated between the parties are likely to end up at the level of actual costs, it is felt that this method would have the advantages of obliging the institution to defend its budget plans in advance, and permit the payor to assert a disallowance of certain costs, for reimbursement purposes, before the expenditure is made. Aside from the tremendous administrative burden of bargaining annually with thousands of individual hospitals, a frequent objection is that such prior control is likely to have a curbing influence upon innovation, as institutions might be pressed into a preconceived and conventional mold.

Other issues are contained in the question as to what types of expenditures should be reimbursed as a cost of patient care. For example, should the costs of education in hospitals be charged to patient care, as they new generally are, or are these general community obligations to be paid for from public funds or philanthropy? Should reimbursements include an allowance for new capital funds for the institution? While such capital payments do not represent the cost incurred for current patients, they are essential if future patients are to be cared for, say the advocates. The opposition points out that such allowances would not distinguish between institutions that need expansion and those that ought not to expand or perhaps even to renew—unless the funds were channeled into a community planning pool for all hospitals. If third-party payors were to become responsible for generating new capital, would they also have to take some authority over how such funds were used?

It should, however, be emphasized that one cannot expect too much from the payment mechanism alone, whatever form it may take. There are many strong inflationary drives in hospitals quite aside from sources of revenue. Efforts to discipline these tendencies exclusively through a reimbursement formula, however designed, are doomed to failure because they ignore the institutional peculiarities of the hospital economy. Incentives should indeed be maximized, but the cost problem will also have to be tackled directly through some sort of regulatory process.[42]

Doctors' fees

Methods of paying for physicians' services are under similar challenge, but for different reasons. The general rule for both government and insurance carriers—who together are paying about 61 percent of physicians' fees—is to pay a "reasonable charge" for each service. The Medicare guidelines, for example, require that the charge be "customary"—it should be the same as the doctor charges other patients for the same treatment; that it be within the range of fees "prevailing" in the community for similarly situated doctors; and that the fee not be more than the carrier (the private insurance company which acts as a paying agent for the government) would pay for its own insureds.

In a seller's market of scarce supply, this too is widely criticized as an invitation to inflation despite the usual requirement of 20 percent copayment by the patient. There is nothing to prevent a doctor from raising his "customary" fees. And, of course, the increase in customary fees will soon automatically raise the "prevailing" levels. In the two decades preceding Medicare and Medicaid, physicians' fees rose at an average annual rate of slightly more than three percent. But in each of the following years, the rate of increase was double the previous rate.

Physicians' incomes have, of course, risen more rapidly since the rate of utilization of their services has also gone up. Median net incomes of physicians rose at an average annual rate of 4.6 percent between 1959–65 and at an average rate of 8.8 percent between 1965–69.[43] In the latter year the median net income of physicians under age 65 was $40,550.[44]

The conspicuous shortage of physicians generally receives the lion's share of the blame. In formal economics, the term "rapidly rising prices" is virtually synonymous with an imbalance between supply and demand. In medical care this is not quite so obvious as is usually the case. As Victor Fuchs has explained:

> . . . it should be recognized that a large part of the demand for medical care is determined by the physician. It is the physician who suggests hospitalization, the physi-

---

[42] For some specific suggestions for containing costs, see H. M. Somers and A. R. Somers, *Medicare and the Hospitals,* The Brookings Institution, 1967, chap. 8.

[43] During the 10-year period 1959–69, average hourly earnings in all manufacturing industries increased at an annual rate of 3.7 percent.

[44] *Medical Care Costs and Prices: Background Book,* Office of Research and Statistics, Social Security Administration; Dept. of Health, Education, and Welfare, January 1972, p. 43.

cian who prescribes drugs, the physician who orders tests and X-ray examinations, the physician who calls in a consultant, the physician who says, 'Come back in a few days and let me take another look at it.' Thus, the physician, in addition to being a supplier of medical care, is also the consumer's chief advisor on how much medical care to purchase.[45]

Steps are being taken to augment the supply of physicians. Even if one accepts the optimistic forecast of the 1972 Manpower Report of the President that the shortage will be met by 1980,[46] we do face de facto scarcity for another decade. The cry is, therefore, to increase the productivity of the existing supply.

But how do we measure physician productivity? The conventional gauge is the number of patient visits handled in a given time period such as a normal week. By this measure, productivity has been rising steadily according to available data.[47] Yet, if for a given ailment Doctor A follows the practice of seeing a patient once a week and Doctor B twice a week, with no apparent difference in result, is Doctor B twice as productive? Are two visits of 10 minutes each twice as productive as one visit of 20 minutes? In the Medicare program, some doctors have been accused of encouraging excessive numbers of visits by beneficiaries.

By the standard measure, there is not much leeway for increased "productivity" under present procedures. Doctors, on average, work a 60-hour week. The time spent with individual patients has been cut mighty fine, often averaging less than 10 minutes. There is considerable doubt whether numbers of visits can be increased significantly without damage to quality which is also a consideration in productivity. The search for increased productivity must be aimed primarily at reorganization. One move is toward development of a new category of health personnel—a "physician's assistant" or "care coordinator" who could take over many of the less skilled aspects of the physicians' job. A number of universities are now engaged in training such personnel, although the market for them is still unknown.

A closely related proposal is to permit existing health personnel, such as trained nurses, to take over many procedures that really do not demand the skills of an M.D. This would require revision of licensing laws in most states. Probably most important is the attempt to move doctors into group practice, which is widely assumed to offer structurally greater productivity potential as well as having a favorable influence upon quality and overall

---

[45] Victor R. Fuchs, "The Growing Demand for Medical Care," *New England Journal of Medicine,* July 25, 1968, pp. 191–192. Elsewhere, in more theoretical terms, Dr. Fuchs has shown that the shape of supply and demand curves do not appear to determine price and vice versa. "Health Care in the United States Economic System," *op. cit.,* pp. 220–229.

[46] See pp. 143–144.

[47] Thirty years ago the average doctor saw about 50 patients a week. In 1967, according to a *Medical Economics* survey, the average number of patient visits was reported to be 131. General practitioners averaged 175 visits per week; some reported seeing 250–299 per week.

economy, particularly where group practice and pre-payment are combined.[48]

Some have suggested attempts to curtail demand. This, in fact, is part of the rationalization for deductibles and coinsurance. In practice, they don't appear to be much of a restraint. If they were, they would then face the objection that they are a barrier to necessary care and prejudicial against low-income people. Moreover, there is still great unmet need. A more adequate, or more equitably distributed, supply of doctors would, for example, almost certainly promote a justifiable increase in utilization among the poor. Several health economists, most prominently Professor Martin Feldstein of Harvard, have been hopefully exploring the possibility of finding more effective, yet equitable, consumer financial incentives for restraining utilization.

While we wait for structural reform, the problem facing government and insurors on how physicians should be paid is immediate and acute. The government and carriers surely cannot indefinitely guarantee to pay fees which are essentially unilaterally established by the profession itself. Many variations of fee regulation—negotiated or administered—are being widely considered. The medical societies are opposed to fee schedules or controls. Until Medicare, most public programs, including Workmen's Compensation and welfare programs, paid according to fee schedules, but these were relatively small matters for the average doctor. Now any change from the "customary" and "prevailing" standards will provoke strident controversy and resistance would be formidable.

Restructuring the system

Government has, of course, done more than just provide finances for purchase of care. In addition to heavy investment in medical research,[49] it has subsidized construction of hospitals and other medical facilities and increasingly financed medical education to accelerate the production of physicians and allied health personnel. Meritorious as such activity may be in its own right, the feeling is growing that such measures do not reach to the real core of the problem. In fact, there is already fear that we may already have an excess of hospital beds, that the educational pipeline is about to pour forth more allied health practitioners than can be employed, and the 1972 President's Manpower Report to Congress surprised many

---

[48] Surveys have indicated that doctors in partnerships or groups can manage an average of about 25 more visits a week than solo practitioners, chiefly because of the extra time the latter must devote to paper work and business matters which in a larger organization are handled by specialized personnel. See discussion of Health Maintenance Organizations below.

[49] The $1.8 billion spent by government for medical research in 1971 was almost 25 times the amount spent in 1950 and represented over 90 percent of the total public and private expenditures in the U.S. See Table 3–1.

people by pointing out that the number of medical school graduates in 1980 will probably be 50 percent above the 9450 graduated in 1971. The number of physicians in this country would then reach about 440,000 (120,000 above the 1970 number of active physicians)—enough to eliminate the overall shortage.[50] Yet, few people believe this will remove the basic problems.

The last few years have witnessed an extraordinary array of investigations and reports of official and expert bodies. All in one form or another have elaborated the thesis advanced some years ago by Harvard economist John T. Dunlop: "It is the fundamental transformation in a variety of our arrangements that I think is signalled by these cost changes. The permanent problem is the need for more productivity . . . brought about by structural changes in the practice and organization of medicine." [51]

For example, the National Advisory Commission on Health Manpower found that the inadequacies in health manpower could not be successfully tackled outside of reform of the institutional framework within which manpower is utilized. It reported:

> There *is* a crisis in American health care. . . . *The crisis, however, is not simply one of numbers.* It is true that substantially increased numbers of health manpower will be needed over time. But if additional personnel are employed in the present manner and within the present patterns and 'systems' of care, they will not avert or even perhaps alleviate, the crisis. *Unless we improve the system* through which health care is provided, care will continue to become less satisfactory, even though there are massive increases in costs and numbers of personnel. . . .
>
> Medicine has participated in the general explosion of science and technology and possesses cures and preventives that could not have been predicted even a decade ago. But the organization of health service has not kept pace with advances in medical science or with changes in society itself. Medical care in the United States is more a collection of bits and pieces (with overlapping, duplication, great gaps, high costs and wasted effort), than an integrated system in which needs and efforts are closely related.[52]

There is a remarkable degree of agreement on necessary general objectives; much less, of course, on specific details; and even less on how any substantial reform can be achieved in view of the scattered authority and influence in this field. Proposals and actions have been proliferating in the attempt to reorder delivery of care. The leading ideas can be classified and briefly described in five interrelated broad categories.

1. **Systemization.** Medical care in the United States has been colorfully described as a technically excellent product thrown into a Rube Goldberg

---

[50] *Medical Economics* magazine is less sanguine. It forecasts a 20 percent increase in total number of M.D.s and D.O.s and a 40 percent growth in demand between 1968 and 1978. (June 10, 1968, p. 91.)

[51] "The Capacity of the U.S. to Provide and Finance Expanding Health Services," *Closing the Gaps in Availability and Accessibility of Health Services,* N.Y. Academy of Medicine, 1965, p. 1327.

[52] *Report of the National Advisory Commission on Health Manpower,* G.P.O., 1967, Vol. I, pp. 2–3. Italics in original.

delivery contraption which distorts and defeats it, and makes it more expensive than it need be, because "we do not have a health care *system* —we have a *happening,* with everyone 'doing his own thing.' " [53] The eminent Barr Committee reported to the Secretary of HEW that "The key fact about the health service as it exists today is this disorganization. . . . fragmentation and disjunction that promote extravagance and permit tragedy." [54]

It has often been pointed out that in the typical American community the various health service resources have little organizational relationship to one another. Individual hospitals are autonomous. Services and equipment may be duplicated unnecessarily, and costly surpluses may abound in several institutions. Other necessary services may be available in none. Excess of facilities for highly sophisticated types of procedures can be dangerous as well as costly. Some hospitals, partly because of the competitive search for prestige, have built and staffed such units (cardiovascular surgery is a not uncommon example) for which there turns out to be an insufficient case load; the staff is thus unable to maintain the skills necessary for optimum performance. Other health institutions in the community —clinics and skilled nursing homes—may or may not have any organizational relationship with a hospital or with one another. A physician may have some affiliation with one or several hospitals (in some cases, none) and for some parts of his practice it may prove to be the wrong hospital. Organization has not been adapted to mesh the efforts of increased specialisms.

For the patient this fragmentation often means confusion, uncertainty, and lack of comprehensiveness in care. Access to appropriate level and site of care is limited by the dispersion of specialized professional personnel and facilities. Quality is restricted by gaps in available services, lack of a point of responsibility for the patient as a whole, and discontinuity of care. Productivity is curtailed by the inherent waste of such dispersion and lack of integration, and cost is increased.

The objective is to bring together the bits and pieces into a system which relates them to one another organizationally, and thus illuminates the gaps as well as the surpluses. At whatever point a patient enters the system—the physician's office, outpatient department of a hospital, or a clinic, the organized system should have responsibility for equal access to the spectrum of services—preventive, diagnostic, therapeutic, and rehabilitative—coordinated to maintain a primary doctor-patient relationship, avoid unnecessary duplication of tests and other services, assuring that the appropriate level of institutional care is assigned, and provide centralized complete medical records for each patient.

---

[53] Peter Rogatz, M.D., et al., "Organization and Quality of Health Services," *Health Services Working Conference,* Fairleigh Dickinson University, 1970, p. 20.
[54] Secretary's Advisory Committee on Hospital Effectiveness, *Report,* pp. 9, 11.

Many proposals have been made and some steps taken towards such a goal. It has become a prominent public policy issue, with leaders of both political parties committed to the pursuit of systemization, as is indicated in the following four items which all relate to that objective.

2. Planning. System requires planning and planning, to be effective, requires controls. The term planning has taken on a specialized meaning in the health field. Originally it related only to construction of facilities. The Hill-Burton Hospital Survey and Construction Act of 1946 was the nation's first significant instrumentality for a very limited form of planning. An attempt was made to relate federal grants to statewide plans, based upon an inventory of existing facilities and needs. Starting in 1960, the U.S. Public Health Service began to render financial support to local and state planning groups. In the main these were voluntary nongovernmental bodies. They interpreted their task to pass upon proposals for new construction or expansion of health institutions in terms of the needs of the area of jurisdiction. The bodies lacked any formal authority and were of limited effectiveness. In 1965 Congress enacted legislation to encourage and help finance official planning machinery in every state. Health planning agencies and health planning councils have been established in all states, but in the main the agencies were not given any enforcement authority.

Recently, the concept of planning has broadened to encompass an organized attempt to introduce rationality in relationships among the autonomous entities in health care, to move towards a coordinated system of facilities and personnel, hopefully enabled to offer comprehensive services to a given area. From a negatively oriented function of saying "no" to unnecessary or duplicatory facilities, it is struggling for an affirmative image of encouraging the development of an appropriate and effective mix of services in an efficient framework. It would provide a mechanism for allocation of area resources to maximize output and accessibility. As one writer put it, it would create a technostructure for what is now essentially a cottage industry.

Most advocates now appear to believe that a planning agency must have legal authority to back its decisions. In the absence of a market regulator and discipline, a framework of external regulation and control must be substituted. By and large the purely voluntary arrangements have not worked satisfactorily. Over the past few years, nineteen states have given some enforcement powers to planning agencies, but only in respect to their authority to reject new construction or equipment proposals.

The Nixon administration is encouraging more vigorous planning authority. It has, for example, secured legislation which would make Medicare reimbursement, and other federal payments, contingent upon prior approval of the facility in question by the appropriate geographic planning body. The American Hospital Association has officially accepted the principle of mandatory planning. Many Blue Cross plans will not pay full reimbursement to hospitals that do not comply with health planning agencies. Insurance carriers have taken a sympathetic stance and some have even proposed that "a moratorium should be declared on building new hospital beds until the need for more beds . . . can be fully justified."[55]

While the planning idea has clearly won widespread support from the parties at interest, experience has been limited and brief and it has yet to prove its effectiveness. There is opposition, mainly from a group of economists who believe that market competition can still be made effective among hospitals and that there should be no restriction upon free entry into the market. They also argue that government regulation is generally ineffective.[56] Probably a more persuasive criticism of the kind of planning we have described is its probable tendency to inhibit innovation, which is sorely needed in this field.

As health institutions profoundly affected with a public interest, hospitals are already under a formidable array of state regulation,[57] and it is unlikely that these will be curtailed. As a practical matter, the real issue for public policy in the foreseeable future will probably not be regulation or no, but rather what kind of regulation is likely to prove most effective.

3. Health maintenance organizations.   Under the pressure of spiraling costs the Nixon administration announced in 1971 that a central part of its "health policy for the 1970s" was to be maximum development of health maintenance organizations (HMO), a concept modeled after prepaid group practice plans. Such plans had been strongly advocated by reformers since the thirties and been developed particularly on the West Coast after World War II, but had long suffered the antagonism of organized medicine.[58] Despite the extraordinary success of many existing plans, growth has been slow and only 7 million Americans are now enrolled in this type of organization.

The administration has defined an HMO as 1) an *organization* that accepts, on a contractual basis, the responsibility to provide or assure the delivery of 2) relatively *comprehensive* health services for 3) a *voluntarily* enrolled group of persons and 4) is compensated by advance fixed periodic payments made by or on behalf of all enrolled members (but individual physicians may be compensated by the organization in any method they agree upon). Although the successful model which inspired the administration's HMO proposal is postulated on centralized multispecialty *group practice,* the administration's definition does not require group practice.

---

[55] *Health Care Delivery in the 1970's,* p. 6.

[56] For example, Jan Acton, Joseph Newhouse, Vincent Taylor and other economists at The Rand Corporation have been writing along these lines.

[57] Anne R. Somers, *Hospital Regulation: The Dilemma of Public Policy,* Industrial Relations Section, Princeton University, 1969.

[58] The American Medical Association dropped its opposition some time ago and adopted a neutral posture, but some offshoot factions, notably the Association of American Physicians and Surgeons, Inc., are still actively opposed.

Existing prepaid group practice plans offer one-door comprehensive services. They enjoy the economies of scale with capacity to maximize the use of allied health or paramedical personnel and adequate nonprofessional staffing for bookkeeping and paper work to permit physicians to devote maximum time to their special skills. Preventive care is encouraged, as it appears advantageous to the plan as well as the patient. Incentives for savings to the plan and better health for the patient are built into the plan as the two are made mutually dependent, unlike fee-for-service practice. Health professionals are encouraged to try new methods and procedures as they share in the savings that improved organization can achieve.

The National Advisory Commission on Health Manpower made a careful case study of the west coast's Kaiser Foundation Medical Care Program,[59] and described the detailed results in glowing terms for both quality and efficiency.

The . . . Program provides comprehensive services to more than a million and a half members drawn primarily from the working population. These services are provided at significant saving by comparison with the cost for equivalent services purchased in the surrounding communities and the country at large. The quality of care provided by Kaiser is equivalent, if not superior, to that available in most communities. . . .

One of the main sources of economy has been the ability of Kaiser to discourage excessive hospital use. After adjustments for age differences, Kaiser subscribers in California were found to have hospitalization rates more than 30 percent below the state average. Between 1960 and 1965, hospital patient days of Kaiser subscribers declined by 12 percent, while those of the United States as a whole increased by 9 percent. Primarily on this account, the Kaiser plan was able to hold the rise in its expenditures for hospital care during this period to 15 percent compared to a 50 percent increase for the United States. The staff study concluded that "the average Kaiser member obtains high quality medical care for 20–30 percent less than the cost of comparable care obtained outside the Plan . . . . the majority of savings achieved by Kaiser results primarily from effective control over the nature of medical care that is provided and over the place where care is given."

It is the Kaiser record that the administration mainly displays in support of its HMO policy, but there can be no assurance that new programs would duplicate the experience of Kaiser, a superbly managed operation.[60] Moreover, as noted, the administration would sanction as HMOs some which substantially depart from some basic principles of the Kaiser model.

---

[59] *Report of the National Advisory Commission on Health Manpower,* Vol. II, Appendix IV; Vol. I, pp. 66–70.

[60] See, Anne R. Somers, ed., *The Kaiser-Permanente Medical Care Program,* The Commonwealth Fund, 1971.

Yet, even these would undoubtedly improve on the prevailing pattern of fee-for-service solo practice.

There is, however, no basis for optimism that HMOs will proliferate very rapidly. The capital investment and start-up costs for most such organizations is very formidable, despite the promise of government assistance. It is estimated that an enrollment of 25,000 to 30,000 is required to make a good plan viable. Under present conditions, there is little incentive for physicians to join such plans. HMOs would operate under regulatory controls, placing them at a disadvantage in relation to fee-for-service practice. At present over twenty states have legal obstacles to the formation of prepaid group practice plans, although the administration does propose to preempt such state barriers.[61] At best, it will be a long time before any substantial proportion of the population experiences the advantages of HMOs.

4. **Organizing around the hospital.** The hub of the present medical care world is the modern hospital. It is where the largest share of the medical care dollar is spent. It is the doctor's indispensable workshop, where the three essential elements of scientific medicine—patient care, research, and teaching—are focused. It is the place where the doctor interacts most frequently with professional colleagues. It is the point of convergence of the informal referral patterns in most communities and between communities. In short, it is the center of whatever degree of systemization has already been achieved in health care.

On the theory that it is most sensible and practical to build on what we already have, and that any realistic system must be related to its most crucial unit, a movement is developing to systematize the whole range of health care further, with the hospital as the ultimately responsible core.[62] This new hospital conception is envisioned as primarily an "organizational arrangement." It would be officially assigned the role of organizational catalyst, referral center, and professional monitor of the quality and quantity of care rendered not only on its own premises but throughout its community. All physicians within its area of jurisdiction would be affiliated with it, as would satellite units such as neighborhood health centers, skilled nursing homes, first-aid stations, and clinics.

The proposal definitely does not mean that all, or even more, community health services actually would be provided within the walls of the hospital. On the contrary, it anticipates that the health system of the future will call for fewer acute hospital beds per capita than at present and will

---

[61] For an excellent analysis of the impediments to development of HMOs, see E. W. Saward and M. R. Greenlick, "Health Policy and the HMO," *Milbank Memorial Fund Qaurterly,* April 1972, Part 1, pp. 147–76.

[62] The leading proponents of this position are Ray E. Brown, Vice President for Medical Affairs, Northwestern University—McGaw Medical Center, and Professor Anne R. Somers of The College of Medicine and Dentistry of New Jersey—Rutgers Medical School. For a fuller description of the proposal, see Anne R. Somers, *Health Care in Transition: Directions for the Future,* Chicago: Hospital Research and Education Trust, 1971, chap. 7.

stress physical decentralization for all services except those that actually require sophisticated technical equipment and highly specialized personnel. There will be increased emphasis on the satellite units: neighborhood health centers, home health programs, long-term care facilities, and other nonhospital services.

The hospital would be franchised or chartered by the state to assume responsibility as coordinator and monitor of community health services and the state would exercise general regulatory authority, somewhat akin to the franchised public utility. Federal payments for health care would be contingent upon state assumption of such franchising and assumption of regulatory authority.

This proposal is not in conflict with the expansion of health maintenance organizations. In fact, the coordinating task of the hospital would be simplified if prepaid group practice plans were affiliated with it, and it is almost universally agreed that HMOs are most effective when combined with a hospital. (The Kaiser Plan owns its own hospitals.) The crucial fact is that the hospital is a ubiquitous reality, while for most of the country the HMO is still a gleam in the eye.

5. **Strengthening management.** The heritage of a "charity institution," the anomalous organizational structure, and the relatively small size of the average organization, together with other special features, have resulted in a neglect of efficient management in American hospitals. Attitudes have shifted in recent years and a corps of professional trained administrators is appearing. But resistant old traditions and built-in diffusion of authority remain formidable obstacles even to highly skilled administrators. *Fortune* magazine headlined a recent article, "Before We Start a New Building Binge, We Had Better Recognize That Hospitals Need Management Even More Than Money."

The difficulties are both external—the relationship of hospitals and other medical institutions to one another—and internal. The most obvious factor in the external category is the autonomy of each institution. About half of all short-term general hospitals have fewer than 100 beds, considerably too small to afford or warrant the employment of adequate managerial talent. The lack of skilled personnel managers, for example, is probably among the explanations of the notoriously poor labor relations of hospitals. Except among proprietary institutions, mergers are almost unknown. In the not-for-profit sector, the incentives are lacking.

There is no good reason, except in tradition and vested interest, that a group of hospitals should not be under a single management. Administrators are aware of the advantages, and in some areas arrangements have been made for joint purchasing, joint laundry operations, and the like, which have proved beneficial. But this is not a substitute for unified management. As a by-product, if all hospitals in a community were under single management, present planning difficulties would be minimized. The management plan of such an operation would itself be a very substantial part of the community plan.

Internally, the authority of the administrator is severely limited and often ambiguous. The physicians, who typically are not employed by the hospital but are privileged to use its facilities for their patients, generally determine or dominate important hospital policies. Yet the doctors are in an essentially irresponsible position in relation to the efficiency and financing of the hospital. Excessive equipment and costly low ocupancy rates (over 20 percent of the average hospital beds are normally empty) are the consequence. Administrators are frequently appalled by a system which uses expensive beds as freely as we do. One has compared it to "using a Mack truck to deliver a suitcase when a taxicab could do the job as well and a lot cheaper."

The crucial role of managerial effectiveness is a source of increasing concern. Proposals for coping with the problem are multifold. One of the more interesting comes from the Secretary's Committee on Hospital Effectiveness which focused its attention on the need to clarify lines of responsibility and accountability by involving the medical staff in the financial and operating phases of the institution.[63] They point out that since the administrator does not make the most important decisions affecting costs—what patients should be admitted, when they should be discharged, what drugs must be stocked, what services provided, and the like—he cannot be held accountable for the financial results. Since the physicians' decisions are key determinants of costs and effectiveness, they should assume some accountability.

The Committee recommended sanctions to assure that every health care institution annually prepares a detailed financial plan of income and expense, and a plan of services and operations; and that the medical staff should be directly involved, along with the administrator, in developing the budget and operating plan. In turn, the trustees shall delegate to the administrator the authority required to enable him to manage the operations of the institution in accordance with the approved financial budget and operating plan.

The principal benefit is expected to derive from the bare discipline of the planning process. The physicians practicing in the hospital will be involved with the administrator in planning the income and expenses of the operation and the extent and type of services to be offered. The purpose is not to interfere with the free exercise of medical judgment in the care of patients, but to increase the physician's awareness of the cost and financial consequences of his practice, to involve the physician in responsibility for establishing both expense and service objectives. It might bring an answer to the question often raised by economists of how physicians can be

---

[63] *Report*, p. 28.

brought to consider the economic as well as medical consequences of their decisions.[64]

Since the Committee's report, proposals have been made that a minimum standard of managerial adequacy be included among the conditions of participation in Medicare and other federal programs. Others have gone further and recommended that management capacity be a condition of licensure.

Financing health services

It has long been obvious that large portions of the population normally lack access to adequate medical care because of insufficient means—and this extends far beyond the poverty class—and that in case of large or complex illnesses most families would find themselves in severe difficulty. Skyrocketing costs have increased public sensitivity to the problem and the question of equitably financing medical care is again a lively public policy issue. Means test programs have not been successful. They are generally associated with personal indignities and fostering inferior quality of care. Multitudes of people fall between the chairs, neither having sufficient means of their own nor being able to qualify under the means test. The effectiveness of several of the previously discussed delivery system reforms would depend upon the removal of financial barriers to universal access to service.

By 1970 virtually all organizational interests had endorsed some form of universal health insurance. Congress has before it over a dozen different proposals from such diverse sources as the AFL-CIO, the American Medical Association, the Nixon administration, the Health Insurance Association of America and the American Hospital Association. Several independent scholars have also developed program proposals.[65]

But this apparent consensus for "national health insurance" can be misleading. The label is being used to embrace a wide diversity of plans whose only evident common factor is the proposed use of enlarged federal financing to increase public access to health services. Beyond this, the plans differ in almost all essentials. As areas of disagreement remain many and large, comprehensive national health insurance is not as imminent as many people have been led to believe.

---

[64] Victor Fuchs has written: "It is a fundamental proposition in economics that decisions involving the allocation of scarce resources to competing goals require a weighing of benefits against costs. However, there is little in the training or motivation of a physician to impel him to think in these terms. In this respect he is not different from any technologically oriented person, but almost nowhere else in the economy do technologists have as much control over demand. About the only exception I can think of is the influence exerted by the military in time of total war." "The Growing Demand for Medical Care," *New England Journal of Medicine*, July 25, 1968, p. 192.

[65] Two of the better known plans are The Feldstein Plan (See, R. D. Eilers and S. S. Moyerman, eds., *National Health Insurance—Conference Proceedings,* Richard D. Irwin, Inc., 1971, pp. 223–226) and the Somers Plan (See, H. M. and A. R. Somers, "Major Issues in National Health Insurance," *Milbank Memorial Fund Quarterly,* April 1972, pp. 204–8).

The legislative bills can be grouped, for convenience, into four broad categories reflecting their most prominent characteristics.

Category 1: Proposals for tax or other incentives to stimulate voluntary purchase of private health insuranoo. Tho A.M.A.'o "Modicrodit" plan offoro a tax credit against the individual's federal income tax; the HIAA plan provides incentive tax deductions. The AHA plan uses a benefit rather than tax incentive. All qualifying policies would be required to include specified minimum benefits.

Category 2: Proposals for mandatory purchase of private health insurance by employers for their employees. This is the core of the Nixon administration's proposal. It also includes provision of a separate insurance scheme, subsidized by the federal government, for low-income families with children and availability of insurance for voluntary purchase by persons not protected by its other programs.

Category 3: Proposals calling for a unitary, all-embracing, federal program, compulsory coverage of the whole population, comprehensive benefits, financed by a combination of payroll taxes and general revenues, and administered exclusivoly by tho fodcral government, without use of private carriers. The Kennedy-Griffiths bill exemplifies this approach.

Category 4: Proposals that call for strengthening and extending Medicare to tho entire population. Financing would be primarily through payroll taxes on employers and employees, as at present, wlth a speclal contribution from general revenues. Private carriers would continue to act as fiscal intermediaries. The program would carry options permitting employees or Individuals to opt out of the program if they purchased insurance at least equal in benefits to those provided by the public program.

Even this oversimplified summary offers some Indlcatlon of tho ooopo of important differences: Should government financing be used to underwrite a program covering the entire population or be confined to developing protection for the poor alone and perhaps also for catastrophic illnoesee for ovorybody? Can a voluntary scheme prove adequate for the desired universality of coverage? What sources of government financing are most feasible: general revenue, social security payroll taxes (in what proportions among the parties?), or a mixture of the two? Assuming a broad government financed program, should it be wholly administered by government or is pluralistic participation by private carriers desirable? Should the financing legislation also comprehend reforms of the health care delivery system or should these be treated independently? Does government have the managerial capacity effectively to operate a single program for the entire nation? How can extending universal access be done without giving further impetus to the inflationary spiral? [66]

These and many other imponderables are dividing and perplexing men of goodwill equally interested in improving the financing of medical care.

---

[66] For a description and critique of the major bills and a discussion of some of these issues, see H. M. and A. R. Somers, "Major Issues In Natlonal Health Insurance," pp. 177–210.

The debate reflects the vast gaps in our knowledge; yet the political realities will not permit the long-time wait for results of the great amount of research still needed.

Given the massive budgetary implications of national health insurance and the extreme sensitivity and complexity of health matters, it seems safe to say that government is unlikely to embrace a full-fledged scheme at one time. We will probably move towards universal health insurance in easy stages, as we have already begun through Medicare.

Concluding observations

Some of the thorny issues besetting health care have been reviewed here. Before closing it may be appropriate to call attention, briefly and summarily, to a few general, even philosophical, problems which seem worthy of the student's reflection, some of which have been broadly alluded to earlier.

1. How much of our national income should be invested in health care? The notion that resources are no longer scarce is false. We must still make difficult choices in respect to scarce resource allocation. We have seen that the share of GNP spent for health has been rising steadily and reached 7.4 percent in 1971. It will undoubtedly continue to rise.

Health improvement has been impressive in this century, although It Is impossible to gauge how much of it can be attributed to health services and how much to other factors. Life expectancy has increased from 46 years at the turn of the century to over 70 years, but it has now clearly plateaued. It may be that as the health of a nation advances, a point is reached where the extent and character of the benefits to be derived from additional expenditures for health services must be appraised in relation to costs and to society's values.

Sheer demand for such services is no adequate criterion. As we have seen, medical care demand does not behave according to the normal laws of the marketplace. Supply can create its own demand. As a distinguished British authority has put it, "Expenditures for medical care can be a bottomless pit." This is an area that requires conscious and informed social decision making in light of immense competing demands on our resources: to rehabilitate our cities, to clean our air and water, to educate increasing numbers of our young, and other urgent needs.

2. Similarly, even if we decide that we should invest substantially more towards health goals, it is not clear whether a given additional economic input into additional health facilities or services will move us more rapidly or economically toward such goals than a like input in housing, or education, or recreation, or better food. For large parts of our population lack of adequate health services is not their most important health problem, We need to know more about the probable relative return from different types

and different combinations of expenditures. The implications for public policy are large.

3. Within the range of practical possibility, irrespective of how much we decide to allocate for health, and even if we succeed in distributing access to health services more equitably, we will face another set of choices of a different dimension. Medical science and technological capabilities are expanding exponentially. Recent years have seen development of cures and controls of deadly diseases, but frequently they are enormously expensive. Persons with kidney failure can now be kept alive and functioning with dialysis, but at a cost of about $10,000 a year. At present, facilities are available for only a small fraction of the many thousands who otherwise die of this disease. Transplants and implantations of artificial organs are at the frontier. Each involves many thousnds of dollars. Many other "miracles" are in the offing. Demand for such services is incalculable; the resources required to meet all potential demands for newly developing technologies are virtually boundless.

In the past, decisions as to who should have access to such costly procedures was determined primarily by individual financial ability. This standard has become unacceptable. We will, through some scheme of national health insurance or other device, soon be attempting to offer relatively equal access to health services to all our population. Since resources are not unlimited, a new way must be found to make socially acceptable determinations. Where will we set limits upon individual health services? How will choices be made as to who will have access to extremely costly procedures and who will not?

4. As indicated, we appear to be moving towards more equitable distribution of access through national health insurance or similar means. In the enthusiasm for such programs, one often reads statements such as, "Every American has a right to good health." Perhaps so, but no national insurance program can assure anybody good health or even better health. As we have said, even if we attain full equality in services for the poor, for example, their health status will remain unequal because health services alone will not overcome the other basic disadvantages of poverty.

Moreover, as has been indicated, we are increasingly recognizing that, at our present stage of social development, for all our population the most important single ingredient of health is personal life style and behavior. In the provision of health services, we may now have to shift our emphasis from traditional therapy to health education. As a population we are appallingly ignorant of how to build or maintain our health in daily behavior and how to use health care services effectively. This is a growing challenge to our communities, educators, health professionals, and to our social values.

5. In similar vein, now that the issue of national health insurance is prominently before the public, we must be clear about what it is reasonable

to expect from such a program and what is not. This writer believes that a comprehensive and equitable program of universal health insurance would represent a large step forward in our social progress, but it is not an apocalyptic cure for all ills, and it is important to recognize its limitations.

Any expectation that it will automatically bring a halt to inflation of health care prices and costs is probably overoptimistic and not in keeping with experience abroad. England and Sweden, which have generally praised but quite different national systems, have each experienced sharp rises over the past decade—about the same rate as our own in the case of England and even greater in Sweden. A national program could provide the potential means to exercise more controls than we now have and perhaps slow down the pace we have been experiencing, but this will depend upon the character of the particular program and the effectiveness of administration. In any case, the multiple factors affecting higher prices and costs cannot simply be regulated out of existence, and it is misleading to make such claims.

Nor will a national health insurance program necessarily or automatically alter the maldistribution of facilities and manpower. This is not primarily a problem of money but a problem of organization. The technology of a modern hospital cannot function effectively in an isolated area. Free societies have found it is neither desirable nor effective to attempt to force professional people to work in places contrary to their wishes.

National health insurance will be costly. Even without new legislation the Social Security Administration has estimated that the nation will spend about $105 billion for health care in 1974. How much more would be added by national health insurance depends, of course, on the particular plan adopted, but estimates indicate that some proposals could result in $120 billion or more. How much of this staggering sum will simply represent a transfer from current private expenditures to public financing varies with plans, but in any case we must expect a substantial increase in public spending and taxation. Together with other rising necessities for more social spending, this will challenge American attitudes towards paying for services through tax bills rather than private payments and their tolerance of redistributive effects.

The operation of so vast and complex a program will add to the already prominent issue of the limits of our public management capacities. Are our governmental institutions compatible with the demands of effective administration for programs of dimensions never before contemplated? Do we know how?

6. Lastly, as we have already indicated, national health insurance is only a generic name for a wide array of different possibilities. In light of the questions we have raised, it should be clear that the choice among different plans is immensely important. Plans may or may not actually be able to achieve the goals they allege or intend. Plans may or may not be manage-

able. The decisions to be made by the American people within the next few years deserve the most careful public deliberation. The stakes are high. In any case, it must be remembered that the current anomolies and needed reforms described in this essay will remain difficult and important issues to be resolved with or without national health insurance.

4

The Economics of
Education: A Survey

DOUGLAS M. WINDHAM

Associate Professor of Economics
University of North Carolina—Greensboro

The widespread interest in the education field manifested by economists in the last decade is an extension of a long-standing concern, reactivated by certain methodological developments.[1] The growth of education itself, in numbers of participants and the aggregate expenditure thereon, is an even more important cause for the new attention. When education was reserved for only a few and did not make great demands upon the public purse, there was little controversy concerning it. Within this century, really only since the Depression of the 1930s, education has grown tremendously in terms of its economic effects and its widespread public support.

This pattern of growth was reinforced by the space competition of the late 1950s and early 1960s, with public enthusiasm for education extending to greater support of post-secondary education. It is only in the last few years that critical questions have again been asked concerning education's appropriate goals and evidenced achievements. The sources of the present dissatisfaction with and questioning of our educational systems, will be

---

[1] In particular, refinement of the concept of investment in education as human capital formation. One of the early formulations of this approach appears in an essay by J. R. Walsh, published in the *Quarterly Journal of Economics,* Vol. 49 (1935), pp. 255–285. The work of T. W. Schultz and Gary Becker some thirty years later began the present era of research in this field.

surveyed in full at a later point. For now, the discussion need only concentrate upon the size of the financial investment in education to understand its importance to the economy.

Table 4–1 presents data on public and private school expenditures by level of instruction for public and private schools from 1930 to 1971. It is worth noting that while the percent of Gross National Product expended on education increased slightly from 1930 to 1950, the percent increased by 50 percent over each of the next two decades to the present total of over $70 Billion.

A pre-survey of the discussion

A systematic discussion of the economics of education is difficult because the topic can be analyzed in so many different ways. One could discuss education level by level; one could concentrate on the dichotomy of costs and benefits; one could compare private versus public education, or emphasize the alternative individual and societal aspects of education. Here the attempt is made to present the subject matter of the economics of education in an issue-oriented manner.

First, the economic tools of analysis will be explained so that the reader may appreciate the contribution which economics can make to educational research. The nature of education as an economic good will then be explored. The public versus private nature of the various levels and forms of education is a crucial point to be resolved. Data on the extent and form of educational attainment will be presented.

The analysis will then proceed to successive discussions of the supply of education, the private demand for education, the social investment in education, and the financing of education. This last topic will include a study of the apparent conflicts which exist between the equity and efficiency goals of our educational systems. Racial, sexual, generational, and regional income inequalities will be noted in terms of their relationship with the educational process.

I.   The tools of economic analysis

What contribution can economists make to the study of education? After all, not just professional educators but sociologists, psychologists, statisticians, and even political scientists have evidenced a long-standing interest in educational phenomena. If the economist is going to make a unique contribution he should show some area of comparative advantage (to use the economist's own jargon).

Efficiency concepts

As economics students know, economics is the "science of scarcity." More specifically, economics attempts to study the manner in which scarce

Table 4-1. School expenditures* by type of control and level of institution, 1930–1971 (in millions of dollars)

Control and Level	1930	1940	1950	1960	1965	1969	1970	1971 (est.)
Total	3,234	3,200	8,796	24,722	40,200	62,000	70,600	75,300
Percent of GNP	3.1	3.5	3.4	5.1	6.4	7.2	7.6	7.7
Current Expenditures	2,700	2,833	7,229	20 603	33,200	53,100	61,300	65,800
Capital Outlay	534	367	1,567	4 120	7,000	8,900	9,300	9,500
Public	2,656	2,697	7,057	19 447†	31,000	49,900	57,300	61,200
Percent of Total	82.1	84.3	80.2	78.7	77.1	80.5	81.2	81.3
Elementary and Secondary	2,367	2,364	5,883	15 613	23,800	35,700	41,000	43,300
Higher Education	289	333	1,174	3 753	7,200	14,200	16,300	17,900
Private	578	503	1,739	5 275	9,200	12,100	13,300	14,100
Percent of Total	17.9	15.7	19.8	21.3	22.9	19.5	18.8	18.7
Elementary and Secondary	237	230	790	2,412	3,500	4,200	4,700	4,800
Higher Education	341	273	949	2,863	5,700	7,900	8,600	9,300

* Expenditures include current expenditures, interest, and capital outlay.
† Includes expenditures for certain Federal schools excluded from breakdown.
Source: Dept. of Health, Education, and Welfare, Office of Education; *Biennial Survey of Education in the United States,* chapter on "Statistical Summary of Education," and annual reports, *Digest of Educational Statistics* and *Projections of Educational Statistics.*

resources may be used to greatest advantage in satisfying society's needs and wants. This process is summed up by the term "efficiency," the least-cost means of achieving a particular goal or the most productive means (in terms of goal-achievement) of using a given amount of resources. It is the efficiency concept, with all of its inherent ramifications in terms of evaluation of alternatives and definition of costs, that represents the primary conceptual contribution economists have to offer in the economics of education.

An individual firm is said to be operating efficiently when it produces the quantity of output where marginal cost equals marginal revenue. If the producer is a profit maximizer, it will be illogical for him to produce at any other level of output than this. This definition of production efficiency is appropriate for any market form: monopolist to pure and perfect competitor.

The individual is said to be maximizing his utility when he equates the ratios of marginal utility to cost for all of the items of expenditure available to him. Any inequality of ratios would suggest that the consumer could increase his total utility by shifting expenditures from the item(s) with a higher ratio to the item(s) with relatively lower ratios. It is assumed that the consumption of all items is subject to the principle of diminishing marginal utility. The maximization of societal utility will be detailed in a later section but it may be noted for now that it follows much the same form as presented here for the individual.

How applicable are these economic concepts to the study of education? Education has been depicted as a heterogenous, multi-input, multiproduct, and, normally, nonprofit institution. The very complexity of education may make economic analysis difficult but would normally pose no impossible barriers. To appreciate fully the problem of judging efficiency in education, it is necessary first to be familiar with the more common evaluation of efficiency of a market. Through a contrast of the normal conditions of production efficiency with the extant production conditions in education, one can begin to understand the problems which face the economic researcher.

Basically for a market system to have efficient results all of the following five conditions should exist:

1. Producers and consumers have perfect knowledge of relevant information for their decision-making;
2. Producers act as profit maximizers and consumers as utility (satisfaction) maximizers;
3. Product prices and resource costs are not controlled by any agency but are freely set by interaction of supply and demand;
4. Firms and resources have freedom to enter and exit their respective markets; and

5. No significant external (accruing to someone other than the parties in-
    volved in the market exchange) production or consumption costs or
    benefits should occur.

All of these conditions need not exist in full for the system to have efficient
results within some acceptable limits. However, few of the conditions presently exist for the production and consumption of education.

Information about educational costs and opportunities is often either
inadequate or nonexistent. Within the limits of their lack of information,
consumers of education may attempt to be utility maximizers but few educational "firms", with the notable exception of the proprietary vocational
schools, do or should act as profit maximizers. Education at the primary
and secondary level operates as either a monopoly or oligopoly market.
Mobility of educational resources is not free. Teachers, for example, become tied to specific jobs and geographical areas because of salary, promotion, and retirement criteria. Finally, the existence and possible extent
of any social benefits or costs is grossly uncertain.

To compound these problems facing the economist as an educational
researcher attempting to apply the concept of efficiency, is the fact that no
adequate alternative measures to the standard of market efficiency exist.
Attempts to solve this and related problems are the basis of the current
expansion of research activity. The status of the discipline at present is
such that the researcher is still grappling with the problem of determining
the significant variables in the educational input–output relationship and
defining operationally measurable goals. The uncertainty over the latter,
the lack of a consensus about the explicit goals for the various educational
systems, is quite possibly the single greatest problem the researcher faces.

Public production and public goods

A problem constantly encountered by economists who work outside the
strict limits of their discipline, is that terminology used by economists has
a different meaning than that in more common usage. It is essential that
such semantic confusions be resolved early to avoid unnecessary mis-
understandings later on. For example, many people would use the term
"public good" to represent all goods which happen to be collectively produced by society. The economist restricts the use of this term to those
products and services which may need to be produced collectively for social efficiency to exist.

A first condition for social efficiency is that the price of a good should
equal the marginal cost of producing the good, a condition which is met
automatically in competitive markets. When such a situation exists, the
sacrifice required of the consumer in terms of alternative forms of consumption is equated with the sacrifice to society in terms of alternative

forms of production. In imperfect markets, however, there is not the same automatic concomitance of price and marginal revenue at the equilibrium quantity of production. Rather, price will be greater than marginal revenue at the quantity where marginal revenue equals marginal cost. The inequality between price and marginal cost indicates the inability of the imperfect market to attain a socially efficient equilibrium.

To resolve this problem, society may choose one of three alternatives: (1) antimonopoly policy to restore competitive conditions to the market; (2) public regulation of prices and quantities so that price will more closely approximate marginal cost; and (3) public production of the good to ensure equality of price and marginal cost.

Unfortunately, in many cases antimonopoly policy cannot be successful because certain economic conditions do not permit the efficient opera- of a sufficient number of firms to assure that competition will exist. An example would be where economies of scale (the cost-saving from producing larger quantities) are so large that only a few firms can operate efficiently. A second example would be where the marginal cost of producing a good is zero, and therefore a socially optimum level of output may require that production be expanded beyond the point where marginal revenue equals marginal cost.

The alternative of market regulation is less satisfactory but often more politically palatable than the actual takeover of production by the public sector. When the good is produced publicly the reason is often the existance of substantial "collective consumption externalities." An externality of this type is the gain accruing to some economic unit or units because of the production of a good whose benefits cannot be restricted but are available to everyone. A "pure public good" is one which is available for equal consumption by all regardless of whether or not they helped pay for it. National defense is commonly cited as an example of a pure public good with these collective consumption characteristics. Education is usually described as a "quasi-public" good because a share of its benefits are available only to the individual educated and not for equal consumption by others.

The human capital concept

It is not uncommon to find references in textbooks to the *three* types of productive resources: land, labor, and capital. Increasingly, however, writers have come to the realization that the inclusion of all human effort as "labor" assumes too much about the homogeneity of the labor force. The use of the term "human capital" as a fourth type of economic resource is one effort to meet this difficulty.

The concept human capital, which to some may appear as a use of seemingly mutually exclusive terms, is the part of labor effort which has been subject to improvement as a result of education or other training. At one extreme, the phrase could describe nearly all human effort since all but the very basic human actions are "learned" in some way. For this reason, the term has been reserved for those skills or traits which are the product of formal training, either within some educational institution or as part of the individual's employment. The latter type, on-the-job training, may be especially difficult to quantify but is no less important because of this reservation.

One advantage of the human capital concept is that it permits, within certain assumptions, a clearer cost-benefit comparison of individual and societal alternatives. Such a comparison is easier to make for an individual, though even in that case it poses some empirical problems, since part of the total expenditure on education is for purposes of consumption rather than investment. This point is elaborated on in a later section.

However, for most people the primary goal of education, especially at higher levels, is probably the addition to his asset value. An individual's human capital at any point in time is represented by those skills which he possesses. The value of his human capital is defined as the present value of the expected lifetime income stream which those skills are expected to generate. Because the expected income will vary with age, the timing of the income stream with age has an important effect upon the present value. The sooner that income is received, the less it is discounted. A formula which has been suggested is:

$$V_a = \sum_{n=a}^{\infty} (Y_n P^n_a \frac{1}{(1+r)^{n-a}}$$

where

V_a = present value of lifetime income at year "a";

Y = the value of expected productivity between year "a" and infinity;

r = rate of discount of future income;

and

P^n_a = probability of being alive at year "n" [2]

There are other economic terms and concepts not discussed here which are quite important to the appreciation of the economics of education. The nature of the age-income profile or the definition and scope of the "social benefits" of education are only two examples. These and other economic terms are elaborated on within the discussion of later topics to which they are relevant. The understanding of the efficiency concept, the public or private nature of education, and of the meaning of human capital are all so basic that they have been presented here in advance of the more specific discussion of topics which follows.

---

[2] Burton A. Weisbrod, "The Valuation of Human Capital," *Journal of Political Economy*, Vol. 69 (October 1961), p. 427.

II. Education as an economic good

Education is certainly an economic good because it is produced under the restraints of scarcity. It is impossible to increase the amount of education produced without sacrificing alternative goods or services. This requires that some device must exist for distributing education among the members of society. The product of the educational process may be represented as a bundle of diverse services which in some way alter the individual's ability to handle certain situations. Learning to speak and write; learning to behave in socially approved patterns; learning to operate a complex machine; all of these are parts of the educational package of which any person might partake.

The complexity of education makes it necessary that some distinctions be made among the various types. Here, the interest is in three main forms of education. The first form is institutionalized education: pre-primary, primary, secondary, and post-secondary (including proprietary school training). The second and third forms are distinct types of extra-institutional education: family and peer influence and on-the-job training. The analysis of each is quite different.

Institutionalized education

Formal education is the most common subject of study by researchers because it is commonly produced publicly and involves substantial public subsidization. Most public production of education is not subject to normal market rules of supply and demand. The result is that alternative measures of efficiency are needed. Before proceeding to the analysis of the supply and demand of education, this section will review the present status of education in the United States.

Table 4–2 presents enrollment statistics for the years 1960 and 1970 for kindergarten, elementary (grades 1–8), high school (grades 9–12), and col-

Table 4–2. Enrollment in public and private schools: 1960–1970 (in thousands of persons 5 to 34 years of age)

| | Number Enrolled | | | | | |
| | 1960 | | | 1970 | | |
Level	Total	Public	Private	Total	Public	Private
Total	46,259	39,027	7,232	58,804	51,562	7,242
Kindergarten	2,092	1,691	401	2,726	2,317	409
Elementary (1–8)	30,349	25,814	4,536	33,950	30,001	3,949
High school (9–12)	10,249	9,215	1,033	14,715	13,545	1,170
College	3,570	2,307	1,262	7,413	5,699	1,714

Source: Department of Commerce, Bureau of the Census; *Current Population Reports, Series P–20.*

lege. The table includes figures for both private and public schools. The largest increases in enrollment between 1960 and 1970 occurred in high schools and colleges where the percentage increase was over 40 percent and 105 percent respectively. Public enrollment increases were greater absolutely and proportionately at all levels. These increases at grade nine and beyond are encouraging in that they reflect increased educational attainment for the school age population. Simultaneously, though, the institutional facilities must be expanded to take care of these increased enrollments and an inability to make this adjustment has caused some potentially serious problems.

More detailed information concerning the pre-primary enrollment of children may be found in Table 4–3. The total enrollment figures for this group are different from those of the kindergarten group in the previous table because the definition of pre-primary schools used here includes pre-kindergarten training but excludes any six-year olds remaining in kindergarten classes.

Even though the total age cohort of three to five year olds is smaller in 1970 than 1960 (reflecting the change in birth rates which occurred during the 1960s), the total number of children enrolled is greater. It is also interesting to note that family income, rather than race, *per se,* appears as the stronger determinant of pre-primary enrollment. The percentages enrolled for whites and nonwhites are quite close: 37.8 to 35.7. But, if one looks at enrollment percentages by family incomes, there are dramatic differences. The $10,000 and over group has almost twice (47.5 to 24.4) the enrollment propensity of the lowest income class. Given other home environmental advantages which might be expected to accrue to children of high-income families, these data suggest a partial explanation as to why low-income children may not perform so well in primary and secondary education.

The enrollment figures by occupation, location of residence, and education of parent follow patterns similar to that found for income. This would normally be expected because these characteristics are highly correlated to income. Therefore, one finds that white-collar (higher-income) workers have a larger percentage of their children in pre-primary education than do manual, service, or farm workers. This last group, farm workers, faces not just an income limitation but also the present limited availability of pre-primary educational facilities in rural areas.

By residence, the suburban ("outside central cities" classification) family is most likely to have children in pre-primary education while farm and other rural families are, again, the least likely to have their children enrolled. Enrollment propensities follow the expected relationship with the education of the head of the household. The greater the household head's level of educational attainment, the greater is his probable income, his likelihood to live in nonrural areas, and, therefore, to have children enrolled

Table 4-3. Pre-primary school enrollment of children 3 to 5 years old,* by selected characteristics as of October 1965, and 1970 (in thousands, except percent)

Characteristic	1965			1970		
	Total Population	Enrolled Number	Enrolled Percent	Total Population	Enrolled Number	Enrolled Percent
Total, 3–5 years of age †	12,549	3,407	27.1	10,949	4,104	37.5
White	10,608	2,957	27.9	9,098	3,443	37.8
Negro and other	1,941	451	23.3	1,851	661	35.7
Family income:						
Less than $3,000	1,719	247	14.4	916	224	24.4
$3,000–$4,999	2,503	525	21.0	1,312	392	29.9
$5,000–$7,499	3,821	1,004	26.3	2,277	737	32.4
$7,500–$9,999	3,744	1,402	37.4	2,321	856	36.9
$10,000 and over				3,320	1,577	47.5
Occupation of family head:						
White-collar	4,177	1,516	36.3	3,807	1,791	47.0
Manual or service	6,264	1,453	23.2	5,231	1,678	32.1
Farm	659	63	9.6	346	82	23.6
Residence:						
Metropolitan areas:						
Central cities	3,500	1,048	29.9	3,088	1,218	39.4
Outside central cities	4,619	1,500	32.5	3,949	1,705	43.2
Nonmetropolitan areas	4,430	861	19.4	3,913	1,181	30.2
Education of household head:						
Elementary, 0–8 years	(NA)	(NA)	(NA)	1,686	397	23.6
High School:						
1–3 years	(NA)	(NA)	(NA)	2,103	734	34.9
4 years	(NA)	(NA)	(NA)	3,831	1,381	36.0
College, 1 year or more	(NA)	(NA)	(NA)	2,977	1,452	48.8

* Relates to civilian noninstitutional population. Includes both public and nonpublic prekindergarten and kindergarten programs; excludes 5-year-olds enrolled in programs above kindergarten and 6-year-olds enrolled in pre-primary programs.
NA Not available.
† Includes children with family income, occupation of family head, and education of household heads not reported, not shown separately below.
Source: Department of Health, Education, and Welfare, Office of Education; annual report, *Preprimary Enrollment Trends of Children Under Six.*

Table 4-4. School enrollment, by race, level of school, and age 1960 and 1970, as of October (in thousands, except percent)

Age	White				Negro and Other			
	Total Enrolled	Elementary*	High School*	College*	Total Enrolled	Elementary*	High School*	College*
1960, total	40,348	27,884	9,122	3,342	5,910	4,556	1,127	227
5–13 years	27,723	27,149	574	0	4,336	4,285	51	0
14–17 years	9,028	731	8,084	214	1,213	268	937	8
18–24 years	2,854	4	431	2,420	312	2	132	178
25–34 years	743	1	33	709	49	1	7	41
1970, total	50,464	30,980	12,723	6,759	8,337	5,689	1,992	654
5–13 years	30,390	30,063	327	0	5,459	5,392	67	0
14–17 years	12,769	898	11,639	230	2,027	295	1,703	30
18–24 years	5,979	14	661	5,304	701	5	196	499
25–34 years	1,326	5	95	1,224	150	0	24	125
Percent change, 1960–1970, for totals	25.1	11.1	39.5	102.2	41.1	24.9	76.8	188.1

* Elementary includes kindergarten; high school, grades 9–12; college includes professional schools.
Source: Department of Commerce, Bureau of the Census; Current Population Reports, Series P-20, and unpublished data.

in pre-primary schooling. The point to be emphasized is that all of these variables—the income, occupation, residence, and educational attainment of parents—are interdependent. This fact requires that one be careful in offering explanations as to why the different groups have different enrollment propensities.

Table 4–4 presents additional information on enrollments at the elementary, high school, and college level by characteristics of race and age. Of special importance are the figures on percentage changes in enrollment at the various levels of education. These amounts are much greater for the "Negro and other" group than for the white group. The high percentages are a function of improved attainment relative to the previously suppressed level of educational success experienced by nonwhite groups. The changes in the relative positions of whites and nonwhites are summarized in the next table.

Table 4–5. Percent enrolled in school, by age and race: 1960 to 1970

	1960		1965		1970	
Age	White	Negro and Other	White	Negro and Other	White	Negro and Other
Total, 5–34 years	56.4	55.9	59.6	60.0	58.6	60.6
5 and 6 years	82.0	73.3	85.3	79.3	89.2	83.6
7–9 years	99.7	99.3	99.4	99.0	99.3	99.4
10–13 years	99.5	99.0	99.4	99.3	99.1	99.4
14 and 15 years	98.1	95.9	99.0	98.2	98.2	97.6
16 and 17 years	83.3	76.9	87.8	84.6	90.6	86.2
18 and 19 years	38.9	34.6	47.1	40.1	48.7	41.9
20–24 years	13.9	7.5	20.2	10.2	22.5	15.2
25–34 years	3.8	1.9	4.9	3.1	6.1	5.2

Source: Department of Commerce, Bureau of the Census; *Current Population Reports, Series P–20,* and unpublished data.

Table 4–5 presents enrollment percentages by age and race for the years 1960, 1965, and 1970. The eight distinct age groups allow for the evaluation of attrition rates for the two racial groups. One of the serious problems facing contemporary education is the relatively higher attrition rates experienced by minority/poverty students. Although family income rather than race alone is more probably the prime causal factor in these disproportionate attrition rates, the acknowledged white/nonwhite income differential makes the present analysis more relevant.

As had been previously indicated in Table 4–4, nonwhites are making sizeable advances. However, it is only above the age of sixteen (the normal limit on legally required school attendance) that any really significant analysis may be made. In Table 4–5, above the age of 16, the nonwhite's enrollment percentage drops behind that of the white student group. One reason nonwhites in the 25–34 year old age group appear to be doing relatively better in 1970 than earlier years may be the effect of training supported by the G.I. Bill. The large participation rate of this same nonwhite age group, may also be a reflection of the longer academic programs which low-income nonwhites often have to follow.

Another view of the attrition problem is depicted in Table 4–6. There, the percentage distribution by year of school completed is presented for persons 25 years or older, by race and sex, for 1960 and 1970. The apparent gains for Negroes may be overemphasized unless one studies the table carefully. For example, while the proportion of Negroes with an education above the eighth grade has increased substantially from 39 to 57 percent, this latter amount is still small when compared with the over 73 percent of whites who have such an education. Even more dramatically, over 57 percent of whites had a complete high school education or more in 1970 while the same figure for Negroes was slightly less than 34 percent.

When one studies only the male group, it may be seen that Negroes have noticeably increased their position absolutely and relative to whites in the high school graduate and above category. In 1960, whites had 41.6 percent of all males, 25 years old and above, in this category. Negroes had only 18.2 percent. In 1970 the respective figures were 57.2 and 32.5 percent. Again, however, the improved situation for Negoes should not be exaggerated. If the 1970 figures for males with some college are compared, white males still lead Negro males, 26.3 to 10.3 percent. In the college graduate and above category, white males lead by an even greater margin, 15.0 to 4.6 percent.

Studying the figures in Table 4–6 by sex rather than race reveals some equally interesting facts. For whites especially, the male is seen to dominate at both ends of the educational attainment spectrum. The male student is more likely than the female student to drop out at the very early grades of school but the male high school graduate is more likely to enter and complete college than is his female counterpart. The same general sexual pattern holds true for Negroes with the noteworthy exception that it is only in the last decade that Negro males have surpassed females at the college graduate level and above. The reduction in employment barriers for highly educated Negro men has made a college education a better investment for this group.

Students of white-nonwhite income differentials may find little satisfaction in the pace of the educational advancement of Negroes, since there has been a simultaneous increase in the educational requirements of the job market. If it now takes a high school diploma to qualify for a job formerly filled by high school dropouts, the Negro can only hope for significant employment and income gains if he increases his education faster than job requirements are increased. This has been partially offset by the

Table 4–6. Years of school completed, by race and sex: 1960 and 1970 (persons 25 years old and over)

Year, Race, and Sex	Persons 25 Years Old and Over (1,000)	Years of School Completed (Percent Distribution)							Median
		Elementary School			High School		College		
		0–4 Years	5–7 Years	8 Years	1–3 Years	4 Years	1–3 Years	4 Years or More	
1960 total, all races	99,438	8.3	13.8	17.5	19.2	24.6	8.8	7.7	10.6
White	89,581	6.7	12.8	18.1	19.3	25.8	9.3	8.1	10.9
Male	43,259	7.4	13.7	18.4	18.9	22.2	9.1	10.3	10.7
Female	46,322	6.0	11.9	17.8	19.6	29.2	9.5	6.0	11.2
Negro	9,054	23.8	24.2	12.9	19.0	12.9	4.1	3.1	8.2
Male	4,240	28.3	23.9	12.3	17.3	11.3	4.1	2.8	7.7
Female	4,814	19.8	24.5	13.4	20.5	14.3	4.1	3.3	8.6
1970 total, all races	109,310	5.3	9.1	13.4	17.1	34.0	10.2	11.0	12.2
White	98,112	4.2	8.3	13.6	16.5	35.2	10.7	11.6	12.2
Male	46,606	4.5	8.8	13.9	14.1	30.9	11.3	15.0	12.2
Female	51,506	3.9	7.8	13.4	17.3	39.0	10.1	8.6	12.2
Negro	10,089	15.1	16.7	11.2	23.3	23.4	5.9	4.5	9.9
Male	4,619	18.6	16.0	11.1	21.9	22.2	5.7	4.6	9.6
Female	5,470	12.1	17.3	11.3	24.5	24.4	6.0	4.4	10.2

Source: Department of Commerce, Bureau of the Census; U.S. Census of Population: 1960, Vol. I and Current Population Reports, Series P–20, No. 207.

encouragement which equal-employment laws has given to minority employment at the higher educational levels: the relative scarcity of Negro graduates has bid up their value.

Table 4–7. Institutions of higher education-enrollment, by characteristics: 1960 to 1970, and projections to 1979 as of fall opening (in thousands)

Characteristic	1960	1965	1970	1975	1979
Total	3,789	5,921	8,274	10,664	12,258
Degree credit	3,583	5,526	7,608	9,702	11,075
Undergraduate	3,227	4,907	6,662	8,368	9,435
Male	2,004	2,952	3,875	4,749	5,276
Female	1,223	1,956	2,788	3,619	4,159
4-year	2,776	4,066	5,178	6,324	6,989
2-year	451	841	1,484	2,044	2,446
Public	1,929	3,255	4,916	6,449	7,471
Private	1,298	1,653	1,747	1,919	1,964
Graduate, resident only	356	619	946	1,334	1,640
Nondegree credit	206	395	666	962	1,183

Source: Department of Health, Education, and Welfare, Office of Education; annual report, *Projections of Educational Statistics to 1979–80.*

Table 4–7 presents the enrollment statistics, for selected characteristics, at institutions of higher education for the period 1960 to 1970 with projections to 1979. There are several noteworthy patterns which emerge from these figures. First, female participation in higher education will continue to increase in the 1970s just as it has so dramatically in the 1960s. Changes in both the supply and demand sides of the labor market for women are responsible for providing incentives for a large part of this change. Women, through choice now and not simply necessity, are increasingly seeking employment opportunities. Employment opportunities for women are simultaneously expanding. Equal-employment regulations have again been a factor.

A second important pattern which emerges is the increasing importance of the two-year college. These community or junior colleges, as they are known, are expected to supply a large part of the increase in educational opportunities which will take place during the next decade. The two-year colleges will have larger and larger demands placed upon them to provide technical/vocational instruction and adult education programs in addition to general college courses. Many states already have "technical institutes" which are quite separate from the transfer-oriented junior colleges.

Those who support private post-secondary education as a valuable alternative to public education, have little to be happy about from the projected figures. While enrollment at public institutions is expected to increase by approximately 50 percent in the next decade, private enrollment will increase by less than 15 percent. Private institutions have suffered from two major sources of difficulty in the last decade: the disadvantageous price competition from subsidized tuitions at public institutions and their own financial mismanagement. Even those private schools whose wisdom has allowed them to avoid the latter problem have not been able to avoid the former.

The problem for private colleges is aggravated by the increase in the quality of many public colleges and universities which has occurred in the 1960s. In many areas, the subsidized tuition at a public institution may well purchase an education equal, if not superior, to that of the formerly preferred private school. Efforts in many states to assist private colleges have been directed at removing the private/public tuition differential through the means of direct financial aid to students rather than institutions. The student receiving such aid is then allowed to use it at either a public or private college or university.

The relative increase in graduate enrollment which is expected in the 1970s may be attributed in part to the increased employment requirements mentioned earlier. Superior students are forced to get additional degrees in order to differentiate themselves sufficiently in the job market. Even if graduate degree holders become too numerous for the positions which they would traditionally occupy, their additional education may serve as an advantage in competing for other previously lower-status positions. Although not discernible from the figures here, it may be expected that by the 1979–80 academic year, the proportion of graduate students working in post-Masters degree programs will also have increased.

The importance of the continuing increase in nondegree credit programs should not be overlooked. The ability of higher education to adapt itself to nontraditional demands is reflected in these figures. Especially important in the 1970s will be the increased enrollment of adults who will return to school for a special course or program of courses but will not seek degree status.

Vocational programs are an increasingly important part of the educational process. In 1969 the U.S. Office of Education reported that the total annual expenditure on such programs was $1,369 million of which $255 million was from federal sources, $467 million was from state sources, and $647 million was from local sources.[3] Table 4–8 presents a summary, for the period 1950 to 1969, of selected federally-aided vocational programs.

The table reveals two dominant areas of change. First, secondary level vocational programs have gained relative to adult programs. These have the ability to reach a greater number of potential students. Second, office

---

[3] U.S. Bureau of the Census, *Statistical Abstract of the United States: 1971* (Washington: GPO, 1971), p. 134.

Table 4–8. Federally aided vocational programs, 1950–69 (for years ending June 30)

Item	1950	1960	1965	1969
Expenditures, total ($ millions)	129	239	605	1,369
Federal	27	45	157	255
Percent of total	20.7	19.0	26.0	18.6
Students, total (in thousands)	3,365	3,768	5,431	7,979
Adult	NA	NA	2,379	3,050
Secondary	NA	NA	2,819	4,079
Other	NA	NA	233	850
Type of Program:				
Home economics	1,430	1,588	2,099	2,449
Office occupations	0	0	731	1,835
Trades and industry	805	938	1,088	1,721
Agriculture	765	796	888	851
Other	365	445	626	1,123

NA = Not available.
Source: Department of Health, Education, and Welfare, Office of Education; annual report, *Vocational and Technical Education.*

occupation training and trade and industry programs have increased more rapidly than either the home economics or agriculture programs.

Another type of education, which is less formal than those discussed above, is the on-the-job training program. This is normally conducted by individual companies. Table 4–9 presents a summary of the programs in 1970 which were administered by the U.S. Department of Labor.

With the exception of the Neighborhood Youth Corps (predominantly a summer oriented program), the largest program in number of enrollees was the Manpower Development and Training Program. The participants in this program were predominantly male, white, and 22–44 years old. This program also included the highest percentage of high school graduates. Women were most heavily represented in the Public Service Careers project and the Work Incentive Program. Negroes and other nonwhites participated at the highest rate in the JOBS (Job Opportunities in the Business Sector) program. Older workers found the most opportunities, when measured as a percentage of all participants, in the Operation Mainstream project.

Analysis concerning the success of such work and training efforts is most available for the Manpower Development and Training Program. Table 4–10 provides information on enrollment opportunities, actual enrollment, completions, and post-training employment for the years 1965-70. It is evident that 1967 was the most successful year for the project, even though 1966 had funding for more enrollment opportunities. In 1967 the program had its largest total enrollment (265,000), largest number of completions (192,600), and the largest number of enrollees finding post-

Table 4–9. Work and training programs, 1970

Year and Program	Total Enrollees (1,000)	Male	Negro and Other Races (Excl. White)	Percent — Age in Years			Education, By Grade		
				Under 22	22–44	45 and Over	Less Than 9th	9th–11th	12th and Over
Manpower Development and Training Program:									
Institutional	130	59	41	37	54	9	15	38	47
On-the-job	91	66	33	35	54	11	17	37	46
Neighborhood Youth Corps:									
In school (enrolled Sept.-May.)	74	50	46	100	0	0	17	82	1
Out of school (enrolled Sept.-Aug.)	46	48	50	98	2	0	32	66	2
Summer (enrolled June-Aug.)	362	54	56	100	0	0	21	78	1
Operation Mainstream	12	71	38	4	46	51	52	28	20
Public Service Careers	4	23	68	21	72	7	13	42	45
Concentrated Employment Program	110	58	74	41	51	8	20	45	35
JOBS Program	87	68	78	47	49	4	15	50	35
Work Incentive Program	93	29	48	23	71	6	24	44	32
Job Corps	43	74	74	100	0	0	37	55	7

Source: Department of Labor, Manpower Administration; 1971 *Manpower Report of the President.*

Table 4–10. Manpower development and training program, 1965 to 1970, for years ending June 30 (in thousands)

Item	1965	1966	1967	1968	1969	1970
Enrollment opportunities *	231.8	281.1	270.9	229.9	198.5	201.4
Enrollment	156.9	235.8	265.0	241.0	220.0	221.0
Completions	96.3	155.7	192.6	164.2	160.0	147.0
Postraining employment	73.4	124.0	153.7	127.5	124.0	115.3

* Number of positions provided for by funding.
Source: Department of Labor, Manpower Administration; *1971 Manpower Report of the President.*

training employment (153,700). More importantly, the completion rate of enrollees was highest for that year (72.7 percent) as was the employment rate of all those completing the program (79.8 percent).

A very special type of general skill training program offered by the federal government is military training. As a member of the armed forces, an individual may expect to receive some education in skills other than those of use only to the armed forces. One approximation of the success of these programs would be their effect upon the later employment opportunities of veterans. Table 4–11 offers the results of a survey of United States Air Force veterans, officers and enlisted men. The survey attempted to determine the effect of service training on the ability to qualify for civilian employment.

As would be expected, officers reported the greatest positive effect from service training. The two positive answers, "helped great deal" and "helped somewhat," were selected by over 60 percent of the officers responding. Enlisted men were less enthusiastic. Only 52 percent of those with crafts or technical background selected the positive responses; of those who received primarily military training and no important skill education only about 35 percent found any employment value in their service experience.

Table 4–12 presents a more recent survey of the employment situation of veterans as compared to nonveterans in 1970–71. The data is presented for all males and then separately for members of nonwhite groups. The most obvious characteristic of the data is the consistant pattern of higher unemployment rates for veterans. All nonwhite groups in the table have higher unemployment rates than do whites. What is more surprising is that nonwhite veterans have lost ground to nonwhites who have not recently been in the service.

To make the picture even gloomier, the employment changes from 1970 to 1971 have resulted in larger unemployment increases for veterans than nonveterans. This is true in both the "all races" classification and in the minority classification. The interpretation that can be made from these data, and those in the previous table, is that any positive effect of military service training is presently being outweighed by other factors. These

Table 4–11. USAF experience and training as qualifying factors for civilian employment (percent distribution)

Influence of USAF Background on Qualification for Civilian Work	Officers			Enlisted Men		
	Scientific-Engineering	Administrative-Managerial	Total	Crafts-Technical	Military Services	Total
Total	100.0	100.0	100.0	100.0	100.0	100.0
Helped great deal	33.8	32.1	33.0	30.2	14.6	25.6
Helped somewhat	29.4	32.5	30.9	22.0	20.3	21.5
Helped very little	16.5	16.0	16.4	15.9	13.0	15.1
No help	10.0	10.5	10.2	27.1	44.7	32.3
Hindrance	3.9	2.4	3.2	.7	3.3	1.4
No response	6.5	6.2	6.4	4.1	4.1	4.1

Source: U.S. Department of Labor, *Transferring Military Experience to Civilian Jobs* (Washington: GPO, 1968), p. 14.

Table 4–12. Employment status of male Vietnam-era veterans and nonveterans 20 to 29 years old, by race, 1970–71

Employment Status	Total, 20 to 29 Years		20 to 24 Years		25 to 29 Years	
	1970	1971	1970	1971	1970	1971
Veterans,* all races						
Civilian noninstitutional population (1,000)	3,436	4,057	1,795	1,953	1,641	2,104
Labor force participation rate	92.8	91.6	90.3	88.9	95.4	94.0
Unemployment rate	6.9	8.8	9.3	12.2	4.3	5.7
Nonveterans, all races						
Civilian noninstitutional population (1,000)	8,885	9,391	5,024	5,499	3,861	3,892
Labor force participation rate	87.1	86.7	80.8	80.9	95.3	94.9
Unemployment rate	6.0	7.3	8.0	9.5	3.8	4.7
Negroes and other minority race veterans *						
Civilian noninstitutional population (1,000)	321	397	179	204	142	192
Labor force participation rate	91.0	90.4	89.0	88.0	93.6	93.0
Unemployment rate	11.6	13.7	15.2	17.5	7.4	10.0
Nonveterans, negroes and other races						
Civilian noninstitutional population (1,000)	1,211	1,271	687	742	524	529
Labor force participation rate	86.2	84.6	82.0	79.7	91.7	91.4
Unemployment rate	9.5	12.0	11.9	15.8	6.6	7.2

* Vietnam-era veterans are those who served after Aug. 4, 1964; they are all classified as war veterans. Over 80 percent of Vietnam-era veterans of all ages are 20 to 29 years old. Not included in this table are post-Korean peacetime veterans aged 20 to 29.
Source: *Manpower Report of the President* (Washington: GPO, 1972), p. 47.

factors include the lack of familiarity among veterans with the domestic job market and a lack of civilian work experience. The hardest hit are the younger veteran (20 to 24 years old) and the minority race veteran.

The rationale for service training emphasizes the manpower needs of the military, not the general manpower needs of society. The same study cited as the source for Table 4–11 noted that, in the period 1957–63, the number of aircraft mechanics who left the service exceeded the total number already employed in civilian industry. Obviously, the probability of a veteran with these skills finding a job where the skills would be directly applicable is slight. Even so, one may be assured that the military continues to train new aircraft mechanics. This interest-bias of service training severely limits its general usefulness.

The statistics in this and earlier tables are presented to give a feeling of the scope and diversity of what we term "education." One of the most important forms of education cannot be easily summarized in such a way. This is the learning process by which the individual is influenced by his parents, siblings, and peers. The preschool environment is an obviously important part of the educational process, a fact recognized by even the strongest proponents of theories emphasizing the role of inherited intellectual ability. Fortunately, researchers are beginning to examine and better understand the difference between inherited and family-related environmental educational influences. The other environmental effects are still less well understood and are not emphasized here even though their potential important is fully appreciated.

The next section will study the conditions which determine the supply of education in the various forms presented above. In this and following sections, the discussion is moving from the descriptive to the analytical aspects of the economics of education.

III. The supply of education

Education has been introduced as a heterogenous, multi-output process which is subject to few of the normal market standards of performance. To understand this process and the manner in which education is supplied to the individual is not a simple matter.

To assist in this understanding, the complex problems which exist may be categorized in two large areas. The first relates to definition, in an operationally measurable way, of the goals of education. Obviously, these goals will differ among the various types and levels of education. At the present time the characteristic which all the types and levels of education seem to share is the lack of such a definition of goals. Homilies and generalization abound; goals which may be systematically evaluated are lacking.

The second area of categorization for the study of the supply of education is the subject of internal production relationships. What economists call educational "production functions" attempt to relate the inputs of eduction to the desired outputs. Definition and qualification are again problems. Because these production relationships can only have meaning in terms of goal achievement, the topic of educational goals will be discussed first.

Educational goals and social choice models

T. W. Schultz has noted the importance of determining standards of performance for our educational systems. In writing "A Comment on Research by Economists on Economic Problems of Education," he stated:

A major unsettled question in our society facing legislators and public administrators in making funds available to schools and to institutions of higher education is the determination of acceptable social and political standards with regard to performance. Responsible government must develop such standards in accounting for the uses that are made of the funds provided for education. It is, however, a most difficult undertaking in view of the social, economic and political diversity of the United States, the multi-objectives of schooling and higher education, the public-private components that are parts of the system, and the importance of strengthening the *incentives* of students, schools and local authorities in using such funds both efficiently and with due regard to equity considerations. Although such standards involve issues that go beyond economics, economic conditions and considerations are exceedingly important.[4]

The problem of defining goals is complicated by the lack of resolve about who should have the authority to set the goals. Politicians who would not attempt to set specific goals for a specialized area such as medical education are quite willing to prescribe for general education. Primary, secondary, and even post-secondary education possess no "mystique" (such as is often encountered in medicine) that deters the politician from registering his value judgments. Education, like economics in general, suffers from an abundance of self-proclaimed experts.

The politician's interest and concern is justified, however. The professional educators who operate the educational systems must be held accountable in some way for the seemingly obvious failures of education. The disturbing question which can be raised is whether the system is actually failing. To parents who wish only day-care provision for their children, the present educational system may appear as a successful one. Unless one knows who determines the goals and what the goals are, little meaningful research can be done.

The ideology of education in the United States has evolved with the belief that the separation of politics from education was essential to the free and democratic operation of the educational system. In fact, this

---

[4] An addendum to Mary Jean Bowman, *Educational Outcomes, Processes, and Decisions,* a report prepared for the National Institute of Education, December 1, 1971.

belief has always been a rather shallow pretense. The operation of the country's educational system has never been separated from the legal and extralegal exigencies of the political system. The pretense has now outdistanced the reality to such an extent, however, that it represents a hindrance to an adequate understanding of the social institution of education.

In the last decade economists and political scientists have increasingly added their abilities and techniques to those of other educational researchers in an effort to increase this understanding. This effort is justified in that, today, political influence in education is not only more common but it is also meeting more resistance than in the past. Rather than ignoring the "political" implications within education, the need is to examine them more thoroughly.

Before proceeding to a description of the specific topics in a social choice model of education, it may be well to clarify what is meant by the general term "social choice model". The formulation of such models has resulted from the work of many individuals but most notably James M. Buchanan and Gordon Tullock. Their book remains the essential primer for any researcher interested in the subject.[5]

The intent of their original formulation was to explain the workings of the decision process of a rational individual in regard to questions of constitutional choice, specifically questions of decision-making rules. The characteristic which separates their work from more general "political" decision models concerns the role of the individual in public decisions. This emphasis on the individual rather than the group reflects the "individualistic" bias of economic science.

In a choice model which emphasizes the individual, the importance of the group need not be ignored. For example, the recognition that a group may behave differently than the sum of its individual components' behavior in isolation might have suggested is not a weakness in the "methodological individualism." It simply requires an alteration of criteria on which an individual bases his decision when the moves from an isolated to a group decision context.

There is no fine line between "social choice" and "political choice" models, but the difference is more than semantic. The social choice model of Buchanan and Tullock stresses two concepts: (1) the importance of the unanimity rule and (2) explicit recognition of the costs of decision making. Any social choice model should start from this methodological base. However, by confining the scope of the social choice model to education, we may enlarge on this base to incorporate a wider range of decision issues. These may range from explicit educational decision criteria of a state or national legislative assembly to the unstated extra-official incentives which operate within an individual school.

---

[5] James Buchanan and Gordon Tullock, *The Calculus of Consent* (Ann Arbor: The University of Michigan Press, 1962).

We may begin by asking to what extent do the individual students and their families control the specification of educational goals.

The answer, of course, depends upon what student and what educational form is being discussed. In primary and secondary education, for example, the immediate control of education is held by local administrative boards. These boards operate under the general supervision of state agencies responsible for public education. Local school board members are either elected or appointed, depending upon state and local law. At the state level, the only elected representative that may exist would be the director of the state agency, Sometimes, even this position is an administrative one and is filled by a professional educator.

Under these controlling agencies, there exists a large number of other professional educators—teachers, counselors, and administrators. It is this group which directly supplies education to the student. Dissatisfaction with minor specific educational problems may be resolved by direct interaction on the part of the student or his family with these individuals. To make larger, more general changes, however, requires direct influence on the professional educators. This influence can be exerted through the political process, but this is a time-consuming and indirect method.

One of the most important contributions that could be made to a social choice model of education would be the formulation of an "influence configuration" for a single school system. This would produce a matrix of lines of authority, responsibility, and incentives as perceived by the various participants in the educational decision-making hierarchy. These perceived lines could then be compared with the "official" lines of authority, responsibility, and influence to point up inconsistencies between the two. An understanding of the perceived lines of influence would aid the decision maker in understanding the workings of his decision system. It would also assist the student or parent in an effort to alter the system. Secondly one needs to determine if it is the implied intent or the explicit content of administraive behavior which most strongly affects the decisions of those who compose the educational system.

All of this suggests that an individual student, either independently or in concert with his family, has little direct influence over the supply of education. In fact, the effective goals of the education system may be inadequately related to the educational needs of society. For example, some degree of inequality of educational opportunity may be acceptable to an elite or even a democratic majority. This same level of inequality, however, may result in a less efficient output of the economic system.

This situation can result because voting laws and individual patterns of voting behavior conspire to restrict political majorities to fewer numbers than represent a social majority. A problem faced by minority and poverty groups is that their low rates of political participation allow other individuals to control the decision process. The latter may be expected to have different, if not at times diametrically opposite, interests to those of the minority/poverty group.

Many problems in education may not be the result of anyone's plan. Rather, incentive systems, which are part of the effect of policies governing employment, job security, teacher assignment, pay, and promotions, have implicit effects upon performance. The traditional economic assumption of self-interest as the motivating force for behavior is quite applicable to this analysis. Administrators, teachers, and students may all be expected to perform in the way which they view as most beneficial to themselves. If the incentive pattern conflicts with the generally stated goals, it is the incentives which will determine behavior.[6]

The ultimate product of research on social choice models of education should be a more adequate understanding of an individual's criteria for decision making concerning collective educational questions. In this way an expanded economic production function model of education may be presented. This model would include the political interaction which affects education in addition to the traditional production function concerns to be discussed below.

Educational production functions

In whatever manner goals are determined, there remains a need for evaluating how those goals may be attained in the most efficient manner. Economists have made a contribution to the evaluation of this efficiency by the formulation of education production functions. The production function states some measure of output in terms of its relationship to its determinant. The educational performance of a system may be viewed as functionally related to student ability, home environment, peer group influences, family incomes, school facilities, teacher/administrator quality, and a residual variable which may simply serve as an error term.

Since the desired outputs of the educational system are defined in terms of the post-educational behavior of the student, the ability variable is obviously necessary. It is the change in the student, from pre- to post-school behavior, that is the effect or product of education. The preschool ability level represents both a base point for measuring change and a determinant of the propensity to change, that is, to be affected by education.

It is not the controversial question of "natural" or inherent ability that is predominant here. That would be the crucial question only if one were

---

[6] J. D. Owen, "The Distribution of Educational Resources in Large American Cities," *Journal of Human Resources,* Vol. 7 (Winter, 1972), pp. 26–38, notes that three factors may promote inequality for the poor and the nonwhite in the allocation of educational resources. These factors are: (1) single, city-wide pay scale offers no additional compensation for more difficult positions; (2) most attractive posts are allocated to most experienced teachers, and (3) some informal pressures continue to exist to keep nonwhite teachers in nonwhite schools.

measuring the effectiveness of the pre-school home environment or, perhaps, pre-primary education. Rather, ability need be defined only in terms of the student's evidenced capabilities prior to the level of schooling to be evaluated. An additional point concerning the relevance of the ability variable concerns the way in which it is complementary to other variables. Particular methods of instruction may be successful for students of a certain level of measured ability but not suitable for those with greater or less ability.

Present understanding of home environment and peer group influences on educational performance is inadequate to establish their relationship to student post-educational behavior. Parental educational attainment is correlated to the attainment of children, but this could be an effect of the inherent ability variable, the factor of family income, or something else. Most writers assert an intuitive feeling that the home environment of the child must have significant effects, but until these effects can be specified little can be done with this variable. The same problem exists with respect to peer group influence.

Family income is considered a separate determinant of educational output because, in addition to its effect on the nature of the home environment, it has a direct causal relationship to the child's educational experience. This relationship exists in its most obvious form at advanced educational levels. There, family income may allow the child to reap greater consumption benefits of education. These benefits may accrue because of the student's ability to finance the social activities normally concomitant to education. Income advantages also allow the student to prolong his education beyond what would be rational for a lower-income student.

School facilities and teacher/administrator quality have been the most frequently studied input variables in the analysis of educational production functions. These studies have had predominantly inconclusive results due to high levels of intercorrelation among the measures of school facilities or quality which have commonly been used, such as expenditures per student, pupil-teacher ratios, age of building, total enrollment, teacher ability (as measured by test performance), teacher/administrator salaries, experience. and turnover in employment.

In addition to the problem of interrelatedness, there are some inherent weaknesses in certain of these measures of quality. The use of expenditures per student as a measure of the contribution of resources ignores the reality that high expenditures can result simply from inefficiency. In that case further increases in expenditures cannot promise improvements in performance. This variable also takes no account of possible economies of scale which would necessitate different expenditure per student levels in different situations.

Other variables, such as teacher pay, experience, and turnover, may be self-fulfilling measures of input effectiveness. Pay and experience are high and turnover rates are low in precisely those schools where the other preconditions for successful educational effort may be expected to be high. Again, all of this reduces the economic researchers ability to differentiate effectively the causal factors resulting in certain educational outputs.

All of the major production function studies to date have concentrated on the cognitive outcomes of education. Herbert Gintis among other authorities, has argued that:

. . . the lack of understanding on noncognitive outcomes of education has led economists consistently to misstate the interactions and performance of education. . . . Their consequent mishandling of the outcomes of education vis-a-vis the economy vitiates much of the concrete policy-oriented analysis of economists. Significant progress cannot be made in the economics of education until considerable attention is focused on the noncognitive outcomes of schooling in relation to economic success.[7]

What then does this discussion, and the preceding comments on social choice models and goals, leave us with respect to knowledge of the supply side of education? If an abundance of research topics and unfinished work can be viewed as encouraging, there is certainly that. If there are conceptual and methodological difficulties to be overcome, there is no reason to believe that they cannot be overcome.

IV.   The private demand for education

This section shall present an analysis of the demand by individuals for education. The survey is again restricted to institutional or formal education, though the reader is reminded that informal types of education also exist.

The consumer in precollege education

In studying the demand for education at each level, pre-primary through post-secondary, it is crucial to determine who the actual "consumer" of education is. For example, in the informal preschool home environment, the parents are both the producers and consumers of educational benefits. The child at the age of two, there, or four is little concerned with education as an abstract idea. Rather, the child learns because of the favorable response which such learning engenders from those around him.

The parents encourage preschool education to the extent that they themselves have been conditioned to view their child's education as a

---

[7] Herbert Gintis, "Non-Cognitive Outcomes of Schooling: Priorities for Research in the Economics of Education," an addendum to the Bowman-National Institute of Education report, p. 1.

consumption good. Depending on the income, occupation, age, race, religion and other characteristics of the parents, they will place greater or less emphasis on the development of the learning processes of their child. These characteristics also affect the ability of parents to produce a favorable learning environment for their children. The child enters into this process primarily as the "raw material." Children differ in the way in which they are suited to learning depending upon differences in inherited and adopted behavioral traits. The value of the expenditure on education at this level may be estimated by the direct costs for books and other materials plus the opportunity costs of the parents (in terms of either the work or leisure alternatives which the latter forgo).

Formal pre-primary education and primary education again are situations in which the parent acts as the choice-making consumer. The alternatives available to the parent are usually limited to enrollment of the child in a public school or one of several types of private institutions. At the pre-primary level the formal education of the child may be viewed by the parent as a substitute for continued preschool learning in the home. Where pre-primary education is publicly subsidized, the saving in parental opportunity costs plus the smallness of direct costs (transportation, clothing and materials for example) contribute to the parents' decision to enroll the child. This is certainly the case in the increasing number of families where both parents either must or prefer to seek outside employment.

The parents' election of a public or private school will be based upon a comparison of the benefit-cost ratios of the alternatives within their budgetary constraint. As parental income increases the family is more likely to choose a private school. The ability and willingness of some private schools to maintain racial segregation has had an important effect in some areas.

The present controversy over busing presents an interesting insight into the parental view of public education. The concern over the poor quality of former minority/poverty neighborhood schools surfaced only when large numbers of children of white, higher-income parents were forced to attend them. It appears that the parents were concerned only with the education received by their children and had little general concern for educational quality in general This interpretation has some important implications for the social investment process.

The "product" which the parent purchases at the primary school level may include psychic benefits as well as real ones. The "good feeling" of fulfilling parental responsibility is just as much a benefit as the "day-care" aspect which frees parents for work or leisure opportunities. The primary school child is still only a resource in the educational process and does not yet exert any important general control.

However, the child soon begins to exert some control over quality. This is done as the child makes choices about the degree of personal effort to be expended on educational activities. The child's decision will be based upon his ability, earlier educational experience, and the manner in which new educational opportunities are presented to him. The degree to which the child exerts such discretionary power may be expected to increase in the junior-high school years as more alternatives are available to him, in school and out.

Two very important changes occur in education as the student enters the high school years (grades 9–12). The first is that education becomes more implicitly an investment process. Actually the student (and his family) have been making an investment as well as consumption expenditure throughout the child's education. But it is in the high school years that the student and his family begin to explicitly recognize it as such. This new perception has several important implications which the discussion will return to below.

The second important change which occurs is that the student begins to exert more control over educational choices. With the legal requirement for attendance removed (generally at age 16), the student must either wish to continue or else the parent must be able to exert some control over the student to cause him to continue. The student's wish to continue or leave will be based upon his comparison of the *perceived* costs of continued attendance with his evaluation of the benefits of more education. Educators, social scientists, and others who are concerned with the problem of high school dropouts often fail to recognize that the student is making a choice which to himself seems exceedingly rational. Some studies have found that high school dropouts may actually gain more in certain situations than those who complete school.

It was mentioned above that during the high school years the student is more likely to view education in the context of a personal investment opportunity (though few could be expected to describe it in those terms). This means that the student recognizes he has two important alternatives to continued education: work or leisure. The net value of the work alternative is the student's expected income (including some estimation of the probability of finding a job) minus the gain or loss of leisure utility expected from leaving school and taking a job. The immediate benefits of leaving school are likely to be perceived as being quite high while the future costs are assumed to be rather low. Within this context, it should be noted that if a high discount of the future is a characteristic of any group of students, they may be expected to have proportionately more dropouts. Similarly, one unexpected effect of programs to find employment for school dropouts may be that more students find it feasible to drop out.

A student doing poorly in school has both a high psychic cost of attendance because of his performance and a low expected value for continuing. The latter is especially true if he does not expect to graduate. This helps to explain the relatively high attrition rates of minority/poverty students shown in certain of the earlier statistical tables. These students are making a rational decision (in their view) based upon the expected benefits and costs of completing high school. Similarly, a part of the explanation for the historically high rates of high school completion among females is the poor employment alternatives which they possessed.

Parents support a child in high school in line with their perception of responsibility and personal wants. They may take pride in their child's accomplishment as well as satisfaction in their reduced responsibility for his welfare. For a majority of parents, high school graduation is the end of their direct financial support for their child's education.

The educational decisions of the parent and student may be internally rational and yet still have unfortunate results for the individual if they are based on poor knowledge. One of the great educational problems at the high school level is the lack of information among students, and often even among their parents, about the true costs and benefits of continued education. The child of a family with a disadvantaged educational background may simply be ignorant of the advantages of post-secondary education. Similarly, an excessively high discount may be made of the probability of unemployment or low-paying employment.

These informational problems are especially important in that they may reduce private educational attainment below the point which is viewed as socially optimal. It would be a mistake, however, to assume that increased informational systems will have more than a marginal effect. To greatly alter the present situation, the actual secondary school environment has to be changed so that the student's educational costs are perceived as relatively less and his benefits as relatively greater.

Those who control education have an unfortunate tendency to treat the time of students as a free good in the organization of educational systems. It is a free good to administrators. Students, however, value their time as does everyone else and make their decisions accordingly. Shorter, as well as more interesting, academic programs may be an asset in reducing the attrition problem.

The consumer in post-secondary education

Post-secondary formal education may be studied in three main forms: the technical or vocational institute, the two-year college, and the four-year college or university. In all of these the investment component of the educational decision process may be expected to be more important than at any earlier educational stage. This is true even though, for some individual students, the consumption aspects may still outweigh the investment aspects.

The student's participation in post-secondary education may be expected to affect his lifetime income in four main ways: (1) The size of the income stream; (2) The timing of the income stream; (3) The certainty of receiving future income; and (4) The form of income received. The increase in income related to educational attainment is greater for the four years of college than for any other equal period of earlier schooling. In 1968 the expected life-time earnings of a male high school graduate 25 years old or over, was $350,000 while that of a college graduate was $586,000. The estimated annual mean incomes for the two groups in the same year was $8,148 and $12,938 respectively.[8]

Students who earned some college credit, but did not graduate had a considerably smaller income gain from their educational efforts. In 1968 males with one to three years of college credit had an expected lifetime income of $411,000 and an annual mean income of $9,397.[9] These figures are noticeably closer to the amounts for high school graduates than those for college graduates. This "diploma effect" may also be found in comparing incomes of high school graduates and high school dropouts. The income differential between these two groups has increased in recent years as more employers have used high school graduation as a minimum qualification for new employees.

The income differential between groups with different levels of educational attainment probably overstates the true effect of education on income. If one assumes that those who attain higher levels of education possess more ability, however defined or measured, then it is likely they would have had higher than average earnings even without the additional education.

Burton Weisbrod has emphasized a special value attached to completing a specific level of schooling.[10] This is the "option-value" inherent in the opportunity to continue education beyond that level. An example would be the case of the high school graduate again. His expected lifetime income or mean annual income are not the full measure of the value which his high school diploma had for him. The "option-value" of continuing education beyond high school was, at least at the time of graduation, worth something to every student. Not taking this value into account would mean an underestimation of the return to educational investment at this level. Today, the option-value of the baccalaureate degree, which is a prerequisite for most graduate and professional degrees, is of extreme importance in estimating the return to a college education.

The role of occupation as an intervening variable in the education-income relationship should be mentioned.[11] Table 13 presents figures for

---

[8] U.S. Bureau of the Census, Statistical Abstract of the United States, 1971 (Washington, D.C.: GPO, 1971), p. 111.

[9] Ibid.

[10] Burton Weisbrod, "External Benefits of Public Education," *Journal of Political Economy* (October, 1962).

[11] For an especially lucid discussion of this topic, see B. Wilkinson, "Present Values of Lifetime Earnings for Different Occupations," *Journal of Political Economy,* Vol. 74 (December 1966), pp. 556–73.

Table 4-13. Major occupation group of employed persons, by sex, race, and years of school completed, 1970

Sex, and Occupation Group	White			Negro and Other		
	Total	Less than 4 Years of High School	4 Years of High School or More	Total	Less than 4 Years of High School	4 Years of High School or More
Male, number (000 omitted)	42,434	14,701	27,733	4,629	2,626	2,003
Percent, by occupation:						
White collar	44.3	18.5	58.0	23.2	8.8	42.1
Blue collar	45.0	64.8	34.6	61.1	71.6	47.3
Service, including private household workers	5.6	7.5	4.6	11.1	12.6	9.2
Farm	5.0	9.1	2.9	4.6	7.0	1.4
Female, number (000 omitted)	25,040	6,926	18,114	3,551	1,656	1,895
Percent, by occupation:						
White collar	64.7	30.3	77.9	35.1	10.3	56.8
Blue collar	16.3	35.6	9.0	18.4	21.5	15.8
Service, including private household workers	17.5	31.0	12.3	45.8	67.0	27.3
Farm	1.5	3.2	0.8	0.7	1.2	0.2

Source: Department of Labor, Bureau of Labor Statistics; Special Labor Force Report, No. 125.

occupation of groups in 1970, by sex, race, and educational attainment. Those with a high school education or more are predominantly employed in white collar positions, with the exception of nonwhite males. Nonwhite females of this educational level are less proportionately represented in white collar jobs than are white females. Quite clearly even for equivalent education levels race too has an important occupational and thereby income effect.

What about the investment value of graduate education? A recent study by Duncan Bailey and Charles Schotta [12] produced the following conclusions:

1. The private rate of return to graduate education is either zero or less than one percent;
2. The social rate of return to graduate education is either zero or less than one percent;
3. The higher estimated rates of return to undergraduate education may suggest that funds should be reallocated away from graduate education;
4. The returns streams are lowest for graduate study in the humanities, education, and certain of the social sciences;
5. The returns to graduate education are predominantly psychic rather than real.

Whether or not one is willing to accept any or all of their conclusions of this single study, or the adequacy of the measure of return on which it is based, it raises significant questions for economic researchers and educational policy-makers alike.

The second way in which post secondary education affects income is in the timing of the stream of occupational income. To understand this effect it is necessary to introduce the concept of an age-income profile. Dependence upon cross-sectional age-income distributions has led some researchers to misconstrue the age-income profile upon which lifetime income estimates should be based.

Cross-sectional profiles are graphical representations of the various levels of income at some one point in time by individuals of different ages but with similar socioeconomic characteristics (education, region, size of place, etc.), These profiles normally show that income increases rapidly for individuals up to age thirty-nine; increases at a slower rate to a peak income at approximately age forty-nine; and then displays a small rate of decline thereafter. The early researchers' fallacy was to assume that an individual's lifetime income would follow the cross-sectional pattern of increase and decline.

As Figure 4–1 shows, the age-income profile of an individual follows a significantly different pattern. The successive cross-sectional profiles for 1950, 1960, and 1970 show an upward shift due to economic growth and

---

[12] Duncan Bailey and Charles Schotta, "Private and Social Rates of Return to Education of Academicians," *American Economic Review,* Vol. 62 (March 1972), pp. 19–31.

Figure 4–1. A comparison of cross-sectional and cohort age-income profiles

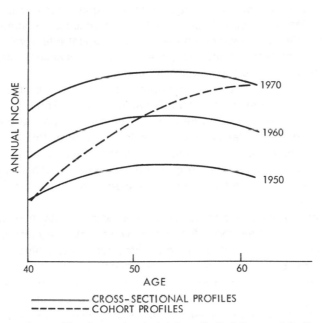

Source: The diagram is adapted from M. R. Colberg and D. M. Windham, "Age-Income Profiles and Invidious Comparisons," *Mississippi Valley Journal of Business and Economics,* Volume 5 (Winter 1970), p. 32.

inflation. While each cross-sectional income profile does show a decline of income past the age of fifty, no such decline occurs if one follows the cohort profile of individuals who were forty in 1950, fifty in 1960, and sixty in 1970.

If the 1960 and 1970 incomes were deflated to reflect 1950 purchasing power, a decline in the rate of increase in the cohort's profile would result. To the extent that inflation, rather than economic growth, is responsible for the higher, more recent cross-sectional profiles, cohort profiles defined in terms of purchasing power became more horizontal at higher age levels.

Another important consideration of age-income profiles is the definition of the group for which the curves are drawn. If Figure 4–1 is for *all* individuals of a certain classification, rather than only the employed individuals, the cohort income profile is more likely to decline at later ages. This may be expected because of the inclusion of zero income levels for those older workers who are unemployed or retired.

Education beyond high school may be said to improve the "timing" in which income is received. It does this by increasing the slope of the age-income profile, at least through age forty. The individual with a post-secondary education should find his income not only higher but increasing more rapidly than those of his less-educated counter-parts. Timing is also improved in that, past age forty, the more highly educated individuals' incomes are less subject to forces which might cause an income decline. For example, the older worker who is "human-capital intensive" does not face the same problem as the older manual worker whose ability to perform is more closely tied to physical condition.

The person with post-secondary training does face two problems which may affect the "wisdom" of his educational investment. The first is that for the period of his education his income will be below what he could have earned by immediately taking a job. The importance of this will vary by individual characteristics, time, place, and the level of education. The degree candidate in a doctoral program obviously has a higher opportunity cost in terms of employment alternatives than does the average college undergraduate.

The second problem faced by the person who invests in education is the necessity to maintain the value of his investment. The more education a person has, the more likely he is to be employed in a position which requires that he continue to update his education. Doctors, professors, engineers, and the like are required (sometimes simply to maintain their present income levels), to stay informed about new developments within their discipline. However, the financial ability to reinvest is likely to coincide with the need to reinvest. One complaint which has been registered, though, is that human capital depreciation does not receive tax advantages in line with those granted for depreciation on material capital. This inequity could only be viewed as a crucial one if, in view of society's interest, there appeared to be a significant underproduction of human capital.

Education, at the high school level and beyond, affects the certainty with which one may expect future income. This is a result of the education-employment relationship. For example, for March 1971, the Department of Labor reported the following unemployment rates for various levels of educational attainment:

5 years of college or more 1.2%
4 years of college 3.0%
High school graduates 5.5%
All labor force 5.8%

Increases in unemployment thus tend to be borne by the least trained workers. If there are fewer jobs for aeronautical engineers or college teachers, these professionals will begin to complete for lower status jobs. Displaced college graduates, in turn, begin to compete with high school graduates, and so on down the employment ladder. This process is not immediate and may not always be fully realized. Seniority provisions may intervene, or employers may wish to avoid morale problems inherent in the employment of "over-educated" employees, for example. But the process does operate over time, and low unemployment rates for higher trained workers constitute an additional private incentive to seek further education, increasing the certainty of a higher stream of lifetime income.

Finally, education affects lifetime income by the form in which that income is received. Income may accrue simply as money wages or salary. It may be received in the form of a package of employee benefits: stock option plans, retirement, health, disability, and life insurance, travel, vacation time, and, in more unusual cases, the provision of housing, transportation, and other personal needs. Finally, income may be received in "psychic" forms which embody all of the satisfaction and dissatisfaction associated with the type of work, place of employment, and relationships with other workers.

Each of these income forms has an effect which is either reduced or enhanced by their respective tax status. Wage and salary income bears the heaviest burden of taxation. For the most part employee benefits are presently either completely or partly excluded from tax liability, though the imputed value of housing and other such personal needs are commonly taxed as income.

Finally, psychic forms are completely free from taxation. Thus, *ceteris paribus,* the income recipient should prefer his income in forms other than direct wage or salary payments. There is a direct relationship between the provision of the nonsalary forms of income and the level of an employee's educational attainment. Thus an additional incentive for investing in additional education is the ability to receive income in one or more of the more favorable forms. The actual relative "income" positions of a coal miner and a college president are underestimated by comparing only the relative money income of the two.

For many workers, their only post-secondary education is on-the-job training. In most cases this may be viewed as both complementary to and a substitute for formal education. The individual firm's decision to train its employees is based on its expectation of receiving additional receipts in the future to offset the present cost increase from the direct and indirect costs of training.

Figure 4–2 shows the relationship of earnings to age for trained and untrained employees of a firm. It is assumed that untrained workers will receive the same earnings regardless of age, as represented by the line *"UU."* This is an oversimplification, of course. In most jobs a worker will gain additional skill simply through experience (a form of training) and this will be reflected by increases in earnings as he becomes older. The result would be a positively sloped *"UU"* line.

Trained workers, represented by line *"TT"* in Figure 4–2, receive lower

Figure 4–2. Age, earnings, and on-the-job training

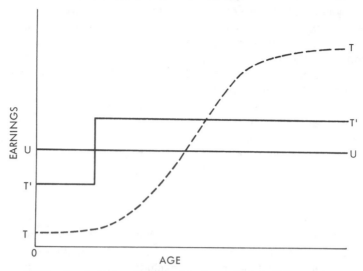

Source: Gary S. Becker, "Investment in Human Capital: A Theoretical Analysis," *Journal of Political Economy,* Vol. 50 (October 1962), p. 15.

incomes while being trained and higher incomes after the completion of training. Thus, they pay the costs of training (including the earnings foregone) at early ages and collect the benefits at later ages. If training affected only the height and not the slope of the earnings curve, the line "*T'T'* " would be appropriate.

The firm may decide to alter its means of payment to the worker in order to encourage participation in on-the-job training programs. It can do this by paying the worker more during the period of training than the worker's immediate marginal productivity would warrant. The firm can then attempt to recoup its excess payments by paying the worker less than the value of his marginal productivity in future years.

Gary Becker has presented this relationship as an identity:

$$MP'_o + G = W_o + C$$

where

MP'_o = what could have been produced in the training period if all workers had been engaged in production;

G = the present value of the excess of future receipt over future outlays resulting from training;

W_o = total wages and expenditures paid during the training period;

and

C = the sum of opportunity costs and outlays on training.[13]

---

[13] Gary Becker, *Human Capital* (New York: Columbia University Press, 1957), pp. 8–11. Also see Jacob Mincer, "On-the-Job Training: Cost, Returns, and Some Implications," *Journal of Political Economy,* Vol. 51 (October 1962), pp. 50–79.

G is defined by:

$$G = \sum_{t=1}^{n-1} \frac{MP_t - W_t}{(1 + i)^t} \text{ where}$$

MP_t = production in period "t"

W_t = wages in period "t"

and

i = discount rate.

The opportunity costs included in "C" are defined as MP_o-MP_o', that is, the decrease in production resulting from part (or all) of the workers engaging in training.

This formulation suggests that the present value of the excess of future receipts over future outlays should exceed the total costs of training by at least the same amount that total wages and expenditures in the training period exceeded the possible production during the training period. If this equality holds, there is no incentive to alter the amount of on-the-job training until there is a change in "G" and/or "C".

The above formula applies only to training which is specialized to the extent that only the firm providing the training will be able to benefit. The worker's marginal productivity in other firms is less than his marginal productivity in the job he has specialized in through training, and at least some of this difference can be captured by the firm as a return on the training it has provided. If a firm has pure monopsony powers it can be almost certain of recouping its training expenses.

However, no excess return occurs to a firm if it provides general training which is useful in other firms in a competitive labor market. Under such circumstances, the worker's marginal productivity would increase for every firm in the market, not just for the one which trained him. The firm which provided the training will have to increase the wage (as a result of a higher market wage) of the trained worker to the same extent which his marginal productivity increased, thus excluding any excess returns for the firm.

To summarize this section, additional education or training has favorable income effects because it improves the size of income, the timing over the worker's economic life, the certainty of future income, and the forms in which income is received. The individual's final choice rationale would involve the comparison of these benefits plus any immediate consumption benefits with the direct and indirect costs of investing in education. The costs must include the foregone earnings which most researchers have found to approximate one half of the total educational costs.

Rates of return to educational investment

Ignoring equity considerations, for the moment, the rate of return may be used to compare the relative value of various types of educational investments. T. W. Schultz has presented a summary of the current research results concerning these rates: [14]

U.S. domestic economy	10–15%
Primary education	35%
Secondary education	25%
College education	15%
Graduate education	15%

All these educational investments appear superior to the average of capital investments in the general economy. The higher rates at lower levels of schooling suggest that a reallocation of funds toward these grades may prove quite beneficial. The high rate of return to graduate education cited here, which contrasts with the Bailey and Schotta results noted earlier, is probably explainable on the grounds that it (1) is for all graduate education and not just that for academicians; (2) includes a return to research which is a joint product of graduate education; and (3) was based upon data from a period when employment opportunities for graduate students were substantially better than they are today.

These rates appear to justify the high level of private investment in education which presently exists. They are not social rates of return, however, and cannot automatically be applied as arguments for increased public spending or a reallocation of the present level of public support. For social investment decisions, these rates are suggestive only.

Effective private demand for education

If a comparison of educational benefits and costs is favorable then an individual can be expected to have a desire for additional education. For this desire to result in effective demand for education, an ability to finance the costs must exist. Moreover, the benefits to education are embodied in a rather extended future pay-back period while the costs accrue within a short period in the present. This situation points up the need for an improved loan market for educational investments. Presently, it is difficult to acquire short-term loans and nearly impossible to acquire long-term loans for the purpose of financing additional education. Some few institutions—notably Yale—are now experimenting with direct loans to students repayable by a low percentage "tax" on future earnings. If such a practice spreads, this will simply shift the need for long-term borrowing from students to universities, at least until the "pipeline" of repayments provides a sufficient cash flow. We shall have more to say about this later.

To review what has been presented here: the private demand for education has been shown to be the result of the comparison of the expected net benefits of the expenditure on education with the net benefits from other alternative expenditures. At early levels of schooling the parent is the

---

[14] T. W. Schultz, "Human Capital: Policy Issues and Research Opportunities," Human Capital Paper No. 70:10, Department of Economics, University of Chicago, revised January 7, 1971, pp. 36–38.

agency for choices concerning education. As age and education progressed, the student becomes more dominant as the choice-maker.

The age-income profile was introduced as a device to illustrate the four income benefits inherent in additional education. The strengths and limitations of the lifetime income approach to human capital analysis were summarized. Finally, the problem of private financing of education has been noted.

Because the individual's expense of education, for purposes of choice, may be viewed as the residual after public subsidization, the discussion in the following section will concentrate upon the rationale for societal investment in education.

V. Social investment in education

The rationale for public rather than private control of production of an economic good has been discussed in an earlier section. It was noted that the public agency had three alternatives for bringing private costs and benefits more in line with social costs and benefits. These were: (1) regulation of production; (2) subsidization or taxation; and (3) direct public production.

"Public" education in the United States represents the third form of control. It involves the crucial variables of the pricing policy of the institutions, the form and extent of any concomitant subsidies, and the manner in which subsidies are financed. For example, a public primary school usually has no tuition charge and perhaps a minimal registration fee. Concomitant subsidies include the provision of transportation facilities, meals, and certain health care either free or at a charge below cost. The method of finance at this level is a combination of consumption, income and wealth taxation that is unlikely to have a progressive rate of incidence.

Why should any subsidy be levied for education? The usual answer is that substantial "social benefits" exist from the consumption of (or investment in) education.

As we know, a social benefit of an activity is any gain which accrues to someone other than the agency which initiates the activity. In education, the initiating agency may be represented as the student or his parents or these jointly. For present purposes, private benefits will be defined as all benefits accruing to the student, his parents, and later his spouse and children. Social benefits, therefore, are all economic gains accruing to individuals outside the student's immediate family.

If private benefits are an adequate incentive for the production of a socially optimum amount of education (however the optimum is defined), then no subsidization is needed. If the expected income from a medical education, discounted to the present, induces enough students to become doctors, then no public support for medical schools would seem to be necessary. If these benefits are not enough to ensure the production of the socially optimum amount of education, then, and only then, is government intervention in the form of subsidization justifiable. There is no *a priori* reason that the intervention must take the form of subsidization, however.

In the discussion which follows the various levels and forms of education will again be surveyed. This time the survey will concentrate on social versus private interests in educational investment. A few additional comments about social benefits may first prove useful. Those who believe that public education provides social benefits, and should be supported for that reason, often embrace the concept of "free" (usually meaning only zero tuition) education.

Such a proposal is meritorious only when (1) tuition charges constitute the marginal barrier to equal access to further education and (2) when the public method of financing the "free" educational system meets some measure of tax equity itself. Present analysis of the effects of low-cost tuition leads to the rejection of the first assumption, and present understanding of local and state tax incidence casts additional doubt on the second assumption.

Those who would support totally free education would logically also have to find means for financing many more educational costs than just tuition. Foregone earnings of students from disadvantaged families may have to be reimbursed if the potential student is to be released from any obligation of working to support his family. Since indirect costs of education are estimated as approximately one-half of direct costs, an attempt to produce totally "free education" assumes a great deal about the public's willingness to pay more for education.

It should also be recognized that social benefits are exceedingly difficult to quantify. While this in no way makes their existence less important, it does present a difficult problem when one wishes to equate the public subsidy with purported public benefits. The implicit assumption of zero-tuition advocates that the hypothetical beneficial externalities, equal or exceed the full instructional costs of all levels of education is an assumption of faith.

Finally, the valuation of much that is described as social benefits is inescapably subjective. Statements that more education is likely to produce individuals who are more socially enlightened, better voters, better consumers, or whatever—can quite obviously lead to disagreements about what these phrases mean. People have highly divergent views as to how a "socially enlightened" person should feel about the race issue for example. Republicans and Democrats are very likely to define "better voters" as those who support their candidates and positions. Ralph Nader and General Motors may be expected to disagree at times over what pattern of behavior is indicative of a "good consumer."

But let us return to social interest in educational investment. Preprimary and primary education can usually be justified as creating social benefits because it is in this educational period that the basic skills of literacy are taught. Except in fragmented societies, the transfer of cultural folkways and the implanting of behavioral attitudes is commonly also deemed a social benefit. Because of the general scope of enrollment there is only a small user-nonuser inequity at this level. Nearly all families have benefited, are benefiting, or expect to benefit from the pre-secondary form of education.

At the secondary school level the phenomenon of selective attrition begins to appear. Individuals of certain income or cultural subgroups of the student population manifest higher than average propensities to leave school before graduation. This creates a divergence between the interests of user and nonuser groups. A second problem is that, in secondary school programs, training is more likely to be oriented toward job skills or preparation for further training than for any immediately obvious social rationale. Unless social benefits may be expected from the employment of the students in occupational or college-preparation programs, it is more difficult to justify public financing of an education program which results in differential private benefits. It may be that parents "exploit" nonparents by having schools take care of their children during the day though the use of the word "exploits" does not imply any necessarily perfidious motive on the part of parents.

The present social consensus concerning secondary education is such that there appears to be little likelihood that these subsidies will be removed. Still, the student of the economics of education should recognize that the motivation for this continued subsidy is political and not economic. The former requires only that an effective majority of the democracy vote to have the public, through governmental agencies, pay for the cost of education. The economic motivation for subsidization would have to be based upon the social investment criterion stated earlier.

It is in post-secondary education that the current controversy over public support is the greatest. This is in large part because of the heightened demand for public funds necessitated by increased enrollment and higher costs. A second contributing factor is a reaction by some against student activism on college campuses.

Finally, studies of income-redistributive effects of higher education conducted by Hansen and Weisbrod in California, Windham in Florida, and Hansen in Wisconsin have all contributed to an increased questioning of higher education as a democratizing influence. In reality, these studies only revealed what members of minority and poverty groups already had come to realize about colleges and universities. This is that these institutions are not presently designed to meet the needs of the minority/poverty student but are largely tradition-oriented toward the needs and abilities of the white middle and upper class. There is no need to read any Marxian interpretation into this. The schools were quite simply oriented toward the income class which had traditionally supplied them with students.

As a result of this questioning, and of minority political pressures, public colleges and universities as well as many private institutions have attempted to increase the enrollment opportunities of low-income and minority students. They are limited in this effort by the lower rate of high school graduation of students from low-income families. Combined with this difficulty is the effort by certain factions to maintain the traditional "quality" standards which are applied to prospective students.

Given that inequalities if not inequities exist in college enrollments, why has higher education continued to receive public support? It appears that any proponent of public subsidies would have a difficult time effectively arguing the case for the existence of social benefits which are not in fact appropriated by private individuals. A proponent would not only have to give evidence that unappropriated social benefits exist but also be able to estimate the size of those benefits and to show that, without public subsidies, they would not be produced.

Such economic rationalism holds little favor with either educational administrators or governmental policymakers at the present. If one accepts that the financing of higher education will continue to involve public subsidization, whether based upon economic or noneconomic reasoning, what rules can economists suggest to minimize any possible harmful effects of such a policy?

First, all public assistance should be on a specific rather than general basis. Presently, the largest single type of financial aid at public institutions is in the form of the general tuition subsidy. This subsidy is available to students on the sole criterion of attendance. If one can assume any degree of price inelasticity of private demand for full-cost higher education, some part of the general subsidy is "wasted" on individuals who would have attended school without the subsidy incentive. In addition, many post-secondary schools offer further subsidies in the form of scholarships whose only effect is to bid a student away from another school. Placing public subsidization on the specific basis of evidenced financial need would greatly increase the efficient use of such funds.

The economist could also recommend that instructional subsidies be given to students rather than institutions. There are two main favorable effects to this "voucher" type approach. The first is that the subsidy is available for use by the student at either private or public institutions. If the production of social benefits is the justification for public subsidies, then students at private institutions are equally likely to produce such benefits as those at public institutions.

The second advantage of the "voucher" approach accrues because of the wider range of choices available to potential students. In addition, increased discretionary power in the hands of students might place competitive pressures on institutions to produce the type of education students demand and in the most efficient manner possible. Society could of course continue to set general standards of performance.

A final contribution that the economist can make is a rather obvious one: no matter what subsidies are given, they should always be provided in the least costly manner. Many economists feel that an improvement in the capital market's ability to deal with human capital financing needs should remove at least part of the need for direct grants. Government loans or loan guarantees, for example, would reduce the need to spend public monies for education and thereby reduce potential user-nonuser inequities.

Manpower policy and public education

Part of the justification for public spending on education has been the stated need to produce certain types of skills required for economic growth. This form of social benefit will be discussed in detail because it is a justification not only for the usual forms of post-secondary education but also for the more informal vocational and training programs including on-the-job and general skill training in the armed forces.

The current interest in the relationship between education and the level of aggregate output may be traced to the pioneering work of T. W. Schultz and Edward Denison in the early 1960s. Schultz calculated estimates of the amount of human capital formation (assumed to be equal to costs of producing the education) for the period of 1900–57 and compared this to the total amount of physical capital for the same period.[15] He found that human capital had increased from 22 percent of the value of physical capital in 1900 to 42 percent in 1957. Schultz also noted that the rate of increase in human capital for the period was nearly double the rate of growth for physical capital. The implication was that changes in the quantity and quality of educated manpower could be expected to have an important effect upon the level of aggregate income.

Denison attempted to measure precisely this relationship. Dealing with the distinct periods 1909–29 and 1929–59, he calculated the effect of various factors contributing to the annual growth rates in real income.[16] (These rates for the two periods were 2.82 percent and 2.93 percent respectively.) For the period 1909–29 he allocated the sources of growth as follows:

Attributable to change in capital stock	.73%
Attributable to change in labor force	1.53%
Attributable to residual change in productivity	.56%

The changes in the labor force included changes in both the quantity and quality of labor. Denison estimated that of the total 1.53 percent labor force effect, .35 percent was attributable to education.

---

[15] T. W. Schultz, "Rise in the Capital Stock Represented by Education in the U.S., 1900–1957," in *Economics of Higher Education,* ed. by Selma Mushkin (Washington, D.C.: GPO, 1962).

[16] Edward Denison, *The Sources of Economic Growth in the United States,* paper No. 13, Committee for Economic Development, New York, 1962.

For the period 1929–59 Denison found the following results when the rate of growth was allocated:

Attributable to changes in capital stock 43%
Attributable to changes in labor force 1.57%
Attributable to residual changes in productivity 93%

The portion of the labor force change which was due to education was found to be .67 percent. Significantly, the effect of education as a percent of all sources of growth nearly doubled, increasing from 12.4 percent in the 1909–29 period to 22.8 percent for 1929–59.

Mary Jean Bowman has contended that the assumptions used in the Schultz and Denison studies overestimate the contribution of educated manpower to the growth of aggregate income.[17] A further study by Denison found that the contribution from education was not nearly as high in other countries as in the United States. Only in Belgium and the United Kingdom was the education factor found to be responsible for more than ten percent of the total growth rate. The principal contribution of Schultz and Denison has been in encouraging interest and further study in the education-growth relationship.

Manpower planning is a specific example of this relationship. Manpower planning is a special form of general educational planning designed to produce certain types of educated individuals. The type of education needed is a function of actual or expected labor shortages within the economy.

One might ask why the normal working of the labor market is not adequate for this task. After all, the labor market should produce incentives, in the form of higher wages and perquisites, for those skill levels which are in the greatest relative demand. The answer is that in many countries, but especially in underdeveloped nations, the labor market infrastructure is not an adequately sensitive mechanism to bring about the desired manpower adjustments.

The problem in a developed economy may be the interference of the noncompetitive forces of business and labor union monopolies. In developing nations the problem is compounded by the primitive and informal nature of the labor market itself. In either type of economy, the labor market cannot be expected to take into account possibly important social costs and benefits.

There are several additional problems which are encountered by governments which attempt to institute a manpower policy for public education. One is the time lag between the recognition of the need for a certain type of trained worker and the actual training of such a worker. Forecasting techniques for manpower programs often leave much to be desired. The ability to forecast the needed amount of various types of educated man-

---

[17] "Human Capital: Concepts and Measures," *Economics of Higher Education.*

power is complicated by the problem of increased specialization. In addition, in an economy progressing through periods of rapid economic change, the determinants of need for skilled manpower may follow similar patterns of change. The work by Allan Cartter on the supply and demand of doctorates serves as a valuable example.

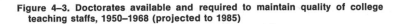

Figure 4–3. Doctorates available and required to maintain quality of college teaching staffs, 1950–1968 (projected to 1985)

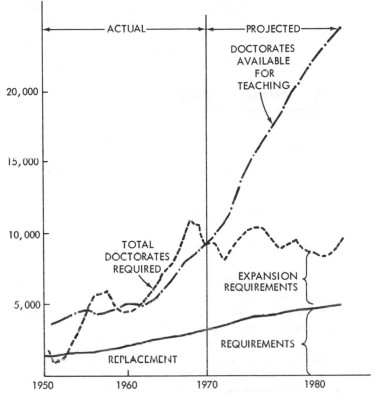

Source: Allan M. Cartter, "The Economics of Higher Education," *Contemporary Economic Issues,* first edition, edited by Neil W. Chamberlain, 1969, p. 169.

Figure 4–3 presents a graphical representation of Cartter's estimates of the total number of doctorates required and available for college teaching. As Cartter expected, the post-1970 period has seen the emergence of a surplus in doctorates,[18] though in the mid-1960s when he first suggested that possibility he encountered strong disagreement from many individuals, in and out of economics.

---

[18] Allan M. Cartter, "The Economics of Higher Education," *Contemporary Economic Issues,* ed. by Neil W. Chamberlain (Homewood, Ill.: Richard D. Irwin, Inc., 1969), pp. 145–184.

As Cartter himself has noted, however, these conclusions apply differently to different doctoral specializations. Also, the doctorate, even within one specialization, is not a homogeneous degree in terms of quality. Thus, we have the assertion that there is still a shortage of "good" economists, chemists, or whatever. To implement a successful manpower policy, more specialized forecasts of employment needs than those presently available even within developed nations would be required.

Does the need for manpower planning require that the government actually subsidize the costs of education? Again, this is necessary only if there is no less expensive alternative to assure the production of the types of workers needed. One such alternative is for the government to promote an improved labor market information system.

VI.   The equity/efficiency quandary and the financing of education

Historically, the views of advocates of public education could be categorized as either emphasizing egalitarian motives or the need for efficiency. The egalitarian view was held by those concerned with reducing the inequality in the supply of educational opportunities to various segments of the population. The efficiency view was maintained by those concerned with maximizing the rate of return on public investment in the educational process. Advocates of these views have often argued in terms which suggest that the two are, to a greater or lesser extent, mutually exclusive.

The egalitarian, for example, would advocate policies which would increase the representation of students from socially or economically disadvantaged families. The efficiency advocate would be expected to give priority to the enrollment of students whose ability and prior training gave them the greatest probability of continued success. That the same student would only rarely meet the standards of both groups is a result of the high coincidence of economic and cultural deprivation in our society. The economically deprived student will more often than not also be burdened with low *measured* ability and a poor educational background.

The traditional means of admission selection and student aid have been such that for any given cohort, beyond the age of compulsory attendance, continued education will be a positively related function of family income. The higher the educational level, the greater the likelihood of more than proportional representation of high income students.

The supporters of the efficiency concept in education have had to rely more on estimates of private rates of return than on social rates of return. This may well have led to a misinterpretation of "efficiency." The social investment criterion mentioned earlier is the best available guide that exists as to the efficiency with which public monies are invested in education. The student from a high income family may have a higher than average private rate of return to his educational investment. The higher rate of return may be due to his innate ability, his preschool environment, his earlier education, or to the greater amount of job- and income-related "connections" which accrue to a member of his social group.

This does not necessarily reflect a high social rate of return on such a student's education, for at least three reasons. (1) As T. W. Schultz has suggested, the average "ability" of low-income students may well be greater than that of high income students, at advanced levels of education, since the low-income student had more barriers to overcome in attaining the given level of academic achievement.[19] (2) For social reasons, there may accrue special benefits to the education of certain disadvantaged groups. The need to assure equal educational opportunity for the poor in order to maintain (or to recover) their faith in the social/economic system would be an example of such a possible social benefit. (3) The education-income effect may not be related to educationally induced changes in productivity. To the extent that this is so, the social rate of return will be substantially lower than the private rate.

There is another problem associated with the use of the word "efficiency" in the educational context. Efficiency in the general economic sense is used to denote a least-cost means of achieving a given goal. A serious problem for educational researchers has been the lack of specific goals for the various levels and forms of education.

Our immediate interest in the efficiency/equity question lies in the manner in which education is financed. We are concerned with who is paying and who should pay for education. The discussion is restricted to formal education because the financing question is of most immediate relevance in this area.

Pre-primary, primary, and secondary education

In the United States the existence of compulsory attendance laws tends to restrict the relevance of the efficiency/equity controversy to higher educational levels. Equality of opportunity appears to be promoted at the lower levels in that students are drawn from all families, regardless of income. In fact, given that average size of family is larger for low-income parents, the low-income family may seem to make more than proportionate use of the pre-primary and primary public systems. This view is further supported by the more frequent use of private schools by higher income parents, even though these parents continue to pay taxes to support public schools.

---

[19] T. W. Schultz, "Optimal Investment in College Instruction: The Efficiency-Equity Quandary," *Journal of Political Economy* (May/June 1972). Schultz asserts that the special ability of the disadvantaged is in the form of entrepreneurial capacity.

As we previously noted, at the secondary school level the efficiency/ equity conflict becomes more apparent. The problem here is not just the higher attrition rates evidenced by disadvantaged students. The curriculum in secondary school programs is more often than not oriented toward the interest of the prospective college student rather than for the terminal high school student. Technical and vocational course offerings are an important exception to this rule.

The taxes which support pre-secondary and secondary education are predominantly local. The local taxes used to support such education have been predominantly property taxes. Public finance economists have long harbored a skepticism concerning the incidence of property taxes. The problem is not the easily assumed regressiveness which is characteristic of consumption taxes. Rather property tax incidence is exceedingly capricious and exists as a function of valuation standards, exemption levels, and other localized procedures.

The protests concerning property taxes have centered upon the fiscal inequalities among school districts which have resulted from use of the tax. For any given amount of revenue needed, the level of the tax rate is inverse to the size of the tax base. The result is that areas with a poor property valuation base have to charge families a higher tax rate. In California it was found that in certain low-income areas families were forced to pay more in taxes per $1,000 of property value than in higher income areas of the state, and yet were unable to spend as much per student.

The property tax controversy has converged with Federal revenue-sharing proposals. The idea is that the Federal government could absorb a substantial part of the instructional costs of pre-primary through secondary education, enabling local jurisdictions to reduce the property tax burden. Some advocates also emphasize that this plan has the additional advantage of shifting taxes to more equitable (more progressive in incidence) forms in that the Federal government uses predominantly income taxes.

The role of the state government under these proposals is not clear. States have generally reserved for themselves the authority to regulate public instruction but have been less eager to assume financing responsibilities. Most states do maintain at least a "minimum-foundation" program which sets a lower limit on what local jurisdictions may provide. Other states, North Carolina and Hawaii, for example have assumed for themselves the primary responsibility for funding public education through the secondary school.

Table 4–14 presents a summary for 1950, 1960, and 1968, of the major sources of revenue and forms of expenditure for public primary and secondary education. The revenue figures show quite clearly the decline in local support, the increase in federal support, and the stable level of state sup-

Table 4–14. Public primary and secondary school finances, 1950–1960–1968 ($ in millions)

	1950 *		1960		1968	
Item	*Total*	*Percent*	*Total*	*Percent*	*Total*	*Percent*
Revenue, total	$5,437	100.0	$14,747	100.0	$31,903	100.0
Federal sources	156	2.9	652	4.4	2,806	8.8
State sources	2,166	39.8	5,768	39.1	12,276	38.5
Other sources †	3,116	57.3	8,327	56.5	16,821	52.7
Expenditures, total	5,838	100.0	15,613	100.0	32,977	100.0
Current	4,723	80.9	12,462	79.8	27,744	84.1
Day schools	4,687	80.3	12,329	79.0	26,877	81.5
Administration	220	3.8	528	3.4	1,249	3.8
Instruction	3,112	53.3	8,351	53.5	18,376	55.7
Plant operation	428	7.3	1,085	6.9	2,075	6.3
Plant maintenance	214	3.7	423	2.7	790	2.4
Fixed charges	261	4.5	909	5.8	2,388	7.2
Other services	452	7.7	1,033	6.6	2,000	6.1
Other current ‡	36	0.6	133	0.9	866	2.6
Capital outlay §	1,014	17.4	2,662	17.0	4,256	12.9
Interest	101	1.7	490	3.1	978	3.0

* Expenditure data for years ending June 30, 1950 excludes Alaska and Hawaii.
† Represent intermediate and local. Include receipts from gifts and tuition, and transportation fees paid by patrons.
‡ Comprises current expenditures for summer schools, adult education, community colleges, and beginning 1960, community services.
§ Prior to 1968, excludes capital outlay by State and local schoolhousing authority.
Source: Department of Health, Education, and Welfare, Office of Education; biennial report, *Statistics of State School Systems, 1967–68*. See also *Historical Statistics, Colonial Times to 1957*, series H 246–261).

port. These figures will change dramatically if the revenue-sharing and property tax reform programs come to fruition.

The increase in total revenue and expenditures is dramatic. The amount expended increased by almost $10 billion from 1950 to 1960 and had already increased by another $17 billion through 1968. While a significant amount of these increases obviously reflect price inflation, substantial increases in the quantity and quality of education also occurred. The present decline in the school age population will relieve some of the quantity pressures, but increased propensities to continue education, further inflation, and more expensive educational technology will still constitute forces for increased costs.

Instructional costs are the largest single expenditure item. The decline in capital outlay (which is even greater than it appears because the table excludes state and local school-housing authority expenditures prior to 1968) should be expected to continue as the demand on facilities subsides. The previous high enrollment periods put extreme pressure on capital facilities and some outdated structures will now be phased out rather than replaced.

College and graduate education

Most proponents of public education suggest that higher education should be *available* regardless of ability to pay. These proponents do not normally suggest, however, that universal higher education is necessary for the United States. If higher education is not for everyone, who is it for?

Traditionally it has been reserved for an income elite and an intellectual elite. Low-income students have been represented less than proportionally. The academically outstanding student, however, has usually been able to find a place in higher education regardless of income.

The maintenance of the income and intellectual elites is now threatened by policies of "open" admissions and need-based financial aid. It is questionable how effective these policies will finally be. Unfortunately, higher education appears peculiarly unsuited to serve as a very successful vehicle for social change. Higher education must work with a student group which represents a skewed distribution of the college-age cohort. This skewness reflects the earlier environment and educational influences which shape the post-secondary educational decisions of individuals. Totally open admissions, with or without increased financial aid, cannot be expected to have any meaningful democratizing influence on society. The group affected is simply too small.

To be effective, educational opportunity must be expanded at the pre-primary level and sustained through the educational progression. Only in this way can higher education be a significant agent for social change. Activists, eager to use the university as a means of attaining their goals, have seemingly failed to realize what a poor vehicle for change they have chosen. Their efforts are not necessarily all in vain, however. They may have the effect of making higher education less inequitable than it has been.

Public higher education is financed primarily at the state level with assistance from federal sources. Local assistance is not great except in the case of community colleges and vocational institutes in certain states. The taxes used to finance state spending are mainly consumption taxes, although the state income tax is becoming more common. The incidence of state taxes may well be regressive and is certainly no more than proportional. As in the case of primary and secondary schools, the federal contribution is from a tax base with a more progressive rate of incidence.

Table 4–15 offers data on the income and expenditure patterns for public and private higher education for 1950, 1960, and 1969. The data on expenditures again presents stark evidence of the rapid cost increase which took place in the 1960s. The pattern of expenditures shows no dramatic changes, a situation which might be surprising in itself. There are several important patterns revealed in the income categories.

Table 4–15. Higher educational finance, 1950–1960–1969 ($ in millions)

Item	1950	1960	1969
Current income	2,375	5,786	18,875
Educational and general income	1,834	4,688	14,330
Student fees	395	1,157	3,814
Endowment earnings	96	207	413
Federal, State and local governments	1,078	2,563	7,932
Private gifts and grants	119	383	605
Organized activities related to instruction	112	245	549
Miscellaneous	35	134	1,017
Auxiliary enterprises and activities	541	1,097	4,545 [1]
Receipts for plant expansion	529	1,309	NA
Increase of endowment and other nonexpendable funds	117	499	NA
Current expenditure	2,246	5,601	18,482
Educational and general	1,706	4,513	13,835
Administration and general expense	213	583	2,278
Instruction and departmental research	781	1,793	5,942
Organized research	225	1,022	2,034
Plant operation and maintenance	225	470	1,338
Organized activities related to instruction	119	303	1,203
Libraries, extension and public services	143	341	1,040
Auxiliary enterprises and activities	476	916	3,832 [1]
Scholarships, fellowships, and prizes	63	172	815
Expenditure for plant expansion [2]	417	1,192	NA
Value of plant and plant funds	5,273	14,612	NA
Endowment and other nonexpendable funds [3]	2,644	5,571	NA

NA = Not available.
[1] Includes major public service programs formerly included in "Educational and general."
[2] Includes grounds, buildings, equipment, and unexpended plant funds.
[3] All funds other than national defense and student loan funds.
1950 excludes Alaska and Hawaii.
Covers universities, colleges, professional schools, junior colleges, teachers colleges and normal schools, both publicly and privately controlled, regular session.
Includes estimates for institutions not reporting.
Source: Department of Health, Education, and Welfare, Office of Education; 1950. *Biennial Survey of Education in the United States,* chapter on Statistical Summary of Education; thereafter, annual reports, *Digest of Educational Statistics,* and *Projections of Educational Statistics to 1978–79.*

Student fees have increased consistently as a percentage of educational and general income. In 1950 they represented 21.5 percent of the total and increased to 24.7 percent in 1960 and 26.6 percent in 1969. Federal, state and local government support represented 58.8 percent of the total in 1950, dropped to 54.7 percent in 1960 and has risen slightly to 55.4 percent in 1969. If endowment earnings are combined with private gifts and grants, this source increased as a percent of the total from 11.7 percent in 1950 to 12.6 percent in 1960. Since 1960, however, this source has declined relatively and now represents only 7.1 percent of all educational and general income. The general income pattern appears to point toward a greater reliance on student fees. The present economic situation should encourage this trend.

Table 4–16 allows for a differentiation of student charges between public and private institutions. The data in the table include estimates for 1962 and 1967 and a forecast for 1972. Public tuition and fees as a percent of private is equal to 24.1 percent in 1962, 22.3 percent in 1967, and 20.9 percent in 1972. For four-year universities only, the same figure was 25.0, 24.7, and 24.4 percent for each of the three years, respectively.

There is a quite obvious public-private price difference, which appears to be widening. Even though students at public schools may be bearing an increasing share of the direct educational costs, they have not experienced the same disadvantage as students at private schools. Board rates and dormitory charges have not shown as dramatic a change because these are not subsidized at public institutions to the same degree as tuition.

Private education

Before we reach the question of who should pay for education, some comment should be made about the position of private institutions in the educational system. Controversy about private education has nothing to do with the legitimacy or even value of its existence. Individuals obviously have the legal right to establish and maintain private institutions so long as these schools meet minimum performance standards set by the state and do not promote policies against the public interest. The controversy occurs over the use of public funds to support private education.

The opponents of such public assistance cite the impropriety of aiding students who fail to take advantage of a public education provided elsewhere. "If one chooses to go to a private school, then one should be prepared to pay the costs" is their view. Many have also raised the constitutional question of public support for private schools which have a religious affiliation. No matter for what specific purposes support is provided, it must free funds which can be used for activities related to religious instruction. Another argument presented is that it is improper to expend public monies on education without public control over the uses to which this money is applied.

Those who advocate public support for education rebut each of these charges in the following ways. They note that it would be impossible to assimilate all private school students into the public educational system. Present public facilities would not allow this and the purchase of facilities presently under private control would be exorbitant. It is argued that the major portion of education even at a sectorian private school is still the general, non religious, instruction offered at all schools, and the private

Table 4–16. Tuition and charges in higher education, 1962–1967–1972

Year * and Item	Tuition and Required Fees †	4-Year 2-Year	4-Year Universities	4-Year Other	Board Rates	4-Year 2-Year	4-Year Universities	4-Year Other	Charge for Dormitory Rooms	2-Year	4-Year Universities	4-Year Other
1962:												
Public	$ 218	$ 88	$ 265	$ 182	$423	$356	$433	$409	$228	$155	$249	$197
Nonpublic	906	537	1,059	838	472	427	500	464	288	234	323	268
1967:												
Public	275	121	360	259	457	376	490	417	294	213	321	271
Nonpublic	1,233	845	1,456	1,162	506	487	548	490	385	347	452	355
1972:												
Public	383	174	527	394	555	451	616	491	418	315	456	400
Nonpublic	1,830	1,351	2,161	1,754	615	633	672	594	556	541	664	512

* For entire academic year ending in year stated.
† Represents average charges per full-time resident degree-credit student.
Source: Department of Health, Education, and Welfare, Office of Education; Digest of Educational Statistics, 1970.

schools are presently saving the public the costs of providing this instruction. Finally, many proponents would accept some level of public control in return for public support.

The current political environment appears very advantageous for the extension of some form of public support for private education. The two questions to be resolved are the amount and form of support and how much public control will be involved. At the primary and secondary level this public support will most likely come in the form of direct grants to institutions. At the post-secondary level the form of support is dependent upon what happens to the tuition subsidy at public institutions. If the subsidy remains, the private colleges will need direct grants to counter its effect (or grants to their students which embody an amount equal to the tuition subsidy). If, as has here been advocated, the public tuition subsidy is removed, grants may be given to students to use at either public or private schools. The advantageous consumer effects of this form of subsidy appear substantial.

The social efficiency criterion requires that investment in private education must create unrecouped social benefits in the least expensive manner. The implementation of needed improvements in the loan market to better serve human capital formation should remove much of the need for direct subsidization of private higher education in the same way it should for public higher education.

Who should pay? Resolving the equity/efficiency quandary

If one accepts the conclusion that society should pay for education at precollege levels, the relevant question is one of tax equity. Substitution of income tax financing for property and consumption taxes reduces the internal equity problem among users and the external user-nonuser equity problem. To the extent that anyone feels he is a nonuser of precollege education, an equitable tax base reduces the nonuser burden. In addition, the nonuser of education may be a more than proportionate user of other public services.

The tax equity solution is not adequate for the problem of post-secondary education. The dichotomy of interests between users and non-users is simply too disparate at this level. In another essay, this author has suggested a system of finance for higher education which is designed to help resolve the efficiency/equity quandary in higher education.[20] The basic outline of the program consists of:

1. Undergraduate tuition equal to the full instructional costs calculated separately at each public institution

---

[20] Douglas M. Windham, "Tuition, the Capital Market, and the Allocation of Subsidies to College Students," *School Review* (August 1972).

2. The creation of a quasi-public body with authority to issue bonds so as to accumulate sufficient potential student loan funds
3. The granting of loans to students at full interest expense with optional repayment periods extending to perhaps twenty-five years

Loans would be available to every full time student in an amount equal to full tuition and special fees, a realistic maintenance allowance, and some compensation for the student's foregone earnings.

The need for full-cost tuition is a result of the impropriety of implicit subsidies through the tuition charge. The reason for having tuition differentials among individual public institutions is that such a pricing system increases the ability of the student to compare private benefits and costs in his attendance decision. There is certainly good reason why the institutions presently classified as public are not homogeneous even within a given state. This variety is a quite appropriate part of market operations, especially when attended by an adequate provision of information about the differences of quality and cost. The alternative of charging the average system-wide cost at each institution would require students at less expensive public institutions to pay more than their share, while students at the more expensive state schools would receive a new form of subsidy.

Tuition set at full cost removes all immediate need of a public subsidy. The public may continue to subsidize research and other noninstructional activities at certain institutions. If enrollment is not to be adversely affected by increased tuition, the capital market must be simultaneously expanded. The student loan authority would pay full market rates in selling its bonds. The requirement that the authority be self-sustaining is obvious if the need for public subsidies is to be avoided.

A major innovation in this program is the freeing of the granting of loans from the need-determination process. As all borrowers pay full market interest there is no requirement that the monies be restricted for the "needy". It appears legitimate to view higher education as consisting of students who will be—potentially—wealthier than nonusers of the system. This potential wealth should both qualify them for the loan as well as remove the need to subsidize their education.

It is impossible to predict how students would react to new, longer term, and more extensive loan programs. It may be necessary for the government to carry out the loan program through repayment guarantees until the risks become more determinable. Reluctance to make long-term loans to college students is probably strongly reinforced by the paucity of experience in this area of the capital market. An important research question which remains is the adequacy of the capital market to handle the increase in loan funds which a program such as this would entail.

Certain parents already have the opportunity (through refinancing of a mortgage, for example) of paying for their child's education over an extended period. In addition to equity considerations, the extension of such an alternative to all students who wish to borrow appears necessary if the reluctance to assume rational indebtedness is to be overcome. Such a reluctance is especially characteristic of low-income families.

With a financing program of the type discussed here, public institutions of higher education would no longer depend on legislative grants. Such schools would probably continue to be governed by state-appointed trustees, but this should not prevent them from being more innovative than they have been under the present system. Private schools would gain students from the public schools only to the extent that they offer attractive programs.

This proposal would not be a panacea for those private schools whose problems stem from an unwillingness or inability to offer a marketable good, i.e., a useful education. The private schools which deserve (by a consumer test) to continue would be helped. If private schools failed they would not be able to blame unfair price competition from the public system as the cause.

The suggested program would also allow greater student independence without totally removing the parents' incentive to help their children. A child would no longer be restricted in his decision to enter college either by his parents' inability or unwillingness to pay for the cost of his education. The parent would, of course, be free to pay for all or a part of his child's expenses as he is with any other consumption activity of his child. Those who wish to free their child of a potential loan obligation or provide him with a higher standard of living while in college could still do so.

Some will probably recognize that the effect of this program is to produce college graduates with various debt burdens and that the burdens are an inverse function of present family income. To the extent that college graduates are recipients of higher lifetime income this is less of an equity problem. The fact that this tuition/loan program would eventually release millions of dollars which each state could invest in its precollege educational systems, is a significant long-run benefit which should increase the future equality of educational opportunity.

This program would advance the cause of efficiency in four primary ways. First, it would place social investment on the rational basis of a least-cost means of producing unrecouped social benefits. Second, it would increase the financial ability of individuals who presently are not able to partake of education. Third, it would place consumer power in the hands of students rather than state legislatures or administrative boards. And fourth, it would resolve the present inequality between treatment of public and private college students.

The program would also attack both of the equity problems which presently exist. The increased financial ability of students would help free them from dependence upon parental income as a determinant of attendance.

Greater numbers of students from disadvantged families should begin to participate in the higher education process. Because it removes the need for taxpayers to subsidize college students, the user-nonuser equity problem would be resolved.

VII. The frontiers of education and educational research

This essay began by examining the nature of education as an economic good. The importance of goal definition and of understanding the production function of education was emphasized. The remainder of the discussion has stressed the present means of financing education and alternatives to them.

The purpose has been to direct attention toward the myriad economic concepts relevant to contemporary educational issues. Space limitations have prevented discussion of all the areas of educational research in which economists are presently engaged.

Two sources of research suggestions and summaries which would prove valuable to anyone interested in further exploring the economics of education are T. W. Schultz's "Human Capital: Policy Issues and Research Opportunities" [21] and Mary Jean Bowman's *Educational Outcomes, Processes, and Decisions: Frontiers of Economic Research and Development for the 1970's.*[22] Schultz has emphasized the interaction of policy and research and has identified a diverse number of research opportunities, such as: (1) equity in schooling and higher education; (2) efficiency in schooling and higher education; (3) postschool investment in human capital; (4) preschool investment in human capital; (5) the human capital approach to migration; (6) health as a human capital investment; (7) the role of information systems; and (8) human capital aspects inherent in the acquisition of children.

The Bowman paper, presented with memoranda from twelve other researchers, encompasses a wide range of research and developmental needs of education. Some topics surveyed are: (1) society and the definition of educational outputs; (2) the production of "changes in students"; (3) education, "ability", and earnings relationships; (4) institutional behavior and the economic analysis of public choice; (5) student decisions, information, and market stability; (6) time paths of learning, earning, and the distribution of incomes; and (7) education, the economics of the households, and inter-generational linkages.

We conclude on the optimistic note that the study of the economics of education is still in its infancy. As it grows and matures, it may offer much-needed assistance in the improvement of our educational system.

---

[21] Human Capital Paper 70:10, University of Chicago, Department of Economics, January 7, 1971.

[22] Report prepared for the National Institute of Education, Washington, D.C., December 1, 1971.

5

Current Issues
in Transportation

WILLIAM VICKREY

McVickar Professor of Political Economy
Columbia University

I. The basic difficulty: economies of scale

The special economic problems relating to transportation are ultimately traceable to the fact that there are very substantial economies of scale in most forms of transportation. This is compounded but not inherently changed by the extreme specificity of transportation services as to time, place of origin, place of destination, and the identity of the thing or person transported. A pound of sugar at one time and place is much the same thing as a pound of sugar at another time or place, and the one can be converted into the other, if need be, by carrying and storing it. A 10 mile trip to town at 8 a.m. is not the same thing as a trip to town at noon, nor the same thing as a 10 mile trip to the beach, nor can one be readily converted into the other, in many cases. We thus have a degree of complexity in the production and sale of transportation services that is an order of magnitude more complex than that associated with most other categories of economic activity.

It is important to understand just what kind of economies of scale cause the trouble. It is not that larger transportation organizations are necessarily any more efficient or operate at lower unit costs than small ones—

this may in some instances be true and in others not. It is that when the total amount of traffic in a given area or along a given corridor increases, the average cost per unit of service will in most cases tend to decline, or possibly the quality or convenience of the service to the users will improve, or both. It is this technological fact that confronts us with a situation where if we attempt to charge each user a price that reflects only the additional cost that his additional use imposes on the system, we will not be able to cover the full costs of the operation from the revenues from such charges. Yet if we charge more than this "marginal cost" we run a danger that many to whom the potential use would be worth more than this marginal cost (but less than the price they would have to pay), will fail to make full use of the service. This would involve a loss of economic efficiency equal to the excess of what the user would have been willing to pay over the cost that would have been incurred in providing him with the service. We may thus be faced with a dilemma: either the service must be operated at a financial loss, and subsidized in some way, or the service must be priced in such a way as to fail to achieve maximum economic efficiency.

This dilemma also exists with respect to other utility services, such as water, gas, and electricity, but to a much less severe degree. In many of these other services the fact that the consumer must be physically connected to the system makes it possible to adjust the rate schedules in such a way that a closer approximation to efficient use is achieved, even under the constraint of having to cover total costs and normal return on investment out of the revenues derived from the charges. Problems comparable to those of inducing transportation users to select the correct routing and mode of transportation, in the light of the relative value of the use to consumers and the relative costs of the alternatives, are also either absent entirely or relatively minor in their impact.

It is important to distinguish clearly between the economies of intensity, which is what concerns us here, and economies of mere size, such as might occur from merger or amalgamation of different entities. It is, for example, no evidence against the existence of substantial economies of scale in this relevant sense that the Richmond, Fredericksburg and Potomac Railroad (a relatively small operation when measured by gross revenue or ton-miles), has costs that compare favorably with those of the Southern Railway, a much larger system by most measures but one with a much lower average density of traffic.[1]

---

[1] See, for example, George H. Borts' study "The Estimation of Rail Cost Functions," *Econometrica*, January 1960, pp. 108–131, reprinted in Arnold Zellner, ed., *Readings in Econometrics and Statistics* (Little, Brown, 1968, pp. 440–462). Economies of scale are here measured in a manner quite irrelevant to the special economics of the transportation industry. Cost is related to the total volume of traffic handled by a railroad corporation and to the average length of haul. That the results show no substantial economies of scale may be significant for mergers of the end-to-end variety (as distinct from mergers of parallel lines offering the possibility of concentrating traffic on a smaller number of routes), but not for the determination of either short- or long-run marginal cost.

Measuring these economies of scale in the relevant sense is, to be sure, not easy and there are many ways in which even fairly sophisticated statistical approaches to the problem are likely to understate these economies. Comparing operating units in terms of the relationship between costs and density of traffic may produce biased results, for example, unless allowance is made for the tendency of high density routes to occur in areas where the entire level of costs is higher, whether because of higher land values, a greater degree of general congestion in the area traversed, or difficult terrain. Another factor is that as the overall level of traffic increases, the density of the network that will most economically serve the traffic also increases, with the result that output measured in terms of ton-miles, for example, will increase less than in proportion to the amount of traffic originated and terminated, even if the relative pattern of origins and destinations remains the same.[2] The quality of the service is likely to improve as traffic density increases, also. Thus even if there were no economies at all in the provision of the service in terms of the usual cost per ton-mile or cost per passenger-mile criteria, nevertheless, if the service is measured in terms relevant to the value of the user, there will often be substantial "increasing returns"—though one might want to distinguish the term "decreasing costs" to exclude such factors. Under extreme conditions, indeed, marginal cost in terms of the user-relevant units might actually be negative.[3]

---

[2] If A, B, and C are located at the vertices of an equilateral triangle 100 miles on a side, and each point ships 10 tons a day to each of the other two, at this level of traffic it may not be found worth while to have a direct link AC, but rather to carry the AC traffic via B, in which case total traffic will be 8,000 ton miles per day. If activity doubles and each point ships 20 tons per day to the other two, it may now be worth while to install the AC link, and to ship direct between A and C, in which case total ton-miles per day will increase by only 50 percent to 12,000, i.e., the marginal cost of the increment in traffic is only half of the former average cost. Measured in cost per ton mile, no reduction in cost level would be recorded; indeed such costs might even increase if the costs on the link AC are slightly higher than on AB and BC. Nevertheless shippers between A and C find their rates reduced considerably.

[3] Consider a bus line served by buses having a capacity of 40 passengers, the cost per bus trip being $12. Suppose that, at a fare of 30 cents and a 15 minute headway, demand is 160 passengers per hour, just filling the four buses, and that of these 160 passengers, 100 value time spent waiting for the bus at $5.00 per hour and 60 at $1.00 per hour. If the head way is shortened to 12 minutes, requiring 5 trips per hour, the average wait would be 6 minutes instead of 7.5, or a saving of 1.5 minutes on the average per passenger, assuming the passengers to arrive at the bus stop at random without reference to the time-table of the bus. The value of the time saved is 12.5 cents each for the 100 $5/hr. passengers, and 2.5 cents each for the 60 $1/hr. passengers or a total of $14, which would be greater than the $12 additional cost of the extra bus trip. If the extra bus were added in order to carry an additional 40 riders, the net cost of the additional riders would be −$2.00, and if these riders valued the ride at an average of say 20 cents each, the total net gain from arranging for the added service would be 40(20 cents) + $2 = $10.00

In practice, however, it may prove difficult to finance the cost of the better service, especially if there is no way to discriminate between the various groups of riders. If the fare is raised to 37.5 cents, which is the fare necessary to break even if all 160 passengers continued to ride, the service would be less attractive by 5 cents to the $1/hr. riders (37.5 − 30 − 2.5 = 5) and some of them would stop patronizing the line. On the other hand the service would be more attractive by 5 cents (30 + 12.5 − 37.5 = 5) to th $5/hr. riders, and some additional patronage by this group might result. But unless this added patronage is

To be sure, increasing cost conditions may be found in some specific areas in transportation. In the short run, increasing costs are likely to be encountered when capacity is inadequate, though often diminishing returns will be felt chiefly in terms of delays, crowding, and other aspects of service impairment rather than in increasing financial costs to the operating agency. In the long run, increasing costs may be encountered due to the scarcity of air space near major air terminals, or scarcity of alignments through built-up areas for right of way that do not require extensive demolitions. More fundamentally, in the long run as transportation networks are built up more and more densely in metropolitan areas, the increased complexity of the network will generally require a more than proportional increase in the number of intersections, grade separations, connecting ramps, and the like, which will cause costs to rise more than in proportion to the magnitude of the transportation task to be performed, even if the nontransportation characteristics of the area are held constant.[4] Thus the generalization that transportation is a decreasing cost industry may not hold within highly industrialized or large metropolitan areas. Without much data to go on, one may hazard the guess that for highway transportation this situation is likely to occur chiefly in metropolitan areas with populations of 1 million or more, and possibly within the central business districts of cities of over 100,000 population. For railroad transportation the only likely instances in the United States are the Chicago area and the New York-Philadelphia area. The great bulk of all transportation is still carried out under conditions of substantial increasing returns.

Marginal cost pricing

It is a commonplace of welfare economics that if we had an idealized situation in which there were frictionless, competitive markets in all goods and services, and if the government had adequate sources of revenue that involved no adverse impacts on the efficiency of the economy at the margin (i.e., all taxes were completely "neutral" in their impact on the choices of individual taxpayers), then an optimal allocation of resources would require that the prices of transportation services should be fixed at marginal cost. In this way users of transportation services would be pro-

---

enough to offset the loss from the $1/hr. riders, the $60/hr. of costs for the 12 minute headway will not be covered. The potential added value derivable from the increased service may be realizable only by discriminatory pricing or by subsidy.

[4] To illustrate the point with a somewhat abstract model, suppose that a transportation network of 12 one-way links connects the four corners of a square, and that each of these links is loaded to the point that no further economies of scale are possible. If traffic doubles, it would be possible to duplicate each link, if land were available, even to the extent of duplicating the terminals, conceivably with only a corresponding duplication of total costs, except where the AC and BD links cross, where the number of grade crossings or the area of the core bridges will quadruple rather than double, even if the approaches only double. Intersections and grade separations are indeed, among the most costly elements of transportation networks.

vided with the information that would permit them to judge how best to use transportation services in the interests of economic efficiency. Requiring them to pay such prices, and no more, will give them just the right incentive to choose correctly among the alternatives open to them, balancing the gain ot themselves against the costs they will thereby impose on the rest of society. Prices in excess of marginal cost would result in wasteful stinting in the use of the service, while prices less than marginal cost would encourage wasteful overuse.

To some this proposition may seem fairly obvious. It does imply, however, the notion that in order to achieve this optimum allocation of resources a subsidy must be provided not merely for those transportation services that appear to be incapable of paying their own way, as seems to bc incroasingly the case for urban mass transportation, but even for situations were charges could readily be set at levels sufficient to cover total cost without driving all users away. Such a generalized subsidy is of course quite contrary to the usual practice throughout the world, and thus the basis for claiming that it is necessary and proper may need to be set out in a slightly more detailed and rigorous fashion. The argument by which this is shown, indeed, is essentially the same as that by which the advantages of the free competitive system are demonstrated for those areas of the economy for which such free competition is possible.

If a situation exists where all prices, without exception, are firmly specified and all economic units are free to buy as much or as little as they wish at these prices, and do buy and sell in such quantities as to maximize their profit (or level of satisfaction, in the case of ultimate consumers), and the aggregate amounts that individual units wish to buy and sell at these prices are in balance, then the result is "Pareto optimal". A Pareto optimum is defined as one which it is impossible to change in such a way as to benefit some person or group without hurting anyone else. If, for example, a situation were such that there were some way in which two or more people could trade with each other to mutual benefit, the original situation would not be a Pareto optimum situation.

The classical idealized perfect competition situation is one which satisfies the above conditions, and is therefore Pareto optimal. Prices are set by an impersonal market mechanism, which each trader in any given market is too small to affect, so that each trader must further his own welfare within the limits determined by these given prices. That the above conditions do indeed result in a Pareto optimum situation can readily be seen by considering that if a change is to be made from this situation that will make any given individual better off in terms of his own preferences, this will imply that his budget will have to be relaxed in terms of these existing prices. This would be necessary because if any combination of goods and services to be bought and sold, attainable within the existing budget at the existing prices, were preferred to the equilibrium combination, it would have been chosen instead and this individual would not have been in equilibrium. And since the market is in balance, enabling one consumer to enjoy a combination of goods and services bought and sold that corresponds to a looser budget at existing prices necessarily requires, if the total amounts bought and sold are to balance, pulling someone else down to a combination implying a tighter budget at existing prices. This pulling down to a tighter budget will require impairing this other person's level of satisfaction, either directly as an individual or through a reduction in the profit situation of a firm in which he has an interest, abstracting from the possibility that the person adversely affected might have been in a position where he could have had more of everything than he really wants.

The relevance of such a proposition to the pricing of transportation and utility services is found in the fact that in such a Pareto-optimal equilibrium, all of the prices will necessarily be equal to marginal cost. If any firm or individual is capable of producing an additional unit of anything at a marginal cost that is less than the ruling market price, he would increase his profits or level of satisfaction by doing so. Conversely if the marginal cost of the last unit produced were less than the market price, it would have paid the firm or individual to have refrained from producing it. Thus the Pareto optimal-market equilibrium requires that all prices be equal to marginal cost.[5]

The difficulty in applying this norm directly to transportation services lies in the fact that an enterprise that is required to meet its total costs out of revenues from sales, whether operated as a private firm or a public agency, cannot, if it is conducting an operation with significant economies of scale, govern itself by the rule of adjusting output so as to maximize profits on the assumption that all current prices will remain fixed independently of how much it attempts to buy or sell. Most such enterprises indeed determine their own selling prices rather than finding them determined in an automatic market. More fundamentally, the difficulty is that an externally fixed price would either be such as to make it more profitable for the firm to sell nothing at all in the given market, or to throw on the market more than the market could in fact absorb at the going price.

Thus one cannot rely on competition to bring about an efficient solution where significant economies of scale persist. Pareto-optimal results can, however, be obtained if the prices of the various services are kept equal

---

[5] Strictly speaking, where discontinuities occur in the marginal cost function, so that there is a significant difference between the marginal cost of the last unit produced and the marginal cost of the subsequent unit, the requirement is merely that price be no greater than the former "downward" marginal cost and no less than the latter "upward" marginal cost. This case can be subsumed under the briefer statement by adopting the convention that marginal cost at such points of discontinuity shall be construed to signify the closed interval between the upward and downward marginal costs, and that equality is satisfied if the price lies within this interval.

to marginal cost and whatever is demanded at this price is supplied.[6] If this is done, however, revenues will not cover total costs, and the resulting "intra-marginal residue" must be covered by some form of subsidy. How this subsidy is to be financed, and what modifications to marginal cost pricing should be made to take account of these difficulties, constitute the main consideration leading to the adoption of a "second best" approach.

Another difficulty with the simple prescription of setting price equal to marginal cost is the fact that while universal adherence to this principle ordinarily assures that no other situation differing only slightly from the situation thus arrived at will be better for some and worse for none, there does remain the possibility that there exist other situations somewhat remote from the existing one, such as those involving complete suppression of some services or the introduction of new ones, which would be better for some and worse for none. Marginal cost pricing is thus a necessary, but not sufficient, criterion for the achievement of a Pareto-optimal equilibrium. It may indeed be fairly difficult to determine which of the various situations that satisfy the marginal cost criterion are actually undominated and thus Pareto-optimal in the global rather than in the local sense, much as it is more difficult to determine which of the two hilltops is the higher, particularly in a fog, than to determine that one is, in fact, at the summit of one of the hills. Generally, however, this uncertainty will be a poor excuse for not climbing to the top of whichever hill one happens to be on.

Second-best approaches

More important, in practice, are the constraints and inevitable imperfections in the market that make it impossible to fully achieve any of the local optima. In the face of such constraints, it becomes desirable to set prices somewhat above, or in rare cases below, marginal cost in order to take account of them. These are principally (1) the costs and distortions that will be introduced elsewhere in the economy by the taxes imposed to secure the revenues required to finance the subsidy, and (2) deviations from marginal cost of other goods and services that are either close substitutes or strongly complementary to the services being priced.

In some quarters, indeed, there is a predilection for attempting to discredit entirely the basing of price on marginal cost on the ground that the departures of price from marginal cost that are required to allow for these imperfections and constraints are too difficult to determine accurately. While in theory a complete and accurate determination of the optimum "second best" prices would require a complete analysis of the entire economy with all of its complex demand and production functions, ac-

---

[6] If the upward marginal cost is greater than the downward, price should be set at whatever intermediate level will limit demand to the output at which this discontinuity occurs.

tually, with the aid of simplifying assumptions that still come reasonably close to representing the actual situation, prices can be determined in relation to marginal costs that will come reasonably close to achieving the second-best optimum, and in any case will produce results far superior to any arrived at by alternative methods such as those based on one or other scheme of full cost allocation.

The cost to consumers of increments in net revenues

The easiest part of the problem is that involved in allowing for the added inefficiencies introduced in the process of raising the revenues for the subsidy. One way of looking at the problem is to attempt to minimize the total cost to taxpayers and consumers of meeting the revenue requirements of the operating agency. As the price of a given service is raised above the marginal cost level in an attempt to increase the net revenues of the operating agency, each dollar of additional revenue is generally obtained at a cost of something more than a dollar of additional burden on the affected customers. This excess tends to increase as the price is pushed further and further above the marginal cost level. The total cost of meeting a given net revenue requirement will then be minimized if one pushes prices above marginal cost in each service category in such a way that this marginal cost to consumers of getting an additional dollar of net revenue will be the same for each of the various prices at which the various categories of services are provided.

This rule can be briefly stated as the rule of equalizing the marginal cost of net revenues obtained from the various services. This (gross) marginal cost of net revenues can be defined as the ratio of (1) the increased amount the consumers of a given service have to pay as a result of the price increase to (2) the increase in the net revenues of the operating organization that is thereby obtained. For example, let the rate for a given service be increased from p to $p + dp$, resulting in a reduction in usage from q to $q - dq$, as shown by a movement from a to b in Figure 5–1; let the marginal cost of producing the service be m. Then the consumers who continue to use the service to the extent of $(q - dq)$ and have to pay a price higher by dp are worse off by an amount $(q - dq)dp$ represented by rectangle A, in the aggregate.[7] Net revenue produced is the extra amount $(q - dq)dp = A$ paid by the persisting customers, less the margin of price over marginal cost formerly contributed to the net revenue by those purchasing the

---

[7] In addition, consumers who no longer use the service give up a consumers' surplus measured by the small triangle abe of area $(dp)(dq)/2$, which is the excess of the amount they would have been willing to pay for the amount dq over the amount they formerly actually had to pay. If the change in price is made suitably small, however, the area of this triangle becomes negligibly small compared to the areas of rectangle A, and can be left out of account without vitiating the analysis.

Figure 5–1

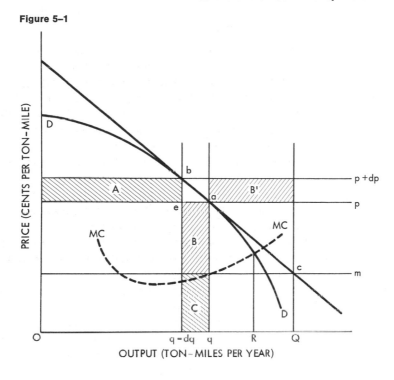

amount dq which is no longer being sold, $(p - m)dq = B$. The marginal cost of net revenue is thus the ratio

$$\frac{(q - dq)dp}{(q - dq) - (p - m)dq} = \frac{A}{A - B} = z.$$

This ratio can be given a meaning somewhat easier to grasp as follows: Project the demand curve as a straight line through the two points a and b to meet a horizontal line representing the current marginal cost, at a point c which will determine a hypothetical output Q. Then draw a vertical line through c at the output Q, and extend the two horizontal lines representing the prices p and $p + dp$. The area B' between the ordinates q and Q and the price lines p and $p + dp$ (equal to $(Q - q)dp$) can readily be shown to be equal to B. Indeed, triangles abe and cad are similar, implying the proportion $\frac{ae}{be} = \frac{cd}{ad}$ whence $(ae)(ad) = (be)(cd)$, or $B' = B$. Since B' and A have the same height, we can write

$$z = \frac{A}{A - B} = \frac{A}{A - B} = \frac{q}{q - (Q-q)} = \frac{1}{2 - \dfrac{Q}{q}}$$

from which we can derive immediately

$$\frac{z}{2z-1}=\frac{q}{Q}.$$

Thus if the marginal cost of net revenue z is to be a constant for the various services supplied, the ratio q/Q must also be a constant.

Equalizing the marginal cost of net revenues, for cases of this type, is thus equivalent to setting prices that will cause the actual output q of the various serives to be a constant fraction of Q, the amount of the particular service that would have been produced had the price for the service been set equal to its current marginal cost, on the assumption that the demand curve were projected as a straight line. If the actual demand curve is not a straight line, the rule is nevertheless to be applied as though it were a straight line tangent to the actual demand curve at the point corresponding to the actual price to be charged. It is irrelevant, for this purpose, that the actual demand and marginal cost curves might intersect at some such output as R in Figure 5–1. This rule of uniform reduction in all outputs as compared with the output projected for a price equal to current marginal cost is especially useful in that it can be applied with good results even in fairly complex situations where capacity constraints occur or where the demands for the various services are interrelated.

An alternative and equivalent representation of the marginal cost of net revenue is as the ratio of (1) the excess of price over marginal revenue to (2) the excess of marginal cost over marginal revenue. Marginal revenue is defined as the increment to gross revenue resulting from the lowering of the price by an amount sufficient to sell one additional unit of the product or service. It differs from price by the amount of revenue lost from the old customers through the reduction in price. In Figure 5–1, the revenue gained from new customers by lowering the price from $p + dp$ to p is $B + c = p{\cdot}dq$, while the revenue lost from the old customers through the lowered price is $A = (q - dq)dp$. The net revenue loss is thus $B + C - A$, and the marginal revenue is $MR = \dfrac{B + C - A}{dq}$. The marginal cost of net revenues according to this representation is

$$z=\frac{p-MR}{m-MR}=\frac{p-\dfrac{B+C-A}{dq}}{m-\dfrac{B+C-A}{dq}}=\frac{pdq-B-C+A}{mdq-B-C+A}=\frac{A}{A-B}$$

In the numerator, the expression $p - MR$ gives the total net loss to consumers through the reduction in the output by one unit, which diminishes the value received by p (since this was the price the users were just willing to pay for this last unit) while MR is the reduction in the total amount paid. In the denominator the expression $m - MR$ gives the change in net revenues, m being the cost saved by producing one less unit, and MR is the reduction in gross receipts.

If two or more services are being provided in circumstances such that the marginal cost of net revenues differs from one service to another, then if more net revenue were derived from the service with the lower marginal cost of net revenues by raising its price, while the prices of services with higher marginal costs of net revenues were lowered to the extent possible while still maintaining the same level of net revenues, the net result will be a reduction in the total cost to the consumers of providing whatever net revenues are called for by the established budgetary requirements. If sucessive adjustments are made in this way until the marginal cost of net revenues is the same for all service categories for which distinct prices can feasibly be charged, then a second-best optimum will have been reached in which the required budgetary constraint is being met in such a way as to detract as little as possible from the gains the consumers are realizing, as compared with the situation where prices were put equal to marginal cost.[8]

---

[8] Suppose, for example, that the independent demands for two services are given by $q_1 = 300 - 5 p_1$, and $q_2 = 144 - 6 p_2$, with the total cost of the joint production process given by $C = 2,804 + 5 q_1 + 4 q_2$. Then strict marginal cost pricing would give $p_1 = 5, p_2 = 4$, $q_1 = 275, q_2 = 120$, gross revenues $R = 1,855$, $C = 4,659$, resulting in a deficit of 2,804 equal to the intramarginal residue, consisting in this case of the fixed costs represented by the first term of the cost function C.

If a policy were followed of setting prices according to the fully allocated costs, with the fixed costs allocated in proportion to the marginal costs, then prices would have to be approximately tripled in order to break even, giving $p_1 = 14.90, p_2 = 11.90$, which would give $q_1 = 225.5, q_2 = 72.6$, $C = 4221.9$, $R = 4223.89$, yielding a slight profit due to rounding of $G = 1.99$. If now we were to increase p_1 by 0.10 to 15,00, this decreases q_2 by 0.5 to 225, increases gross revenues by 15.05, and lowers costs by 2.5, resulting in a gain of 17.55 in net revenues. This gain, however, has cost the consumers 0.10 for each of the 225 units they continue to consume, or 22.5, plus a further loss of .05 on the average with respect to the 0.5 units no longer consumed that were considered to be worth at least 14.90 but not more than 15.00, giving a total loss to the consumers of product 1 of 22.525. Dividing the increased cost to consumers by the increase in net revenues gives a ratio of 1.29 of cost to consumers for each unit of increase in the net revenues of the operating agency.

If on the other hand p_2 were raised by 0.10 to 12.00, this would decrease q_2 by 0.6 to 72, gross revenues would be increased by 0.06, costs would be decreased by 2.40, and net revenues would be increased by 2.46, but the customers would be paying 7.2 more for the units they still buy, in addition to suffering a loss of an average of 0.05 on the 0.6 units no longer bought, for a total cost to consumers of 7.23, or a ratio of cost to consumers to gain to the operating enterprise of 2.93, as compared with 1.28 for category 1. There would thus be a net gain on balance obtainable from reducing p_2 and rising p_1 in such a way as to maintain the net revenue constant at the required level, until the marginal cost of net revenues has been equalized.

As was shown above, in a case of this type equalization occurs when the amount of each category sold is the same fraction of the amount which would be sold at marginal cost prices. In this case the constant fraction that will produce the required net revenue is $\dfrac{q}{Q} = 0.8$, with $q_1 = (0.8)(275) = 220$, $q_2 = (0.8)(120) = 96$, $p_1 = 16$, $p_2 = 8$, and the marginal cost of net revenues in both categories is

$$z = \frac{0.8}{2(0.8) - 1} = \frac{1}{2 - 1.25} = 1.333.$$

As compared with the situation where prices were made proportional to marginal cost, at $p_1 = 14.9$ and $p_2 = 11.9$, the consumers of q_1 are worse off by $(16 - 14.9)(220) + (0.5)$ $(16 - 14.9)(225.5 - 220) = 245.025$; the consumers of q_2 are better off by $(11.9 - 8)(72.6)$ $+ (0.5)(11.9 - 8)(96 - 72.6) = 328.77$, with a slight reduction of 1.99 in the net revenues of the operating agency for an overall net gain on balance of 81.755.

The optimum level of subsidy

The concept of the marginal cost of net revenues can be a useful tool for arriving at the optimum level of subsidization. In balancing the cost of obtaining additional net revenues by raising prices of transportation services and thus reducing the required level of subsidy, against the cost of raising revenues by other means, it is desirable to equate the marginal cost of net revenues from the transportation agency with the marginal cost of obtaining additional revenues by other means such as taxation. Most taxes do, in fact, impose costs on taxpayers over and above the net revenues realized by the levying agency, whether in the form of administrative costs, taxpayer compliance costs, or a general interference with the efficiency of the economy resulting from the fact that most taxes do drive market prices further away from marginal costs. For a government with a well-designed and well-administered tax system, under moderate degrees of fiscal pressure, this "marginal cost of public funds" coefficient may be in the neighborhood of 1.1, indicating an "excess burden" of taxation of 10 percent at the margin. For a government struggling along on the brink of disaster and able to balance its budget only by extreme measures, or having resort to inflationary finance to any considerable extent, the figure may be closer to 1.5.

For example, a recent increase in the subway fares in New York, involved, according to data developed by Steven Fischer on the elasticity of demand at various times, as evidenced by subsequent reductions in traffic volumes, a marginal cost of net revenues of about 1.4. It would seem that it should be possible even in New York City to find sources of revenue with a lower marginal cost that this.

Reconciling the interests of gainers and losers

A frequent objection to such a principle of rate making is that it equates the gains of one class of users with the losses of another, or perhaps the burdens of the taxpayers, and that such interpersonal comparisons are illegitimate and the whole procedure therefore unwarranted. Transportation in general, however, and freight transportation services in particular, are largely intermediate products. Hence the benefits or burdens of any rate change will eventually be diffused very widely, so that to a considerable extent the gainers from a reduction in the rates for one class of service will be the same individuals as the losers from the concomitant increase in other rates, or from the increase in the general level of taxation, acting in a different capacity, so that the balancing off is largely with respect to the same individuals. When the question is posed not in terms of whether a specific rate change should be adopted, but rather whether rates in general should be based on a principle of maximizing the excess of gains over losses as measured in this way, rather than by an arbitrary method of cost allocation, it would probably prove difficult to find any individual who would be made worse off as a result of the whole series of changes.

To be sure, if there is a major salient change in a given area that is to be considered as a separate issue, such that one can suppose that there will be a substantial class of net losers as well as net gainers, and if there were reason to suppose that the losers are generally either better or worse off economically than the gainers, or are in other ways more or less entitled to consideration, then some appropriate differential in evaluation of the marginal cost of net revenues derived from the two groups might be called for. The degree to which this should be done, however, is in large part a political decision which cannot ordinarily be decided on in terms of strictly objective economic analysis. But a refusal to make adjustments where no such considerations intervene, on such grounds as that abstract justice or fair competition requires that prices be based on some form of full-cost allocation, or some principle in conflict with that of maximizing aggregate net gains, would in many cases amount to taking $2 out of a man's left hand pocket in order to be able to put $1 in his right hand pocket. This procedure is often accompanied by solemn assertions that justice or equity requires it, but the individual concerned might not think much of such justice if he fully realized what was happening.

Allowing for the presence of close substitutes

Another type of situation where the equality of the marginal cost of net revenue criterion requires modification is when a particular service is a close substitute for another, or that users are prepared to switch from one service to its substitute depending on the relative level of rates charged. If this elasticity of substitution were extremely high, so that a relatively small price differential would induce large numbers of users to switch, the applicable rule would require that the price differential between the two services should correspond closely to the marginal cost differential as long as both services are likely to be used. Otherwise users will make wrong decisions in deciding which of the two services to use. The equality of differential aimed at is an absolute differential in terms of the units of the two services that substitute for each other, in order that the user in choosing between the two services shall choose correctly in terms of a comparison of the relative value or convenience of the services to himself and their relative costs in terms of resources supplied by the remainder of the community.

Proportionality is in most cases not the correct relationship. For example if it costs $2 to provide a rush hour round trip from suburb to city by commuter train, and $6 per round trip to provide the highway space needed for the same trip during rush hours by private automobile, a proper choice of mode will not be induced by a system in which each mode is subsidized by 50 percent, so that the highway round trip costs the commuter $3 in highway user charges and the rail trip only $1: the commuter would then be induced to use his car when he considers the advantages to him might be $3, or $1 more than the difference in the cost he must himself bear, but $1 less than the difference in the cost to the community. If a $1 subsidy is provided to the rush hour commuter, then the sudsidy for the private auto round trip should be no greater than $1, leaving a level of charge of $5 per round trip. On the other hand, should the subsidy to the auto user be fixed at $3 per round trip, then the only way to induce an efficient choice on the part of rush hour commuters would be to subsidize the train round trip to the tune of $3, i.e., to *pay* each commuter train rider $1 per round trip, rather than charging him a fare. Obviously this in turn would have disadvantages in inducing a number of trips to be made in order to collect this bonus that clearly are not worth their true cost.

An example that illustrates the complexities that can arise even in a relatively simple real life situation is the ingot molds case decided June 17, 1968, by the Supreme Court. Here the marginal cost of carrying ingot molds from Pittsburgh to Steelton, Kentucky, had been determined to be $4.69 by rail, while the marginal cost for the competing barge-truck service was determined to be $5.19. Faced with barge-truck competition for the traffic at a rate of $5.11 (which would seem to indicate that the barge-truck route was offering to haul the traffic at a net loss!) the railroads had applied in 1963 for permission to lower their rate from $11.86 to $5.11. That application had been turned down by the Interstate Commerce Commission, on the ground, apparently, that since the "fully allocated" costs were determined to be $7.59 for rail and approximately $5.19 for the barge-truck route, the latter had the "inherent advantage" and was entitled to have its carriage of the traffic protected. Here, efficient allocation of the traffic would call, on the above principles, for the maintenance of a rate differential of 50 cents for the rail rate below the barge-truck rate, so as to reflect the difference in marginal cost, so that only those shippers to whom the service provided by truck-barge shipping would be worth 50 cents more than the service provided by the railroad would ship by truck-barge. This condition could have been met by requiring the barge rate to be raised to $12.36, 50 cents above the rail rate, or by lowering the rail rate to $4.61, or by any other combination establishing this differential. In the case at hand, it was claimed that the shippers fairly uniformly preferred the rail service, and that all traffic would in fact move by rail unless the truck-barge rate were significantly below the rail rate. Thus any rate pattern with the barge rate above the rail rate would have, for the time being at least, produced an efficient routing. Maintenance of the appropriate differential would, however, be desirable in order to faciliate the economic use of barge lines by an future shippers who might locate themselves more conveniently to the water than the rail route: for example if a plant were at the water's edge with a dock but no railroad siding.

In the above case, the Supreme Court upheld the ICC position, holding, in effect, that the meaning of the phrase "recognize and preserve the Inherent advantages of each" (mode of transportation) in the Transportation Act, and of the proviso in section 15a(3) that "rates of a carrier shall not be held up to a particular level to protect the traffic of any other mode of transportation, giving due consideration to the objective of the national transportation policy declared in this Act," were insufficiently definite to warrant the Circuit Court's reversal of the ICC position, and that the ICC was entitled, though not required, to use fully allocated cost in determining inherent advantage.

The Supreme Court decision can possibly be defended on the ground that it was upholding the authority of an administrative tribunal whose competence in the special economics of transportation could be presumed to be greater than that of the Court. It is difficult to defend the ICC position on economic grounds, however. In terms of the traffic under consideration, it should have been amply clear that efficiency required that the shipment move by rail. Even in terms of fully allocated costs—while truck taxes may be considered the equivalent of an allocation of the cost of the highway—nothing was Included in barge costs to reflect any significant allocation of the cost of waterway Improvements, let alone any rental payment for use of the scarce carrying potential of the waterway in its natural state.[9] About the only justification one could adduce for the result would be to the effect that an extra cost of 50 cents per ton, plus whatever added inconvenience the use of the barge-truck route entails for shippers, would be an acceptable price to pay for the preservation of the multiplicity of modes of transportation—though how one would determine the importance of this objective remains obscure. Possibly, too, at this point the ICC was trying to refute those who had claimed that the ICC had become a captive of the railroad industry that had been for so long a period its dominant concern.

From a longer run point of view, there is not only the substitution between modes and routes between given points, but substitution between alternative origins or destinations to be considered. If the existence of a competing mode such as water transportation, is allowed to cause a reduction in the available freight rates along the favored routes, this may cause an uneconomical concentration of Industry along the favored routes, if the excess of freight rates above marginal cost is smaller along these routes than elsewhere. As long as the water mode rates are relatively close to marginal cost—either because the economies of scale are inherently

---

[9] As with any scarce natural resources, when the capacity of a natural waterway is so limited that costly expansion is called for, proper resource allocation involves the imputation of a rent. Significant congestion does apparently occur on the Ohio river: see "Congestion Tolls and the Economic Capacity of a Waterway", by Lester Lave and Joseph S. DeSalvo, *Journal of Political Economy*, Vol. 76, No. 3, May/June 1968.

smaller than for railroads, or because the overheads are financed by government and not fully covered by tolls—it will be impossible for unsubsidized railroads to lower rates generally to where their margin above marginal cost is no greater than for the water mode, and distortions will occur. If subsidy to railroads is ruled out, the only really general solution to this problem would be to raise the rates on the water mode so that they will exceed their marginal cost by as much as the rail rates do. This might involve the earning of a substantial profit on that part of the traffic that continues to move by water at such rates, which might be absorbed by higher tolls on improved waterways, by special taxes, or by combining water and rail transportation into one organization that could handle internally the cross-subsidization thus called for.

In many cases, however, the choice may be between moving by water and not moving at all; or between using a remoter, cheaper source of raw material rather than a closer more expensive source that involves less transportation or even using no common carrier transportation at all. In such instances, the raising of transportation rates on route A above the marginal cost to prevent undue diversion of traffic from other routes B (where rates have to be higher than marginal cost for financial reasons), may cause even more damage by suppressing traffic that would never have moved by route B in any case but which could afford to pay something above the marginal cost for route A.

On a political level, if a locality is served by a mode having an especially low average cost (e.g., waterways) indignant howls are likely to arise from the local Chamber of Commerce if impediments are placed in the way of lowering the rates on at least one mode to a level reflecting this "inherent natural advantage" of the location.

This protest would be fully justified if the average cost of the localized mode (e.g., water) were actually below the marginal cost of the generalized mode (e.g., rail). They would be somewhat less fully justified if merely the full marginal cost of the localized mode, (inclusive of whatever externalities may be involved) is les than the marginal cost of the generalized mode. In the latter case the justification is in terms of making economical use of a facility already in place and in operation, regardless of whether the original outlay for its construction could be fully justified by the subsequent cost savings. Even in such a situation, a rate differential larger than the differential in marginal cost would be conducive to inefficiency through giving the favored locality a degree of advantage not warranted by the relative costs. If the only effect of the availability of the localized or specialized mode would be to secure particularly favorable rates for traffic which actually (on a marginal cost basis) would be most cheaply handled by the generalized mode, complaints of this sort would be entirely unjustified.

It is, however, politically very difficult to deny a group of shippers the right to use a transportation mode at rates that cover its own full cost. Indeed, the language of section 15a(3) would seem to bar the ICC from raising water rates to protect the traffic of a competing rail route. And in some cases the competing mode may be open to exploitation on a private or contract basis that would make regulation of this sort extremely difficult. On the other hand, politically significant protest is also likely to arise if rates for given commodities in a particular locality are markedly higher, for comparable distances and by the same mode, than for other comparable communities. Such differentials are much easier to defend against public criticism if they are between different modes—even though the implications for economic efficiency and locational choice may be no different. Thus if a shipment by rail to Steelton, Kentucky were granted a lower rate because of potential waterway competition, there would be a greater tendency for, say, Sparrows Point, Maryland, to complain that it was being discriminated against by higher rail freight charges than if the lower rates to Steelton were confined to barge—even though the competitive relationships would be substantially the same whichever mode was actually used. The outcome in the ingot mold case may, indeed, represent the torturing of the statutory language and the perversion of economics to reach a result selected (consciously or otherwise) on the basis of its being expected to be relatively free of political repercussions of this kind.

Allowing for monopoly user and complementarity situations

Another situation in which deviation from the simple rule of equalizing the marginal cost of net revenues may be desirable on grounds of economic efficiency is when the consuming industry is itself a monopoly, whether contrived or natural, regulated or unregulated. In such cases the selling price of the monopolized output will generally be substantially above the marginal cost to the monopolist. If an increase in the transportation charge is made this will result in (1) lowering the profit-maximizing output in the case of the unrestrained monopolist, (2) lowering the output at which a normal rate of profit can be earned in the case of a regulated monopoly, or (3) causing a monopolist who for one reason or another is pricing his output on an average-cost-plus-reasonable-profit basis to raise his price and thus lower his output. In such instances, there will be an additional loss of efficiency due to the increase in transportation charge. For each unit by which the output of the final product is reduced, the additional loss will be measured by the excess of the price of the final product over the marginal cost to the monopolist. This loss will be over and above the loss indicated by the marginal cost of net revenues as calculated in terms of the demand and cost curves for the transportation service supplied to the monopoly. An upward adjustment must be made to the initial estimate of the marginal cost of net revenues, to allow for this additional loss of efficiency, and this will result in the appropriate rates for such services being lower than they would be adjudged to be without this adjustment.[10] This implies, perhaps somewhat surprisingly, that for economic efficiency the freight rates for shipments to a monopolist should be lower than for shipments to a firm operating in a highly competitive field. On the other hand, if one were to take the position that providing an additional dollar of profit to a monopolist should not weigh as heavily in the setting of freight rates as the providing of an additional dollar of consumers' surplus to ultimate consumers, one might want to modify this position somewhat, or even reverse the indicated rate discrimination.

A very similar analysis applies where the particular transportation service is highly complementary to some other service being sold at a price that is substantially above its marginal cost. Here again, an increase in the rate for the particular transportation service will reduce the use of the complementary service and induce a loss of efficiency in the use of that service as well as in the use of the particular transporation service. Here also, an upward adjustment in the marginal cost of net revenues for the transportation service is called for, with a corresponding reduction in the rate charged.[11]

---

[10] Suppose, for example, a monopolist selling a product in a market with a demand of $Q = 500 - 10P$, requiring one unit of transportation purchased at a price of $p = 5$ for each unit of output, and other marginal costs of 15 per unit. Maximum profit will occur at a price $P = 35$, $Q = 150$, $G = 2250$. If the transportation rate is raised to 6, his maximum profit will occur for $P = 35.5$, $Q = 145$, $G = 2102.5$, so that consumers will have lost $(35.5 - 35)(145) + (0.5)(35.5 - 35)(150 - 145) = 73.75$, while the monopolist will have seen his gross profits before fixed charges fall by $2250 - 2102.5 = 147.5$. Gross transportation revenues will increase by 120 from 750 to 870. If the marginal cost of the transportation service is 3 per unit, costs will increase by 15, leaving a net revenue gain of 105 attained at a cost of $147.5 + 73.75 = 221.25$, giving an incremental cost of net revenues of $221.25/105 = 2.107$. If the incremental cost of net revenue had been computed from the demand curve for transportation, with $Q = 150$ at $p = 5$ and $Q = 145$, at $p = 6$, the cost to the user would have been calculated as $145(6 - 5) + (0.5)(150 - 145)(6 - 5) = 147.5$ (which happens to coincide with the loss of profits to the monopolist without taking account of the loss to ultimate consumers), for an indicated incremental cost of net revenue of $147.5/105 = 1.405$.

[11] Suppose, for example, a rail service with a marginal cost of $5 per passenger connecting with a boat service with costs consisting of $80 per day of fixed costs plus variable costs of $1 per passenger. Demand for the through trip is given by $Q = 100 - 5P$, where $P = P_r + P_b$ is the combined charge for the through trip, equal to the sum of the fares for the separate legs: there is no separate demand for either portion of the trip. If the rail price is set at $9, and the boat company operates as a profit-maximizing monopolist, taking the rail price as given, the boat fare wil be set at $6, bringing the combined through fare to $15, at which rate there will be 25 passengers per day, yielding a profit for the boat service of $45. If the rail fare were raised to $9.40, a profit maximizing monopolist would be induced to lower the boat fare to $5.80, for a total fare of $15.20, at which fare 24 passengers per day would make the through trip, yielding a profit to the boat operation of $35.20, a reduction of $9.80. In addition, passengers would lose $24($15.20 - $15.00) + (25 - 24)(0.5)($15.20 - $15.00) = 4.90, for a total net loss of $14.70. Rail revenues would be increased from $25($9.00) = 225.00 to $24 ($9.40) = 225.60, and costs would be reduced by $5(25 - 24) = 5, so that net rail revenues would increase by $5.60, implying a marginal cost of net revenues of $14.70/5.60 = 2.625$. If the loss had been measured solely in terms of the demand for rail service, without regard to the impact on the efficiency of the boat service, the loss would have been $24($9.40 - $9.00) + (25 - 24)(0.5)($9.40 - $9.00) = 9.80, giving a marginal cost of net revenue of $9.80/5.60 = 1.75$, a substantial understatement of the full cost.

If, on the other hand, the boat service were operated on a break-even basis, as a result of regulation or otherwise, then if the rail rate is set at $9.00, the boat rate required to just

If the affected enterprise making use of the service as an input or producing the complementary service is effectively regulated or is publicly owned or is organized as a cooperative so that the rate reduction will be passed on to ultimate consumers, one can view the indicated rate adjustments in favor of such users not only as economically efficient but also as not obviously unjust or improper. If the affected enterprise or industry is characterized by unrestrained monopoly, on the other hand, the results would be subject to modification unless one were willing to consider a dollar placed in the pockets of the monopolist to be just as significant for the welfare of the community as a whole as a dollar placed in the pockets of consumers generally. Considering the likelihood that there would be considerable political demurrer to any such proposition, a fairly wide consensus might be expected for a policy of not carrying out such adjustments quite to the full extent indicated by the pure efficiency criterion. Just how short one should stop would, to be sure, be difficult to determine: such a question is fundamentally a political matter rather than one of pure economics.

Imperfect competition among users

In a large number of cases the user industries are neither fully competitive nor completely monopolized, but operate in that ill-defined and often somewhat chaotic state variously termed imperfect competition or monopolistic competition. It is tempting to assume that since such situations are in some respects intermediate between the extremes of perfect competition and perfect monopoly that the appropriate policy to adopt would be one intermediate between that appropriate for monopoly users of the service and that appropriate for competitive users. However, such is not necessarily the case. It is quite possible for situations to arise where a reduction in the transportation charges to a given industry would simply result in a proliferation of varieties and an intensification of nonprice competition through advertising, promotional efforts, or embellishments of the product in ways such that the ultimate gain to the consumer would be only a fraction of that indicated by the demand curve for transportation.

The opposite, to be sure is also possible: the monopoly case is sufficient evidence for that. Moreover, if attention is focussed on transportation

---

cover expenses will be $3.00, resulting in a combined through fare of $12.00 and 40 passengers per day. If the rail fare is raised to $9.29, the boat rate required to break even will rise to $3.11, for a total of $12.40, at which rate there will be 38 passengers per day, resulting in a slight profit for the boat operation, due to rounding, of 18 cents. The rail revenues will be increased by $38($9.29 − $9.00) − (40 − 38)($9 − $5) = 3.02 net, after allowing for the reduction in costs of $5 each for the 2 passengers no longer travelling. The cost of this addition to net revenue will be the loss to the passengers of $38($9.40 − $9.00) + (40 − 38)(0.5)($9.40 − $9.00) = 15.60. Allowing for the small profit of $.18 gives $15.42 as the net cost of securing the $3.02 of net revenues for the railroad by this rate increase, or a marginal cost of net revenues of $15.42/3.02 = 5.11$. If the cost had been computed solely in terms of the demand for railroad service, we would have had $(38 + 40)(0.5)($9.29 − $9.00) = 11.31 as the burden on the customers, giving a marginal cost of net revenues of $11.31/3.02 = 3.75$, a very high figure but still substantially below the actual figure of 5.11.

charges for highly differentiated finished goods—as contrasted with reatively more uniform raw materials—a lowering of transportation charges may have a significant effect in increasing the competitiveness of the industry by making products produced in different locations closer substitutes for one another. The result would be a greater range of choice for the individual cosumer, lower profit margins, and greater efficiency generally. This is over and above the effect calculable from the economies of scale that are likely to exist in at least mild form in any firms producing highly differentiated products.

Actual results that are likely to be produced under conditions of imperfect competition are however so highly uncertain, depending as they often do on intangibles of posture, attitude, and expectations, that even for situations specified in considerable detail it is difficult to make reliable estimates of the specific consequences of transportation rate changes. It is probably not too wide of the mark to treat these situations as lying somewhere between the monopolistic and the competitive user cases. The one exception is the proposition that in general economic efficiency may be promoted by setting rates on differentiated final products somewhat lower, relative to rates on standardized commodities, than would otherwise be indicated.

II. Externalities, congestion, and peaks

Any attempt at evaluating marginal costs for purposes of determining the appropriate level of a particular set of rates must take into account the direct nonmarket impact of the transportation operation on the environment and in particular on the costs associated with other traffic. Such effects are often substantial, and their neglect and lead to a serious loss of efficiency.

The externalities most commonly thought of involve the contribution of various forms of transportation to the impairment of the environment through smoke, noise, smog, fire hazard and the like. Concern for such externalities is of long standing, early examples of the concern being the banning of steam locomotives from Manhattan Island, requirements for spark arresters on locomotives, and the like. Currently, increased concern is being expressed over the contribution of the automobile to air pollution. It has been estimated that the contribution of the automobile to air pollution in New York accounts for damages amounting $400 per car annually. Drastic pollution reduction requirements have been established by law for automobiles produced beginning in 1975, with lesser standards in earlier years, but it remains to be seen whether these standards will in fact be insisted on in the face of assertions from the automobile industry that they are unable to meet them within any reasonable cost limits. A recent proposal in Washington, D.C. for a special tax on cars entering downtown parking lots during the morning rush hour and remaining more than four hours was premised on the proposition that this would help the District meet the standards set up by Federal anti-pollution legislation.

Ideally, externalities such as air pollution should be dealt with by evaluating the impact of the emission of a given amount of additional pollution on the remainder of the community, and then levying a corresponding charge on the activity responsible for the emission. This will then serve as an incentive for those responsible for the pollution to take appropriate steps to diminish their contribution to it, as well as raising the cost of products whose production involves pollution. Thus consumers will be stimulated to shift their consumption to other less polluting substitutes. There will be a tendency for pollution abatement expenditures to be distributed among different sources of pollution so as to achieve the maximum of pollution abatement for a given direct and indirect cost or conversely to minimize the cost of achieving any given level of abatement. Achieving a given level of pollution abatement by administrative or legislative standards of performance runs the serious danger that inadequate incentives will be provided for those who can readily do much better than the standards require and that many activities will be required to bear extremely high costs in order to meet the Federal standards relative to the contribution they thereby make to the level of abatement.

As applied to transportation, the imposition of appropriate charges for air pollution, noise (especially of aircraft), and other externalities would mean that a fairly steady and uniformly applicable incentive would be provided for all forms of externality abatement. This would include the development of cleaner and quieter running engines not only as new models but in terms of modifications to existing engines, shifts to mass transit and to less polluting forms of propulsion, and shifts in routing and timing to minimize the impact of the externalities. High-pollution automobiles could be relegated to rural use to finish out their useful life, with urban transportation supplied by vehicles with better pollution performance. In the event that a change to electric vehicles for certain purposes becomes desirable, appropriate incentives would be given to users to make the shift (in those cases where the characteristics of the electric vehicle make this easiest), avoiding at the same time the knotty problem of how to maintain an equitable balance between the users of the two types of vehicles during the inevitable interim period when vehicles of both types will necessarily be operating currently.

The practical problem with the application of such charges is in the measurement of the amount, time, and place of pollutant emission by each unit. The difficulty is sufficiently serious for stationary sources, but with transportation, the source typically moves about between densely populated areas where pollution effects can be serious and unpopulated areas where it may be of relatively little concern. For railroads, airlines, and possibly some common carrier trucks, the problem may in fact be solvable without too much difficulty through establishing pollution ratings for different categories of vehicles. The ratings could be determined on the basis of tests made on a random sample of vehicles at random times, and by estimating the contribution of the fleet to the relevant types of pollution from records of the schedules operated by the various vehicles. For private vehicles, however, the problem is much more serious. Nevertheless it may be possible to adapt methods of levying congestion charges, to be discussed below, to assess charges with respect to pollution externalities as well.

Highway congestion costs

While air pollution is the transportation externality currently most in the public eye (literally, in the case of some irritants!) the externality with respect to which the greatest immediate gains are possible is the congestion of automobile traffic in downtown city streets and on expressways and arterial highways in large metropolitan areas. Indeed, while the nominal pretext for the proposed $1 per day parking tax for Washington mentioned above was the need to diminish air pollution, the particular form of tax adopted was largely justifiable in terms of congestion. Congestion costs are not only high, they are also heavily concentrated at specific times and locations, and possibilities for substitution of other routes, modes, or times are often available at relatively low cost or inconvenience. Failure to charge the individual user for the very high costs of the congestion he generates so that he will take them into account in his choice of the manner and extent to which he will use facilities is especially serious. The absence of adequate charges relating to congestion is responsible for major easily avoidable wastes in terms of inefficient utilization of current facilities, costly constraints on the way new facilities to be constructed are planned, and substantial distortions in the patterns of development of metropolitan areas.

It might seem at first glance that since motorists impose congestion costs on each other, so that the costs are largely borne within the automobile-using sector, this represents an adequate account of the cost. This is far from the case, however. A motorist who plans a trip under congested conditions may correctly anticipate that it will take him 5 minutes longer than under uncongested conditions, and will ordinarily take this into account in making his choice as to whether to make the trip then, or by another mode, or at another time, or perhaps not at all. The making of the trip under congested conditions is likely, however, to cause additional delays adding up to at least 5 minutes and possibly as much as 20 to 30 minutes to other motorists. The impact of any one motorist on any other motorist may be slight and even imperceptible, but in the aggregate when many motorists make similar decisions based only on the delay they themselves expect to experience, the result may add up to an almost catastrophic traffic jam.[12]

The implication of congestion costs for current types of rate-making policy is, of course, that in setting rates for modes competitive with the congested mode one must take into account the fact that full marginal cost on the congested mode will usually be higher than the marginal cost as computed without regard to congestion. If the rates or costs to the users for the congested mode are lower than the full marginal cost, there is then reason for setting the rates for the competing mode below marginal cost by a corresponding amount, revenue requirements permitting. At

---

[12] In "Traffic Studies and Urban Congestion, *Journal of Transport Economics and Policy*, January 1968, p. 34, R. J. Smeed indicates that a formula of the form $q = a - bv^2$ will fit quite closely to the data for central cities in England, where q is the volume of traffic per unit width of roadway and v is the speed. For central London, values of $a = 68$ vehicles per hour per foot of width and $b = .13$ vehicle hours per foot per square mile were found to fit the data. If we put v_o for the speed under light traffic conditions ($q = 0$), the equation can be written

$$q = a[1 - \frac{v}{v_o}{}^2].$$

If we put

$$z = \frac{1}{v} - \frac{1}{v_o}$$

for the delay for one vehicle going on mile, then $Z = zq$ is the total delay per mile per unit width of roadway, and

$$\frac{dZ}{dq} = z + q\frac{dz}{dq}$$

is the increment in the delay caused by increasing traffic by one unit. Of this, the first term z is the delay experienced by the additional motorist himself, and $q\frac{dz}{dq}$ is that imposed on others. If we look at the ratio of delay caused to others to the delay experienced by oneself, we find that

$$r = \frac{q\frac{dq}{dz}}{z} = \frac{k(k + 1)}{2},$$

where

$$k = \frac{v}{v_o};$$

k is thus the ratio of the no-congestion speed to the actual speed. Under low congestion conditions where $k = 1$, delays inflicted on others are about equal to those experienced oneself; if congestion is such as to cut speed down to half the no-congestion speed, $k = 2$, and the congestion imposed on others is three times that experienced oneself.

The situation may be considerably different on expressway and other routes not dominated by delays at intersections. Here, significant delays are less apt to be encountered until volumes are substantial, but are then likely to set in much more sharply. Data for the Lincoln Tunnel in New York were fitted very closely with a curve of the form $z = A q^B$ with $B = 4.5$. In this case, $r = B$, and the delay imposed on others in the Lincoln Tunnel case turns out to be uniformly 4.5 times that suffered oneself.

Where queuing conditions develop, the relationship between delay inflicted on others and delay experienced oneself may become quite erratic, depending on the total duration of the queue subsequent to the passage of the vehicle in question. If a bottleneck begins to back up a queue at 7:30 a.m. which is not worked off until 9:30, a motorist arriving at 7:35 may find that the queue is still quite short and he may accordingly be delayed himself for only a minute or so; he nevertheless causes the length of the queue to be increased by one car from the time he arrives to the time the queue is worked off at 9:30, or a total added delay of 115 minutes. Conversely, a car arriving at 9:15 may be delayed for 10 minutes but cause only 5 minutes of delay to others if the drop-off in the volume of traffic after the peak is fairly sharp.

least, the competing mode rate should be lower than if congestion were not a factor.

Congestion tolls

A more important implication is that charges for the use of congested facilities should be designed to bring these matters home to the user. It is not enough to include these costs in some overall set of user charges as rough average amount. Because the costs vary so widely according to time and place it is essential that the charges vary also according to time and place so as to conform reasonably well to the pattern of costs or they may do more harm than good. Fortunately, recent technological developments have made possible a number of techniques for assessing such charges in close conformity to the requirements of assessment related to current marginal cost.[13] One relatively unsophisticated method would involve prepaid licenses to be exhibited during the chargeable use, after tabs have been detached or stamps affixed in appropriate combinations to indicate the time and nature of the usage being paid for. It would be possible to arrange for used licenses to be returned for credit of the unused portions of the prepaid value against the purchase prices of additional licenses. This would permit the schedule of charges to be varied in a more flexible manner so as to produce efficient utilization of the available facilities. Another device is a license that can be chemically activated at the time use is initiated, as by stripping off a protective sheet, with the chemical reaction then turning the license a different color after a fixed lapse of time, to indicate that the license is then no longer valid. A scheme that involves a somewhat more advanced technology involves cables laid in thoroughfares to be energized in various combinations at various times so as to trigger a counter on all cars passing by, payment being made periodically according to the reading of the counter. Still another uses devices for scanning response units of various kinds located on the vehicle, the response determining the identity of the vehicle and its location at the particular instant, either as within the range of one of a large number of scanners or by triangulation of the time phase of the response at a smaller number of scanners, the information being assembled and processed by a central computer to produce an appropriate monthly bill. There is no dearth of methods for imposing whatever scale and pattern of charges may be considered appropriate, and at reasonable cost.

Queuing costs and peak-hour tolls

The need for pricing on such a detailed basis, and especially for varying charges according to time of day is illustrated most vividly in queuing

---

[13] See R. J. Smeed: *Road Pricing—the Economic and Technical Possibilities* (London: H. M. Stationery Office, 1964).

situations. In such situations an appropriately graduated toll can often, by reducing the waste involved in waiting in the queue, raise substantial revenues without imposing any substantial burden on the user at all, and indeed in many cases leave the typical user better off paying the toll and spending less time in the queue than he was in the original situation.

The way in which this rather striking result can be achieved is as follows: we first observe, over a suitable number of typical days, the average delay that a car passing the bottleneck point at a particular time during the morning rush hour will have experienced in the queue, at, say, five or ten minute intervals throughout the normal duration of the queue. Using some assumed average value which the typical motorist is thought to place on a reduction in the delay for the car and its occupants, a provisional toll pattern can be determined. The imposition of this toll pattern should result in approximately eliminating the queue, while maintaining traffic flow throughout the period at close to the capacity of the bottleneck, on the assumption that flow through the bottleneck was largely independent of the length of the queue as long as a substantial queue persisted. Subsequently, further adjustments in the toll schedule can be made in the light of experience, the toll being increased at any time when a substantial queue, longer than necessary to smooth out random fluctuations in traffic, regularly persists, and the toll being lowered whenever the average flow through the bottleneck at that time drops substantially below capacity.

In the simple case where all motorists plan with full knowledge of conditions, in terms of the time they wish to arrive at their destination, and place the same value on the loss of time in the queue, each motorist will find that his preferred time for passing the bottleneck is the same with the toll as it was with the queue, so that motorists will in general pass through the bottleneck at the same time as they did previously. The only difference will be that they will leave home later by the time they formerly spent in the queue, and pay a toll which is the equivalent of this time saving. They are, individually, no worse off than they were before; the toll revenue is being collected without imposing any net burden on them at all. The waste represented by the waiting in the queue has been converted into a revenue to the community. Here, indeed, is a fiscal bonanza: a source of public funds with a marginal cost of zero!

But this is not all! The above result was obtained on the assumption that all motorists had a uniform value of time per car.[14] But this value will in fact be higher for some cars than for others; it will tend to be higher for cars with several occupants than for one, for motorists on urgent missions, such as trips to a hospital or when trying to meet a tight schedule and for motorists with high incomes. If, for example, we have a situation where 60

---

[14] Actually, the same qualitative results will be obtained if we assume merely that the value of time varies only with the time the cars pass the bottleneck, with all cars passing the bottleneck at approximately the same time having approximately the same value of time.

percent of the motorists value their time at $2 per hour, for this purpose, and 40 percent at $5 per hour, the level at which the toll must be set will in general be governed by the preferences of the $2 per hour motorists, who will tend to adjust their travel times to the availability of bottleneck capacity at various times, whereas the $5 per hour motorists will to a greater extent ignore the (for them) relatively small toll variations and travel at their preferred times. In this situation the $2 per hour motorists will in general be no worse off than before, even though they have shifted their time of travel: the inconvenience of the shift to them is less than the saving in toll, and they would have been just as well off as before had they travelled at the same time. On the other hand the $5 per hour motorists gain substantially by in effect paying $2 per hour for time saving. Those prepared to pay the toll can now get to their destinations without delay at any time, a privilege which formerly was not available at any price.

Another source of net gain to motorists from the imposition of such tolls is in the incentive it gives for increasing the number of persons per car. With queuing, there is no saving in queuing time *to the individuals involved* if they ride in fewer cars, whereas with the toll there is the toll saving as an inducement. To the extent that this occurs, it can only be at a further net gain to those involved, since they continue to have the option to ride separately and pay the added toll, which on the above assumptions was shown to leave them no worse off than originally. To the extent that this happens, the total number of vehicles using the facility will tend to fall, the level of toll required to eliminate the queue will be lowered, and motorists generally will find themselves paying a lower toll than that which they would have been willing to pay to save the time wasted by the queueing delay.

A flat toll undifferentiated by time of day would have a much less salutary effect, since there would be no financial inducement to travel at one time rather than another. If off-peak traffic demand is relatively more responsive to changes in toll levels than peak hour traffic, which seems frequently to be the case, and if the off-peak traffic is a fairly large part of the total, the net effect of an increase in the toll on the off-peak traffic might lead to so much inefficient underutilization to the facility during those hours as to outweigh the beneficial effects during the peak, so that the overall effect would be a reduction in efficiency.

Moreover, it is of considerable importance that the toll vary fairly smoothly rather than in one or more large jumps. If substantial jumps in toll occur at times of heavy traffic, briefer periods of congestion just before each increase or just after each decrease are likely to be generated, along with a certain amount of jockeying by motorists attempting to beat the increase or dawdling to wait for the decrease. If the toll is flat throughout the peak period and is raised or dropped only at times when traffic is well below peak, in order to avoid creating these "mini-peaks", relatively few of the present peak hour motorists will be willing to make the substantial shift in timing needed to take advantage of the lower toll, so that less peak abatement would occur than by several individuals shifting each by a small amount, as would occur with a smoothly varying toll.

Even if sophisticated general roadway pricing methods have not yet been instituted, where toll collection facilities of the conventional type exist, it would be a relatively simple matter to institute a system of varying the toll smoothly according to time. For frequent users it would be possible to issue charge cards which would be inserted by the user in a slot at the toll gate, where a record would be made of the user's number and the amount charged (the amount charged also being displayed), and the card returned to the user, the records would then be processed at suitable intervals and bills sent to the user, together with a charge card for an appropriate subsequent period in the case of users that are not delinquent in payment. Users without charge cards could be charged a gross toll at the maximum rate, but given a refund voucher for the difference between the amount paid and a net toll slightly above that charged on the charge cards. These vouchers could then be cashed when presented in suitably large batches. Or occasional users could simply be charged a maximum flat toll, or a toll changing in large jumps but remaining sufficiently above the charge account toll to keep the number of such users down to a level where any bunching or delay at the time of toll change would be inconsequential. It is essential to keep the time required for toll collection down to a level approximately that required for present tolls, otherwise the capacity of the facility may be impaired unless costly enlargements of toll plazas are undertaken.

There may be a small minority who could be adversely affected by the institution of such queue-eliminating tolls, specifically those who value their time at substantially less than the bulk of the users, so that the reduction in queuing time is of less moment for them than the increase in the toll. Many such persons, however, will receive adequate compensation through the benefits they obtain from the services financed from the toll revenues, whether or not related to transportation, or from the reduction in other taxes that these revenues make possible. For example if peak-hour toll revenues are used to reduce tolls formerly charged at off-peak times, the peak-off-peak differential required to eliminate the queue may be reached with a smaller net increase in the peak toll than otherwise; moreover the motorists with low time preference rates would have the opportunity to travel off-peak at a lower charge than before.

Optimum routing of traffic

Another situation of some importance where tolls seem essential if efficient use of facilities is to be obtained is where traffic divides between routes through urban centers and circumferential routes. If the volume of the through traffic is large and the route through the center is sufficiently shorter so that under relatively uncongested conditions it is faster than the bypass, the tendency may be for the through traffic to divide between the circumferential and the central routes in such a way that the time required by the two routes is equalized. If an attempt is made to improve access from *A* and *E* at opposite sides of the city in the situation illustrated by Figure 5–2 by improving the central artery *ACE,* the net result may

Figure 5–2

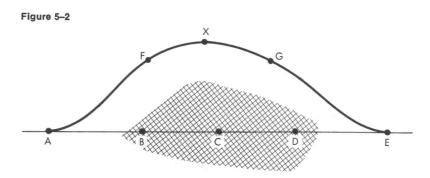

simply be to attract more through traffic to this route and off the circumferential route until the time required for the *ACE* route is again the same as that for the circumferential route *AXE.* In the extreme case where there is a relatively large volume of through traffic and the circumferential route *AXE* was ample enough to have relatively little congestion originally, the traffic may switch rather rapidly from *AXE* to *ACE* until the time required to go from *A* to *E* on this route is just as great as via *X,* and since this is roughly the same as before, the net result may be that nobody can get anywhere any faster after the "improvement" than before. If a suitable toll were imposed on the central route, it could be preserved for those who have no attractive alternative. Again, the toll revenues may be obtained almost without any net burden being imposed on motorists. The toll-free improvement may, indeed, be worthless precisely because it is free!

Even though the improvement may not become absolutely worthless, and indeed even in the worst cases there are likely to be substantial periods of the day or week when total traffic volumes are sufficiently low so that it does provide a significant improvement in access to *C,* its potential value to the community will be substantially impaired if it is underpriced. The alternatives to some form of pricing seem to be the following: (1) Tolerate a substantial degree of congestion on central arteries, at least during peak hours. (2) Deliberately degrade the central artery, as by leaving out a short link near *C,* making the route fairly satisfactory for trips to or from the immediate neighborhood of *C,* but inhibiting the use of this route by through traffic between *A* and *E.* Unfortunately this will also similarly impair the potential usefulness of the route for traffic between *A* and *D, B* and *E,* or *B* and *D,* for which no good alternatives may be available. (3) Build the ACE link to such capacity that it can handle all the through traffic likely to develop, relegating the circumferential route to the service of such traffic as that between *A* and *G* or *F* and *E.* This last, indeed, is what seems to be happening in many areas. It can be done, but the cost often becomes astronomical. Building high-capacity arteries in the core of a metropolitan area can cost three to five times as much as routes of comparable capacity in outlying areas, while the adverse neighborhood effects in terms of pollution, noise, and interference with cross traffic can also be considerably more serious.

In those areas where tolls actually exist, their pattern is, more often than not, quite perverse from the standpoint of optimum routing of traffic. Tolls on the San Francisco Bay area bridges are lowest on the heavily congested Bay and Golden Gate bridges, and higher on the Dumbarton, San Mateo and Richmond-San-Rafael bridges that are almost never seriously congested. With the exception of the Golden Gate bridge, all of these are operated by the same authority so that overall budgetary constraints do not seem to explain the pattern. Rather the explanation seems to be that there is a tendency to adhere slavishly to an "every tub on its own bottom" dogma and potential political opposition rooted in local particularism to any too obvious subsidization of the facilities used more heavily by residents of one area out of excess revenues generated by a facility used more heavily by residents of another locality. From the standpoint of the region as a whole, there would be everything to be gained and nothing to lose from an increase in tolls on the Bay bridge and possibly on the Golden Gate bridge, coupled with the elimination of tolls on all the other bridges in the area. Again, traffic between O'Hare airport and Indiana points has a choice of using the uncongested Illinois Tollway or of avoiding tolls by contributing to heavy congestion on the Dan Ryan and Northwest expressways passing close to the Chicago Loop. Traffic from the Holland Tunnel to Brooklyn can either run down West Street and pay a toll to use the Brooklyn-Battery Tunnel, or cross Manhattan along Canal Street to contribute to some of the heaviest congestion in New York to reach the free Manhattan Bridge. Instances of this sort could be multiplied.

Congestion and stationary vehicles

The problem of congestion is not limited to moving vehicles, but arises also with respect to stationary vehicles, even aside from their impact on movement in cases where such vehicles block or impede movement. In many areas the inability of vehicles to find space in which to make deliveries or even to park reasonably close to their destination is a major source of inefficiency in roadway utilization. Some of the worst congestion in New York is in the garment district, where in spite of drastic restrictions on truck lengths and other regulations the lack of any charge for the use of the street generates conditions that have already driven considerable segments of the industry out of town. Trucks appear to preempt parking space early in the day and to a considerable extent remain without making any adequate attempt to do their business promptly and clear the space for others. If a suitable rental were charged for the occupancy of this space, a proper incentive would be created for expeditious loading and unloading, possibly using manpower more intensively for this purpose; greater encouragement would also be given to increased nighttime deliveries and pickups. In the long run a more nearly adequate number of off-street loading bays would be provided, even in the older buildings where it is difficult to make the owners provide them by fiat. The difficulty of determining administratively for which buildings such bays would be worth the cost would be bypassed by giving owners an incentive to provide them and avoid parking charges.

The issue arises in a more familiar context in connection with the parking of passenger cars. Here a rather strong sentiment has grown up that a kind of "freedom of the road" entitles a car owner to park his car on the public street either without charge or at purely nominal charges that usually fall short of reflecting the real scarcity of the space involved. Even off-street parking is often provided with an outright subsidy or is provided in excess of the amounts that would be demanded at rates sufficient to defray the full costs as a result of various types of zoning requirements and building codes, sometimes in a frantic attempt to lure motorists to drive downtown in order to patronize the various attractions of the central city.

Not only is the resulting diversion of additional resources to the provision of parking space of highly dubious long-run economic efficiency in itself, but the patterns of utilization of the existing space seriously compound this inefficiency. Much of the regulation of curb parking is in terms of time limits which are only very imperfectly correlated with the relative urgency of the errand for which the car is being used. Even where parking meters are used, the maximum time limits and the rates charged are typically such that it is the time limit and not the rate that is the controlling factor. Curb parking rates are almost universally far below the level of rates charged in nearby commercial off-street parking facilities, in spite of the fact that for most purposes the curb parking, if available, is more convenient than the off-street space.

In terms of strict economic efficiency, the ideal curb parking fee structure would be one in which the rate per hour varies from time to time in such a way that space is nearly always available within a reasonably short distance for those willing to pay the rate, while on the other hand as long as the number of vacancies exceeds that necessary to assure would-be parkers of being able to find a space promptly and conveniently, no charge would be made. Here the marginal cost of occupying a space consists of the added expenditure of time and effort by someone who would have liked to have used the space but is driven to search elsewhere. When alternate space nearby is readily available, marginal cost of space occupancy is close to zero, while if finding an alternate space involves extended search or possibly the use of much less convenient space, the cost can be very high.

The common parking meter is at best a clumsy device, in that even when no limit is placed upon the amount of time for which prepayment can be made, there is no way of charging different rates for different periods of the day, and even a permanent change in the rate, such as might be called for by shifts in patterns of demand or the availability of nearby space, involves a fairly expensive mechanical alteration of the meter. Meters also cut up the curbside into bays of fixed length that must be large enough to accommodate the larger cars, resulting in inefficient use of the space by smaller cars. A number of alternatives are possible that avoid the rigid demarcation of bays, permit prepayment for any required length of time, and permit the rates to be varied in a fairly sophisticated way according to time of day and also to be changed readily to meet changing conditions.

One method that has already had a certain amount of use in other contexts is to provide vending machines set up at suitable intervals in the area in which parking is to be controlled, from which the parker can buy one or more time-stamped tickets to be placed in the window of his parked car. The amount of time paid for can be determined by the number of tickets bought in accordance with a posted schedule. Overtime parking would not be quite as conspicuous as with meters, but with a little practice enforcement personnel should be able to cover the ground almost as quickly as with meters. If this causes difficulty a slightly more complex vending machine should be able to be made to issue a single ticket with an expiration time stamped on it. A possible alternative or adjunct to such ticket-vending machines would be to allow regular or frequent parkers to buy packets of licenses which they could validate for the specific use just before use. Another possibility is that regular parkers could provide themselves with clockwork meters which could be rewound at servicing stations upon the payment of the appropriate fee in advance, then set to run down when the car is parked at a rate appropriate to the space occupied and the time, with suitable indication to outside inspection of the rate at which it was running. By stopping the meter when he returns to the car, the parker would have to pay only for the time actually parked, rather than, as at present, paying for the maximum time he expects to be away when he originally parks. There may also be ways in which payment for parking can be integrated with payment for movement on the streets, with or without the use of meters.

The important point is that by such means it should be quite feasible to create a situation where anyone can be fairly sure of finding a convenient parking space at any time, and almost anywhere where parking space is available at all, provided that one is willing to pay the corresponding price. This could be accomplished with only a relatively minor reduction in the number of cars parked on the streets in the areas of high demand: a 5 percent vacancy ratio should be sufficient to make the difference between a situation in which many potential private car trips are just not made (or are made by other modes because of the difficulty of finding a convenient parking space at the destination), and a situation in which such trips can be made with confidence and convenience. Parking space that is free, or underpriced, is thereby made, if not worthless, at least worth very little, if it is then in fact available only to those who can so organize their lives as to be on the spot at a time when they can preempt it to the exclusion of later comers who would derive much greater advantage from its use, at least in terms of what they would be willing to pay.

Costs of providing for peak traffic

It might appear that the higher levels of congestion costs during peak hours occur only because the facilities are inadequate and that if over the years an adequate highway system were constructed the occasion for these high charges would disappear. Indeed until relatively recently there appeared to be a tendency on the part of the general public—stemming primarily from automobile interests but not effectively opposed by others—to demand that roadspace be supplied in sufficient abundance to reduce congestion to a negligible level, even in the absence of tolls other than for a limited number of specific facilities. We are becoming increasingly aware, however, that the costs of doing this are likely to be extremely high, both in financial terms and in terms of environmental impact. For intelligent decision making, however, we need more than a general impression of high cost, or rough determinations of the overall costs of providing added facilities to take care of peak hour use.

How heavy these costs are, when reduced to a vehicle-mile basis, will of course depend on the duration of the peak. It is obvious that to provide facilities to take care of peak loads that occur for, say, only one hour a year on the average would be absurdly costly. But the standard proposed on occasion by the Bureau of Public Roads—that roads should be built to have a capacity sufficient for the thirtieth busiest hour during the year—is, under some circumstances, hardly less extravagant. To begin with, it is patently absurd to use the same standard for rural highways and for urban highways costing up to ten times as much. The situation is also quite different if the thirty hours of maximum traffic are three evening hours on ten summer Sundays, (with traffic rarely reaching a fifth of thiis level for most of the remainder of the year) than where the thirty hours of maximum use are the rush hours on a couple of weeks in December, with the corresponding rush hours of other weeks of the year close behind. Even on a basis of 3 hours of peak use for each of 300 weekdays a year, or 900 hours per year, the costs can be sufficient to give pause.

Construction costs for grade-separated expressways can vary from around $300,000 per lane mile in favorable rural locations with few grade separations or building demolitions and no severe grading or right-of-way problems to from $1 million to $5 million per lane mile and even higher in high-density cores of metropolitan areas. Taking $1 million per lane mile as a basis, charging 8 percent for interest, amortization, and maintenance related to weathering, amounts to $80,000 per year. Figured at 50 weeks per year, this is $1,600 per week, which at 18 peak hours per week, is about $90 per hour. At a capacity flow of 1800 cars per lane per hour (average headway 2 seconds), which is rather more than can usually be achieved with reasonable safety except at relatively few points under ideal conditions, this works out at 5 cents per car mile, as contrasted with roughly 1 cent per car mile that is paid in user taxes of all kinds. The more expensive $5 million-a-lane-mile stretches would on this basis be costing 25 cents per car mile for peak hour use. At this rate it is not difficult to run into cases where providing for commuters making a 15 mile trip each way each day during peak hours would involve costs of from $3 to $5 per day and even more, in addition to any parking or vehicle operating costs.

To be sure, it is overstating the case somewhat to charge the full cost of the system against the peak-hour user, even though significantly fewer lanes and routes would be considered an adequate system were it not for the peak hour traffic. Having a six-lane rather than a four-lane expressway is of some value to the offpeak user in that it permits slightly higher speeds; more importantly, it appears to reduce in most cases the risk of accidents, and also may considerably reduce delays that occur as a result of accidents or breakdowns that block one of the lanes. Also if two routes are available in a corridor rather than one, some off-peak travellers may be able to select a shorter route. But even when full allowance is made for these factors, It is clear that the private rush-hour private-car commuter is often paying in user charges only a minute fraction of the costs which he is imposing at the margin on the rest of the community. He is, in effect, being subsidized, often to an extent measured in hundreds of dollars a year. The subsidy can be thought of as being paid in part by off-peak users of the same facilities, in part by users of rural arterial highways that often generate revenues substantially in excess of their costs, and by the failure to make any charge, in the balancing of the highway receipts against the highway costs, for rental of the area used for, or the taxes on the capital invested in, public street and highway facilities.

Commuter fares and peak-hour charges

This subsidy to the private-car commuter has had an almost catastrophic impact on mass transit systems as the competition of the automobile has increased. In many cases, even if mass transit were offered on a completely free basis the annual subsidy per passenger for the peak hour transit or suburban train rider would be far below that being offered the private-car commuter. With present highway user charges it would be necessary to offer the commuter a bonus for using the transit facility if optimal choice between the modes is to be induced.

The development of a rational fare structure for rapid transit service has been seriously hampered by this competition. Were it not for this competition rational fare structures would involve drastically lower fares for off-peak as compared with peak-hour riding, providing a suitable incentive for those who can do so to avoid the peak hours. In cities such as New York and other large cities throughout the world the degree of cross-elasticity between transit and automobile is still slight enough for many of the transit services (though possibly not for railroad commuter lines) so that such fare differentiation would be well worthwhile, even though to maintain the financial balance it might be necessary to raise the peak fares at the same time that the off-peak fares are lowered. Elsewhere, however, especially in the medium sized and larger cities in the United States, an attempt to charge peak hour transit riders a fare corresponding to the full marginal cost of the longer trips would, without corresponding charges on automobiles, cause a serious increase in rush-hour highway congestion, by driving peak-hour commuters to increased use of private automobiles.

On the other hand, in most cases the elasticity of demand for rush-hour travel is less than that for off-peak travel, so that if the externality involved in the increase of rush-hour automobile traffic is either negligible or is not a consideration to the transit operator, substantially better results can be obtained with a differentiated fare than with a given uniform fare. Even where marginal cost is uniform (as where an adequate schedule frequency requires substantial numbers of empty seats at all times), the elasticity differential would be sufficient reason for lower off-peak rates, and *a fortiori* if marginal costs are higher during peak hours. Nevertheless, in spite of a few modest attempts to offer reduced rate "shopper's special" or "senior citizens' " off-peak fares, the prevailing pattern, where differentiation exists at all, remains one of lower rates for regular commuters who are predominantly rush-hour passengers.

Transit operators are prone to defend the low rates offered regular commuters on the ground that regular riders are entitled to a discount for their regularity and predictability. Indeed, considerable sentiment has been expressed in the transit and commuter railroad industry in favor of charging a premium fare for "snow-birds" who flock to the transit system when weather conditions make driving difficult (in Europe the phenomenon occurs in rainy weather with respect to bicycle riders), partly to preserve the amenities of the system for the regular riders. But since the congestion in bad weather will be alleviated just as much by the shifting of the travel of a regular customer off this special peak as by the discouragement of a snow bird, there would be no reason to exempt the regular passenger from a bad weather surcharge, if one were applied. Some discount to the regular commuter is, to be sure, justified on the basis of the reduced costs of collecting the fares, but commuter fare reductions usually go considerably beyond this modest level.

When low off-peak fares are considered by transit operators, they are often rejected on the ground that they do not pay—i.e., that the elasticity of off-peak demand is less than unity, so that, for example a reduction of 20 percent in these rates results in an increase of traffic of less than 25 percent and hence in a reduction in gross revenues and an even greater reduction in net revenues to the extent that total costs increase as a result of the increased traffic. This, in effect, ignores the fact that a reduction in rates to off-peak riders, even if it lost net revenue, would benefit those paying these lower rates by an amount substantially greater than the loss in revenue, and that presumably the benefit on account of these rides could be made to justify a required increase in the peak rate to recoup the revenues. Indeed, since in many cases the peak and off-peak riders are the same persons, or at least members of the same families, the offsetting would be immediate. In terms of the marginal cost of net revenues, this cost is in such circumstances very much higher for revenues obtained from off-peak riders than from peak riders, both because price exceeds marginal cost by a higher margin and because marginal cost exceeds marginal revenue by a lower margin.

Free transit service

In the smaller cities and towns the maintenance of a satisfactory schedule frequency often implies a peak load per bus of considerably less than the seating capacity of a full-sized bus. In such a case, the long-run marginal cost even of peak service is likely to be measured by the incremental cost of operating a larger rather than a smaller bus, which can be relatively negligible. If in these circumstances the operation is in the hands of an agency that is eligible for subsidy, the optimum positive fare that would balance the marginal cost of net revenues with the marginal cost of public funds from other sources might be quite small, and the cost of fare collection might loom large relative to the other gains in efficiency produced by collecting this optimum positive fare rather than no fare at all. The alternative of providing free service can in such circumstance well prove the best alternative.

The gains from instituting free service rather than a given positive fare would consist of (1) the excess of the value of the additional riding over its marginal cost for those passengers who would have been willing to pay more than the marginal cost but less than the fare previously charged, (2) the savings in the cost of collection, including the maintenance of the collection apparatus and the time personnel spend in checking out their receipts, (3) the improvement in the quality of the service through eliminating the delays involved in fare collection and the inconvenience to the passengers of paying fares, and (4) the improvement in conditions on congested highways from which the additional passengers have been diverted. The costs to be offset against these gains would consist of (1) the costs of securing the equivalent revenues from other sources and (2) the excess of the marginal cost over the value of the service for those additional passengers carried who would not have been willing to pay a fare equal to this marginal cost. A further consideration would be that the fare revenues would be derived largely from lower and middle income groups on very close to a per capita basis, so that nearly any alternative source of revenue likely to be seriously considered as a source of the replacement revenues would have a more progressive incidence. Indeed, if one had started from a situation where transit service had historically been considered a free public service and were considering the institution of a fare as a form of tax, this tax would in many cases rate as one of the worst substantial taxes in the lexicon of public finance, as judged in terms of its high cost of collection, its adverse impact on the economic allocation of resources, and its highly regressive incidence.

Critical financial situations

Much the same can be said concerning increases in a fare that is uniform over peak and off-peak periods when this fare is substantially above the off-peak marginal cost level. In extreme cases where the transit operation is close to the point of being unable to operate profitably at any fare level, increasing fares in an attempt to balance costs with revenues can involve an extremely high marginal cost of net revenue, indeed approaching infinity as the point is approached where even an unconstrained monopoly could barely make ends meet. Under such circumstances a subsidy to transit operations can yield very high returns indeed.

Again, where severe limits are for one reason or another placed on the degree to which a transit operation can be subsidized, imposition of congestion tolls may also pay very high dividends through increasing the demand for transit service at ranges of fare where the marginal cost of net revenues is very high. In some cases, a service of great value to the community can be preserved that would otherwise succumb.

Effects on the need for separate rights-of-way

In some of the larger cities the problem is not one of complete abandonment of mass transit but rather of whether to undertake major investments in specialized transit facilities. In such cases congestion tolls may make it possible in many instances to avoid the high cost of providing a separate right-of-way for transit vehicles, whether bus or rail. Without tolls, heavy congestion may make it difficult or impossible to provide an attractive transit service on public streets and highways, particularly as transit vehicles may be constrained to use congested routes in order to provide convenient intermediate loading and discharge points. A costly separate right-of-way which can often be utilized only to a small part of its capacity may in the absence of congestion tolls be the only satisfactory means of freeing the transit service from this congestion. With congestion tolls, a flexible and diversified bus service on the public highways and streets may be quite satisfactory, possibly even more so than a service constrained by the need to use a limited number of separate right-of-way routes.

Accident costs

Transportation externalities occur not only as noise, air pollution, and congestion delay, but also in the form of accidents. The total cost of highway accidents in the U.S. in 1967 was estimated at from $8 to $12 billion, depending in part on the extent to which allowance is made for "pain and suffering" as distinct from strictly monetary loss. This is of the same order of magnitude as the entire outlay out of highway funds for construction and maintenance of highways. More recent estimates making fuller allowance for intangible costs have put the figure for the annual cost of accidents as high as $40 million.

Not all of this cost is borne by roadway users as such, even in an average sense. For one thing, much of the cost of injuries to pedestrians, damage to wayside property and the like is borne by the victim, either through lack of legally demonstrable fault on the part of the operator of the vehicle, failure to press a valid claim because of the costs and inconvenience involved and the uncertainty of recovery, inability to identify the guilty party, lack of insurance coverage or financial resources on the part of the offending party, or other reasons. In addition, much of the cost is borne by other segments of the community in ways which do not become part of any charge for highway use, such as payments under various forms of non-automobile insurance, Blue Cross, and the like; employers' sick-pay provisions; social security and welfare payments, and so on. It seems not unlikely that there is a subsidy to highway users through such channels of around $1 to $3 billion per year, or possibly more.

It is not sufficient, even so, to consider merely the average cost of accidents and their impact on the non-automobile community, for the impact at the margin differs considerable from the average impact. For example, if two cars collide, the entire cost of the accident is in an *ex post* sense a part of the marginal cost of *each* of the trips involved, on the assumption that no such accident would have occurred had either car not been there. Double counting would be correct, here, for purposes of computing marginal rather than average cost. To some extent this double counting may be thought of as being a counterpart of a rental charge that might be made for the use of the scarce roadway space: if each vehicle had had its separate roadway, the accident would presumably not have taken place. If each participant is required to pay, as part of the price of his trip, the full cost of the accident, the duplicate payment could be thought of as a rent being paid for the use of the facility, and a high level of such payments would be indicative of a need for improved facilities.

Accidents are, by and large, not paid for by motorists on an *ex post* basis, but almost entirely by the payment of the insurance premiums *ex ante,* and even where the payment is *ex post,* as in the case of accidents not covered by insurance, the decision on whether or not to make a given trip is based on expectations as to this cost, to the extent that such decisions are influenced at all by expectations regarding accidents. If the impact of decisions as to the making of trips on the cost of accidents is to be correctly brought home to the decision maker in such a way as to have an appropriate influence on his decision, it is the effect of added trips on accident cost that is relevant. Unfortunately, this relation is far more complex than even the above example of the two car accident would suggest: some accidents involve more than two cars, some only one, and the presence of an additional car may even under some circumstances avert an accident that would otherwise have occurred. Data bearing on the relation between traffic flow and the incidence and costs of accidents for given characteristics of the highway, time of day, and weather conditions are scarce and such data as there are have generally been collected with other objectives in mind. It seems fairly clear, however, that for the bulk of the conditions encountered by highway traffic, increases in the flow of traffic on a given roadway produce an increase in at least the total number of accidents, and probably also in their total cost, that is greater than in proportion to the increase in traffic flow. For instance data for freeways in California, covering four-, six- and eight-lane sections over a period of three years from 1961 to 1963 show fairly clearly that the marginal incidence of accidents is about 1.5 times the average incidence. That is, a

10 percent increase in traffic flow on a given facility of this type will result in a 15 percent increase in the number of accidents.

Even this figure must be treated with some caution. There is some indication that at very low levels of traffic the accident rate per vehicle mile declines slightly with increasing traffic, but it is not clear whether this is a genuine long-run phenomenon accounted for perhaps by the beneficial effect of a minimum amount of traffic in keeping drivers alert and warning of curves and obstructions at night, or whether it is simply a transitory phenomenon resulting from the fact that most of the very low traffic flows are recorded on segments relatively recently opened to traffic, with lesser familiarity on the part of drivers and possibly unfinished exits and entrances contributing to a higher accident rate. Moreover these data relate to the number of accidents and not to their cost, and a complete analysis would have to allow for differences in the average severity of accidents under different conditions. There is also some indication that deaths are less frequent per vehicle-mile on high density routes than on low density routes, but the average cost per accident may nevertheless be higher on the high-density routes because of the greater likelihood of multiple vehicle involvement. At any rate, it is clear that even if highway users paid, on the average, the full costs of highway accidents, this would fall short of a payment intended to bring home to users, at the time of their decision as to the nature of their use, the impact of their decision on probable accident costs, at least in terms of a short-run analysis.

The faulty impact of insurance premiums

Even to the extent that highway users as such do bear the burden of accident costs, it is largely done in a manner not conducive to their being taken suitably into account in decisions affecting highway use. Insurance premiums are usually paid on the basis of the automobile year, and while some attempt is made to vary the premiums in accordance with the mileage the insured expects to drive during the year, this is usually in terms of very broad categories. Categories are based on such indicia as whether or not the car is driven to work and if so whether the trip distance is over or under a specified limit. To a considerable extent the classification of the risk is based on statements of the insured that are often difficult to check, and competitive pressures keep the variation in rates relatives to such criteria within relatively narrow limits. In most cases there is very little to cause a driver to consider the impact on the cost of accidents of decisions he might make concerning the use of a car already insured, at least to the extent that this cost is covered by insurance.

An exception to this may occur when a decision is being made as to whether or not a younger member of the family is to be allowed to drive the car, as this does have a significant effect on the premium, at least if such driving becomes known to the insurer. However, while cars having younger drivers do as a class have a substantially higher loss experience than others, and thus from the standpoint of the insurer require a substantially higher premium, in those cases where the decision is so marginal as to be likely to be affected by the premium differential, the use contemplated to be made of the car by the younger driver is likely to be minor and so lead to actual exposure much lighter than the average exposure with respect to which the premium is adjusted. In this case the deterrent provided by the premium differential is likely to be far greater than would be appropriate to represent the additional expected average accident cost involved in the decision and thus lead to undue stinting in the incidental or occasional use of cars by younger drivers. For drivers having an exposure more nearly corresponding to the premium charged, the decision as to whether or not to drive at all is much less likely to be sufficiently marginal to be affected by the premium differential.

A similar phenomenon occurs with respect to decisions as to whether or not to maintain a car at all, especially if it is a second or third car. Even though discounts are often offered for a second or third car insured by a given household, in cases where the question of maintaining the car is sufficiently marginal to be influenced by the cost of the insurance, the amount of exposure the maintenance of the car would add (as distinct from the amount the particular car happens to be driven, if another car would be used for many trips if the given car were not maintained) is likely to be relatively small, and the actual increment to the accident cost that would be involved in the decision is likely to be substantially less than the added premium cost. Thus the structure of insurance premiums is in general one which leads to excessive use of a given stock of cars and undue stinting with respect to the stock of cars held for use.

Correction of this situation would require that the cost of insurance against accidents be allocated more nearly in proportion to mileage driven. For driving in uncongested areas where the incidence of accidents is generally lower (as indicated by insurance rates) and does not vary too widely, a suitable means of assessing this cost on motorists would be by an increment to the motor fuel tax. For driving in congested areas, the cost of the added incidence of accidents over what is covered by the fuel tax could readily be added to the congestion cost proper in establishing the level of congestion tolls discussed above.

Such a payment for accident costs through added fuel charges or congestion tolls would, indeed be a substantial step in the direction of greater governmental or public agency participation in the accident compensation process than at present. But since present policy writing and premium collection procedures appear to cost as much as 30 percent of the amount collected, such a method of collecting the charges would represent a very substantial saving in unproductive overheads, a consideration probably much more important than any element of abstract justice associated with the variations in premium rates obtaining under present classificatory practices of the underwriters. Indeed, since the single, 19-year-old unmarried male driver could not avoid the payment of an especially high premium even if he drove with consummate skill and caution, the justice of the present scheme could well be characterized as guilt by classification. And as we have seen above, the incentive pattern provided by the suggested mode of payment would be greatly superior to that provided by present premium scales.

Collection of charges through governmental or public channels in this way need not, however, entail the payment of claims through a governmental agency. One possibility would be simply to farm out to the lowest bidders the liability for settling claims against various groups of registered automobiles. With suitable packaging of groups of automobiles for such bidding, it should be possible to get the job done at about the same cost as this phase of the operation is currently costing. Nevertheless, when it is realized that at present only about 45 percent of the value of the premiums collected ever reaches the ultimate claimants, the rest being absorbed in commissions, underwriting expenses, costs of investigation, litigation, and the like, it is readily seen that wide scope for improvement on this score exists, and even the most inefficient conceivable social insurance system would find it difficult to do worse.

"No-fault" Insurance

Indeed as a result of dissatisfaction with this situation, and especially with the rapid increase in premium rates over the past few years a considerable sentiment is gathering momentum in favor of so-called "no fault" insurance, the main thrust of which is to eliminate the costly and time-consuming procedures associated with the presently required determination of which party is at fault in an accident in order that the indemnity payments can be assigned accordingly. To the extent that these costs can be eliminated or reduced, this represents a real reduction in the overall cost of accidents, as well as a reduction in the congestion in the courts, though the opponents of no-fault claim vigorously that this is done only at the expense of reducing the deterrent to accident-courting behavior embedded in the fault principle. As was seen above, however, by the time this principle is filtered through the process of the writing of insurance, very little of this deterrent is left. If this point of view were followed to its logical conclusion, the recommendation would have to be that automobile tort liability insurance, far from being compulsory, as it increasingly is, should be forbidden, or at the very least that all tort liability insurance policies should contain a substantial deductible amount to be borne by the party at fault without recourse to insurance, the insurance covering only that part of the risk that the insured could not well afford to carry personally. Actually, of course the reverse is true: collision insurance can be purchased with various deductible amounts, but with respect to liability to others the insured is always covered for the full amount and thus in practice gets off scot-free.

However, while the no-fault principle avoids litigation over the issue of fault, leaving injured parties in most cases to recover from their own insurance companies, it leaves open to dispute the amount of damages, which in the case of bodily injury can also be a costly procedure unless, indeed, the amount to be paid for various types of injury is tied to a standardized scale. But while a standardized scale can be reasonably satisfactory in workmen's compensation cases where the circumstances of the victims vary only within a relatively narrow range, the circumstances of automobile accident victims vary much more widely and make any such standard scales much less satisfactory. Genuine reductions in costs of claim settlement, therefore, are much less than might at first be assumed. In order to obtain the maximum possible reduction in accident insurance costs on behalf of motorists, promoters of no-fault insurance have included in their proposals various measures to limit the amount of the awards to be paid claimants. Thus provisions are frequently inserted severely limiting or eliminating the amounts presently payable under the heading of "compensation for pain and suffering" and requiring victims to make use of other sources of compensation such as sick pay, hospital insurance, and income tax deductions and limiting the compensation receivable from the automobile insurers to the resulting net balance. The net effect is to further reduce the extent to which motorists bear the costs of the accidents which result from their actions, increasing the subsidy to the automobile sector from outside sources, and doing little or nothing to bring premium payments closer into line with the extent of actions leading to accidents, even if it be admitted that in a broad sense every motorist is "at fault" the moment his car leaves the garage.

While it may be entirely proper, through abating claims to the extent that other sources of compensation are available, to eliminate situations where the victim can actually profit from his misfortune through duplicate compensation, and it may also be desirable to eliminate or curtail payments for pain and suffering on the ground that the determination of the amounts in individual cases is too difficult or costly, this does not detract from the desirability of requiring the motorist to pay, as a price for engaging in his dangerous activity, a premium covering a full estimate of the costs on both of these counts, or even one that is higher than this to the extent that marginal accident costs exceed average accident costs. Even if the funds generated by such premiums cannot, for practical reasons, be distributed to victims, these amounts should still be collected and the excess not required to make payments to victims collected by the state as a kind of rental payment for the use of the roadways.

Congestion in mass transit

Congestion cost is a feature of other forms of transportation also. In railroad operations, for example, the time spent by a freight-train crew waiting on a siding for a passenger train to pass is a marginal cost of operating the passenger train (as well as a marginal cost of operating the freight train), though it is likely to show up in the cost accounting exclusively as a cost of freight train operation. Double counting is again correct here for purposes of computing short-run marginal cost: to some extent, again this is the approximate counterpart of the rent of the physical plant that would be included in a long-run marginal cost: if a separate track were constructed for the passenger train the passenger service would be paying for this track instead of for having the freight train wait its turn for the use of the joint track.

In subway service, congestion is often felt in terms of slower operations resulting from extended station stops, and in discomfort due to crowding or inability to find a seat. In the short run, additional traffic may occasion no additional costs to the operating agency; the marginal cost may be entirely a matter of discomfort to fellow passengers. Ideally, if there were no excess burden of taxation so that the marginal cost of public funds is 1.0, and if the operating agency adjusted the service optimally, the medium run marginal cost, calculated as the marginal cost to the operating agency of increasing the service so as to accommodate added traffic while maintaining the same quality of service, would be equal to the short run marginal cost in terms of deterioration in the quality of service due to added traffic being crowded into the same number of cars operating.

In practice, imperfections in the tax structure make it desirable to stop short of such a balance, and here again the concept of the marginal cost of net revenues can be brought into play. Given imperfections elsewhere in the economic system, it would be appropriate to adjust service so that the short-run marginal costs, in terms of added discomfort to passengers due to crowding, exceeds the medium-run marginal cost, in terms of outlays for expanding the service at constant quality, by a ratio corresponding to the marginal cost of net revenues that is being used as a basis for other adjustments of the system. In effect, the marginal cost of an increment in net revenue secured by cutting back on the service is the short run marginal cost in terms of the discomfort experienced by the passengers.

Not many transit operators are prepared to look at the matter in this light, however, Whereas highway agencies have often used a figure of about $1.55 per vehicle hour in evaluating benefits from projects involving savings in vehicle time (equivalent to about $1.00 an hour on the basis of an average occupancy of 1.55), transit operators often pay no attention to opportunities to spare their passengers waiting time on unprotected street corners and far from cozy subway stations at a cost of 20 cents per passenger hour or even less. Considering the far greater comfort enjoyed by those sitting in cars held up by traffic as compared to those waiting for a bus or train, this seems a relationship scandalously out of line, even considering the relative affluence of transit and automobile riders.

Airport and airway congestion

Another important type of congestion is found in and around airports. For most airports serving small and medium sized cities, an airport capable of handling the larger commercial airliners is nearly always able to handle most of the traffic that normally offers itself under current conditions, at a marginal cost that is either entirely negligible or is readily reconciled with the usual scale of landing fees and other charges, and that in any case varies relatively little with traffic volume. But in perhaps a dozen to a score of the busier airports in the United States and perhaps an equal number in other parts of the world, traffic is already so heavy that serious delays frequently occur, and while the impairment of safety does not transgress established standards, the impairment may be of some economic significance.

The marginal cost of allowing a plane to land at Kennedy during a busy period when there are perhaps 100 transport planes due to land subsequently before the stacked queue is finally worked off during an ensuing period of slack demand can easily be evaluated at several hundreds of dollars. The cost is, to be sure, not completely independent of the size of the plane, but while data that permit an appraisal of the way in which this cost varies are scanty, it is clear that in most cases the cost varies, for planes of various sizes landing at a given time, much less than in proportion to the weight of the plane, which is the basis for most landing fees. A better basis, in most cases, would be a classification of the plane according to which of the various types of runways available at the airport are normally capable of handling the landing and take off of the plane. Even more important than the landing or takeoff characteristics of the plane is the time at which the operation occurs: the cost can vary over time both systematically according to the regular daily and weekly traffic pattern and erratically with weather conditions.

Another factor affecting landing costs is the sequence of planes and the traffic mix. A light plane in the middle of a sequence of transports can require substantially more rather than less runway time than a transport would in the same position, because of the difference in approach speeds and the greater susceptibility of the lighter plane to the residual turbulence in the wake of the large plane. Constructing a schedule of landing fees or other charges to reflect the influence of all of these variables on marginal cost is thus a potentially quite complex matter.

There may be some doubt as to whether charges should vary according to adventitious weather conditions. While costs certainly vary rather sharply with the weather, and charges that take the weather into account would probably exert a considerable influence on some of the nonscheduled traffic, the difficulties of administering such charges, involving assigning a classification to the weather status at each point in time, with consequent disputes, plus the fact that for a major part of the traffic the variation of the charges with the weather would be unlikely to exert a significant effect on decisions as to whether or not to cancel schedules, are strong arguments for setting the charges independently of actual weather conditions. If the schedule of charges is to be the same for bad weather conditions as for good, it should probably be based almost entirely on the good weather conditions: any increment in charge large enough to have a substantial effect in curtailing the number of bad weather operations that are attempted and hence in curtailing the wasteful queuing and stacking on such occasions is likely to have a serious impact in curtailing the operations in good weather below the capacity level. But even if it be considered necessary to have a predetermined schedule of charges, there is no doubt that a schedule of charges high enough during periods of heavy demand to reduce queuing under normal conditions to relatively brief delays needed to even out uncontrollable momentary fluctuations in traffic volume would have a salutary effect in improving conditions at the busier airports.

One beneficial effect would be to sharply curtail interference by general aviation planes with transport operations. A large proportion of such flights can be diverted to other airports with relatively slight inconvenience to those involved in them; the flights that would persist in using congested airports at times of congestion would be chiefly those where the urgency of using the particular airport at the particular time, usually for the purpose of connecting with a transport plane, would be sufficient to warrant the payment of the large fee. A flat ban on the use of such airports at such times by non-scheduled or smaller aircraft, as has at times been suggested, would be far too indiscriminate, in that many important uses of the airport would be precluded, and an important and growing source of revenues available for public purposes, with a very favorable marginal social cost, would be forgone.

Even with the commercial transport sector, such a charge would have a substantial favorable effect in promoting a reorientation of such service so as to make more efficient use of facilities. For example, a fairly large proportion of traffic at such airports as Atlanta, Dallas, OHare, and even Kennedy and Miami consists of traffic making connections that could be shifted to other airports if schedules were rearranged. Another impact would be to induce airlines to work to higher passenger loads per plane for arrivals and departures at the congested times, whether through the use of larger planes or by being more cautious about scheduling trips likely to be lightly filled. Still a further impact would be through the shifting of schedules away from the most congested hours, though to carry this out to the fullest extent would require passing the cost differential on to the passenger in some way.

Passing the cost on to the passenger would help divert traffic to surface routes for short trips where the advantage of air travel would not justify the imposition of the added congestion delays on the longer haul passengers.

In the long run, there is of course the possibility of adjustment through the construction of additional airports, though if the full cost of such additional airports were allocated to the peak traffic, the cost might be more than the traffic would bear. In some cases, moreover, such as in the Washington-Boston corridor, the congestion may arise as much in terms of sheer airspace limitations as in terms of runway capacity. In such a case, the congestion charge emerges as a pure economic rent collected with respect to the use of this inherently limited natural resources, differing from land rent charged for occupancy of the underlying metropolitan land area only in that the occupancy is of shorter duration for any one user.

Short-run marginal cost of reserved service

Even where no congestion in the usual sense occurs, as with reserved seat service, a short-run marginal cost can be derived from the impact of a given use in other users. In reserved seat service there is an *ex post* marginal cost (which is very low if in fact there are several empty seats), limited to the relatively negligible lesser comfort of passengers not able to spread themselves or their belongings over the seat occupied by the marginal passenger, plus the cost of meals, reservation services, and the like. The marginal cost will have been relatively high if a would be passenger has been turned away as a result of an individual's having made a reservation, but failing to show up. In such an event the cost is measured by the value of the trip to the person displaced, in the light of the alternatives available. That under present operating practices an average of the marginal cost so measured is in most instances far less than the marginal cost of operating more seat miles is an indication of the inefficiency of these practices, chiefly in offering far more space than would be optimal for the purpose of carrying the volume of traffic generated by the present level of fares.

One could not, of course, charge passengers retrospectively on the basis of such an *ex post* marginal cost: even if the evaluation and collection were feasible, no useful purpose would be served in this case by requiring the passenger to take his chances on how much he will eventually be charged.[15] Nor would it be satisfactory, in most cases, to auction off the entire available space on the spot just prior to departure of each schedule; not only would the procedure itself be costly and difficult to organize smoothly so as to avoid undue delays, but those turned away will have been put to fruitless effort in preparing for a trip they are unable to complete at the expected time.

A very promising procedure, however, would be to sell firm reservations in advance at a price based on the marginal cost as estimated at the time of sale. Such a marginal cost would be an *ex ante* expected value of the *ex post* marginal cost. What the *ex post* marginal cost will turn out to have been is, in turn, in part dependent on the price policy followed for subsequent sales. If subsequent sales are made at relatively high prices so that the likelihood of empty seats is high, the marginal cost will be low, and conversely if subsequent sales are made at too low a price, with the consequent likelihood of having to turn away customers for whom the value of the seat would be higher, the marginal cost will turn out to have been high. Consistency and a good approximation to the maximum attainable efficiency will be achieved, however, by following a policy of charging at any time a price which—if maintained from then on—would be expected on the average, according to the information then aivailable, to just sell out the remaining capacity by the time the schedule departs. Such a price could be considered a reasonably accurate approximation of the *ex ante* marginal cost.

This is approximately what could be expected to happen in an ideal speculators' market in seat reservations, if such a market could operate without overhead costs and with full interchange of information among speculators as to past and current sales and unsold stocks on hand, a situation very roughly approximated by organized markets in commodity futures. For travel reservations, however, any actual market of this sort would be excessively costly, given the relatively small size of the typical transaction. A reasonably close approximation to the results of such a market could, however, be achieved by setting up an appropriate scheme for determining the price at which reservations will be sold by the operating agencies to the customers, so that the price for reservations on a given schedule would

---

[15] This case differs from that of congestion tolls and parking charges, where it may be in some cases desirable to determine the charge retrospectively on the basis of conditions actually experienced at a given time, on the ground that the motorist may have prior knowledge, at the time he commits himself to a trip, of events or circumstances affecting the congestion to be expected that is either not available to toll-collecting authority or is of a nature too varied and complex to permit it to be incorporated in a prepublished schedule of tolls. In the case at hand, where most users make relatively infrequent use of the service, there is less reason to suppose that individual travellers would generally have better information about the probable demand than the selling agency, and the amount typically at stake is generally too large for the uncertainty to be borne with complete equanimity, or averaged out over a large number of occasions.

fluctuate from time to time in a manner roughly similar to that produced by the speculators' market.

One way to do this would be to establish for each departure a price to be used as the standard price, and a normal pattern of sales over time, so that if sales actually conform to this normal pattern, the expectation generated by the prior experience would be that if the price is held at the standard level the schedule will be just fully booked at the time of departure. Whenever sales run ahead of this normal time pattern, the price would be correspondingly increased, so that in spite of the apparently higher than usual demand and the smaller than usual number of seats remaining to be sold, the expectation is restored that at this (higher) price the schedule will still be just fully booked at the time of departure. Conversely, if sales run behind this normal time pattern, the price would be decreased sufficiently to create the expectation that if this lower price is maintained for the balance of the selling period, all space will just be sold at the time of departure. Prices might on occasion tend to vary fairly sharply as the departure time is approached, and sales would have to be considered final, subject to the resale at the current price for the account of the passenger if he changes his plans after purchasing his reservation.

For the longer trips especially, it should be possible to achieve average load factors of 95 percent or more, as compared to the current load factors of around 45 percent that are common. Average cost per passenger mile would be cut nearly in half, so that the average level of fares needed to break even would likewise drop drastically. For travelers with some flexibility in their plans so that they can select the schedules having the lower fares the effective fare reduction would be even greater than this, and those willing to adapt their plans to relative fares on fairly short notice would be in a position to pick up real bargains. Travelers making firm plans considerably in advance would be able to make reservations correspondingly early at rates fluctuating within a relatively narrow range, averaging much less than current fares. Executives and others needing to make a trip on a specific schedule at the last minute would be relatively certain of being able to find space even during periods of peak demand; to be sure the price might on occasion be fairly high, but rarely as high as current prices.

While a scheme of this sort might have been unworkable before the advent of electronic reservations systems, with current technology it could be implemented at relatively little immediate cost to the operating agencies. It would, of course, tend to involve travelers wishing to adapt their plans to the pattern of available prices, together with their agents, in considerable additional effort, and the multiple inquiries that this would generate would be an added burden on the airline reservations systems. This added effort would often not be worth while for the shorter trips, but for the longer trips the resulting increase in utilization and saving in overall cost would make something of this sort highly worth while.

Such a pricing scheme could be adopted fairly readily by a publicly owned transportation agency, and also perhaps without too great difficulty on main trunk routes where a substantial potential for competition exists. In situations where there is a substantial degree of monopoly, however, it would be necessary to counter the tendency of such a scheme to offer the monopolist a strong temptation to cut back on the volume of service offered so as to produce an increase in the average level of rates and hence of profits. A regulatory agency might find itself called upon to regulate not only the formulas by which levels of reservations at given times determine prices, but the volume of service to be scheduled. One way around this difficulty would be to resort to an escrow fund into which the excess of the fares charged when reservations are running ahead of the normal pattern over the standard rates would be paid, and from which the operator could draw amounts sufficient to make up the deficiency of the fares actually collected, below the standard fares, on occasions when reservations are sluggish. Insufficient service would then cause the escrow fund to grow, but the company could realize its interest in this fund only by increasing the level of service sufficiently to drive the average level of the actual "reactive" rates down below the standard rates. This would require fairly close auditing to ensure the integrity of the escrow fund operations, but should provide an adequate incentive for an operating company to maintain an adequate volume of service.

III. Congestion, returns to scale, and rents

It is sometimes claimed that highway tolls or user charges based on marginal congestion costs are not based on true costs in the same sense as prices arrived at under competition. Another claim also frequently made is that if congestion charges are collected, then any revenue derived in excess of current costs, including a return on the capital invested, should be used to finance expansion, by analogy to the tendency in competitive areas for an activity yielding more than a normal profit to attract additional investment. The answer to both of these claims, in terms of a correct understanding of the relation between current costs, congestion costs, economies of scale, and rents, is perhaps best arrived at by considering what would happen if the provision of highways could be carried on under conditions of perfect competition.

To make perfect competition conceptually possible, it is necessary to assume constant returns to scale, so that it would be possible to provide a multiplicity of small capacity roads competing with each other without sacrifice of efficiency. If highways were perfectly divisible in this fashion, so that instead of one roadway 24 feet wide we could carry the same total volume of traffic equally well on 24 roadways each 1 foot wide, and we assume for simplicity a steady level of traffic without daily or seasonal fluctuations, we could, on such assumptions, expect to find a multiplicity of roads constructed between any two given points, with a variety of toll rates and a variety of degrees of congestion to suit varying tastes and preferences of individual users. We can show that in the resulting competitive equilibrium the toll charged on the various roads by the competing entrepreneurs will at one and the same time equal both the long-run average cost per vehicle of providing the roadway and the short-run marginal quality deterioration or congestion costs associated with an increment of traffic on any one road.

That the equilibrium must have these properties may be seen as follows. Put p for the price per vehicle, q for the number of vehicle trips per hour, w for the width of the roadway, or any other measure proportional to capacity, and c for the average cost (in terms of annual capital charges including normal profits plus maintenance expenses) of the roadway per unit of width or capacity w. For simplicity we will ignore any wear and tear, which if necessary can be thought of as being financed directly by a separate charge. Then if there are to be no losses or above normal profits that would tend to induce a change in the pattern and be a symptom of disequilibrium, we must have $pq = cw$. This can be written

$$p = \frac{cw}{q} = \frac{c}{h},$$

where

$$h = \frac{q}{w} \; ;$$

h is the density of traffic relative to capacity. Thus, the price on the various roads will vary inversely with the density of traffic: users will in general have a choice between a given toll for travelling on one road, or a toll 25 percent greater for the privilege of traveling on a road having only 80 percent as much traffic per unit of capacity, and hence having less congestion. They can, in effect, rent as little or as much roadspace (in terms, for example, of acre-minutes) as they wish to occupy in the making of their trip: the more space they rent, the less congested the conditions under which they will travel. We assume an approximately continuous range of densities is available for users to choose from.

To evaluate the marginal cost of adding traffic to a particular road in terms of the resulting deterioration in the value of the service of that road to its other users, we can first put $v_i(h)$ for the value placed by the user on the ith use when that use is at a density $h,$ defined as the price the user would be willing to pay for use under those conditions rather than forgoing the use entirely. (We assume that users are indifferent as between roads with different width w but the same density h.) Then

$$(\frac{dv_i}{dh}) \, dh$$

is the change in the value of the ith use resulting from an increment in traffic density dh produced by an increment $dq = w \, dh$ on the roadway in question. Now for any use i that in equilibrium uses a roadway priced at p corresponding to a density $h = \dfrac{c}{p}$ we must have

$$\frac{dv_i}{dh} = \frac{dp}{dh},$$

otherwise the user would find it to his advantage to move either to a higher priced and less congested road or to a more congested but lower priced road, depending on the sense of the inequality. In the one case, he would value the gain in quality more than the increase in price, and in the other he would consider that the reduction in price more than compensated for the deterioration in quality. Thus, if, as assumed, the variety of roadways available provides a continuous spectrum, then although different uses of the same roadway may have different values, the differential between the value of any of these uses at a particular density h and the value of that use at adjacent densities $h + dh$ or $h - dh$ as given by

$$\frac{dv_i}{dh}\, dh = \frac{dp}{dh}\, dh$$

must be the same for all uses i for which a roadway operating at a given density h is selected. Accordingly, the marginal cost $m\, dq$ of an increment of traffic dq as measured by the total value of the impairment of service enjoyed by the other users of the same roadway, associated with the resulting increase in the density of traffic

$$dh = \frac{dq}{w}$$

is given by

$$
\begin{aligned}
m\, dq &= q\left(\frac{dv}{dh} \right) dh \\
&= q\left(-\frac{dp}{dh} \right)\left(\frac{1}{w} \right) dq \\
&= \frac{q}{w}\left(-\frac{d}{dh}\left(\frac{c}{h} \right) \right) bp \\
&= h\left(\frac{c}{h^2} \right) dq \\
&= p\, dq
\end{aligned}
$$

so that

$$m = p$$

and the competitive price obtained as the average cost per unit of traffic for the particular facility is equal to the marginal cost computed in terms of congestion. There is, therefore, in a long run competitive equilibrium under constant returns to scale no conflict between ordinary notions of a competitive price based on average cost to the operator and a marginal cost charge based on an evaluation of the adverse impact on fellow users.

In the short run in which the total roadway capacity has not yet been fully adjusted to the demand, price on the different roads will still vary inversely according to the intensity of use, at a level higher or lower than the equilibrium. Returns to road owners will constitute Marshallian quasi-rents. Any deviation from a relation $ph = k$, instead of $ph = c$, with k constant for all roads, greater than c if total capacity is below the equilibrium level, and less than c if total capacity is greater than at equilibrium, would be symptomatic of a failure on the part of an individual road owner to maximize these quasi-rents. On the other hand traffic, not being directly concerned with the cost of the roads to the owners, will still be distributing itself over the various roads in such a way that

$$\frac{dp}{dh} = \frac{dv}{dh}$$

and the above argument that the competitive price must be equal to the marginal congestion cost still holds, with k instead of c. Thus in the short run a truly competitive price would still be equal to marginal congestion cost, even when it cannot be said to equal the average cost inclusive of a normal return on the value of the capital used.

Competitive price would also be equal to marginal congestion cost if the deviation from the steady state were the result of seasonal or other fluctuations in demand, in which case the situation could persist as a long-term equilibrium. In such a case there would be no way in which the competitive price at any instant could be derived from any cost of roadway data: the only relation available is to the congestion cost, which reflects the market forces to which the competitive price responds. The above analysis also holds when the cost of accidents is added in to the congestion cost: a rational user would pay more to travel on a less heavily used route by reason of the lower risk of accident, even if the traffic is not heavy enough for there to be any appreciable delay due to the lighter density of traffic. If he is called upon to bear a charge equal to the sum of the marginal congestion costs associated with time delay and in addition the marginal accident cost, then the excess of the accident charge over the average cost of the accidents on that road will be a surplus over and above the portion of the accident charge required to compensate the victims, both those at fault and innocent parties, and this surplus, if it accrues to the road operators, would be just sufficient, under constant returns to scale, to finance the expansion of the total roadspace that would be justified in terms of lowering the accident rate, through lowering the average density of traffic, for a given total traffic flow. Thus under constant returns to scale everything just balances out nicely, at least in the long run.

Economies and diseconomies of scale in road transport

Constant returns to scale is however the exception rather than the rule (let alone the degree of divisibility that would make the above perfectly competitive model at all realistic). On the one hand in rural areas significant economies of scale will predominate, so that otpimal user charges collected with reference to the use of such roads would be insufficient to finance the optimal system of roadspace in such areas. In densely populated areas, on the other hand, it is less easy to generalize. Much depends on the way in which land has in the past been designated for street and other use, on the degree to which the street pattern is adapted to modern conditions, and on the way in which values are attributed to the land devoted to highway use. Especially if land originally platted as streets has been given little if any value in the accounts and little or no rent is charged for its current use, and if the streets happen to be narrow relative to current traffic, or laid out in an inefficient pattern, the fact that appropriate congestion charges at rates representing marginal cost would yield a substantial surplus over and above any actual current outlays, plus capital charges with respect to past outlays, as recorded in the accounts, is no warrant for attempting to use the surplus to enlarge roadway facilities in such areas by demolishing valuable buildings or constructing expensive viaducts or double-decked structures.

Such a surplus could, indeed, be regarded as a rent generated by the scarce street space, the rent being the higher the more niggardly the original planners were in allotting space to streets, and not necessarily bearing any very close relation to the rental value of nearby building lots, except in those rare cases where transfer of space between building lots and street space is feasible without heavy conversion cost or the creation of inefficient irregularities in the street plan. Conversely, if congestion charges at levels representing marginal congestion costs should fall short of covering a cost figure inclusive of a land rental charge comparable to that earned by adjacent property, one might conclude that one is faced either with a situation in which too much land had been devoted to streets, or perhaps the street widths are down to a point where critical indivisibilities begin to play a heavy role, as can often be the case for narrow streets used primarily for immediate access to abutting property. Generally speaking, however, optimum congestion charges in urban areas will yield very substantial revenues over and above that yielded by existing user charges, and probably more even than a meticulous cost accounting would show as the full cost of urban streets.

In the United States, where highway user charges are not too far out of line with respect to users of rural roads and highways, any excess revenues developed by urban congestion charges may well serve as a welcome succor to the budgets of hard-pressed core cities. In some European countries where the level of highway user charges constitutes often a substantial overcharging of rural roadway users even if urban users are undercharged, revenue produced by the institution of congestion charges could well be used, at least in part, for the abatement of the unduly heavy user charges bearing on the use of rural roadways.

Land rents and long run transportation planning

In the short run, we have seen, setting prices on the basis of marginal congestion cost is the only feasible way to guide users to an approximately optimal manner of using existing facilities. But there is no warrant, in general, for using the relation between the revenues so generated and a total cost derived from the various more or less arbitrary ways in which highway accounts are kept as a signal to govern increases or decreases in the amounts invested in additional roadway facilities. Such decisions are appropriately made by a cost-benefit analysis of each set of projects, or combination of projects, where they are interrelated, in which gains and losses are estimated, with future values subjected to appropriate rates of discounting, and the worthwhile projects selected. In this process, however, there is a danger that in taking, as is usually done, the market price of land as a measure of its social opportunity cost, a serious bias may be introduced into the process. This is because the rental value of land as established by the market tends seriously to understate the social opportunity cost of using land for transportation rather than for other purposes. In making decisions, therefore, between land-hungry forms of transportation, such as the private automobile, and land-saving forms, such as mass transit, the use of current market prices for land in comparing costs of alternatives seriously biases the decision to the disadvantage of the land-saving forms.

This understatement of the cost of taking land for transportation comes about because urban land values are intimately related to the cost of transportation. Much of the high land values observed at the centers of large cities can be explained as the premium paid in order to reduce the transportation costs (inclusive of the cost imputable to the time individuals doing business at the central locations spend in travel) connected with the activities carried on at a given location. It has been said that if transporation were costless and instantaneous, urban land values would fall to the level of surrounding agricultural land values. Currently, indeed, there are those who prophesy an eventual collapse of rental values in urban cores because of projected advances in communications technology that will, in effect, place individuals in instantaneous visual and oral communication with each other and thus eliminate the need for physical proximity. For the time being, however, transportation remains costly in time and money, and rents remain high where people can save on these costs.

In a scheme of perfect competition, indeed, rental values at the center of the city would correctly reflect the marginal social opportunity cost of the occupancy of that land by a given set of activities, in compelling other activities to move to where transportation costs would be higher. Perfect competition, however, is an extremely severe condition: it implies that each commodity or service have a well-defined delivery price at every point in the urban space, that for each commodity or service these prices will differ, as between two different locations, by the amount of the transportation cost for any two points between which the transportation actually takes place, and that they will never differ by more than this transportation cost.

Actual urban patterns differ widely from those required by the competitive model. Delivered prices are often uniform over a wide area. Trips often serve more than one purpose, so that the transportation cost for a given commodity or service between one point and another becomes poorly defined, as when a delivery truck drops off small shipments at a number of locations along its route. A great deal of cross-hauling occurs, as when individuals of similar skills pass each other going in opposite directions on their way to work. Price differentials are thus generally much smaller, from one location to another within the city, than the competitive model would require. The result is that firms and households generally, in considering whether to locate in a central high-rent location or in a more peripheral lower rent location, fail to take into full consideration the savings in transportation costs that would result from the more central location, since many of these savings will accrue to others rather than be captured by themselves through more favorable prices. Accordingly they will fail to bid the rental price for central locations up to the levels that would fully reflect the transportation advantages of locating there, and thus the cost involved in displacing activities from such locations.[16]

If this analysis correctly describes elements of the actual situation, then if market values for land are taken as a basis for cost-benefit evaluation of transportation projects, more land is likely to be taken for transportation than the amount that would minimize overall costs, and decisions are likely to be unduly biased against the forms of transportation requiring less land, such as mass transit, and in favor of forms using more land such as private automobiles. This bias is likely to be even more severe in the absence of congestion tolls, in that firms considering alternative locations will be underestimating the true social cost of the location involving he larger amount of transportation. For similar reasons, the bias will be the greater the greater the role of the noncentrally-focussed types of transportation and cross-hauling movements generally, including, for example, recreational trips to the surrounding countryside. Failure to levy conges-

---

[16] To take a somewhat simplified extreme example, suppose that in a given town every producer periodically loads his output into a truck and proceeds to deliver throughout the town, covering the entire area in one trip. If this is the major form of transportation in the town, each producer finds that it does not matter at all where he locates, since the cost of traversing the route is independent of where along the route he begins and ends. Since nobody cares where he himself locates, none of the land within the town will command a premium, and each firm will proceed to spread its activities out horizontally and the distance each delivery truck will have to travel will be greatly increased. This is bad enough, but planners, forecasting this situation and predicting correctly a very low value for land, use this low value in their calculations and come up with a plan calling for very wide avenues, which further spreads the town apart and lengthens delivery truck routes.

tion charges contributes to the underpricing of land for other purposes as well, with consequent overuse of land for unduly low productivity purposes.

In practice the matter is further aggravated by the weight of the property tax, which tends to be capitalized in a lower market price for land. If the market value of the land is taken to represent its full social opportunity cost when taken for transportation purposes, without either an allowance for the value it would have in the absence of property taxes or for the loss of the property tax revenue to the government (to do both would of course be double counting), there is a further bias introduced in the same general direction. Failure to allow for the property tax loss is sometimes defended on the ground that transportation improvements will enhance the value of the remaining property in the area. In the long run and for the region as a whole, however, improvements in transportation may well decrease total land values, and indeed must do so at some point, if the proposition that instant and costless transportation would eliminate land value differentials is given any credence.

Heavy versus light vehicles

A great deal has been written on the proper way to adjust relative charges for highway use between heavy and light vehicles, usually by an attempt to "allocate" some figure deemed to represent total cost. Among the many methods employed have been "top drawer" methods in which a highway is first conceptually constructed to standards sufficient for light vehicles, and then the difference between this cost and the full cost of the highway assigned to the heavy vehicles, and a "bottom drawer" method in which the reverse practice is followed, first building a highway sufficient for the heavy vehicle traffic and then assigning the additional cost required for the full traffic mix to the light vehicles. Attempts have also been made to assign costs on the basis of the wear and tear impacts of the different types of traffic. However, as long as the loads are within the limits for which the roadway is designed, the amount of cost associated with the wear and tear factor is relatively minor. To be sure, if loads exceeding the design loads are imposed on a road, rather serious costs can result even from a single passage, ranging from fracture of concrete slabs to complete failure of bridge spans. Such uses of the roadways are preferably to be banned altogether, except in exceptional cases, as clearly involving a cost in excess of the benefit, rather than merely discouraged through the assessment of charges. For traffic permitted to move at all, once the road has been constructed in such a way as to support such traffic, no useful purpose is served by attempting to levy charges on such traffic in relation to the past outlays required to prepare the road for such traffic. If such outlays prove to have been ill-advised, it is only to compound the error to refuse to make full use of the facilities provided in an often vain attempt to recover the costs from specific classes of user. Efficient use requires that charges be based on the current contribution of such traffic to congestion costs and to wear and tear, regardless of what past outlays may have been.

There is, actually, something of a paradox inherent in this principle, in that it may imply that a decision to raise the standards to which roads are to be built so as to allow their use by heavier, wider, or higher vehicles in the long run will result in increasing the level of charges to be levied on light vehicles. This is because at these higher standards the cost of increasing the capacity in vehicles per hour of a roadway system, whether by adding lanes to existing highways or adding new routes, will be higher than otherwise, and therefore it will become economical to wait until a higher degree of congestion occurs on existing roadway systems before making additions, and this higher degree of congestion will call for higher charges even on the lighter vehicles.

To be sure, if a substantial part of the roadway system consists of parkways and other roadways from which the heavier vehicles are effectively banned, then conceivably the cost of enlarging the parkway system to take care of increased traffic might be significantly less than that of enlarging the general purpose system so that it would be economical to enlarge the parkway system at a point where the congestion is somewhat less, and congestion on that system would be maintained at a somewhat lower level with the charges for its use correspondingly less. For light vehicles using the general purpose system, however, charges would still be somewhat higher, and the more liberal the limits of weight and dimensions for which the general purpose system was designed, the higher would tend to be the charge imposed on light vehicle traffic for the use of this system. This is one more case in which the system of charges clearly indicated by efficiency considerations seems to involve what some may interpret as unfair treatment.

IV. Organization of the industry

The substantial economies of scale that pervade most forms of transportation make it almost inevitable that a considerable degree of monopoly will characterize the organizations that make up the industry. The exploitation, discrimination, and economic inefficiency that result from unregulated monopoly have generally led either to the subjection of the industry to varying degrees of regulation by public commissions and similar agencies, or to direct participation by government in the operation of the industry.

Throughout most of the world, the trend has been fairly strong toward nationalization of at least the railroads in one form or another. While in the 19th century privately owned railroads flourished in France, England, and several other countries, the United States is now the only major industrial country with a predominantly privately owned and operated railroad system. Canada is unique in having a railroad system that is about evenly split between national and private. Even in the United States, the current trend is running in the direction of public ownership of local transit lines, while rail intercity passenger service is largely, though not entirely, being handled in trains operated by the private railroads for the account of a governmental agency, AMTRAK. The picture in common carrier aviation rather closely parallels that of the railroads. Highway transportation, however, carried on as it is in relatively small units on a common right-of-way provided publicly lends itself more readily to private, specialized forms of operation, along with common carrier operations, and remains more generally in private hands, at least outside the socialist countries.

Even where transportation is carried on by a government agency, it is often operated subject to a nominal budget constraint that requires that aggregate revenues be sufficient to meet at least the nominal cots as reflected in the books of account. In such a case, there would, ideally, be relatively little difference between the pricing practices appropriate for a nationalized agency and those that would be desirable practice under regulation: in both cases one would want to see the marginal cost of net revenues equalized over the various services and price categories at a level that meets this budgetary requirement.

Subsidized operation

Overall economic efficiency would, in principle, however, be better served by eliminating the specific budgetary constraint. Instead, one would first estimate an overall marginal cost of public funds, representing the cost of securing additional net tax revenue from other sources in terms of the purchasing power surrendered by taxpayers, plus the marginal collection cost, plus the marginal compliance cost, plus the incremental inefficiency induced by the increased tax rates. Publicly owned transportation agencies should then adjust their rates so that the marginal cost of net revenues obtained from each of their services matched this marginal cost of public funds. Whatever deficit, or in rare cases surplus, that results from this operation could then be absorbed in the general governmental budget. In a sense, the amounts by which the prices charged for the various transportation services exceed their respective marginal costs can be viewed as taxes, and the problem is one of adjusting these and other taxes so as to impose the smallest possible excess burden on the economy.

In practice, such a principle has not yet gained any wide currency. Indeed, there is a considerable body of opinion to the effect that fiscal autonomy for agencies operating publicly owned transportation facilities is highly desirable as promoting efficient management and that any attempt at subsidy is undesirable on the ground that it relieves pressure for economy, diverts the attention of management from the job of efficient operation to that of making the case for a larger subsidy, presents a temptation for labor to make unreasonable demands, and for potential customers to demand service that may be unwarranted. These objections to outright subsidy would not be nearly so crucial, however, if the subsidy took the form of removing the burdens of various forms of special taxation, or even to exemption from judiciously selected types of general tax to which utilities are often subject.

Even where an outright subsidy is given, its amount is not, in practice, usually determined by any calculation of the marginal cost of public funds or even in terms of providing some optimum adjustment however defined. More often, such subsidies as are given are based on a need to prevent the service from breaking down entirely or from suffering some drastic impairment. In some instances the subsidy has been determined by an arbitrarily selected cost element, as when New York City subway operations were subsidized to the extent of the capital charges, with the requirement that all operating expenses be met out of fare and other incidenal revenues. This arrangement arose in part as a result of historical accident,[17] but was in part rationalized in terms of an analogy with surface transportation where the right-of-way is provided out of tax revenues. This arrangement has, however, had seriously distorting consequences in that as a result the tendency has been to lay on capital improvements of all kinds with a relatively lavish hand while skimping on current operating expenses to a truly Draconian extent as a means of deferring fare increases as long as possible for political reasons.

Thus where subsidies are determined by a cost element, there is a considerable danger that costs eligible for the subsidy will be uneconomically expanded, especially where opportunities exist for substitution between subsidized and unsubsidized inputs (as for example was the case in New York with respect to choices between better maintenance of older equipment versus the purchase of new). There would be a good deal to be said for a subsidy set as a fairly rigidly determined percentage of gross revenues. This at least would provide some incentive for making the service more attractive to the public so as to increase its use, as contrasted to an incentive for increasing cost items. If the percentage were set fairly rigidly for a sufficiently long term, so that it could be regarded as not readily subject to change, the tendency for the various interested parties to make extravagant demands on the assumption that the subsidy would be enlarged to cover the cost might be minimized, even though this would mean the abandonment of the attempt to achieve a continuing close equality be-

---

[17] The subway lines were originally built by the city when it proved difficult to find private funding for undertaking the work in terms of the franchise arrangements that had previously been the usual practice, and leased to private operators for a rental intended to be remunerative to the city, subject to a contractual five-cent fare. When the increase in price levels and operating costs during World War I resulted in insufficient net revenues being obtained to cover these rentals, they ceased to be paid.

tween the marginal cost of public funds and the marginal cost of net revenues.

Regulation and the scope of competition

Where private operation is the rule, as with railroads in the United States, it has become widely accepted that some form of regulation is required, though there remains considerable disagreement concerning the principles to be applied in carrying out that regulation. To be sure, there are some who would maintain that even though regulation is still required in areas such as water distribution, telephone service, and the like, where the degree of monopoly is still quite substantial, the widespread availability of competitive highway transportation as an alternative would make regulation of railway rates unnecessary and even harmful. But while it would be possible to maintain that existing regulation has been so wrong-headed as to make no regulation at all a preferable alternative, it is doubtful whether the possibilities for competition are so general in the transportation field as to leave no room for well-conceived forms of regulation. Heavy bulk commodities often move by rail at a cost substantially lower than could possibly be achieved by highway, so that potential highway competition could be only a very mild restraint on the monopolistic exploitation of this traffic by the railroads. And while there are competing rail routes between many of the major centers, this number is rapidly being diminished through mergers; moreover there are many important points that never did have competitive rail connections, and even where competition of sorts exist, it often involved incurring the costs of unduly circuitous routings for a substantial fraction of the traffic. Removal of all constraints on railroad ratemaking is thus still not an acceptable alternative, although one might possibly be satisfied with some form of general rule prohibiting the grosser forms of local discrimination so that competition for shipments where alternate routings exist would operate to protect shippers not having such alternatives.

Even where competition exists, however, it is often far from being so close as to yield a reasonable approximation to the optimal result. In piggyback and containerized service, for example, the degree of advantage of rail over all-highway routing may vary considerably according to the locations of the origin and ultimate destination of the shipment, the suitability of the available schedules, risk of theft or damage, and the like, in ways not readily made the basis for variations in rates, so that the rates the railroad would find most profitable are likely to be higher than those which would achieve an optimal degree of utilization of the service. Moreover, while much of this type of service is between cities connected by alternate routings, the corresponding terminals are often located some distance apart, so that for many origins and destinations the force of competition between the alternate rail routes is considerably diminished.

The case for eliminating the regulation of highway transportation, other than possibly that involving rates for common carrier service to and from small and relatively isolated communities, and that necessary to secure safety and fair dealing practices generally, is considerably stronger. Here, the ease of entry is generally such as to preclude the maintenance of excessive rates on any large scale. One can, of course, maintain that given the economies of scale in rail transportation, as contrasted with public provision of the highway infrastructure, together with the rigidities in rail rates that inevitably develop as a result of regulation, it is desirable to control highway rates to protect the rail rates and traffic from undue attrition through "cream-skimming" selection by the highway carriers of the most profitable segments of traffic and other forms of specialized competition. This may be especially likely to lead to inefficiency when even though the highway mode has the higher marginal cost, this is below the established rail rate. But it is difficult to distinguish rate maintenance thus motivated from that which aims primarily at maintaining the profit levels of the established highway carriers in the name of stability and order in the industry. Indeed, it is difficult to see how the multiplicity of constraints on the routes and areas that particular carriers are permitted to serve—and especially the restrictions on highway operations by railroads—serve any public purpose other than to abate the rigors of competition among highway carriers and increase the potential short-run profits of the industry, much of which, in the end, is likely to be frittered away by the development of wasteful nonprice traffic promotion practices and general inflation of costs.

Standardization of investors' returns

Once regulation of rates is embarked upon, one important consideration in any rate determination is its impact on the net revenues of the operating entity and the level of these revenues in relation to what investors in the industry can legitimately expect. A determination of what investors are entitled to is, in part, a matter of resource allocation, but the primary consideration is usually one of equity between the investors and the public, with the corollary consideration of assuring that funds for needed future capital expansion can be secured on favorable terms.

If one were starting from scratch, the main concern would be to provide investors, at the time they make the decision to commit their funds, with a clear specification of what returns they can expect under various future eventualities. If these specifications are carried out and they have committed their funds voluntarily on this basis, they can have no cause for complaint even if, in the event, they suffer severe losses. The problem lies in how to make the specifications sufficiently clear and sufficiently general so that what they call for is unequivocally determined under a wide variety of possible future eventualities.

On grounds of simplicity, one very attractive method would be to finance the utility on the basis of limited dividend shares, with regulation committed to allowing whatever rate increases the management deems necessary to protect this limited dividend, and to imposing rate decreases only when reserves and surplus accumulate to a point beyond what is considered reasonably necessary to protect this stipulated divided. The critical level of reserves may, indeed, be further stipulated in terms of some formula. In one variant or another, such barometer-fund types of regulation have found fairly wide application outside the United States and have enjoyed considerable success.

Regulatory practices akin to this have, on occasion, occurred in the United States. In Massachusetts, for a time, the utility commission appeared to be following *de facto,* though never quite expilicitly, a policy of requiring that all new equity capital be raised by competitive underwriting on the one hand, and on the other hand taking substantial deviations from par in the market value of the stock as a signal for appropriate rate adjustment. Carrying this out too explicitly and precisely might well introduce a critical circularity in the procedure, in that current high earnings would be inhibited from driving the stock much above par in consideration of the fact that any such price would be a signal for rate reductions that would eliminate the excess earnings. For a long time, too, a steady $9.00 per share dividend on the stock of A.T.T. was regarded as a fixed return that the regulatory authorities were committed to maintain, as indeed, it had been from 1922 to 1958. Beginning in 1959, however, the Federal Communications Commission gave in to pleas that the real value of the dividend had been eroded by inflation and that utility stockholders should not be placed in a position distinct from that of other stockholders with respect to growth and continued prosperity, and allowed the dividend to be effectively increased following a stock split, reaching the equivalent of $13.20 in 1966. No attempt was made, however, to redefine what investors were entitled to receive in terms of any general price index or index of yields.

Regulation in terms of fair value

Regulatory practice in the United States has, indeed, developed a character all its own. This is partly because effective regulation developed only gradually in a context where much of the investment already in place had been committed in an atmosphere of boosterism, freewheeling enterprise, public subsidy, and often outright corruption, in which little thought was given to any clear delimitation of the legitimate expectations of investors. In the process of attempting to determine, long after the original investment, what these legitimate expectations should be for the future, regulatory authorities had to deal with the intervention of courts seeking to protect the property interests of investors from impairment "without due process of law", according to the wording of the 14th Amendment to the Constitution. Protection of investors was a far cry from this amendment's original purpose of protecting the rights of newly freed slaves, but this usage eventually became one of its most frequent applications. As a result, there has developed a complicated and contention-creating body of doctrine that maintains that investors are entitled to a "fair return" on the "fair value" of the property used in providing the service.

Out of the multitude of principles adduced for the determination of fair value, two contrasting basic principles have survived as respectable contenders: prudent investment or historical cost, on the one hand, and reproduction or replacement cost, on the other. Of the two, the replacement cost principle, suitably interpreted, conforms more closely to the requirements of efficient allocation of resources in that in theory it causes the prices of the service to vary in accordance with current price levels and technological developments, and faces the investor with a corresponding risk of loss in the case of a general price decline or unexpected rapid technological advance, with corresponding profits in case of general price inflation or failure of technological advance to come up to previous expectations. In practice, however, the ascertainment of replacement cost has proved to be so costly, time consuming, and subject to errors and differences of opinion and judgment as to threaten a complete collapse of regulation based on this principle.

Replacement cost

One of the difficulties of applying this principle is that if it is to retain any rationale in terms of promoting economic efficiency it is not the cost of replacing the identical plant that is relevant but the cost of replacement of the service capability. In earlier cases, indeed, it was sometime claimed that the identical structure had to be hypothetically reconstituted even though no such structure would ever, in fact, be built in current circumstances: brick structures had to be replaced with brick structures at a time when the cost of laying brick had become prohibitive relative to that of pouring concrete. In railroad cases, estimating the cost of acquiring a new right-of-way through built-up areas is a highly problematical exercise, with the results depending on what assumptions are made about the existence of buildings in the path of the route and what land values would be encountered, when, in fact, the current values of adjacent land may themselves be largely determined by the proximity of the transport facility. The problem is complicated in cases where trackage already in place might never be sufficiently needed (under modern dispatching methods) to take care of projected traffic levels to warrant installing it, if it were not there. However, it may be sufficiently useful to justify its retention and maintenance rather than scrapping it. While in some cases these problems can be sidestepped for practical adjudication by resort to arbitrary criteria, the resulting valuation will usually have lost all relationship to the theoretical concept according to which the use of the replacement cost notion has been justified as a means to economic efficiency.

In theory, indeed, the application of the reproduction cost principle in its full rigor would involve asking what kind of generally comparable service would be justified if one were starting afresh, what the hypothetical cost of that service would be, and so what the actual service is worth, basing the rates on such a calculation, and imputing a value to the facilities used on the basis of how much of the proceeds from such rates is available after defraying the other current costs to provide a rental return for the use of the property. But even then, one would not be resolving the problem in a manner most conducive to economic efficiency, since it is marginal cost, not total cost, that is of significance for this purpose.

Historical cost

While the replacement cost principle in one or other of its variants retains some adherents, the unsatisfactory experience with it has led to an increased tendency to rely on some form of historical cost as a basis for determining the level of net revenues to which the stockholders are entitled. In its naive form, this involves taking the amounts "reasonably and prudently" invested by the utility in property "used and useful" in the rendering of the regulated service, as the "rate base" and multiplying this rate base by a "fair return" derived from observations of what other investments of a comparable degree of risk are generally yielding, to get a "revenue requirement" which rates are to be made to yield, after allowing for operating costs, and an appropriate charge for depreciation, which depreciation charge in turn is to be eventually deducted from the current rate base in arriving at the rate base for the succeeding year. Subject to the caveat that obviously improper or unwise outlays may be excluded either from the rate base or from current costs,[18] regulation on this basis can be accomplished with relatively little delay, largely from the properly kept books of the utility, without costly field investigations or hypothetical engineering studies. Stockholders are placed in a position comparable to holders of preferred stock or debentures in that no hedge against inflation is provided them, but given the market preference in most cases for assets with relatively certain and fixed yields in money terms,

---

[18] As this is being written, the New York Public Service Commission is reported to have refused to permit charging as an allowable operating expense the cost of self-congratulatory or general institutional advertising not related to promoting the use of the service or providing useful information to customers.

this should still permit the financing of the utility at a cost lower than would occur with other methods of regulation.

Adherence to a naive historical cost approach has on occasion resulted in somewhat anomalous results in circumstances of fairly rapid inflation, whether used as a basis for regulation or as the basis for the budgetary balance of a publicly owned enterprise. In effect, the loss in real terms suffered by the bondholders or stockholders in the enterprise—though no different, from the owners standpoint, from what would have happened with any other obligation defined in money terms—has been used to subsidize the enterprise. If the inflation is mild, the result may coincidentally be rather close to the optimal degree of subsidy, but if it is severe the resulting rates may actually fall below marginal cost. In the opposite situation of a decline in the general price level, the gain in real terms to the security holders will be at the expense of the consumer, and prices will be driven still further from the optimum level set by marginal cost.

There is no real difficulty in modifying the prudent investment or historical cost principle so as to allow for variations of the returns allowed investors according to an appropriate price index. This would give up the odd chance of being able to improve the allocation of resources in the event of a favorable degree of inflation, but on the other hand would protect the economy from having rates set on an inappropriate basis in other cases. So far, however, no regulatory authority in the United States appears to have explicitly adopted any such principle, though such adjustments have been vigorously advocated by the interested parties.

Depreciation, obsolescence, and technological development

A slightly different form of the same difficulty arises when unexpected technological developments drastically alter the economics of the situation. Here, it is difficult to define the circumstances in which and the degree to which investors should be called upon to bear the burden of failure to foresee the development and charge rates sufficient to cover depreciation allowances adequate to write the investment down to a level reflecting its obsolescence (or to reap the gain from overdepreciation in the case of a development making the assets more valuable than had been expected). In terms of equity, indeed, it would seem that if in the period prior to the time the imminence of the innovation became apparent, consumers were benefitting from inadequate depreciation, it is probably fairer that subsequent consumers, many of whom will be the same persons, should pay for the dead horses, rather than that this burden should fall on the shoulders of the investors, particularly where, as frequently happens, the previous depreciation charges have been held down by regulatory commissions acting in the interests of the consumers at the time.

Making the investors bear the risk of unforeseen technological change would make the determination of the depreciation rates to be charged a critical and difficult problem, since in such circumstances there would never be any objective criterion of what depreciation charges are correct, even *ex post,* nor would there be opportunity for redress in case of error, through later reevaluations. Yet saddling consumers with the burden of paying for the dead horses may, in extreme cases, seriously inhibit the full exploitation of new developments that permit a service to be produced at drastically reduced costs. On the other hand, to threaten investors with loss in the event of technological improvements in excess of those allowed for in previous depreciation charges would be to introduce a significant counter-incentive against energetic research, development, and innovation within the industry. In a context of private operation, or of public operation under a requirement that the operation break even if possible, making consumers bear the burden or enjoy the gain arising from past errors in depreciation policy seems the preferable alternative, even though this would run counter to the objective of economic efficiency.

In some cases, of course, the impact of change may come through the competition of alternative services that are beyond the competence of the regulatory authority to control, and in such cases there may be no possibility of maintaining the promised return to the investors. It is primarily with respect to such risks that the investor may be entitled to demand a higher rate of return than that obtained on gilt-edged investments. In practice, however, it is likely that investors would be asked to shoulder risks somewhat higher than this, for there are likely to be limits to the degree of monopoly exploitation that an operating agency would be permitted to exercise in an attempt to achieve an allowable rate of return, or to attempt to maximize profits at a lower level if this allowable rate of return cannot in fact be achieved. Indeed, unrestrained exercise of monopoly power implies an infinite social cost of net revenues at the ultimate margin, and it is hardly conceivable, if the facts were fully recognized, that an operating agency would not be required to forgo at least a modicum of its final and extremely costly potential net profits for the sake of the very much larger gains which would accrue to the consumers if rates were lowered somewhat from their unconstrained monopoly level.[19] Situations of this sort appear to have occurred, for example in many marginal transit operations during the decline of the street-car and trolley-bus. The problem of unrecoverable sunk costs is much less likely to arise with fuel-powered buses, where the salvage value through sale

---

[19] In terms of the example presented in footnote 8, maximum profit would occur at $p_1 = 32.5$, $q_1 = 137.5$, $p_2 = 14.0$, $q_2 = 60$, which would be just sufficient to cover total costs if the fixed cost were increased from 2,804 as in the example given, to 4,281.25. If the return to which the operator is considered to be equitably entitled is at this level or higher, strict application of the prudent investment principle would require that he be permitted to charge these unrestricted monopoly prices in an attempt to come as close as possible to securing that to which he is deemed to be entitled. If, however, he were to reduce p_1 from 32.5 to 32.4, the net reduction in profits would be only 0.05, while the gain to the consumers would be 13.775, a ratio of better than 275 to 1.

of the equipment is likely to be a relatively high proportion of the book value.

Where such intolerably high marginal costs of net revenues are threatened, the alternatives are either to inflict losses on investors over and above those which they would incur in any case if regulatory restraints were removed, or to bail them out through a subsidy of the continuing operation. Unfortunately, regulatory commissions have generally lacked the sophistication and foresight to consider in any specific undertaking what the reaction of investors would be to such developments. Even were they prepared to consider their own response to future contingencies, they of course have generally lacked the power to promise any contingent subsidy. The uncertainty of governmental action is thus added to the uncertainty inherent in the economic ambience of the investment. This uncertainty must be paid for, in the long run, of course, through added risk premiums in the rates of return.

Mergers and consolidations

The organization of the transportation industry, especially in the United States, has recently been undergoing a fairly rapid sequence of changes and there is every indication that this will continue for some time, with abandonment of railroad passenger and low-density freight services and local bus services in smaller towns, the taking over of some of these services by public agencies such as AMTRAK, and the merger and consolidation of transportation companies, especially of railroad companies and airlines. Mergers and consolidations are nothing new, of course: most of the large railroad systems were built up by the consolidation of a number of shorter lines. What is new is that many of the important recent railroad mergers, such as the Penn-Central and the Erie-Lackawanna are of railroads that to a considerable extent were competitive rather than complementary in their relationships. There is an important difference between the economic significance of these two types of mergers, in that mergers between complementary monopolists can often redound to the benefit not only of the monopolists but of their customers as well, whereas a merger between competitors is more likely to operate to the disadvantages of the customers, and may even fail to produce the hoped for profits, witness the bankruptcy of both the Penn-Central and the Erie-Lackawanna.[20]

---

[20] The advantages of complementary merger can be illustrated in terms of the rail and boat service model of footnote 11. If the railroad and the boat company both act as unconstrained monopolists, each in turn adjusting his price so as to maximize his own profits on the assumption that the other will continue to charge his current price, then an equilibrium will be reached when the rail fare is set at $9.67 and the boat fare at $6.67 for a total of $15.33. If, however, the two firms combine and now seek to maximize profit, the resulting fare is reduced to $13.00, and the total profit is increased by $27.22 per day. Thus merger of complementary monopolists facilitates a cooperation in the reduction of fares that is to the benefit of all concerned.

The situation is the dual of the classical Cournot duopoly case with the role of price and quantity interchanged. Each party takes the price, rather than the output, of the other as

The potential economies from the merger of complementary monopolies could have been achieved by negotiation between them, while on the other hand the merger does not in itself guarantee that the operations of the various divisions will be fully coordinated in a way that would maximize the profits of the combined firm. But in practice the offering of improved joint service or lower through rates for traffic involving two or more companies is more likely to be severely retarded by haggling over how the profits are going to be divided, or over which company will adapt its service to coordinate properly with the other, and even by differences of opinion as to whether the proposed joint service or through rate will in the event prove profitable, or at least as to what type of service or level of rates will be the most profitable, than would be the case if the negotiations are between different divisions of the same company. It is perhaps significant that for many decades the only through transcontinental passenger service offered was that from Montreal and Toronto to Vancouver, where the entire run could be handled without intercompany collaboration. In the United States, no regular through transcontinental passenger trains have ever been operated in spite of the far greater passenger potential, and such through car service as has been offered, beginning in 1946, has involved layovers of several hours in Chicago or overnight in New Orleans. The interchange of freight cars, often acclaimed as a triumph of coordination—from one standpoint, perhaps it is—is a miserable failure if one considers what might have been expected from a more highly integrated system. Rigid per diem rental rates, often inadequate and inappropriate, paid to freight car owners for the use of their cars on other lines, have contributed to perennially recurring car shortages, to reluctance to invest in high-performance or specialized equipment, and to such ridiculous spectacles as trailers being off-loaded at a piggyback terminal on one side of a city, trucked through the congested heart of the city, and loaded onto flatcars on the other side, in part to ensure that the special flatcars would not leave the home rails and become unavailable to the owner for several weeks.

Indeed, while linear programming and other similar algorithms exist for routing freight cars from areas loading fewer cars of different types than are unloaded to areas where the reverse is true, so as to minimize empty mileage [21], actual movement of cars in the U.S. is motivated primarily by the per diem charges, which at best are far too rigid to perform the job efficiently. Though empty car movements are also nominally subject to a

---

fixed, and the prices are added to get a total price that determines the quantity purchased, instead of the quantities of output being added to get a total output that determines the price at which sales will take place. With a linear demand curve, equilibrium occurs when each party absorbs one third of the margin between the total marginal cost of $5 + $1 = $6 and the maximum demand price of $20 (= 100/5). Thus each party adds ($20 − $6)/3 = $4.67 to his own marginal cost to arrive at the above prices. Given the price of the other party, each party maximizes his own profits by setting his own price half way between his own marginal cost and the price which would result in a combined price of $20.

[21] See, for example, "Short Haul Routing of Empty Box-cars," in Beckman, McGuire and Winsten, *Studies in the Economics of Transportation* (Yale, 1956), pp. 195–218.

set of car service rules intended to keep cars moving in the general direction of their home rails, in practice these rules are frequently ignored. One advantage of complementary as distinct from competitive mergers is that it would be much easier to get cars back to their home rails, since the distance to the nearest bit of home rail would tend to be shorter, and better utilization of the freight car fleet would result.

While the question of through rail passenger service is no longer a matter of any great moment, the establishment of through freight rates and services that will attract traffic and promote efficient utilization of equipment is still seriously hampered by the independence of complementary transport agencies, whether of the same mode or of different modes. Much of the difficulty under which the New Haven line labored prior to its absorption by a reluctant Penn-Central system can be traced to the lack of any substantial amount of traffic within its own territory with hauls long enough to permit rail transport to compete effectively with trucks, combined with the fact the most of the long-haul traffic in which it participated involved two or more other railroads: its chief western freight connection, at Campbell Hall, was with the Lehigh and New England, the Lehigh and Hudson, and the Erie. Again, if the New York Central had merged with, say, the Santa Fe rather than the Pennsylvania, prospects for improved coordination of service between California and Texas on the one hand and Ohio and New York on the other would have brightened, and errant freight cars would have had a better chance of being returned promptly to the widened range of home rails.

Mergers of competitive routes do have their legitimate cost-saving objectives, however, which tend to offset whatever disadvantages may be attributed to the resulting lessening of competition. Before the advent of effective truck competition, the disadvantages from impairment of competition seemed to be a more dominant consideration in the attitude of regulatory authorities. Recent mergers have been more often of the competitive kind, as the advantages of lowered costs have seemed more important to management than have the advantages of developing better service, while regulatory authorities, being less concerned than formerly with the reduction in competitive pressures, have been more willing to accept such merger proposals.

The possibilities for economies through mergers of parallel routes are, indeed not insubstantial, particularly where previous competitive practices were strikingly wasteful, as is especially likely to occur in passenger service. There was at one time, for example, the spectacle of three overnight passenger trains struggling for the business between Kansas City and St. Louis; or the Pennsylvania operating trains from Washington to Chicago via Baltimore while the B&O operated trains from Baltimore to Chicago via Washington, with the best Washington-Chicago time being an hour longer than would easily have been attainable by a train using the B&O tracks to Pittsburgh and the Pennsylvania from there to Chicago. Currently, trains operated for AMTRAK by the Santa Fe between Chicago and Los Angeles still wind their way up to the Raton tunnel whereas if the traffic were routed over the Rock Island-Southern Pacific route between Hutchinson, Kansas, and Vaughn, New Mexico, some 100 miles in distance, some 4,000 feet in total ascent and descent, and curves equivalent to some 20 full circles would be eliminated. Parallel mergers would tend to improve situations such as the above, as well as even more extreme practices in the handling of freight, and to achieve other economies through consolidation of routings and schedules, but it does seem that economies available from such mergers are more likely to be reflected in reductions in service along with costs without any significant reduction in rates, whereas end-on mergers have a greater tendency to lead to improvements in service and reductions in rates.

But comparably wasteful competitive practices are now arising in the air transport field. Wherever two or more airlines offer service on a given route, there is a tendency for the one with the more frequent schedules to capture a share of the business greater than in proportion to the number of schedules offered, which leads to intense rivalry in schedule frequency over the more profitable routes, often with duplication of schedules and correspondingly low load factors. This is especially noticeable on the longer flights, where the relation of the cost per seat mile to the average fare is especially favorable. For example, of four daily nonstop flights from Dulles (Washington) to San Francisco, two are scheduled to leave simultaneously at 9 a.m., and the other two within ten minutes of each other at 5:45 and 5:55 p.m., while the two daily nonstop flights from Friendship (Baltimore) to San Francisco both leave at noon. The extreme of competitive duplication of service occurs in Australia, where on most main routes the two major airlines, Ansett (private) and Trans Australia (public) offer identical schedules flown with identical models of aircraft. Another form which the more intense rivalry on the more profitable routes takes is elaboration of services, extra lounge space, entertainment and the like, often at a cost to the competing airline far greater than the value the average passenger would place on the added amenity. Some of the wasteful practices arise specifically from regulation, as when international flights are prohibited from carrying local passengers on the domestic legs of a flight. The purpose, obviously, is to protect domestic airlines from foreign competition, but such rules seriously lower the load factors and thus raise costs, in some cases inhibiting the offering of through service between interior and foreign points.

Taxicabs

Taxi service is an often overlooked element in the transportation picture, although in terms of gross revenue its importance is of the same order of magnitude as urban mass transit. Regulation of taxicabs has developed a number of patterns somewhat distinct from those found in connection with other modes of transportation. Indeed the range of forms of regulation is quite wide, including at the one extreme leaving the situation largely open to free competition and individual bargaining as often occurs for trips across jurisdictional lines, monopoly with regulated rates at the other, as well as free entry to anyone who can satisfy appropriate standards of capability and responsibility with rates fixed by regulation, and special licensing, either in terms of issuing a limited number of licenses or in terms of substantial license fees, with varying provisions, tacit or explicit, as to the terms on which license will be transferable or renewable.

Rate regulation is justifiable in this instance not so much on grounds of outright monopoly or inadequate competition but rather on grounds of mitigating the haggling and possible exploitation of strangers that is particularly likely to arise in a case such as this where neither party has any ready means of seeking the other out for a subsequent transaction and comparison shopping is generally not feasible. With free entry, the criterion governing the level at which regulated rates should be set is simply one of setting a rate level that will assure a satisfactory degree of availability of taxis, though even here it is not at all obvious just where the compromise should be made between low rates, high occupancy ratios needed to attract capital and labor away from other opportunities, and hence a level of availability that makes it difficult at times of peak demand to secure taxi service, on the one hand, and high rates of fare, low occupancy ratios and a high level of availability that makes it easy to secure service at nearly all times, on the other.

It is more difficult to justify restrictive licensing. One excuse may be that limiting the number of cabs operating in a given area helps to alleviate congestion in the downtown areas. But restrictive licensing is likely, intentionally or otherwise, to generate windfalls for the licensees, unless, indeed, they are limited as to duration and periodically auctioned to the highest bidders or otherwise priced so as to clear the market.[22] Existence

---

[22] In New York, taxi medallions representing the right to operate a taxi for an unspecified period into the future, originally issued for a nominal fee, have sold for in excess of $20,000. Even with this market price as evidence of windfall profits to cab owners, fares were further increased on the ground that the drivers were entitled to higher earnings, in the face of the obvious possibility of securing at least some increase in their income out of the surplus earnings of the medallion owners that were apparently sufficient to justify the high medallion market price. While it would be possible to argue for an increase in the rates on the basis of keeping the demand for taxis down to a reasonable relation to the fixed supply and thus improving the quality of the service for those able to afford the higher fares, this consideration, if it existed at all, was not widely aired. Recently there has been a rapid growth in non-medallion, or so-called "gypsy" cabs, operating with meters at comparable or slightly lower rates, and officially, at least, required to respond only to telephone requests and prohibited from picking up casual fares on the streets. This service arose initially to meet a serious shortage in the service provided by the medallion cabs in ghetto areas, but seems to be growing to the point of supplying a significant fraction of the total service, though as yet this development does not appear to have caused any marked fall in the market value of the medallions.

of long-term licenses having a high value, whether the licenses are directly marketable or not, is likely, moreover, to make decision difficult when a change is to be made in the situation that might seriously affect these values; for example issuing new licenses in sufficient numbers to eliminate much of the windfall value imposes a loss on recent purchasers, while selling additional licenses to the highest bidder tends to commit the issuing authority to underwrite the value thus established whether by maintaining rates at a high level or restricting the number of cabs licensed. Once an inappropriate pattern is established, it is often difficult to move to an appropriate one.

Even where no undue barriers to entry are imposed and rate regulation is the only issue, significant problems remain. Where meters are used, the typical rate combines a time element when the vehicle is stopped or traveling slowly with a distance element applicable at most normal speeds. Not only is this alternative basis of charging somewhat at variance with the way costs behave, but it gives taxi drivers an unfortunate incentive to drive at full speed up to stoplights and the like so as to maximize the amount of waiting time registered. Even so, relatively little of the total fares charged is generated on a time basis, whereas well over half of the costs of taxi operation vary with time rather than with distance. A meter which charged a time rate in terms of total elapsed time, as well as a distance charge, with the time rate accounting for a major part of the total would reduce these undesirable incentives and produce a combined charge more in line with costs, particularly in the relative charges for trips in slow-moving downtown traffic on the one hand and trips in fast-moving freeway traffic on the other.

Nevertheless, it might be desirable to stop somewhat short of raising the time charge to fully reflect this element of costs, lest there be a temptation to dawdle, particularly in periods of light demand for taxis. There would be a good deal to be said for allowing premium time rates to be charged in bad weather and at other times of peak demand, if only to improve the availability of taxis at such times for people who need them particularly badly. Another possibility would be to have one time rate for running time and time taken up by traffic delays, stop lights, and the like, and another slightly higher rate, applicable for continuous standing in excess of one minute, to take care of waiting time incurred for the convenience of the passenger. It would in any case be illogical for a mileage charge to vary according to the weather or state of demand: mileage costs depend very little, if at all, on whether a given amount of mileage was accumulated largely at times of peak demand or at times of slack demand.

Another problem with meter rates is in fixing the initial charge at a suitable level. An excessively high initial charge has the effect of attracting cruising taxis to downtown areas where average trip lengths are shorter. A substantial initial charge also makes more sense where taxis are despatched on the basis of telephone calls and thus cause a taxi to be unavailable to others for a certain time prior to the start of the trip, whereas a taxi hailed on the street or taken from a rank is tied up only for the duration of the trip. Some variation in the initial charge might thus be warranted according to the circumstances under which the trip starts. Some of these factors indeed can be better taken account of in a zone type of fare in which the fare depends somewhat crudely on the zone of origin and the zone of destination, though most zone fares permit a rather wide range of trip length for a given fare. Achievement of reasonable efficiency in a fare structure of an acceptably low level of complexity requires the ingenious balancing of a number of considerations.

Institutional roadblocks—the case of rail passenger service

Many of the current inefficiencies in the transportation industry are traceable not so much to faulty economic analyis as to the impact of institutional rigidities. One example of this is the overly rapid and extensive disappearance of rail passenger service in the United States. To be sure, the shifting of most of the premium-rate long-haul passenger business to the airlines has been largely inevitable. The cost of providing porter, dining car, and other personal services on a train at 80 miles per hour is sufficiently higher, per passenger mile, than the cost of comparable personal services on a plane traveling 600 miles per hour to make it difficult to keep even the marginal cost of the rail service down to a level competitive with the plane. For most passengers who would be potential Pullman passengers, the time saving or the greater comfort of a hotel room after a couple of hours of flying as compared with an overnight train trip are decisive. Attempts to preserve the traditional de luxe service on any substantial scale for the benefit of a relatively few passengers with idiosyncratic tastes can only burden the service with high costs that threaten the continuance of such service as could be fully justified.

The loss of traffic to buses, and to some extent to private cars, is less inevitable. There is, of course, an important place for intercity bus service where rail connections are circuitous or stations inconveniently located. But given comparable route mileages and terminal locations, rail service should, in technological terms, be able to give a higher quality of service at a lower incremental cost. That buses continue to compete successfully on these terms seems to be due to a combination of artificial constraints, including unjustifiable and costly work rules imposed by labor unions, regulatory authorities, and sometimes by law; safety standards that often kill more people than they save by driving passengers to more hazardous alternatives; and managements afflicted with a kind of megalomania that insists on thinking in terms of 5, 10, or even 15 car trains when smaller units would be more appropriate.

There seems, indeed, to be no good reason why the operation of a rail vehicle of a capacity comparable to that of a bus should require any more manpower or skill to operate: if a bus driver can handle local baggage, sell and collect tickets, assist handicapped persons on and off, give information, and guide the bus and control its speed on a crowded highway where almost anything can happen at any instant, it should not be unreasonable to ask a rail-car operator to perform similar functions, minus that of continuous guidance, in much less arduous circumstances, over comparable distances at a comparable wage. Nor does there seem to be any inherent reason why the incremental costs of operating such a vehicle, given the maintenance of the right-of-way for freight traffic, should be any higher than that of the bus, especially if the bus were charged with the full costs of the congestion it produces, particularly in its departure from and arrival at downtown terminals.

Emphasis on long, high-speed trains operating on infrequent schedules and accepting only long-haul traffic between major cities has not succeeded in keeping traffic from airlines, but it has largely deprived way-station communities of a service which, while not particularly lucrative to the railroads, was of a value to the relatively small number of individuals served that in all probability exceeded the incremental cost of providing it. For a time, buses filled the gap with service to intermediate communities that was in many cases more convenient and frequent than that actually provided by the railroads, though even then perhaps not more so than the railroad service that would have been optimal from a cost-benefit standpoint. With the shifting of bus service to expressways that largely bypass intermediate towns, bus service to these towns can no longer be offered as a by-product of the through service without unreasonable delay to the through passengers, and the service frequency has again declined to the level that can be supported by local traffic alone. In many areas, railroads now have a substantial potential comparative advantage in being able to combine local and through traffic without undue sacrifice of speed in a way that will permit either comparable service frequencies in larger units or improved service frequencies in units of a similar capacity, or some compromise between the two.

Smaller operating units would also lend themselves to the revival of the flag stop as a means of offering service at times and places where traffic on a particular occasion would frequently be nil for a regularly scheduled stop. In the past, no attempt was made, as a rule, to assess the cost of such stops directly against the passengers served, so that where such stops were offered there was a tendency for stops to be made that were not warranted by the added passenger convenience, on the one hand, and on the other for restrictions to be placed on the use of the flag stop in terms of the length of trip involved, to insure that the revenue generated would be sufficient to cover the cost. From the standpoint of profitability, this may indeed have been a suitable approach; however, the value of the flag-stop service to the passenger or passengers may be just as great for a relatively short trip as for a longer one. A more rational approach would be to make a suitable explicit charge for the special stop, sufficient to represent the costs involved, and let the prospective passengers judge for themselves whether or not it is worth it in any particular case.

A somewhat analogous situation occurs when the use by local passengers of through trains is prohibited, motivated by the need to avoid local overloads and inconvenience to through passengers. Between New York and Washington, for example, local passengers have often not been allowed to ride through trains to or from points south of Washington. Carried to this extreme, this practice virtually guarantees a needlessly low level of utilization of the capacity being provided and impairs the effective frequency of service from the standpoint of the passenger. Imposing a modest fare differential could have taken care of the problem of overloading and interference with through traffic with much less impairment of utilization.

If full advantage were taken of the technological potentialities of the situation, it seems likely that nearly all present long-haul intercity bus traffic would be carried by rail, in units small enough to afford schedule covenience comparable to that now provided by the bus service. Intermediate stop service would be available at nearly all points on nearly all trains, at least on a flag-stop basis subject to an appropriate stop charge, except possibly on a few medium haul routes of high traffic density, such as the Boston-Washington corridor, where a serious attempt could be made to compete with air travel over the shorter distances, and where a variety of stop combinations can be offered at a suitably high frequency. Elsewhere, such traffic as places a high premium on saving in travel time is already largely going by air or by private automobile in any case, so that little is lost by relaxing schedules sufficiently to permit a reasonable number of such stops on any one trip without jeopardy to the maintenance of the schedule. Local traffic willing to pay the stop charge would be welcome, no matter how short the trip, with local fares being suitably raised if a local overload should threaten.

A prerequisite to any such development, however, is the introduction of labor practices that will permit bringing costs down to levels comparable to those of bus service for units of comparable capacity, and to correspondingly lower levels for larger units. The outlook for this is not bright. Most of the developments that are taking place in the field of "high-speed ground transportation" seem based on the operation of large units necessitated by the high minimum costs per unit imposed by current labor practices. The intrenched position of railway labor unions, inherited from a period of railroad monopoly and buttressed by prospects for continued exploitation of freight traffic, has brought matters to a point where it appears that even with the takeover of most rail passenger service by AMTRAK, rail passenger service may continue at a level far below its technical and economic potential.

Labor utilization in transit and commuter service

Another situation where the interaction of recalcitrant unions, viscous regulation, staid management, and even, on occasion, short-sighted or irresponsible public officials, have combined to frustrate efficient solutions is in transit and commuter railroad service. A major element in the high cost of rush-hour service is the high cost of labor required to man the peak-hour schedules. Job specialization and demarcations, plus requirements for minimum daily wages and for overtime based on the total spread of hours worked combine to place the marginal cost of manning rush-hour schedules at a very high level. While the existing rules have in the past served a desirable function of protecting labor against undue exploitation and unduly arduous working conditions, their rigid and inflexible application has led to increasing inefficiency as off-peak traffic has dropped off and the duration of the peak has narrowed, sharply limiting the extent to which work at other hours can be found for the personnel required for the peak.

There should be, in a free and open situation, any number of ways of manning rush-hour schedules that would have a far lower genuine social cost than that incurred at present. One obvious approach would be to open up such jobs to individuals to whom a short working day is relatively attractive. Under present practices, the more lucrative and shorter working schedules are often bid in during a pick of runs by those with higher seniority, usually without substantial sacrifice in pay over runs involving more nearly a full day's work. Given the lack of correspondence between pay differentials and differentials in hours actually worked, the tendency is, moreover, to set up the runs so as to spread these "hours paid for but not worked" around much more evenly than would best accommodate the assortment to the preferences of the labor force. Thus not only is there often no way for the worker with little seniority to satisfy a strong preference for a particular job schedule, but in addition the assortment of job schedules offered does not present as wide a variety as would be desirable if such selection were possible.

The problem of organizing the process of setting up work schedules and arranging the pick so as to produce a result that is reasonably efficient (which may be defined as one approximately satisfying the Pareto-optimality criterion) is a fairly difficult one, given the current institutional constraints. A free competitive market solution would, of course, be one of simply opening up the various runs to competitive bidding by the qualified employees in terms of the wage for which they would be willing to undertake a particular schedule. Management would then be motivated to package the various runs into work schedules in such a way as to meet the preferences of the employees and thus secure lower bids. Such a proposal runs too sharply counter to the entire idea of collective bargaining to be seriously considered, however, even if the difficulties involved in providing reasonable job and income security and continuity could be dealt with.

A modification that might conceivably be acceptable would be to have the union contract specify a lower quartile and a minimum hourly rate for various categories of employment. The pick could then be by competitive bidding in terms of a nominal rate; after the pick has been completed, the nominal rates would all be multiplied by a factor selected so as to bring the lower quartile hourly rate thus produced into line with the contract stipulation, after which the minimum rate would be applied. In the case of the tie bids, which would be limited chiefly to minimum and maximum bids, seniority could still be used as a tie breaking device, though a preferable criterion might be the degree of similarity between the run being bid for and the run previously worked by the bidder, if a suitable measure of similarity can be worked out. The procedure for carrying out such a bidding and adjustment sequence might be a fairly complex one, but the results in terms of better adaptation of the jobs to individual preferences should make it well worth while.

Standardization on the basis of the lower quartile rather than the average hourly rate would serve to given the employer an incentive to adapt the assortment of runs to the preferences of the working force, so as to diminish the divergence of the average rate above the quartile, though even in the absence of this incentive one might expect a reasonable effort to be made in this direction. Possibly some form of participation of a labor representative in the process might prove helpful. In any case, explicit daily minimums, overtime rates, night and holiday premiums, or spread allowances would no longer be required, since anyone assigned to a short day, or to a holiday or evening would be doing so as a result of a bid voluntarily made, indicating a preference for this work on relative terms substantially similar to those emerging from the process, over full-time or regular-day work, which would normally carry an hourly rate fairly close to the stipulated lower quartile. Indeed, it would be essential that such explicit daily minimums and premium rates be eliminated if the system is to produce the best possible results for the working force as a whole for a given total wage bill for the work to be done; to the extent that such differentials are called for by workers' preferences they will develop automatically out of the system itself.

Another potentially complementary approach to the problem of manning rush hour trips is through reversing the trend to increased job specialization and demarcation. It is absurd, for example, to require that a motorman who has just brought a rush-hour train into a terminal for lay-up and is about to go off duty substantially short of having done a full day's work must turn his train over to a hostler for a trip to the lay-up siding or yard. On a somewhat broader level, it should not be hard to find work in a terminal office that could readily be performed by a rush-hour conductor, either after his inward run in the morning or prior to his outward run in the evening, so as to provide him with seven or eight hours a day of reasonably continuous productivity. Unofficially, a considerable amount of such daylight moonlighting already exists, even in the face of the individual's having to make his own arrangements and in some cases be subject to the periodically recurring hazard that his arrangements might be upset at the next pick of work schedules, especially if his seniority is low. It would obviously be much better for such arrangements to be directly coordinated insofar as possible, even though this might fly in the face of a considerable remnant of the job-protection philosophy that has been especially rampant in railroad labor circles. In Wellington, N.Z., where an extremely low and long continued level of unemployment has lowered labor resistance to such arrangements, job dovetailing between office work and service on commuter trains is actually in effect to a considerable degree.

Another element contributing to the high cost of labor in publicly operated transit services involves the way pensions are arranged. In many cases fringe benefits provided through liberal pension provisions inure preferentially to the union members with the most seniority, in that the benefits are less remote in time and more certain to be realized than for the younger members who will not only have longer to wait for any benefit to materialize but run a substantially greater risk that because they change jobs before any of their pension rights become vested, or for other reasons, they fail to qualify. Because of the uncertainty concerning what proportion of the labor force will eventually qualify for the specified pensions, it is quite possible either to underestimate the present value of accruing pension rights, or to neglect to fund the pensions completely, or in other ways to defer the cost involved in a wage settlement in a labor negotiation that involves increased pension rights. The interests of a labor leadership biased in favor of the members with seniority may thus combine with the interests of elected local government officials who are not averse to terms of settlement that will inconspicuously shift the resulting budgetary problems to the shoulders of future incumbents to produce a strong predilection for pension terms that may eventually prove an extravagant way in which to secure labor services.

The problem may be compounded if the pension provision calls for a pension determined in terms of the final year's salary. In many organizations it is frequent practice to reward faithful members with a promotion just prior to retirement so that the pension can be based on this higher pay; in transit service, however, this practice takes the form of those about to retire exercising their seniority to bid in all of the premium and overtime jobs that they possibly can with a result that the pension rights become inflated by a much higher factor than occurs in other cases. When this potential is not fully anticipated, the result can be a serious underestimate of the cost of the labor settlement on the part of the government negotiators. Moreover the very high premium thus placed on retirement at the earliest possibility may result in a serious labor turnover problem and a shortage of experienced employees, especially if the age or term of service requirements for retirement are suddenly reduced.

Technological lags in urban transit

Still another problem is the accommodation of automation in rapid transit. So far great difficulty has been encountered in giving full scope to automation in any but entirely new systems, such as the Lindenwald line in the Philadelphia area and the Bay Area Rapid Transit System. Actually, the point where introduction of automated train operation would be most advantageous is in heavily loaded existing systems where the lack of uniformity of performance and the time lags in the control process that are inherent in any human response generate serious unevenness in the loading and greatly reduce the capacity of the system and increase the degree of overcrowding. Another crucial area for automation is in fare collection on commuter lines. Closed station operation on commuter lines in England permits suburban trains to be operated by a crew of two, comparably to rapid transit trains, while elsewhere open or quasi-open station operations with spot checking have reduced the cost of collection. The process of fare collection by conductors on trains as practiced in this country is absurdly costly; although steps are being taken to reduce this cost in some instances, there remains a tremendous potential for economy here. Automation in some form may also be the key to the provision of an adequate frequency of service in off-peak hours.

Overall, indeed, the rate of technological advance in mass transit seems at times agonizingly slow. A minor absurdity is that until relatively recently electrically propelled multiple-unit cars for suburban service were provided with compressed-air signal lines: more costly, slower, and more subject to error than a simple electric buzzer. A more disconcerting fact is that none of the various highly elaborate train control systems developed in the course of the planning for the Bay Area Rapid Transit system apparently made any use of the speed of the preceding train in controlling the following train: the assumption is, in effect, that the preceding train can stop instantaneously at any time from any speed. While for most new systems under consideration this may not be of any great immediate importance in the context of service frequencies likely to be needed in the near future (though the system being planned for Caracas may be an exception), in

New York, Paris, London, Tokyo, and similar situations where service is being operated at minimum headways even a slight reduction in minimum headways permitted by assuming even a minimum emergency braking distance for a moving preceding train would be of strategic significance in improving conditions. Relatively undisciplined drivers of heterogeneous vehicles ranging from Volkswagens to buses and tractor trailers are enjoined to keep 75 feet apart in the Lincoln Tunnel at speeds of over 30 mph on a 6 percent downgrade when the minimum stopping distance on the level is of the order of 120 feet—relying on the impossibility of an instantaneous stop by a preceding vehicle. It would then seem that rapid transit vehicles, operating in a uniform manner with trained personnel (in an environment not subject to the serious fire hazard of gasoline vehicles in a tunnel) could with adequate safety be controlled in terms of reasonable assumptions about the minimum stopping distance of the preceding vehicle. If 3 seconds or less of vacant space between vehicles is adequate in the Lincoln Tunnel, it would seem that adequate safety could be maintained in transit service with a minimum vacant space between trains of substantially less than the 40 seconds that appears to be the minimum under present practices. If traffic in the Lincoln tunnel were suddenly to insist on being able to stop short of the current position of the preceding vehicle, peak-hour flows would be cut drastically and traffic would be backed up in queues for miles further than it already is. Here again is an instance in which signal engineers in concentrating exclusively on performance in their own areas of responsibility have (by insisting on excessively high safety standards that result in lower levels of service), actually killed more people indirectly than they have saved directly, as the lower service frequencies have caused overcrowding to reach such levels that potential passengers resort to other even more hazardous forms of transportation on the surface.

Another area in which short-headway transit service is amazingly backward is in the matter of scheduling, which is still very largely on a predetermined timetable basis. With inadequate control over the inherent instability of the system, any unevenness in the intervals tends to become accentuated because any unit that lags even slightly behind its schedule thereby tends to begin picking up more than its normal share of passengers and thus is made to lag still further. Effective methods of dealing with minor irregularities promptly at their inception so as to prevent their building up into major irregularities and bunching have yet to be applied in any thoroughgoing manner. The long layovers at terminals and checkpoints and delays that are imposed by the slow schedules adopted in part to keep this instability under a degree of control constitute an unduly costly way of providing for variations in operating conditions. What is needed is an automated and computerized dispatching and control system that will automatically signal transit vehicle operators to take action at the earliest possible moment to keep the spacing between vehicles from becoming irregular. If this is done it may be possible in many cases to eliminate the fixed timetable altogether, and simply have a given number of vehicles circulating on a given route, evenly spaced, and at the maximum frequency that the current traffic and other conditions will allow. In other cases routes may be combined end to end so as to reduce the need for transfers and the accompanying delays without thereby creating intolerable degrees of instability.

Actually the development of computer techniques for the dispatching of vehicles may make not only the fixed schedule but the fixed route a thing of the past, at least for trips outside the most heavily traveled corridors. In an affluent society, something better than fixed-route transit and cheaper than taxi service may be required to compete effectively with the private automobile or provide conveniently for the needs of those unable to drive themselves. This is especially true in urban conglomerations that increasingly generate desires for trips that do not lend themselves to being served by fixed route transit. Indeed, a number of experiments have been carried out in recent years with shared taxi, "dial-a-ride," variable route minibuses, and the like, though none of these experiments has been on a scale or has operated with the degree of sophistication that would really test the viability of large-scale and highly automated systems of this type. One can imagine, indeed, a service in which an individual would indicate his transportation request by first dialing the telephone number of a transportation center (or perhaps at some locations simply pick up a direct line phone connection), then dialing further digits identifying the general area of the intended destination, number of passengers, and class of service. The class of service might be individual taxi, shared taxi with priority, group taxi door-to-door, variable route minibus from a nearby corner, direct service or via connections. A computer combining this information with information concerning the location of vehicles under its direction secured by radar triangulaton, the destinations of the riders already en route, and possibly other pending requests would select a vehicle to be used for the requested trip and compose a recorded message to the prospective passenger indicating the time and place he will be picked up and the applicable fare. On hearing this the prospective passenger would dial a further digit to indicate that arrangement is satisfactory or to request a different class of service, or to cancel the request. If the arrangement is accepted, the computer would then transmit signals to the driver of the selected vehicle at suitable stages in his progress indicating to him how he should proceed. On boarding the vehicle the passenger may place his charge card in a slot and tell the driver his specific destination, which the driver would key into the system by a suitable code to be transmitted to the computer, the serial number of the passenger being also transmitted. This information would be used by the computer to develop the optimum route for the vehicle to be indicated to the driver as he proceeds, and to bill the rider for the service at the end of the month.

There is nothing in the above scheme that cannot be accomplished by putting together currently available techniques. The main question is what the optimal configuration of routes and vehicles would be, how to develop the computer program, how the system should be priced, and in what circumstances it would turn out to be financially self-supporting, or at least worth while on an overall cost-benefit basis. It is, indeed, not at all clear from the somewhat uneven results of the small scale experiments that have thus far been attempted, just what the implications might be for a larger system on the above lines, operating over a period long enough to affect habits and patterns of travel and location decisions.

Summary

The transportation industry is a complex giant, resultant of countless decisions, many of which have been made with poor coordination and on the basis of parital and often misleading analysis. In the circumstances, one is often amazed, as with the infant prodigy, not that it performs well, but that it performs at all. The opportunities for improvement are enormous. The mere application of marginal-cost pricing principles throughout the industry, even when severely limited by institutional and financial constraints, not only would change the transportation industry almost beyond recognition but also would have far-reaching impacts on patterns of urbanization.

To be sure, when one considers the tortuous and often illogical patterns into which the industry has so often worked itself in the past, it would be absurd to hope that any large part of the potenital for improvement that can be discerned will be realized overnight. But with ingenuity and perseverance a great deal can be accomplished.

6

Population

RICHARD A. EASTERLIN

Professor of Economics
University of Pennsylvania

The subject of population is an increasing source of uneasiness to economists. In the half century or so before World War II, it was considered off limits, and happily left to demographers and sociologists.[1] But as so often happens, the pressure of events is forcing reconsideration of accepted views. At home, there has been the unexpected swing in fertility since World War II, with its manifest impact on the economy. Recently, concern has grown about the longer term implications of continued American population growth. In less developed countries the population explosion—population growth rates rapidly rising as mortality declines sharply and fertility remains relatively constant—has engendered fears about the possibility of economic growth in less developed areas—indeed, about the adequacy of the earth to support prospective levels of population.

The questions raised by these developments are challenging and disturbing. But the plain truth is that economists—indeed, social scientists generally—do not have reliable answers. Only in the past decade or so has the subject of population started to be considered seriously by economists, and even this is a peripheral development. Contrast this with the

---

[1] The works of Joseph S. Davis [18], Alvin Hansen [45], and Joseph J. Spengler [66] were early and outstanding exceptions. For bracketed numbers, see references at end of chapter.

long record of scholarship underlying the policy prescriptions on business cycles offered by economists today.

Nor is the situation better in sister disciplines. Demography, the scientific study of population, is a creature of the 20th century. The great bulk of work to date has aimed to establish the *facts* of population change—an essential first step in any field of science. But work on the causes and effects of population change is still in a very early stage. It is chastening to recognize, for example, that while the historical record of fertility has now been established for a number of countries for the last half century or more, there exists not a single widely accepted and empirically tested explanation of the experience of any one of these countries.

In these circumstances, a survey of population problems will necessarily reflect the personal judgments of the author on the state of knowledge. It is best that this be understood in advance. The following discussion ranges over many of the issues of population growth today, first at home and then abroad. An attempt is made to use economic theory and relevant facts to illuminate the issues. No claim is made to exhaust any given question; the appended bibliography gives leads for those who want to pursue the literature further. Some may feel a disproportionate role is given to economic theory (though most economists will feel the opposite). Besides reflecting the author's professional bias, this is partly intentional. It is my belief that economics may eventually contribute significantly to clarifying these questions, and if the present discussion helps stimulate further work along these lines it will have served much of its purpose.

American experience

Fertility behavior

The central questions with regard to American fertility are the causes of the long-term decline, which antedated those in most other developed nations, and of the post-World War II upsurge and more recent downturn in fertility. The factors responsible for these developments are the central concern of this section. First, however, it is necessary to set out briefly the economic theory of fertility, since this is not ordinarily included in the standard textbooks.

The theory of fertility.[2] The point of departure is the theory of consumer choice. Let us suppose households view children as a type of consumption good, yielding satisfaction like economic goods in general. Household desires for children can then be conceived in terms of an indifference map with number of children on one axis and commodities on the other. Any given point on the map expresses the degree of satisfaction attaching to

[2] The presentation here is highly simplified. A fuller exposition is given in [31]. Writings of special interest on the economic theory of fertility are [1, 3, 4, 38, 41, 54, 61, 65, and 67].

that particular combination of children and commodities. One can think too of a price tag attaching to children. This would consist of the discounted cost of the various expense items required to have and raise children (including the opportunity cost of the time devoted to child care), due allowance being made for their prospective contribution, if any, to family income. Together with product prices and household income, this establishes a budget line constraint. The interaction of this externally determined constraint with the subjectively determined indifference map identifies the combination of children and goods which will yield most satisfaction under given conditions of tastes, prices, and income. If the relative price of children were higher, because, say, the prices of child care items rose more than the average price of goods generally, the optimal combination would shift toward more goods and fewer children. If, subjectively, the attractiveness of commodities rose relative to that of children, a similar shift would occur. Finally, if the level of household income were higher, the optimal combination would include both more children and more goods, though the increase would not necessarily be proportionate. Thus, in equilibrium, the number of children people have would vary directly with household income and with the price of goods relative to children, and inversely with the strength of desires for goods relative to children.

Admittedly, it seems unrealistic to view household decisions about having children as such a highly rational process. But several considerations suggest a certain plausibility to the approach. First, if one takes commodity purchases proper, to which the theory of consumer choice is ordinarily applied, economic theory does not claim that households actually go through precise calculations. Rather, the argument is that purchase decisions involve a rough weighing of preferences against constraints of the type spelled out rigorously in the formal theory. More importantly, if the constraints or preferences change, behavior will change in a way predicted by the theory. Thus, confronted with higher prices for certain goods, a typical household will tend to substitute other goods. Again, if the household's income rises, it will feel freer to expand its purchases generally. While typically there are no actual calculations—indeed, reactions may be in a sense automatic rather than the product of conscious deliberation—behavior does change in a way implying the type of subjective balancing of preferences against constraints envisaged by the theory. Similarly, with regard to fertility decisions, children, like commodities, are a source of satisfaction. Indeed, just as one observes that one household differs from another with regard to the intensity of its desire for a given good—say, a vacation trip abroad—so, too, we detect differences in the strength of desires or tastes for children. Moreover, children, like commodities generally, are not costless. From prenatal medical expenses through college education, a child involves a long succession of outlays, of which the typical household is painfully aware. Finally, just as different commodities compete with one another for the household's dollar, so, too, do children compete with goods. Having another child this year may mean sacrificing a new car or a long-awaited month at the shore. Desires, costs, income—these do enter people's thinking about having children. And if this is so, then there is some plausibility to supposing that decisions about having children involve a rough balancing of preferences and constraints, maybe largely subconscious, of the type described in the economic theory of household commodity purchases.

For the explanation of actual fertility, however, the theory of consumer choice is not sufficient in itself. For one thing, fertility as usually measured relates to births, whereas the consumption good represented in an indifference map is surviving children, for this is what parents really want. This means that the state of infant and child mortality needs to be added to the analysis as a determining factor. For households to achieve a given number of surviving children, the necessary number of births would be higher, the higher the level of infant and child mortality.

Further, in the case of children, unlike most goods, households are producers as well as consumers. Since coition is itself a satisfaction-yielding activity, there is a consequent tendency for the number of children produced to exceed the optimal number. Production and consumption can be brought into line by resorting to various methods of fertility limitation. Practices of this sort range from those governing the formation and dissolution of unions during the reproductive period, through time-honored methods of fertility limitation such as abstinence, withdrawal, and induced abortion, legal or illegal, to modern contraceptives such as the IUD and oral pill. But this means that observed fertility behavior will depend in part upon attitudes toward and the extent of information about fertility control practices as well as access to such practices. If there were a variety of commonly known and costless fertility control practices, and no taboos on the use of such practices, then the actual number of births would tend to conform to the optimal number. But, in fact, fertility control practices at any given time are limited in number and they are not costless. Moreover, knowledge about such practices is imperfect, and different methods have varying degrees of social acceptance. As a result, in any actual situation, the use of fertility control will be less than perfect, and actual births will exceed the optimal number. The greater the supply of methods of fertility control and the lower their cost, the wider the diffusion of information about them, and the fewer the taboos on their adoption, the more nearly will actual fertility approach the optimal level.

To sum up this brief discussion of the theory of fertility, the following causal view is suggested. Tastes, prices, and income determine the optimal number of children. The latter, together with infant and child mortality conditions, determines the optimal number of births. Finally, actual births exceed optimal births to an extent depending upon attitudes toward and extent of information about fertility control practices, and the supply conditions of such practices. (A fuller model would need to allow also for the extent of uncertainty in households' evaluation of the determining factors.)

To apply this framework to the interpretation of actual fertility experience, it is necessary first to expand the discussion of tastes to include the factors shaping preferences for children and goods. While people's attitudes or tastes are doubtless influenced in part by current conditions, it seems reasonable to suppose that an even more important part is played by their prior experience. Where they were born and brought up, the kind of religion and education they had, how well off their parents were—these are all circumstances which go into the formation of attitudes regarding desirable life styles as adulthood is approached. These aspirations as to life style embrace among other things preferences with regard to number of children and level or standard of living.

Although a wide variety of factors enter into the formation of attitudes toward goods and children, we are especially interested here in those whose influence might change over time, since the subject of explanation is temporal variations in fertility. Three aspects of the process of economic development stand out as altering the intensity of desires for goods versus children. One of these is the growth of per capita income itself and the consequent secular uptrend in the level of living. The others are the progress of education and the introduction and diffusion of new goods. All of these tend to alter tastes in a manner adverse to fertility because they create or strengthen consumption outlets competitive with children as a source of satisfaction. Consider, for example, the secular growth in income. This means that typically young adults in a given generation come from more prosperous family backgrounds than those of the preceding generation, and their views on the material attributes of the "good life" are correspondingly enhanced. Goods which to one generation of young adults may have been luxuries become necessities of existence to the next—the automobile is a case in point.[3] Similarly, education creates awareness of and opens access to new modes of enjoyment. Thus while children are a recognized source of welfare to all, it is usually only those of higher educational status who consider foreign travel as a serious consumption alternative. The progress of education during economic development means that a growing number of households experience such a

---

[3] Economists are generally reluctant to analyze tastes or their determinants. The above reasoning is, however, basically a variant of one widely accepted proposition in economics relating to the determinants of preferences: of two families with equal current income, if in one income was previously higher than at present that family would be expected to spend proportionately more on consumption in order to maintain a standard of living to which it had become adjusted. In other words, *experience* with previous higher income levels alters tastes and thereby consumption behavior [8, 24, 55].

widening of consumption alternatives. And clearly, the development of new goods directly widens the range of items in competition with children.

With this view of taste formation added to our framework for fertility analysis, we are ready now to turn to the interpretation of actual experience. The next section takes up the recent swing in fertility, while the following considers the secular trend.

The recent swing in fertility. A summary picture of the movement of American fertility over the past half century is provided by the total fertility rate. As an indicator of movements in the rate of child-bearing from one year to another, this measure is superior to others such as the crude birth rate, because it is unaffected by variations in the age and sex composition of the population. Conceptually, the rate is the sum for a given calendar year of the age-specific birth rates for women in each single year of age between 14 and 49. As such, it indicates the total number of births per thousand women that would be produced by a hypothetical cohort of women which experienced these age-specific rates in successive years during the course of its reproductive career.

Figure 6–1. United States fertility rates, annually, 1917–1970 (rate per 1,000)

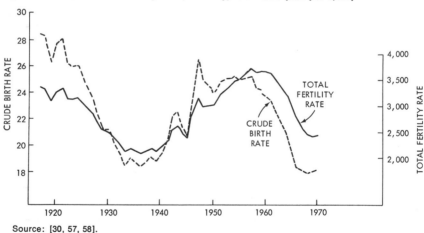

Source: [30, 57, 58].

By this measure, American fertility, after declining in the 1920s, reached an all-time low during 1933–39 (Figure 6–1). In the next eighteen years, it moved upward, reaching a peak in 1957. In that year, the high point of the half century, the rate was about 75 percent higher than its mid thirties trough. When this upsurge first occurred, it was interpreted as the usual rise in births which follows a war, but as the fertility rate remained at high levels into the 1950s, it became increasingly apparent that a new and wholly unexpected phenomenon in fertility behavior was taking place. Then, beginning in the late 1950s fertility started to drop off, at first slowly and then must much more precipitously. Within thirteen years, the fertility rate returned almost four fifths of the way toward the previous low. This abrupt decline was as unexpected as the postwar baby boom. The steeper decline in the crude birth rate (the annual number of births divided by total population) reflects that a decline was taking place in the proportion of women of child-bearing age in the total population—a negative influence on the birth rate which was foreseen. But the major part of the decline in the crude birth rate is due to the age-adjusted total fertility rate—a movement not anticipated. The upsurge in fertility since the 'thirties and the subsequent decline have generated a corresponding wave of population growth, described in one comprehensive study of the postwar economy as "perhaps the most unexpected and remarkable social feature of the time" [46, pp. 161–62].

The explanation presented here for the fertility swing builds on three factors in the preceding theory of fertility. By far the most important are income and tastes, but as regards the recent fertility decline, some weight is also given to contraceptive innovation, notably the oral pill.

With regard to income and tastes, the interpretation focuses on the changing balance between the income earning possibilities of young adults (the income variable) and their desired living levels (the taste variable). The basic idea is that if young men—the potential breadwinners of households—find it easy to make enough money to establish homes in the style desired by them and their actual or prospective brides, then marriage and childbearing will be encouraged. On the other hand, if it is hard to earn enough to support the desired style of life, then the resulting economic stress will lead to deferment of marriage and, for those already married, resort to contraception to avoid childbearing, and perhaps also to the entry of wives into the labor market.

A young man's view of his earning potential is likely to be shaped by his labor market experience. If times have been good and jobs easy to come by, then his assessment of his income prospects is likely to be correspondingly favorable. On the other hand, while recent experience may play some part, the material aspirations of a young adult are probably formed to an important extent by his earlier economic socialization experience. Thus young persons who have been raised in households where goods were abundant are likely to have developed relatively high consumption standards. The state of affluence of one's parents' household depends, in turn, on the parents' income, and this is typically a function of the labor market experience of the father. Thus, the balance between income earning possibilities of young adults and their desired living levels may be seen as depending largely on the comparative earnings experience (or labor market experience) of young adults and their parents.

While the available data do not permit very precise testing of this argument, a rough approximation is possible for the recent fertility decline.

The basic idea is conveyed in Figure 6–2. This shows the movement since 1940 in the fertility of married women aged 20–24—first up, and then down —much like the pattern for all women of reproductive age shown in Figure 6–1. The two curves in the lower panel of the figure are an attempt to approximate the time series movement of the income (curve *A*) and tastes

Figure 6–2. Marital fertility of females aged 20–24, estimated absolute and relative income experience of young adults, and percent of women married less than five years not using oral contraception, varying periods, 1940–1970

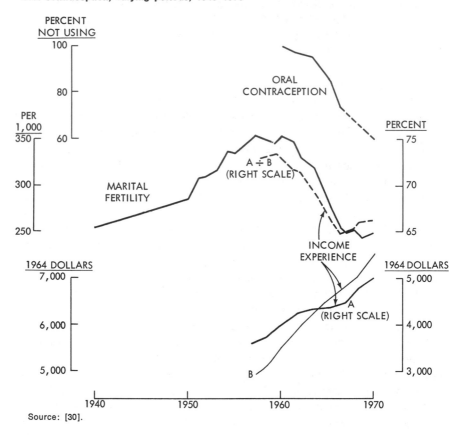

Source: [30].

(curve *B*) of these women and their spouses.[4] One can see from curve *A* that the income experience of successive cohorts of young couples was generally improving during this period, though not at a uniform rate. If this were the only fertility determinant that was changing, there would have been an upward pressure on fertility. Curve *B* shows, however, that

---

[4] The precise derivation of these magnitudes is described in the source article [30]. This article gives also a fuller discussion of other aspects of the recent fertility swing which are taken up only briefly in the present section.

during the course of this period these couples were coming from progressively more affluent households. Thus, while their income prospects were moving upward, so too were the life style aspirations that they had acquired in their parents' homes. The broken line in the middle panel *(A÷B)* shows the relative movement in their income—how income prospects were changing relative to desired living levels. This reveals that although the absolute income of successive cohorts of young couples was typically moving upward, their relative income was declining—especially in the first part of the 1960s. Thus they were experiencing what one might call an "economic squeeze"—a decreasing ability to live in the manner to which they aspired. Because of the crudity of the estimating procedure, not much confidence can be placed in the precise magnitudes of change shown. But the figures seem sound enough to infer that the balance between earnings possibilities and desired living levels of young adults was shifting in an adverse way in the 1960s, and especially in the first part.

If, now, one compares the relative income curve in the middle panel with that showing the marital fertility of young couples, the similarity in movement is striking. Both show a pronounced downward movement concentrated in a period of about seven years. However, the amplitude of the decline is somewhat greater for the fertility series, and in the later 'sixties it levels off rather than turns upward as does the relative income curve.

The explanation for the disparity between the two curves is most likely due to the introduction of oral contraception starting around 1961. In the upper panel of Figure 6–2, the percent *not* using the pill is shown, so that a downward movement in the pill series would lead one to expect a correspondingly downward movement in fertility. From this it appears that the diffusion of oral contraception exerted a consistently negative influence on fertility during this period. As a result the fertility decline in the first part of the 1960s is somewhat greater than might have been expected from the relative income curve alone. Similarly, in the latter part of the 1960s fertility tends to level off rather than rising, as one would have expected from the movement in the relative income curve alone.

It is important to realize that the impact of the pill on fertility is much smaller than one would expect from the figures on adoption of the pill alone. The graph indicates that by 1970 over 40% of young married women were using oral contraception. But if the pill were not available most of these women would have been using some other type of contraception. The available evidence indicates that the appearance of the pill has had rather little impact on the extent of contraceptive use; rather, its chief impact on fertility appears to have arisen from replacing less efficient techniques (especially the practice of rhythm by Catholic women) [64].

Thus, considering the fertility decline in the light of the changes in both relative income and oral contraception, one is led to the conclusion

Figure 6–3. Birth rate of females aged 20–24 and estimated absolute and relative unemployment experience of young adults, 1930–1970

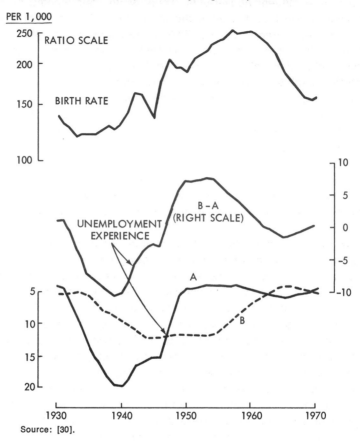

Source: [30].

that relative income has been the dominant factor in the fertility movement since the late 1950s. However, its influence has been modified by the appearance and spread of the pill.[5]

Figure 6–3 is an attempt to illustrate the plausibility of the relative income argument for the full period of the fertility swing, including the upsurge from the 1930s. In this case the estimating procedure is even cruder. The assumption is that the relative income of young adults depends

---

[5] One other factor, a "marriage squeeze", appears to have had some impact in the recent fertility decline, though its influence has been largely confined to fertility of 15–19 year olds, especially those who are less well educated. Since women typically marry men somewhat older than they are, the postwar baby boom has produced a situation in which an upsurge in the number of young females eligible for marriage has not been matched by a contemporaneous rise in the number of males available for marriage. The resulting "marriage squeeze" has consequently led to a decline in the proportions of young women marrying and a corresponding reduction in their fertility.

on how the general unemployment rate during the period in which the sons were in the labor market compares with that during the period their fathers were in the market. For example, if a given cohort of sons experiences much poorer labor market conditions than did their fathers and a second cohort experiences better conditions than did their fathers, then one would expect that the relative income of the first cohort of sons would be lower than that of the second.

The unemployment experience curves for the sons (curve *A*) and fathers (curve *B*) are plotted in inverted fashion in the lower panel of Figure 6–3. Thus an upward movement in a curve indicates more prosperous conditions (reduced unemployment). In the middle panel, the two curves are differenced to obtain a measure of the labor market experience of sons relative to their fathers, and hence implicitly of the relative income of the sons. An upward movement of the *B-A* curve signifies an improvement in the relative position of sons, and conversely for a downward movement. The movement of this curve indicates a decline in the relative position of sons in the 1930s, a marked improvement to the 1950s and then a noticeable decline to the mid 1960s. In the latter period, however, the relative status of sons was still considerably higher than it had been in the 1930s. As a comparison with the birth series in the upper panel shows, these movements accord reasonably well with the ups and downs shown by the fertility rate. There is some suggestion that the economic series leads the fertility series in timing in the post-World War II period, but in view of the much greater crudity of this relative position index than that used in Figure 6–2, it is probably best not to make much of this timing difference. What is noteworthy is that the amplitude of the recent fertility decline leaves the series at present in much the same position relative to its preceding trough and peak as the *B-A* series. It seems, therefore, that the evidence, crude as it is, is consistent with the hypothesis that shifts in the relative income position of young adults have played a major role in the swing in their fertility performance since the 1930s.

The secular fertility decline.   At the start of the nineteenth century, American fertility was extremly high. According to two authorities, the birth rate at this time "was markedly higher than that ever recorded for any European country and is equaled in reliably recorded data only by such unusually fertile populations as the Hutterites and the inhabitants of the Cocos-Keeling Islands." [14, p. 35] The reproductive performance of a number of today's high-fertility nations is modest by comparison with the early American record.

The astounding thing is that from about 1810 on, American fertility started to decline. And this, shortly after a vast expansion of natural resources had been accomplished through the Louisiana Purchase! While the data are not perfect, by 1860, for the white population, the ratio of children under five to women 20–44 years old (the fertility measure most generally available) had fallen by a third from its 1810 level, and by 1910, by over a half. Put differently, in 1790 almost half of the free families contained five or more persons; by 1900, the proportion of families with five or more persons had fallen to less than a third.

How can one reconcile this dramatic reduction in fertility with the seemingly abundant state of natural resources throughout much of this period? The present analysis builds on the economic theory of fertility, sketched above. The population is subdivided into several component groups, each subject to rather different conditions. Attention is focussed on a classification in terms of location—frontier areas, settled agricultural areas, new urban areas, and old urban areas. The argument is that the basic fertility determinants—in particular, the cost of children, fertility control practices, and factors other than income change influencing tastes —vary among these locations in such a way that fertility tends to be progressively lower as one moves from the first to the fourth of these situations. Since the course of American economic growth in fact involved a population shift in just this direction, the result was a continuing secular pressure toward fertility reduction.

To take up first the matter of tastes, as we have seen two determinants directly bound up with economic and social development are the progress of education and the introduction and diffusion of new goods. Both tend to alter preferences for goods versus children in a manner adverse to fertility, because they create or strengthen consumption outlets competitive with children as a source of satisfaction.

Considering different locations at a given time, education was typically more advanced, and hence this influence stronger, in older rural areas than on the frontier, in urban areas than rural, and in older urban areas than in newer urban areas.

Much the same type of argument may be made regarding new goods. New products were more available in older rural areas than on the frontier, because the marketing system was more advanced; hence a wider range of items competed with children in the older areas. Similarly, people in urban areas were more exposed to new goods than people in rural areas by virtue of the greater market potential offered by the denser populations, residents of older urban areas being more exposed than those in newer.

As for costs of childbearing, both the outlays on and returns from children tended to create cost differentials among areas with an effect on fertility similar to that of tastes. On the frontier, with its demands for breaking and clearing new land, the potential labor contribution of children was greater than in established agricultural areas. Also, with land relatively abundant, the problem of establishing mature children on farms of their own was less serious. Nevertheless, in the established agricultural areas, the labor contribution of children on family farms was higher than in cities where work possibilities were more restricted. At the same time the costs of raising children were higher in the cities, since food and housing were typically more expensive there than in rural areas. Thus, taking account of both costs and returns, children were increasingly expensive as the situation changed from frontier to settled agriculture to an urban location.

Finally, consider the situation with regard to methods of fertility limitation. In general, knowledge and availability of a variety of fertility control practices were greater in urban areas than in rural. Similarly these conditions were better in settled agricultural areas than on the frontier, which was at the periphery of the communications network.

Putting together these influences—tastes, cost, and fertility control practices—leads one to expect the following ordering of areas from high to low fertility at any given time: frontier, settled agriculture, new urban areas, old urban areas. Also since frontier areas gradually become transformed into settled agriculture and new urban areas into old, one would expect that over time fertility would decline as new areas "age". Moreover, since "new" and "old" are matters of degree, not of kind, one might expect that even in settled agricultural areas and older urban areas, fertility would continue to decline, at least for some time, as "aging" continues.

These expectations are supported by the available evidence, though much more work is needed. In Figure 6–4, the ratio of children under

Figure 6–4. Number of children under 5 years old per 1,000 white women 20 to 44, United States, 1800–1969, and rural, by division, 1800–1840 and 1910–1960

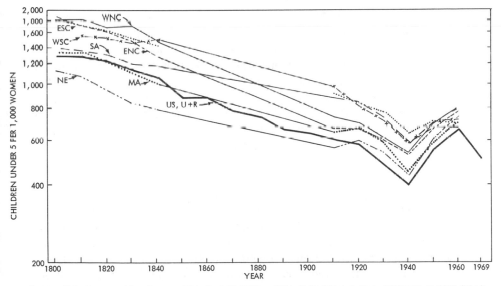

Source: U.S. Bureau of the Census, *Historical Statistics of the United States, Colonial Times to 1957* (Washington, 1960), and *Historical Statistics of the United States, Colonial Times to 1957; Continuation to 1962 and Revisions* (Washington, 1965) Series B39–B68. Urban and rural classified by 1940 Census rules.

five to females aged 20–44 is shown for the rural white population in each geographic division from 1800 to 1960; Figure 6–5 presents similar data for the urban white population. In both figures the United States ratio is depicted by a heavy line. This is the average for the population as a whole, rural and urban combined, and therefore provides a common reference point in the two figures. Unfortunately the rural-urban data are not available from 1850 to 1900; hence the 1840 and 1910 observations for each division are connected with a thin line. The Mountain and Pacific divisions have been omitted, because of the absence of data for the period when they were being settled. One would expect these divisions to be somewhat different from the others, however, because of the importance of mining rather than agriculture in their early development. Similarly, the nonwhite population has been omitted for lack of data. It is the white population, however, which predominantly accounts for the national patterns.

The child-woman ratio used here as a fertility measure typically exceeds the crude birth rate by a factor in the neighborhood of 20 to 25. Analytically, this reflects that fact that the child-woman ratio is computed from (a) a denominator about one-fifth as large as that for the crude birth rate (females aged 20–44 instead of the total population), and (b) a numerator four to five times as large. (Implicitly, birth experience over a five-year period is totalled rather than averaged, and is multiplied by a survival rate on the order of .80 to .95 to exclude those dying before the end of the period.) Although the child-woman ratio is an imperfect measure of fertility, it provides a reasonable basis for a preliminary test of the implications of the foregoing analysis.

Consider first the differentials by location in the early part of the 19th century. As shown in Figure 6–4, among rural areas, fertility was lower in the older settled areas in the East than in those undergoing settlement, the areas west of the Appalachians. This differential between new and old areas existed in both the North and the South. Differences among areas in the age distribution of women of reproductive age, whether due to vital rates or migration, had little to do with this fertility differential. The same differential between newer and older regions holds also for urban areas (Figure 6–5). Thus it is the three older East Coast divisions which are grouped together at the bottom of Figure 6–5. Even the seemingly partial exception, the West South Central division, is not really an exception, because the figures are dominated by Louisiana, an area which was settled early. Finally, within every division, urban fertility is lower than rural fertility. This is quickly seen by comparison with the U.S. reference line in the two figures. Virtually all of the urban ratios are below the U.S. average, and except for New England, almost all rural ratios are above. Thus, there is a clear and consistent pattern of fertility in frontier areas exceeding that in older established areas, and of rural fertility generally exceeding urban.

Figure 6–5. Number of children under 5 years old per 1,000 white women 20 to 44, United States, 1800–1969, and urban, by division, 1800–1840 and 1910–1960

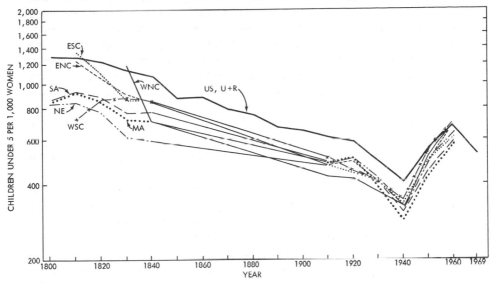

Source: Same as Figure 6–4.

With regard to trends, the U.S. ratio declines from 1810 on, and this is seen to occur in both rural and urban sections of all geographic divisions, though with some differences in timing. Frontier areas become progressively settled and new urban areas are transformed into old, while within the older rural and urban areas the process of aging continues.[6]

Mention should be made of another possible influence in the secular fertility decline, the lowering of infant and child mortality. The child-woman ratio fails for the most part to reflect this influence, since it relates not to births but to surviving children as of the census date. The trend in American mortality for much of the 19th century is uncertain. But it is clear that from the late 19th century onward, there was a substantial reduction in infant and child mortality, and this probably strengthened the tendency toward fertility decline, since fewer births would be needed to obtain a given number of surviving children.

The question arises whether the growth of per capita income associated with economic development may have exerted a strong counter force tending to raise fertility. The answer to this, suggested by our previous analysis of the recent fertility swing, is that income growth is a two-edged sword. On the one hand, it tends to make for higher fertility by augmenting the resources available to a household. On the other, it tends to lower fertility through an "intergeneration taste effect," because in a steadily growing economy successive generations are raised in increasingly

---

[6] For further evidence consistent with the interpretation here, see [35, 79].

affluent households and hence develop successively higher living aspirations in the course of their normal upbringing. Thus, while, on the one hand, each generation on reaching adulthood normally has more resources at its command, on the other, it has greater goods aspirations. If long-term growth is not steady, but fluctuating, temporary disparities can result between the growth of resources and that of aspirations with consequent swings in fertility, such as the United States has been experiencing in recent decades. Secularly, however, the two influences tend to cancel out in their effect on fertility. Whether they do so completely remains an open and important empirical question. It is clear, however, that if this view is adopted, then the presumption no longer holds that secular per capita income growth tends to raise fertility—the net effect could be positive, negative, or zero.[7]

It is worth noting that the fertility declines of the past were accomplished entirely by voluntary action on the part of the population. To some extent marriage was deferred. But also there were declines in fertility within marriage. These developments took place in a situation where not only was there no public policy to help those interested in fertility limitation, but attitudes, and even laws in many states, were hostile to the practice or even discussion of contraception or other fertility control practices. To emphasize the voluntary nature of this development, however, is not to suggest that there was no need for family planning policies then or, for that matter, that there is no need today. What historical experience shows is a voluntary decline in fertility, but this is not necessarily the optimal rate of decline from the point of view of social welfare. One can only conjecture how many households suffered from the miseries of unwanted children because of the hostile public environment. Today, as we shall see below, our evidence on this matter and on the need for intelligent public policy is straightforward.

Effects of the fertility swing

Age structure. A great swing in fertility of the type recently experienced in the United States results in striking differences in the rate at which various age groups of the population grow at any given time. The following are the recent and prospective percent changes of young age groups

---

[7] Evidence in support of the view is provided by recent research on Taiwan by Deborah S. Freedman:

". . . [T]he findings of this study suggest that the convergence of non-traditional family goals—namely, the achievement of new modern consumption standards—which may conflict with supporting a large family, influences couples to desire fewer children and can have an appreciable influence on the use of contraception to achieve family size goals. The steadily increasing income levels in Taiwan have not encouraged couples to have more children. Instead, these higher incomes have served to develop new wants particularly for the new kinds of goods and services development has made available and these new wants, in turn, have encouraged couples to take positive steps to limit family size" [37, p. 40; cf. 36].

according to the current series D projections of the Bureau of the Census [74, p. 7].

Age Group	1965 to 1970	1970 to 1975	1975 to 1980	1980 to 1985
5 to 13 years	+ 2.3	− 9.4	+1.7	+15.9
14 to 17 years	+12.4	+ 5.6	−8.1	− 7.5
18 to 24 years	+21.6	+12.5	+5.9	− 6.6

The figures in the first two columns can be accepted with substantial confidence; those in the second two columns for age groups below eighteen years rest on less certain assumptions.

Compare the prospective growth rates between 1965 and 1975 of 18 to 24-year-olds with those aged 5 to 13. Whereas young adults increase during the decade by over a third, the younger group actually declines in absolute size. That this difference stems directly from the swing in fertility can be quickly seen by comparing the birth years of the two age groups at successive dates.

Age Group	1965	1970	1975
5 to 13 years	1952–60	1957–65	1962–70
18 to 24 years	1941–47	1946–52	1951–57

The 5- to 13-year-olds of 1965 were born in 1952–60; those of 1970, in 1957–65; and of 1975, in 1962–70. Thus, this age group at quinquennial dates from 1965 through 1975 hails from periods in which the birth rate was successively lower. The impact of this on the size of this group over time is correspondingly reflected in the net decline projected for it. The opposite is true for the 18–24-year-olds. Those who will be in this age group during the decade 1965–1975 come from the period of rising and high fertility of the 1940s and 1950s, and this group's size is accordingly growing markedly in the current decade. Thus, the historical turn-around in fertility in the late 1950s leaves its imprint currently on the population in the form of differing magnitudes and even directions of growth for virtually adjacent age groups.

The age structure effects of the fertility swing, in turn, have further consequences on the economy. Consider, for example, the area of education. The age groups selected above correspond roughly to those at three different levels of schooling—elementary, secondary, and higher education. Through 1980, there will be little need for additional facilities or teachers at the elementary level, aside from needs associated with changes in population distribution. In higher education, however, requirements will be rising noticeably. But, if the projection above proves correct, by 1980–85 this situation will have been reversed; at that time, pressures on elementary school will be rising, while at the college level they will be declining. Clearly, the adjustments necessitated by fertility swings call for a flexible and adaptable economic system.

Labor force and household growth. Echo effects of the fertility swing may be seen also in the rate at which the economy's labor force and households grow. This is illustrated in Figure 6–6.

Compare first the upper and middle panels. The upper panel shows the course of the birth rate since the 1920s. The lower curve in the middle panel, showing labor force growth attributable to population change, relates to a period starting 18 years later, when the impact on the labor

Figure 6–6. Labor force and household growth due to all sources and to population growth, compared with birth rate 18 years earlier, 1940–1980

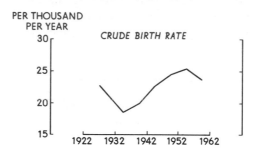

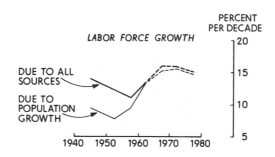

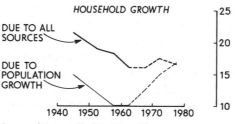

Source: [29, pp. 190, 218; 57, p. 2.]

market of those born in a given year shown in the upper panel would principally be felt. Although the birth rate curve is not the only factor influencing this labor force curve, the similar movements of the two show clearly the dominant influence of the birth rate.

Actual labor force growth, the upper curve in the middle panel, differs somewhat from the lower curve. The difference reflects the fact that with a given size population the labor force may change as a result of variations in the proportion of the population participating in the labor force. Even with regard to this curve, however, the echo effect of the fertility movements is apparent, for it does not differ markedly from the one reflecting population change alone.

To some extent, the same can be said if one compares the birth rate pattern with the two household growth curves shown in the lower panel. In this case, however, it is noteworthy that the curve showing the influence of population change on household growth lags both the corresponding curve for labor force and the birth rate. This is because the median age of household formation is several years later than that of labor force entry. For example, according to the projections used here the recent fertility decline makes its first impact on labor force growth in 1975–80. In that period, however, household growth due to population change is still rising. Not till the following quinquennium would the impact of the fertility downturn on household growth become apparent. Thus, echo effects of fertility movements of the past appear subsequently in different economic magnitudes but with variations in timing and amplitude.

Economic-demographic interactions: An illustration

This discussion has explored, first, possible ways in which economic factors may bear on the fertility swing, and then effects of this swing on the economy. But the economy may react again on fertility, which, in turn, further influences the economy, and so on. So far, little research has been done to explore such interactions; but a simple model of one, perhaps relevant in some measure to ongoing experience, can be presented as illustration.

Note has already been made of the impact of fertility variations on age structure. But the age structure may itself influence fertility through mechanisms of the type suggested earlier. This can be briefly illustrated by a model based on very simple assumptions: (1) fertility varies directly with the income of young adults relative to that of their parents, and (2) the relative income of young persons varies directly with the proportion of older persons to younger. The second assumption follows from economic theory which suggests, other things being equal, that if older workers are plentiful relative to young, their wages will be depressed relative to those of younger workers—i.e., the relative income of the younger group will be raised.

On these assumptions, in a period when the number of older persons is growing relative to young, the relative income position of the young and, correspondingly, their fertility would tend to rise. Conversely, when the number of older persons is declining in proportion to younger, fertility would tend to decline.

Figure 6–7. Fertility rate and relative number of young adults, 1940–1985

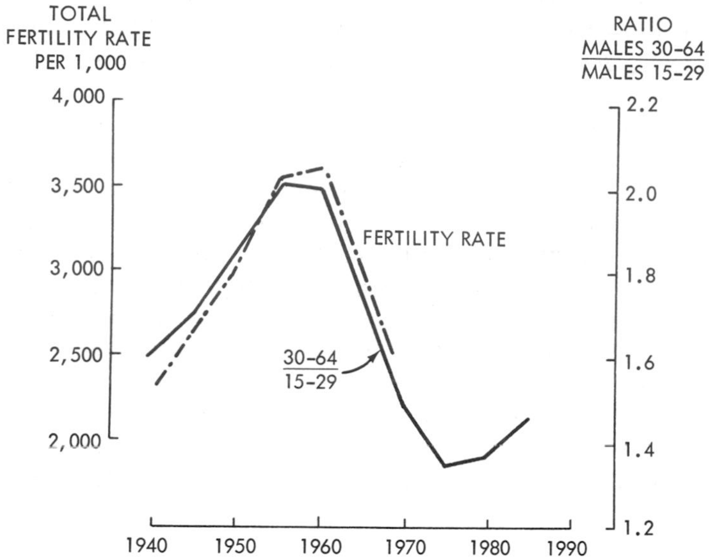

Source: [29, p. 216; 57, p. 6.]

As shown in Figure 6–7, from 1940 on, the proportion of older to younger persons rises and then turns down in a manner remarkably similar, both in timing and magnitude, to the fertility rate. Conceivably, this age structure shift operating via relative income effects may have been one of the factors behind the fertility swing.

But the fertility rate with a lag itself affects the age structure. Thus, the rise in fertility from 1940 to the midfifties, through its eventual impact on the growth in the number of young persons, is principally responsible for the current decline in the proportion of older to younger persons. Similarly, the decline in fertility now going on presages an eventual turn-around in the proportion of older to younger workers. As shown in the chart, after 1975 this ratio starts up again, similar to the 1940s. If such a rise were one of the important influences behind the earlier baby boom, it might betoken another in the future. One could even imagine a self-generating mechanism whereby, other things being equal, age structure changes operating via relative income caused fertility changes, but the fertility changes with a lag reversed the age structure changes, and hence fertility, and so on.

All this is highly simplified and speculative, and, as with most of the subjects in the chapter, much more research is needed. One useful lesson, however, may be drawn. In thinking of the future outlook for U.S. fertility, it would be unwise to assume that the fertility rate is likely to level off at some constant value. Rather, it is possible that continued fluctuation of the type experienced in recent decades may characterize future experience as well.

Longer term issues of population growth

Major swings in fertility and thereby in the rate of population growth cause important fluctuations in various supply and demand conditions in our economy. These clearly discernible effects, however, pale by comparison with the dire consequences attributed to growth of population over the long run, as in advertisements such as the following:

A hungry over-crowded world will be a world of fear, chaos, poverty, riots, crime and war. No country will be safe, not even our own. . . . What can we do about it? A *crash* program is needed to control population growth both at home and abroad. . . . It's the best, most humanitarian, least expensive way we know to secure the future peace and prosperity of our nation and the world.

The quality of living in America—as well as the peace of the world—is threatened by the Population Explosion. As our numbers grow the water we drink becomes more polluted day by day. The air we breathe may endanger our health. And we go out at night in our overcrowded cities at the risk of life and limb.

Our city slums are packed with youngsters—thousands of them idle, victims of discontent and drug addiction. And millions more will pour into the streets in the next few years at the present rate of procreation. You go out after dark at your own peril. Last year one out of every four hundred Americans was murdered, raped or robbed. *Birth Control is an answer* . . . [from advertisements quoted in 50, pp. 95, 97, 101; as quoted in 16, p. 3; emphasis in original].

These and similar themes have been taken up by newspaper columnists and television commentators, with an apparently major impact on public attitudes toward population growth. According to a 1971 survey of American attitudes:

More than half [of those surveyed] think government should try to slow population growth . . .

An equally large number believe people should voluntarily limit the size of their families even if they can afford more children [63, p. 22].

This widespread concern about the effects of population growth is manifested in the emergence of an organization advocating immediate adoption of a national policy of zero population growth (ZPG) and the proposal by

President Nixon in July 1969 for establishment of a Commission on Population Growth on the grounds that:

One of the most serious challenges to human destiny in the last third of this century will be the growth of the population. Whether man's response to that challenge will be a cause for pride or for despair in the year 2000 will depend very much on what we do today [15, p. xv].

In March 1970, Congress responded to this proposal by establishing a Commission on Population Growth and the American Future "to examine the probable extent of population growth and internal migration in the United States between now and the end of this century, to assess the impact that population change will have upon government services, our economy, and our resources and environment, and to make recommendations on how the nation can best cope with that impact" [ibid.].

Assertions about the adverse consequences of population growth often have such apparent plausibility that one tends to accept them almost without question. But such statements are propositions in social science and should be evaluated as such. Are the claimed causal linkages valid? If so, what is the quantitative importance of population growth versus other factors in causing the phenomenon under study? Consider, for example, the presumed connection between population growth and pollution. Since there are obviously other causal factors contributing to pollution, e.g. the types of technology used, what one really wants to know is to what extent cessation of population growth would in itself serve to reduce pollution.

As has already been suggested, the amount of systematic research on the long term effects of population growth is quite limited. We now have the benefit, however, of the substantial effort of the Commission on Population Growth (CPG) to survey and synthesize the relevant literature in its recently issued report. Since for some time to come, this is likely to be taken as authoritative, the present discussion will center on the Commission's views on the long term effects of American population growth. As shall quickly become apparent, these views are themselves controversial, which is hardly surprising in view of the limited amount of basic research on the subject.

Unwanted fertility.   It is desirable to distinguish between two arguments underlying the Commission's recommendations, one relating to the existence of unwanted fertility, and one dealing with the issues just posed about the adverse effects of population growth. The former argument centers on a table presented in the Commission's report, reproduced here as Table 6–1. This shows that 15 percent of all births to currently married women between 1966 and 1970 were reported by the parents as having never been wanted. For those with low levels of education the figure rises much higher. The Commission notes that while not all unwanted births become unwanted children, these figures imply important social, psy-

Table 6–1. Unwanted fertility in the United States, 1970*

Race and Education	Most Likely Number of Births per Woman	Percent of Births 1966–70		Theoretical Births per Woman without Unwanted Births
		Unwanted	Unplanned †	
All Women:	3.0	15	44	2.7
College 4+	2.5	7	32	2.4
College 1–3	2.8	11	39	2.6
High School 4	2.8	14	44	2.6
High School 1–3	3.4	20	48	2.9
Less	3.9	31	56	3.0
White Women:	2.9	13	42	2.6
College 4+	2.5	7	32	2.4
College 1–3	2.8	10	39	2.6
High School 4	2.8	13	42	2.6
High School 1–3	3.2	18	44	2.8
Less	3.5	25	53	2.9
Black Women:	3.7	27	61	2.9
College 4+	2.3	3	21	2.2
College 1–3	2.6	21	46	2.3
High School 4	3.3	19	62	2.8
High School 1–3	4.2	31	66	3.2
Less	5.2	55	68	3.1

* Based on data from the 1970 National Fertility Study for currently married women under 45 years of age.
† Unplanned births include unwanted births.
Source: Reproduced in full from [15, p. 164].

chological, health, and financial costs to the children and parents involved, and concludes:

The Commission believes that all Americans, regardless of age, marital status, or income, should be enabled to avoid unwanted births. Major efforts should be made to enlarge and improve the opportunity for individuals to control their own fertility, aiming toward the development of a basic ethical principle that only wanted children are brought into the world.

In order to implement this policy, the Commission has formulated the following recommendations . . . :

The elimination of legal restrictions on access to contraceptive information and services, and the development by the states of affirmative legislation to permit minors to receive such information and services.

The elimination of administrative restrictions on access to voluntary contraceptive sterilization.

The liberalization of state abortion laws along the lines of the New York State statute.

Greater investments in research and development of improved methods of contraception.

Full support of all health services related to fertility, programs to improve training for and delivery of these services, an extension of government family planning project grant programs, and the development of a program of family planning education. [Ibid., pp. 166–167.]

Note that the above argument for these measures is not based on any claim that population growth has adverse effects. The idea is simply that unwanted births imply serious reductions in human welfare. The aim of programs to reduce or eliminate unwanted fertility is not to reduce the rate of population growth as such, though this effect would probably occur, but to improve welfare directly by reducing the human costs attendant upon unwanted births. A logical counterpart of this argument would be a proposal for programs to help persons who have fewer children than they want to increase their fertility. The Commission report does in fact advance proposals for research in reproductive biology to help persons with problems of infertility, though the attention devoted to such problems is extremely small [15, pp. 179–180, 185].

Adverse effects: Summary of CPG views. The CPG Report estimates that prevention of unwanted births would reduce fertility in the United States by about 60 percent of that needed to stabilize population growth. The Commission favors going further than this, however, and while rejecting an attempt to attain zero growth immediately, recommends "that the nation welcome and plan for a stabilized population" [15, p. 192]. While CPG nowhere specifically says so, essentially this amounts to recommending that families be encouraged generally to adopt a two-child norm. (An eventual zero rate of population growth could be attained with cohort fertility of about 2.25 births per woman.) The basis for this is the Commission's findings on the effects of population growth. The argument is summarized as follows:

We have examined the effects that future growth alternatives are likely to have on our economy, society, government, resources, and environment, and we have found no convincing argument for continued national population growth. On the contrary, the plusses seem to be on the side of slowing growth and eventually stopping it altogether. Indeed, there might be no reason to fear a decline in population once we are past the period of growth that is in store.

Neither the health of our economy nor the welfare of individual businesses depend on continued population growth. In fact, the average person will be markedly better off in terms of traditional economic values if population growth slows down than if it resumes the pace of growth experienced in the recent past.

With regard to both resources and the environment, the evidence we have assembled shows that slower growth would conserve energy and mineral resources and would be a significant aid in averting problems in the areas of water supply, agricultural land supply, outdoor recreation resources, and environmental pollution.

.   .   .   .

For government, slower population growth offers potential benefits in the form of reduced pressures on educational and other services; and, for the people, it enhances the potential for improved levels of service in these areas. We find no threat to national security from slower growth. While population growth is not by any means the sole cause of governmental problems, it magnifies them and makes their solution more difficult. Slower growth would lessen the increasing rate of strain on our federal system. To that extent it would enhance the likelihood of achieving true justice and more ample well-being for all citizens even as it would preserve more individual freedom.

Each one of the impacts of population growth—on the economy, resources, the environment, government, or society at large—indicates the desirability, in the short run, for a slower rate of growth. And, when we consider these together, contemplate the ever-increasing problems involved in the long run, and recognize the long lead time required to arrest growth, we must conclude that continued population growth —beyond that to which we are already committed by the legacy of the baby boom— is definitely not in the interest of promoting the quality of life in the nation [15, pp. 116–117].

These statements are somewhat more moderate than those in the advertisements cited at the beginning of this section. There is no attribution, for example, of "crime in the streets" to population growth. Indeed, in several cases the argument is not about the adverse effects of population growth, but simply against the view that high growth may be beneficial ("Neither the health of our economy nor the welfare of individual businesses depend on continued population growth." "We find no threat to national security from slower growth.") There are, however, some specific indications of adverse effects. While it is not possible to go into each of these effects here, we can at least look at those which involve substantial economic aspects, and these comprise an important part of the Commission's argument.

The basic procedure followed by CPG is to try to estimate the prospective situation in the year 2000 on two alternative assumptions—one that American families will have an average of two children per family, the size the Commission favors, and the other, an average of three children, the size for cohorts which have recently completed their childbearing. (In both cases immigration is assumed to continue at its current levels.) As shown in Table 6–2, from the CPG report, the two child average would yield a total population in the year 2000 of 271 million, almost 16 percent smaller than that which would result from the three-child average. The question is, then, how much better off the United States would be with the two-child rather than the three-child rate of population growth.

Per capita income. One major economic argument of CPG relates to the level of real per capita income—in the CPG's words, above, "the average person will be markedly better off in terms of traditional economic values if population growth slows down than if it resumes the pace of growth experienced in the recent past." The Commission's argument is spelled out as follows:

. . . [I]n the year 2000, per capita income may be as much as 15 percent higher under the 2-child than under the 3-child population growth rate. The main reason for the higher per capita income under the 2-child projection is the shift in the age composition resulting from slower population growth; as we saw earlier, people of working age will constitute a larger fraction of the total population under conditions of slower population growth. A secondary reason is that with lower birthrates the percentage of women in the labor force is expected to rise somewhat faster than it would otherwise. Taken together, these trends mean relatively more workers and earners, and relatively fewer mouths to feed [15, p. 46].

Table 6–2. U.S. population, 1970 and 2000 (numbers in millions)

	1970	2000	
		2-Child Average	3-Child Average
Total all ages	205	271	322
Under 5	17	20	34
5 to 17	53	55	80
18 to 21	15	17	24
Under 18	70	75	114
18 to 64	115	167	179
65 and over	20	29	29
Dependency Ratio * ...	78	62	80

* Number of persons 65 and over plus under 18 per 100 persons 18 to 64.

These data are based on the Census Bureau's *Current Population Reports*, Series P–25, No. 470, "Projections of the Population of the United States by Age and Sex: 1970 to 2000." These projections served as the basis for much of the research reported in this volume. We examined how the population would grow between now and the year 2000 under the 2-child family projection (Census Series E) and under the 3-child projection (Census Series B).

Series B assumes that in the future, women will be giving birth at an "ultimate" rate averaging out to 3.1 children per woman over her lifetime. The transition from the 1969 rate of 2.4 to the "ultimate" future rate is not instantaneous in the projections, but most of the change is assumed to occur by 1980. The 3.1 figure is an average for all women, regardless of marital status. In the United States today, almost all women (95 percent) marry at some time in their lives, so the Series B rate of childbearing represents a reasonable approximation to an average family size of 3 children.

Series E assumes an ultimate rate of childbearing that works out to an average of 2.1 children per woman over a lifetime. This is the rate at which the parental generation would exactly replace itself. The extra 0.1 allows for mortality between birth and the average age of mothers at childbearing, and for the fact that boy babies slightly outnumber girl babies.

Different generations born in the 20th century have reproduced at widely varying average levels, some exceeding three children (as did the women born from 1930 to 1935) and some approaching two (as did women who were born from 1905 to 1910). The fact that major groups in our modern history have reproduced at each of these levels lends credibility to projections based on either of these averages.

It is assumed in both projections that future reductions in mortality will be slight. The net flow of immigrants into the United States is assumed, in the projections, to continue at the present level of about 400,000 persons annually.

Source: Reproduced in full from [15, p. 20].

The reasoning turns on the third term of the formula:

$$\frac{\text{Output}}{\text{Population}} = \frac{\text{Output}}{\text{Labor Force}} \times \frac{\text{Labor Force}}{\text{Population}}$$

For any given value of output per worker (the second term), output per capita will be higher for two reasons—there will be relatively fewer persons (specifically, young persons) outside the prime working ages 18 to 64, and women in the child bearing ages would be more likely to be in the labor force. The former effect, the "dependency effect", can be estimated at 11 percent from the dependency ratios shown in the last line of Table 6–2

$$\left(\frac{1.80}{1.62} - 1.00\right) \times 100.$$

The latter effect, that of the greater labor force participation of women of childbearing age, would account for the rest of the 15 percent additional per capita income, or 4 percentage points. Prorating these two effects over the whole period from 1970 to 2000, they would together raise the annual per capita growth rate by about 0.5 per cent per year, not an insubstantial increase over the typical rate of around 2 to 2.5 percent.

However, there are some reservations about this argument which must be noted. First, consumption requirements vary among persons of different ages; generally speaking, youths and aged persons have lower requirements than those in the prime working ages. The disadvantage of the three child situation is somewhat reduced by this fact. For example, if it were assumed that those outside the prime working ages had a consumption requirement that averaged one-half of those in the working ages, and a calculation were made of output per "equivalent consumer", the advantage of the two-child family would be found to be cut by over one-fourth—from 15 to 11 percent. Second, it is possible that the time devoted to work or the intensity of work effort on the part of parents might be greater in the situation where dependency is greater—this would produce an increase in the second term of the formula tending to compensate for the decrease in the third term. Third, while lower fertility among women of reproductive age would result in more of them entering the labor force, this might force some older women out of the labor force. The reverse of this was seen in the 1940s and 1950s, when the greatly increased fertility of young women during the baby boom led to a reduction in their labor force participation and a sharp rise in that of women over age 35 [29, chs. 6, 7]. Taken together, these observations would lead to a more qualified view than that of CPG on the addition to material well-being that might occur with a two-child rather than a three-child rate of population growth. There is, in addition, the question whether one would want it, if such a gain were possible, a point which will be taken up subsequently.

Resources and the environment. The issue at stake here is to what extent more rapid population growth will add to the economy's demands for resources and exacerbate strains on the environment. A key consideration is the prospective size of total GNP in the two-child versus three-child situations. The Commission's view is as follows:

Regardless of future population growth, the prospect is that increases in output will cause tremendous increases in demand for resources and impact on the environment.

What happens to population growth will nevertheless make a big difference in the future size of the economy. In the year 2000, the difference in GNP resulting from the different population assumptions could amount to one-fourth of today's GNP. By the year 2020, this difference amounts to more than the total size of today's GNP.

In short, total GNP, which is the principal source of the demand for resources and the production of pollutants, will become much larger than it is now. But if population should grow at the 3-child rate, GNP will grow far more than it will at the 2-child rate [15, p. 57].

Thus, while the Commission recognizes that GNP will grow enormously, irrespective of population growth, it argues that greater population growth makes an important difference—"in the year 2000, the difference in GNP resulting from the different population assumptions could amount to one-fourth of today's GNP."

Again, however, the CPG's case is not clearcut, and critics can point to counter arguments. Consider, for example, the statement above on the comparative size of GNP on different population assumptions. The underlying calculations had not yet been made public at the time this was written, but on the face of it the projection is quite puzzling. Total GNP can, of course, be viewed simply as the product of population and per capita GNP. As we have just seen, the Commission concluded that in the year 2000, per capita income might be 15 percent higher in the two-child situation. Since, according to the Commission's figures shown in Table 6–2, total population in the two-child situation would be just about the same proportion less (a little under 16 percent less), it is hard to see how they arrived at any substantial difference in total GNP between the two population situations.

Suppose, however, that one were to accept the CPG statement that the difference in GNP resulting from different population assumptions amounts to as much as one fourth of total GNP today. In assessing this statement, one should recognize that on either population assumption, there would be an implied increase of GNP by the year 2000 on the order of *nine* fourths of total GNP today. Hence, reducing the rate of population growth would relieve the additional demands on resources and environment by no more than one-ninth. And this is setting aside the problem of the inconsistency between the CPG's projections of population, per capita GNP, and total GNP.

As the foregoing indicates, a crucial issue in assessing the population problem is how much contribution lower population growth may make to solving a particular problem. This point is further illustrated by the CPG analysis of pollution. The discussion focusses on "the major products of combustion—carbon monoxide, carbon dioxide, oxides of nitrogen, oxides of sulfur, hydrocarbons, and particulates—and several measures of water pollution, including biochemical demand for oxygen and suspended and dissolved solids," since other pollutants, such as radiation and pesticides, "are very difficult to link to population and economic growth in any simple and quantitative fashion" [15, p. 67]. Hydrocarbon emissions are used for illustration, since the relationships for this pollutant hold generally for the entire first class of pollutants mentioned. Hydrocarbon emissions in the year 2000 are estimated under different assumptions regarding, not only population growth, but also technology, GNP, and abatement policy. As shown in Figure 6–8, a reproduction of a CPG chart, the key to reducing this source of pollution is an active abatement policy. In the Commission's words:

> In the next 30 years, most of these pollutants can be eliminated by enforcing treatment standards for pollution emissions. Slower population and economic growth would help; but over this period, by far the biggest reduction in pollution can be achieved by a head-on attack [15, p. 67].

The Commission goes on to note that "[w]hatever we assume about future treatment policy, pollution emissions in the year 2000 would be less with the two-child than with the three-child rate of population growth—from five to twelve percent less, depending on the pollutant" [15, pp. 67, 69]. This statement derives from comparing emission values in Figure 6–8 such as 34 with 37 or 254 with 270, and is clearly dealing with a minor part of the pollution problem. It is on grounds such as this that Barry Commoner, a prominent ecologist, recently stated:

> One issue . . . is to determine whether there are *scientific* grounds sufficient to warrant the conclusion that improvement of environmental quality in the United States requires that the present fertility level be reduced to the point of achieving zero growth in population size (or as some would have it, to reduce the size of the population).
> In fact the scientific evidence regarding the role of population size in United States environmental problems shows that population size is *not* a decisive factor [16, p. 29, emphasis in original].

Urbanization. Many of our most pressing domestic problems today are associated with urban growth, and population increase is frequently cited as an important cause of this urban growth. The implication is that stabilization of population growth would result in substantial abatement of these urban problems. The CPG position on this is similar to that on the problem of the environment—population stabilization would help, but it's not the whole answer:

> Perhaps the most significant effect of population stabilization on the distribution of population is the most obvious: Zero growth for the nation will mean an average of zero growth for local areas. It may be that the most effective long-term strategy for stabilizing local growth is through national stabilization, not redistribution.
>
> .   .   .   .
>
> However, even if the population of our country were to stop growing today, we would still have problems associated with rural depopulation and metropolitan growth. Our large metropolitan areas would still have problems of congestion, pollution, and severe racial separation [15, pp. 43–44].

The present discussion will be addressed specifically to the issue of how important population growth is as a cause of urban problems.

The first point to be noted is that the problems under discussion arise from the geographic concentration of population, not its absolute size or rate of growth. This point is made by Professor Ansley Coale of Princeton University in his presidential address to the Population Association of America:

Figure 6-8. Hydrocarbon emissions, 1970 and 2000 (millions of pounds per year)

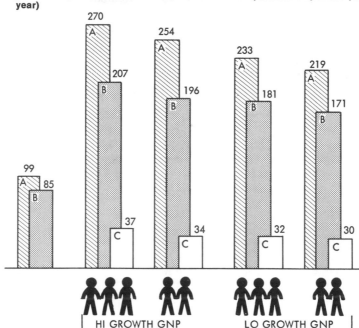

A population half or three quarters the current one in the United States could ruin the potability of our fresh water supplies and poison our atmosphere by the unrestricted discharge of waste. Australia has a population of less than 12 million in an area more than 80% of the United States. Yet Sydney has problems of smog, water pollution and traffic jams. In fact, most of the social and economic problems ascribed to our excessive population in the United States or to its excessive rate of growth are affected more by how our population has chosen to distribute itself than by its size. *The problems arise from excessive concentration in the metropolitan areas, not from excessive total numbers.* More than half the counties in the United States have *lost* population in each of the last two inter-censal decades. The density of population is 4.5 times greater in France, 10 times greater in the United Kingdom, and 30 times greater in the Netherlands than in the United States, yet pollution, traffic jams, and delinquency are no worse in those countries than here. Even if our population rose to a billion, its average density would not be very high by European standards. It seems to me that we must attack the problems of pollution, urban deterioration, juvenile delinquency, and the like directly, and if sensible programs are evolved, continued population growth in the order of one per cent annually would not make the programs tangibly less effective. [12, p. 5; italics in fifth sentence added].

To this, the objection may be raised that rapid population growth forces

Figure 6-8 (continued)

The generation and emission of hydrocarbon pollutants is shown under different assumptions about future population growth, economic growth, changes in technology, and pollution abatement policy.

The bars labeled A, shown for background purposes only, indicate the levels of hydrocarbon wastes that would be generated under present technology: These waste levels would be generated if there were no changes in technology between the 1967–1970 base period and the year 2000.

The bars labeled B show actual emissions of hydrocarbon pollutants in 1970 and expected emissions in the year 2000, assuming no change in pollution abatement policy. The difference between A and B shows the extent to which the introduction of more efficient, less wasteful technology between now and the year 2000 is expected to reduce the generation and emission of pollutants below the levels generated if technology remained unchanged. Such changes in technology are likely to come anyway; they do not depend on public pressure to reduce harmful residuals.

The B bars show that, even with improved technology, pollution levels would be much higher in the year 2000 than they are now. These levels would, however, be somewhat lower if population grew at the 2-child rate rather than the 3-child rate, and if the economy grew at a slower rate rather than a more rapid rate (lo-growth GNP vs. hi-growth GNP).

The bars labeled C show hydrocarbon emissions in the year 2000 assuming an active pollution-abatement policy. The assumed policy is the Environmental Protection Agency's 1975 standard for emissions into the air. The changes in production and waste treatment processes induced by this policy would have a greater effect than would any of the other changes shown—in technology, population growth, or economic growth.

Source: Reproduced in full from [15, p. 68].

---

population concentration in cities. In this view, while superficially urban problems are associated with excessive population concentration, the concentration, in turn, stems from high population growth.

This argument mistakes the cause of urbanization. Consider a few facts. Between 1880 and 1940, while the U.S. population grew by about 80 million persons, the urban percentage rose from 28 to 50 percent. If this population increase is deemed to be the cause of the substantial rise in urbanization, how is one to explain the following: between 1881 and 1941, the population of prepartition India rose by around 130 million, but the percentage urban hardly changed—in 1881 it was 9.3 per cent; in 1941, 12.8 per cent? Moreover, this much greater absolute growth of the Indian population occurred on a land area less than half that of the United States. It is clear that substantial population increase in India did not force urbanization, while in the United States a much smaller increase on a much greater land area was accompanied by a major rise in the geographic concentration of population. Furthermore, in France, population scarcely changed between 1840 and 1940; the growth rate averaged 0.1 percent per year. Yet in this real world example of virtually zero population growth, the proportion urban rose during this period from 24 to 52 percent.

The characteristic which the United States and France share in common as opposed to India—and which accounts for rapid urbanization—is not rapid population growth, but the adoption of modern technology. Before the era of modern economic growth, in any society of considerable size the mass of the population was necessarily concentrated in rural areas, engaged chiefly in agricultural production. The massive concentration of a nation's population in urban centers is a new phenomenon on the world scene. At bottom, it is owing to the nature of modern technology underlying economic growth. This technology has brought major economies of scale in a number of lines of nonagricultural production, and has drastically reduced transportation costs. The influence of this in promoting concentration of nonagricultural production has been reinforced by what are known as "agglomeration economies" and a shift in consumption patterns toward a smaller proportion of food, as per capita incomes rise. This urban concentration reflects, at bottom, a reallocation of resources in response, not to population growth, but to the technology and demands that go with modern economic growth.

Indeed, as Coale observes, in the United States, as in many of the countries which have developed, the movement toward urban concentration has proceeded to the point where rural areas are being depopulated. Even in areas as large as states, a significant leveling off of population and in some cases absolute declines have appeared—examples are the Dakotas and Nebraska, West Virginia, Mississippi, Arkansas, Oklahoma, and (since 1960) Wyoming. Thus after several centuries devoted to settling this vast continent, the American population is now in the process of vacating large parts of it.

Granted that population growth is not the cause of urban concentration, the fact is that the American population is now highly concentrated in urban areas. "Population growth *is* metropolitan growth in the contemporary United States . . ." [15, p. 25, emphasis in original]. Moreover, "our metropolitan population at the end of the century will be nearly 50 million greater if American families average three rather than two children" [15, p. 37]. Should we not opt now for slower population growth in order to prevent the aggravation of urban problems that this growth implies? The answer is that this is like saying that if we could stop our population from growing, our future unemployment or poverty problems would be less because fewer people would be around to be unemployed or poor. The solution to unemployment and poverty calls for direct attack on the factors in our socioeconomic system that produce these malfunctions. In the absence of public policy measures specifically directed toward unemployment and poverty, these problems will still be with us even with a zero population growth rate. Correspondingly, appropriate public policies should be able to solve these problems whether we have a two- or three-child rate of population growth. This point is aptly illustrated by the previous discussion of pollution due to hydrocarbon emissions. The public policy appropriate to this problem is abatement policy. With such a policy we can drastically reduce pollution; without it, we cannot. In either case, whether we have a two- or three child rate of population growth makes little difference in the result. Similarly, in the present case of excessive urban concentration, the problem is one of a misallocation of resources—the price system has not adequately registered the full costs attaching to different productive locations. Clearly the solution to such problems must lie in trying to modify in the public interest, not household decisions regarding family size and migration, but those of business firms and nonprofit organizations regarding the location of their economic activities—decisions which heretofore have omitted the social costs of increasing geographic concentration. It is ironic indeed to see, on the one hand, the changing course of economic opportunity pull the American population first westward and then, even more strongly, cityward to such an extent that numerous areas begin to empty not long after they are filled, and to find, on the other, that population increase rather than economic development is charged for urbanization and its problems.

Social goals and population policy. We have examined a number of arguments about the adverse effects of American population growth, including most of the principal ones. A more extended survey would not alter the basic finding, namely, that population growth is not the *bête noire* that some make it out to be in popular discussions. While there may be some adverse effects of population growth, these are usually exaggerated, and the contribution which stabilization of population growth can make to specific problems is typically small.

Then why, it may be asked, all the concern about population growth? Several reasons come to mind. In part, concern about population growth at home is a natural corollary of the fears which have been created by publicity about the "population explosion" in today's less developed nations. (We shall look into this question shortly.) If population growth is bad for "them," why not for "us"? In part, it reflects a search for answers by the general public in a time when fundamental beliefs and institutions are being challenged. Malthus was not the first exponent of the view that population growth constitutes a major obstacle to human progress. But he came forward with this view in the aftermath of the French Revolution, and his argument quickly became a keystone of the reaction. The population explanation of the baffling problems confronting the nation today has appeal because it is simple and plausible. But it does not stand up to serious scrutiny.

The question may be asked: Even if the adverse economic and ecological effects of population growth are unproven or greatly exaggerated, why not initiate policies to stabilize population growth just to be "on the safe side"? While we may not be sure that a smaller rate of population growth would noticeably raise the growth rate of per capita income or substantially relieve environmental pressures, what harm is there in adopting policies to lower population growth? After all, we know that population growth cannot continue indefinitely. According to CPG, "no substantial benefits would result from continued growth of the nation's population. This is one of the basic conclusions we have drawn from our inquiry" [15, p. 191].

This view leads into the question of social goals. Heretofore we have been dealing with questions of social science—what effect does population growth have on specific social phenomena? The above viewpoint, however, goes beyond the realm of social science into the area of value judgments. As a citizen, in forming one's judgment on public policy proposals, one must consider not only whether a proposed policy is likely to have the desired effect, but also the desirable goals of society—the "good life" toward whose achievement public policy should be directed. This last is a matter of personal value judgments, on which social science can say neither "yea" nor "nay". Because judgments on the good life fall outside the realm of social science as customarily construed, conclusions on policy issues may legitimately differ because of personal differences regarding the ends of society.

The relevance of social goals to the present issue may be shown by a simple illustration. Consider two societies initially identical with regard to GNP, population, and per capita GNP. If the initial values for each of these magnitudes are set at an index value of 100, we have at the first date:

Society	GNP	Population	GNP per Capita
A	100	100	100
B	100	100	100

Assume now that GNP grows fourfold in both societies, but in A total population remains unchanged, while in B it doubles. Thus, at the second date, we have:

Society	GNP	Population	GNP per capita
A	400	100	400
B	400	200	200

In society A, per capita GNP has grown twice as much as in Society B; in B, population has grown twice as much as in A. The question is: which society is better off?

To judge from popular discussion and the CPG statement the answer would unequivocally be society A. Before jumping to that conclusion, however, it is useful to translate the example into personal experience. Suppose "society" is replaced by the term "family," and the example is viewed as relating to the experience of two households starting from the same position and moving through the child-bearing ages. Both families experience the same growth in total income. In one, the husband and wife use this income partly to bear and raise children. In the other, they use it entirely to increase the economic goods at their own disposal; for example, they may take trips abroad, an enjoyment beyond the reach of the couple facing the costs of child-raising.

Couched in these terms, it is less clear which family is better off. If, given the same resources, one family prefers children to foreign travel, and conversely for the other, who is to say which is happier? Perhaps the most that can reasonably be concluded is that, given their preferences, each would be less happy in the position of the other.

Correspondingly for the comparison of the two societies: If one recognizes that children are a source of satisfaction for which parents may sacrifice other pleasures, then the possibility follows that in situation 2 the members of B may consider themselves more fortunate than those of A, and vice versa. It further follows that advocacy of policies aimed at shifting B into A's position may not be in the interest of the best welfare of the residents of B, *as they conceive their welfare.*

Too much can be made of this simple illustration. For one thing, when the discussion shifts to the level of society, it is, of course, wrong to suppose that the unchanging population total of society A implies that households have no children. Under mortality conditions in the United States today, for example, constant population size over time is consistent with an average of somewhat more than two children per couple. Nevertheless, the issue raised by the example remains. The population trend of society B implies, let us say, one more child per family than in A, and hence positive population growth. If one's judgment of the good society embraces free choice on the number of children, as well as cars, on which families spend their income, then it is far from clear that B is worse off than A. On the other hand, if one's view of the good life excludes the welfare value of children, then A is clearly better off. To reiterate, there is no scientific basis for choosing between these views of social ends; each individual must make up his own mind.

Let us revert to the previously discussed CPG projections of real per capita income for the two-child versus the three-child rate of population growth. The Commission's approach sees the two-child situation as better because real per capita income would be 15 percent higher (by its estimate), and "no substantial benefits" would result from the extra population growth. But is it not conceivable that, despite higher per capita income in the two-child situation, parents might feel themselves poorer because they have only two rather than three offspring? When CPG says there would be "no substantial benefits" in the higher population growth situation, it is disregarding the welfare value of children.

It is worth emphasizing that proponents of early population stabilization are often advocating a special view of human welfare, since they themselves are sometimes seemingly unaware of this. CPG itself says, for example:

> We are concerned with population trends only as they impede or enhance the realization of those values and goals cherished in, by, and for American society.
> What values? Whose goals? As a Commission, we do not set ourselves up as an arbiter of those fundamental questions [15, p. 118.]

Since children are obviously one of the goals cherished by American society, the Commission, in its advocacy of a two-child norm, is certainly setting itself up as an arbiter of social values. In a similar vein, the Commission says:

> Our immediate goal is to modernize demographic behavior in this country: to encourage the American people to make population choices, both in the individual family and society at large, on the basis of greater rationality rather than tradition or custom, ignorance or chance [15, p. 7].

Few students of society would deny that "tradition or custom, ignorance or chance" influence behavior. But few would suggest that such influences are peculiar to demographic behavior. Is it more rational, for example, to prefer having a sports car, camper, and power boat to having three children? This is the logical implication of the Commission's preference for per capita income growth over population growth. (Indeed, when the comparison is stated in this way, one can quickly see why the higher per capita income and lower population situation may create more pressure on the environment.)

The point of these remarks is not to argue for one or another set of social goals, but to make clear that the issue of social goals is intimately involved in the advocacy of programs for stabilizing population growth soon, as in the CPG report. In the absence of solid evidence on sizeable adverse effects of population growth, such programs would unnecessarily penalize those whose preferences especially favor children.

If nothing is done to limit population growth, won't population go on growing until intolerable conditions result? This question implies that human reproductive behavior does not voluntarily respond to environmental conditions. Instead, man, like animals, following his natural instincts, will "breed" without restraint and population will grow until environmental limits force a halt through higher mortality.

Our earlier survey of the historical trend in American fertility provides no support for this view. Rather the historical record suggests an adaptation to changing environmental conditions of dramatic magnitude. There is little reason to suppose that this adjustment process has exhausted itself, though swings in fertility may obscure the basic trend. Indeed it seems likely that the three-child family which plays such a prominent and unfavorable role in the CPG analysis, represents a recent peak of one of these swings, and that the average over the next three decades will be below this, even if unwanted fertility remains as high as estimated in the CPG report.

Conclusion. Does all this mean, then, that there is no need for public programs relating to fertility? No, only that it is difficult to build a strong case for such programs in terms of the adverse effects of population growth. But, as the CPG report shows, there are more direct considerations which point to the need for public policy in this area. We know that American families often have children earlier than they intended, and sometimes have in total more children than they would like. We know too that extralegal abortions are all too frequent in our society. Circumstances such as these imply serious welfare losses to the persons involved. When unwanted children are present, child care generally is likely to be poorer and the intellectual and physical development of children suffers. The parents are subjected to serious strains and emotional stress. Clearly welfare would be advanced by programs aimed at helping parents to have the number of children they want when they want them. Nor should such programs be biased in an antinatalist direction; they should also aim to help those who are having trouble in achieving their family size goals. Similarly, welfare would be advanced if access to knowledge and techniques of family size limitation were freer. Given the intensely personal nature of these matters, on the one hand, and the heretofore negative disposition of government and society on the other, the welfare return per dollar spent on population programs may be high, quite aside from any economic or ecological effects.

The world population explosion

The facts of the population explosion speak for themselves. Table 6–3 presents estimates of the world rate of population growth by broad geographic area since 1750 and the UN's medium projected rate through the year 2000.[8] In the three half centuries before 1900, world population grew at a rate of about 5 percent per decade. Since then, the growth rate has been twice as large, and the projected rate for the remainder of the century is larger still—17 percent per decade. Stated differently, at the growth rate prevailing in the century and a half before 1900, it took about 115 years for world population to double; at the growth rate projected through the

---

[8] This discussion of world population growth rates draws on the presentation of Bourgeois-Pichat [7]. The data are preliminary estimates by John D. Durand, a revised version of which has been published in [25].

end of this century, population would double in about 40 years. World population, which was slightly short of 3 billion in 1960 would be almost 6 billion by the year 2000.

This recent acceleration in world population growth arises from trends in the less developed parts of the world—Africa, Asia, and Latin America. As the detail in Table 6–3 shows, population growth rates in Europe and

Table 6–3. Estimated average rate of growth of world population by region, 1750–1960, and projected, 1960–2000 (percent per decade)

Area	Medium Estimates				
	1750–1800	1800–1850	1850–1900	1900–1960	1960–2000
World total	5	5	6	10	17
Asia	5	5	3	10	18
Africa	. . .	. . .	8	10	26
Europe	5	5	8	6	5
U.S.S.R.	8	9	12	8	13
Latin America	10	11	12	20	27
U.S. and Canada	. . .	30	23	15	15
Oceania	. . .	. . .	. . .	16	17

Source: [7, p. 7].

the overseas areas settled by it have come down in this century. In contrast, those in the other continents have risen to virtually unprecedented levels, matched or surpassed only in the early settlement stage of Northern America and Oceania.

This phenomenon reflects major reductions in death rates in less developed areas, toward levels more like those in the now-developed countries. The improvement in life expectancy which this betokens is a major advance from the viewpoint of human welfare. Europe, too, went through a phase of declining mortality and rising population growth rates, but the decline in birth rates in this century has, as noted, brought population growth back down to lower levels. In the less developed areas so far, there have been only a few small indications of fertility declines—in Singapore, Taiwan, Korea, Hong Kong, and Malaysia, among others. The question naturally arises whether the persistence of high population growth rates does not seriously imperil economic growth in these areas—indeed, whether there is space enough in the world to support such unusually high rates for very long.

Although the principal concern in this part is with the effects of population change on economic growth, a few words, at least, should be said on the matter of physical space. Some writers have noted that at the world's present population growth rate, the density of the earth's population would reach one person per square meter in seven and a half centuries—a period of time which, while not negligible, seems alarmingly close.[9] We are thus "sitting on a demographic time bomb," "a growth process which . . . within 65 centuries and in the absence of environmental limits, could generate 'a solid sphere of live bodies expanding with a radial velocity that, neglecting relativity, would equal the velocity of light.' "[10]

Such calculations are designed to show, among other things not only that there is a physical limit to the world's population—an obvious point— but that, at the present growth rate, this limit is being rapidly approached. If *at the present growth rate* a density of one person per square meter is only some seven centuries away, it is natural to ask whether the world can afford, in terms of physical space alone, a half century, let alone a century of high population growth, even if the rate may subsequently come down.

The catch lies in the lesson that all children learn when they eagerly deposit their pennies, expecting them to blossom promptly into dollars. Compound interest takes time to work its awesome effects. This may be seen most readily by starting seven and a half centuries hence with a world population of 135,000 billion—1 person per square meter—and working back in time. Given a growth rate which doubles population every 40 years, moving back 4 decades would yield a population one half the terminal figure, moving back 8 decades would yield a population one fourth the terminal figure, and 12 decades, one eighth the terminal figure. Doubling the entire time span again—roughly to 2½ centuries—would yield a population $\frac{1}{8} \times \frac{1}{8}$ or $\frac{1}{64}$, of the terminal population; and doubling it once more— to 5 centuries—$\frac{1}{64} \times \frac{1}{64}$, or less than 1/4000 of the terminal figure. In other words, of the increase from 3 to 135,000 billion that the present world growth rate would produce in 7½ centuries, most would take place in the last 150 years of the period projected. The present population of the world is about .00002 of that corresponding to a density of 1 person per square meter. At the present growth rate, it would be .00004 in 40 years, and .00010 a century from now. A quintupling of population density in a century is no insignificant matter; on the other hand, it hardly implies the exhaustion of physical space. Let us turn, therefore, to the more pressing question of the effect of population growth on per capita income.[11]

Theory

First, what does economic theory have to say? The most common reasoning, the Malthusian analysis, is rooted in the law of diminishing returns.

---

[9] The concept of population density is an ambiguous one and difficult to quantify. It is used here, as customarily, simply as the ratio of population to total land area.

[10] [66, p. 21]. The reference within the quotation is to [11, p. 36].

[11] The treatment below follows the somewhat fuller presentation in [28]. For a valuable recent discussion of many of these issues, see Kuznets [49]. Important studies stressing the adverse effects of population growth are [13, 51, 59]. A good survey of the literature prior to the early fifties is given in [68, chap. xiii].

With due allowance for the lag between birth and labor force entry, population growth implies growth in the labor supply. However, growth in the labor supply does not in itself yield a proportionate growth in output. Labor is but one of the inputs in the production process, and only if all inputs were increased in the same proportion would it be reasonable to expect output to grow correspondingly. If they are not, and if production methods remain unchanged, then one would expect output to grow less than proportionately to labor. To put it differently, if technology is assumed fixed, then population growth coupled with slower or zero growth in one or more other productive agents implies that there will be progressively less material, equipment, and/or natural resources per worker and, hence, that output per worker will tend to diminish.

In this reasoning, the fixity of natural resources, particularly land, is most often emphasized, and the inference is drawn that agricultural productivity and thus food supplies per capita will become progressively less. (Of course, if the new workers provided by population growth simply increase the number of unemployed and do not add to the actual labor input in the economy, the productivity of *employed* labor will be unaffected, but total output will have to be shared among greater numbers so that per capita output will decline).

Some recent variants of this analysis are concerned with the relation, not of natural resources to population, but of reproducible capital—structures, equipment, and inventories—to population. The stock of reproducible capital is taken as normally growing, rather than constant, at a rate varying with the proportion of national income invested. If population and labor force were constant, then capital per worker and, hence, output per worker would normally grow over time. Population and labor force *growth* would imply a reduction in the increase of capital per worker—part of the addition to capital being required simply to keep the stock of capital per worker constant—and a consequent slowing down of the growth of output per worker. This viewpoint thus sees high population growth not necessarily as reducing the *level* of output per head but as lowering the rate of increase—the higher the rate of population increase, the greater the reduction in the growth of output per head.

Such reasoning is often used in discussions of development plans in less developed countries. For example, in response to a recent U.N. inquiry on problems resulting from the interaction of economic development and population changes, the reply of the government of Ceylon stated:

> . . . unless there is some prospect of a slowing down in the rate of population growth and relative stability in at least the long run, it is difficult to envisage substantial benefits from planning and development. It is not so much the size of the population in an absolute sense; but rather the rate of increase that tends to frustrate attempts to step up the rate of investment and to increase income per head. Apart from the difficult process of cutting present levels of consumption, the source for

increasing the volume of investment is the "ploughing back" of portions of future increases in incomes. This task is handicapped if these increases have instead to be devoted each year to sustaining a larger population.

. . . Population growth has obviously an impact on the magnitude of the economic, social, and financial problems which we have to solve. For instance, the Government's current expenditure on food subsidies, education and health is now considerably higher than it would have been if our population had increased at a slower rate. The same applies to our import requirements and the scarcity of foreign exchange [69, pp. 19, 20].

While the Malthusian approach is most commonly emphasized, economic theory also recognizes the possibility of favorable effects from population growth. The most common argument is that relating to economies of scale and specialization. Within a productive establishment, there tends to be at any given time an optimum scale of operation, large in some industries, small in others. If the population is small, then the domestic market will not be able to support the most efficient level of operation in some industries. Extending one's view from an establishment in a given industry to the economy as a whole brings into view additional productivity gains associated with increased size. George Stigler has put it as follows.

The large economy can practice specialization in innumerable ways not open to the small (closed) economy. The labor force can specialize in more sharply defined functions . . . The business sector can have enterprises specializing in collecting oil prices, in repairing old machinery, in printing calendars, in advertising industrial equipment. The transport system can be large enough to allow innumerable specialized forms of transport, such as pipelines, particular types of chemical containers, and the like [17, p. 61].

The view is frequently expressed by economists that economies of scale are significant in accounting for the high productivity of the United States economy.

It does not follow, however, that any given nation must have a population large enough to realize all or even most of such gains if it is willing to participate in international trade. Through specialization in particular branches of economic activity and exchange with other nations, it is possible for a nation to achieve high levels of economic development. This is one important argument for customs unions and free trade areas among smaller, less developed nations today. It also helps explain why among the richest nations today are some with small populations, such as Switzerland, Norway, Finland, Denmark, Israel, and New Zealand. But to recognize this is not to gainsay that increasing population size within a given geographic area widens the alternatives available for productivity gains.

A second view makes the point that accelerated population growth in less developed areas today is a reflection of sweeping reductions in the death rate, and that the health advances that have made this possible have themselves expanded productive capacity and promoted attitudes favorable to economic development. Thus, a major survey of the world social situation points out:

Medical services and medical advances are often pace-makers of social change. Penicillin (and the whole range of antibiotics which followed its discovery) and DDT (and the other insecticides) have already transformed the lives of millions, not only by benefiting the individual directly, but also by increasing capacities and changing the attitudes of whole communities [70, p. 22; cf. 34, pp. 271–82].

A concrete example of the impact on economic productivity of the health advances which have at the same time raised population growth is offered later in the report:

. . . disease is a considerable factor in the incapacity of people to feed themselves. In Mymensingh, a district in East Pakistan, malaria control not only diminished infant mortality ("more mouths to feed") but increased the production of rice by 15 per cent—from the same acreage ("more and better hands to work") without any improvement in methods of cultivation or the variety of rice. This increase was due to the fact that whereas in the past three out of every five landworkers had been sick of the fever at the critical seasons of planting and harvesting, five out of five were available for the manual operations when the malaria had been controlled. In other areas, removal of a seasonal malaria has made it possible to grow a second crop. In still others, hundreds of thousands of acres of fertile land, which had been abandoned because of malaria, have been recovered for cultivation. People who are sick, ailing and incapacitated by disease lack the energy, initiative and enterprise needed to adopt new methods and improve their means of food production and so increase the yields from existing acreages [70, p. 36].

It should be noted that in this argument, the line of causation is not from high population growth to improved productivity. Rather, high population growth *and* improved productivity both arise from the same source— the reduction in mortality and associated improvement in health. It could be argued that if the mortality reduction were accompanied by a fertility reduction, so that population growth did not accelerate, then the productivity increase would be higher, for the positive effects of better "quality" workers would not be partially offset by the tendency toward diminishing returns produced by a greater quantity of workers. Thus, while this analysis does, on the one hand, point up a dubious aspect of the usual Malthusian argument as it bears on the present situation in less developed areas— the assumption that the quality of labor is unchanged—it does not deny that the stimulus to increased numbers as such is adverse.[12]

Another argument, however, is based directly on accelerated population growth—or at least natural increase—as the cause. The key element in this analysis is the impact of the pressure of increased family size on

---

[12] Barlow [2] has constructed a simulation model of Ceylon's post-World War II experience which assumes only adverse productivity effects from the rapid population growth there due to malaria eradication and related mortality-reducing developments. The model recognizes, however, the positive stimulus these developments themselves had on productivity, and this is found to more than offset the negative effects of population growth for several decades.

individual motivation. It may be illustrated by comparison with the Malthusian approach. Assume in a population initially with a zero growth rate that a substantial cut occurs in the infant mortality rate owing, say, to new public health measures. The effect will be to raise dependency and, with a lag, the labor supply. Assuming no change in production methods or other productive factors, the employment of this extra labor will reduce output per worker and consumption per head of the population.

At this point, a question might be asked whether human beings are likely to be totally oblivious to these Malthusian implications. Clearly, the rise in dependency creates a threat both to the maintenance of existing consumption levels and to future improvements therein. Will individuals passively accept this consequence? Or may the threat posed by this population pressure provide the motivation for changes in behavior?

At least three broad alternatives to passive acceptance come to mind. One, stressed in Kingsley Davis' presidential address to the Population Association of America, is a change in demographic behavior such as a reduction in fertility or rise in out-migration. Looking back at Western European experience over the past century and a half, Davis asserts:

Although generally overlooked because of our preoccupation with the contraceptive issue, the fact is that every country in northwest Europe reacted to its persistent excess of births over deaths with virtually the entire range of possible responses. Regardless of nationality, language, and religion, each industrializing nation tended to postpone marriage, to increase celibacy, to resort to abortion, to practice contraception in some form, and to emigrate overseas [21, pp. 350–51].

The stimulus to this, in Davis' view, is the decline in mortality and sustained natural increase to which it gave rise.

Mortality decline impinged on the individual enlarging his family. Unless something were done to offset this effect, it gave him, as a child more siblings with whom to share whatever derived from his parents as well as more likelihood of reckoning with his parents for a longer period of life; and, as an adult, it gave him a more fragmented and more delayed share of the patrimony with which to get married and found his own family, while at the same time it saddled him, in founding that family, with the task of providing for more children—for rearing them, educating them, endowing their marriages, etc.—in a manner assuring them a status no lower than his [*ibid.*, p. 352].

The second alternative is a change in productive behavior—e.g., the adoption of new production methods or increased saving to utilize more capital in production. Population pressure arising from mortality reduction may provide the spur to work harder, search out information, increase capital formation, and try new methods. Recent exponents of this view have been Colin Clark, A. O. Hirschman and Ester Boserup [6, 9, 47]. Boserup argues that what are typically regarded as more advanced agricultural techniques have actually required more labor per unit output—that is, the sacrifice of leisure. Historically, populations which have been aware of the availability of more advanced methods have often resisted their adoption until growth raised population density to a point compelling the adoption of such methods in order to maintain consumption levels. With this shift may come better work habits and other changes facilitating sustained economic growth. Whether or not one accepts this specific argument, it seems clear that the initiation of new forms of economic acitvity might be a possible response to population pressure.

A third alternative is resort to political action. This possibility is noted in studies of both historical and contemporary experience.[13] In an analysis of Italian emigration before World War I—a situation of intense population pressure—J. S. MacDonald suggests that in some areas, rather than emigrate, populations chose to "[remain] *in situ* while attempting to change the *status quo* through militant working-class organization . . ." [52, p. 61]. With reference to today's less developed areas, J. E. Meade, in his presidential address to the Royal Economic Society, notes the potential for social conflict in Mauritius because of the institutional conditions under which the "population explosion" is occurring [53]. Marshall Wolfe, generalizing about experience in Latin America, observes that "the nuclei of small cultivators . . . undergoing a multiple squeeze from population increase, deterioration of their land through unavoidable over-use, and declining opportunities for seasonal labour on the large estates" turn, among other things, to "organized demands for division of the land of the large estates, in some areas reaching a point of chronic violence . . ." [78, p. 459]. Writing of experience in Asia and the Far East, Ulla Olin notes that "what is not often explicitly stated, but probably sensed, is the fear that continued population growth may, through its adverse effect on economic development, lead to social unrest and possibly to the overthrow of the existing social order" [60, p. 314]. She develops this as follows.

Take a large city in an Asian country today. Its population contains typically a very large number of young in-migrants, preponderantly male, who have come from towns and villages in search of employment and the "new" life. They hope the city will offer them the opportunities they feel are denied them in their place of origin. A few will make good and adjust without undue difficulty to city life. The majority, whether successful in their bid for employment or not, will find city life frustrating. The freedom from traditional bonds is obtained at a price: employment—if secured at all—is not a sure thing; housing is expensive and usually inadequate; in times of trouble there are often no friends and relatives to turn to; wives—if found—may not be able to adjust; the day of work may be long and hard, etc. In short, the sum total of frustration (irritation) is staggering. As has been shown in numerous incidents, this is an atmosphere in which any appeal to injustices suffered falls into fertile ground. It makes little difference whether the alleged cause of grievance is imagined or real; the need for an outlet (counter-irritation) to the pent-up frustrations is far stronger than any incentive towards a rational assessment of the situation, which, in any case, would require the possession of information and a power of analysis beyond what is

---

[13] A recent study by Chamberlain [10] examines a number of the arguments touched on in this section.

available to any but the elite of society. This kind of situation is the main explanation for the sporadic outbursts of riots and disorders of various magnitude that have characterized the last two decades in Asia and the Far East [60, pp. 314–15].

All three of these alternative arguments involving the possibility of demographic, economic, and political responses to population pressure— take a view of human nature which contrasts strikingly with that underlying the Malthusian analysis. Whereas the Malthusian approach assimilates human to animal behavior (an analogy with an experiment involving fruit flies in a jar is frequently used), these alternative arguments center on decision making by human beings based on an awareness and assessment of their changing situation. In this respect, they link up with the seemingly remote analysis of recent American fertility presented in the preceding section. In both cases, a basic element in the analysis is what may be called the Deusenberry-Modigliani principle: previously experienced consumption standards influence current behavior. In secularly static societies, where change arises chiefly from random forces such as climatic conditions, behavior may appear to be dominated by custom and tradition, but this is because the secular environment typically changes little from one generation to the next, and so no new conscious assessment is required. But if a drastic improvement takes place in the survival of children, households will find themselves with larger families than anticipated, and corresponding pressure on their material living levels. In the terminology of economics, the actual (ex post) situation proves substantially different from the one envisaged (ex ante). The result is to force on households a need for fresh examination and assessment of the situation. Instead of mechanically persisting in customary behavior, new decisions may be forthcoming in one or more areas of behavior—migration, fertility, effort, saving, innovation, political activity, and so on.

Obviously, this line of reasoning does not lead to the conclusion that economic development will necessarily result from the pressure arising from accelerated population growth. It does question the view that human beings will passively breed themselves into a state of starvation without trying to do something about the situation. But since change is often painful, adjustments may be minimized and little or no advance in income per head take place. Nor is the possibility of social conflict, even if it ultimately fosters economic development, necessarily appealing. Clearly, the nature of the changes in behavior, if any, depends on many associated circumstances, such as the education of those involved, the supply of information, and perhaps most important of all, institutional conditions affecting mobility and the pursuit of opportunity.

But these arguments do in common point to a valid possibility typically overlooked in discussions of this subject: the possible role of population *pressure* in *inducing* new thinking and altered behavior. It may be that population pressure is one of the first important ways, though not necessarily the best, in which the process of modernization makes itself felt among the masses of the population. It may thus make for attitudes more receptive to change, including the kind essential to economic growth. If there is any validity in this view, government planners who consider high population growth only a liability are perhaps assuming to themselves too exclusive responsibility and influence in promoting economic growth. Perhaps population pressure is opening up opportunities for promoting widespread participation in new endeavors by the mass of the population, a development ultimately essential to the achievement of sustained economic growth.

The record

Although the theoretical possibilities include both favorable and unfavorable effects of population growth on per capita income, it is possible that one or a group of factors on either the positive or negative side may be so overwhelming in the size of its effect that it dominates actual experience. The history of the past two centuries embraces countries exhibiting a variety of population growth patterns both in time and space. Unfortunately, relatively little has been done to analyze carefully the implications of these for economic development. However, it is at least possible to ask, to the extent data are available, whether variations in population growth rates show any consistent relation to growth of product per capita. This question is no more than a start, for it fails to allow for variations among nations or through time in other growth-affecting factors which may obscure the actual relationship between population and economic growth. But if the effect of population growth were very strong relative to these other factors, then it might be expected to show up even in such a simple two variable comparison. Unfortunately, estimates of per capita income even for this century are generally not available, except for very recent years, and experience has shown that short periods are not necessarily reliable indicators of secular tendencies.

For what it is worth, Table 6–4 summarizes recent data on growth rates of population and per capita income for 50 less developed countries, those with populations under 1 million having been omitted. The table shows that since 1959–61, when population growth rates in most of these countries are among the highest ever experienced, per capita income has generally increased (line 1). Moreover, if India, where long period income estimates are available, is representative, it is likely that in a number of cases the current rates of per capita income growth are noticeably higher than earlier in this century [56]. Thus, accelerating population growth in recent years has not generally precluded positive per capita income growth, and has perhaps even been accompanied by accelerated income growth.

Table 6–4. Frequency distribution of developing nations by growth rate of real per capita income cross-classified by growth rate of population, 1959–61 to 1966–68

Rate of Population Growth, (percent per year)	Total	Rate of Growth of Real Per Capita Income (percent per year)						
		Less than Zero	0 to 0.9	1.0 to 1.9	2.0 to 2.9	3.0 to 3.9	4.0 to 4.9	5.0 and Over
Total	50	6	5	14	14	6	3	2
3.5 and over	4	1	0	1	2	0	0	0
3.0–3.4	17	0	2	5	2	4	3	1
2.5–2.9	17	2	3	3	6	2	0	1
2.0–2.4	8	2	0	3	3	0	0	0
1.5–1.9	2	0	0	1	1	0	0	0
Less than 1.5 . . .	2	1	0	1	0	0	0	0

Notes: The countries included are noncommunist ones in Africa, Asia, and Latin America (except for Israel, Japan, and the Union of South Africa) with populations of around 1 million or more, for which data were available. In a few cases, data for one of the two variables were not available for the specified period, and the nearest overlapping period was used.

Source: Organisation for Economic Co-operation and Development, *National Accounts of Less Developed Countries 1959–1968* (Paris, June 1970).

Even if per capita income growth is in most cases positive, do those nations with relatively low growth of per capita income usually exhibit relatively high population growth, and vice versa? It is clear from the table that there is little evidence of any significant association, positive or negative, between the income and population growth rates. Cases of high per capita income growth are associated with both high and low population growth, and the same is true for cases of low per capita income growth. If the now-developed nations were added to the comparison, one would find that there was some indication that countries with higher growth rates of per capita income have lower population growth rates [49]. But if one were to go back before World War I and perform a similar analyis, including both developed and less developed nations, the reverse conclusion would be obtained: those with higher per capita income growth rates (the now-developed nations) would typically have higher population growth rates.[14]

On the whole, then, simple empirical comparisons between economic and population growth rates are, like a priori theorizing, inconclusive. None of this means that per capita income growth would have been the same if population growth rates had been markedly higher or lower. But the effect of population growth, whether positive or negative, is not so great relative to other growth determinants as to stand out in a simple comparison. This cautions against preoccupation with the effect of population growth on economic development to the exclusion of other deter-

---

[14] [7, p. 15] gives comparative data on population growth in developed versus less developed areas for earlier periods. A statistical analysis similar to that above, and reaching like conclusions, appears in [49].

minants. At a minimum, the evidence, as far as it has been touched on here, suggests that in the past two centuries accelerated population growth has not typically prevented growth in per capita income, let alone compelled a decline.

Concluding observations

The theories and evidence surveyed here do not, it seems, add up to any clear-cut generalization as to the effect of population growth on economic development in today's less developed areas. Indeed, it may well be that no single generalization is appropriate for countries differing as widely in growth rates, densities, and income levels as do these areas. Clearly there is need for more basic research on the actual experience of nations, currently and in the past.

To some Western observers, the population explosion is a fearful threat, the world's foremost problem. The excessive and irrational breeding of human beings is seen as a major obstacle to curing many of the world's principal ills—in some cases, a root cause itself of these ills.

The feelings of those experiencing the "population problem" are likely to be rather different, however. To parents in less developed areas, it means that new babies are more likely to survive the rigors of childbirth and infancy. It means that the suffering and sorrow caused by the illness and death of much-loved children is drastically reduced. It means that the parents themselves are less debilitated by disease, and are able to work harder and live fuller lives. It means that homes are less frequently saddened by the death of one of the spouses.

In time, the "population problem" may mean also the emergence of a new and real family problem—more offspring surviving than had really been wanted. If Western experience is any guide—and there is no reason to suppose that Westerners are in some way a distinctive and exceptionally rational species of mankind—this problem of excess fertility will eventually induce voluntary action by parents to regulate their fertility. Indeed, fertility declines are already occurring in some of today's less developed areas [71; 72, pp. 18–20, 29–30]. Government population programs in these countries may accelerate the adjustment of fertility to lower levels, and thereby reduce the heavy emotional and other costs of unwanted children. Such programs are more likely to succeed, however, if they are sensitive to the real concerns of parents than if they seem to force population control on them in order to halt their "excessive breeding".[15]

Rapid population growth in today's less developed countries is not an isolated occurrence in otherwise static societies, without any parallel

---

[15] For an excellent example of how a family planning program may backfire if imbued with a population control philosophy, note the effects of the "loop and run" tactic described in [73, p. 3].

whatsoever in historical experience. Along with the rapid mortality decline and consequent surge in population growth, drastic changes are occurring, too, in economic, political, and social institutions, and in educational systems [27, 70]. Many less developed societies are currently exhibiting characteristics which, in broad outline, are like those which appeared in the early phases of modernization in Europe, its overseas descendants, and Japan. The current surge in population growth is thus symptomatic of the further diffusion of modernization to today's less developed areas, of a social transformation which in the past has brought with it, in due course abatement of the initial wave of population growth and higher living levels for the mass of population.

References and suggestions for further reading

1. Adelman, Irma. "An Econometric Analysis of Population Growth," *American Economic Review,* LIII, 31 (June, 1963), pp. 314–39.
2. Barlow, Robin. *The Economic Effects of Malaria Eradication,* Bureau of Public Health Economics, Research Series No. 15 (Ann Arbor, Michigan: School of Public Health, University of Michigan, 1968).
3. Becker, Gary S. "An Economic Analysis of Fertility," in Universities—National Bureau Committee for Economic Research, *Demographic and Economic Change in Developed Countries* (Princeton: Princeton University Press, 1960).
4. ———. "A Theory of the Allocation of Time," *Economic Journal,* LXXV, 299 (September, 1965), pp. 493–517.
5. Blake Judith. "Income and Reproductive Motivation," *Population Studies,* XXI, 3 (November, 1967), pp. 185–206.
6. Boserup, Ester. *The Conditions of Agricultural Growth: the Economics of Agrarian Change Under Population Pressure* (Chicago: Aldine, 1965).
7. Bourgeois Pichat, Jean. "Population Growth and Development," *International Conciliation,* 556 (January, 1966).
8. Brady, Dorothy S., and Rose D. Friedman. "Savings and the Income Distribution," in Conference on Research in Income and Wealth, *Studies in Income and Wealth,* X (New York: National Bureau of Economic Research, ﹍﹍﹍ –65.
9. Clark, Colin. *Population Growth and Land Use* (New York: St. Martin's Press, 1967).
10. Chamberlain, Neil W. *Beyond Malthus: Population and Power* (New York: Basic Books, 1970).
11. Coale, Ansley. "Increases in Expectation of Life and Population Growth," in Louis Henry and Wilhelm Winkler, eds., *International Population Conference* (Vienna, 1959).
12. ———. "Should the United States Start a Campaign for Fewer Births?" *Population Index,* 34, 4(Oct.-Dec. 1968), pp. 467–74.
13. Coale, Ansley, and Edgar M. Hoover. *Population Growth and Economic Development in Low-Income Countries* (Princeton: Princeton University Press, 1961).
14. Coale, Ansley J., and Melvin Zelnik. *New Estimates of Fertility and Population in the United States* (Princeton: Princeton University Press, 1963).
15. Commission on Population Growth and the American Future. *Population and the American Future* (New York: The New American Library, 1972).

16. Commoner, Barry. "The Humane Preservation of Human Life," mimeo (May 6, 1971).

17. Conference on Research in Income and Wealth. *Output, Input, and Productivity Measurement, Studies in Income and Wealth,* 25 (Princeton: Princeton University Press, 1961).

18. Davis, Joseph S. *The Population Upsurge in the United States* (Stanford: Food Research Institute, War-Peace Pamphlet No. 12, 1949).

19. Davis, Kingsley. "Population Policy: Will Current Programs Succeed?" *Science,* 158 (November 10, 1967), pp. 730–39.

20. ————. *The Population of India and Pakistan* (Princeton: Princeton University Press, 1951).

21. ————. "The Theory of Change and Response in Modern Demographic History," *Population Index,* XXIX, 4 (October, 1963), pp. 345–66.

22. Davis, Lance E., et al. *American Economic Growth: An Economist's History of the United States* (New York: Harper & Row, 1972).

23. Day, Lincoln and Alice T. *Too Many Americans,* 2d ed. (New York: Dell, 1965).

24. Duesenberry, James E. *Income, Saving, and the Theory of Consumer Behavior* (Cambridge, Mass.: Harvard University Press, 1952).

25. Durand, John D. "The Modern Expansion of World Population," *Proceedings of the American Philosophical Society,* III, 3 (June, 1967), pp. 136–59.

26. Easterlin, Richard A. "Does Human Fertility Adjust to the Environment?" *American Economic Review Papers and Proceedings,* Vol. LXI, No. 2 (May 1971), pp. 339–407.

27. ————. "Economic Growth: An Overview," *International Encyclopedia of the Social Sciences,* 4 (Macmillan, 1968), pp. 395–408.

28. ————. "Effects of Population Growth on the Economic Development of Developing Countries," *Annals,* 369 (January, 1967), pp. 98–108.

29. ————. *Population, Labor Force, and Long Swings in Economic Growth: The American Experience* (New York: Columbia University Press, 1968).

30. ————. "Relative Economic Status and the American Fertility Swing" in Sheldon, Eleanor B., ed., *Social Structure, Family Life Styles and Economic Behavior* (Philadelphia: J. B. Lippincott for Institute of Life Insurance, Forthcoming 1972).

31. ————. "Towards a Socio-Economic Theory of Fertility: A Survey of Recent Research on Economic Factors in American Fertility," in *Fertility and Family Planning: A World View* (Ann Arbor: University of Michigan Press, 1969), pp. 127–56.

32. Enke, Stephen. "The Gains to India from Population Control: Some Money Measures and Incentive Schemes," *Review of Economics and Statistics,* XLII (1960), pp. 175–81.

33. ————. "The Economic Aspects of Slowing Population Growth," *Economic Journal,* LXXVI (March, 1966), pp. 45–56.

34. Fein, Rashi. "Health Programs and Economic Development," in *The Economics of Health and Medical Care,* Proceedings of the Conference on the Economics of Health and Medical Care, May 10–12, 1962, sponsored by the Bureau of Public Health Economics and the Department of Economics of the University of Michigan (1964), pp. 271–282.

35. Forster, Colin and G. S. L. Tucker. *Economic Opportunity and White American Fertility Ratios, 1800–1860* (New Haven: Yale University Press, 1972).

36. Freedman, Deborah S. "Consumption Aspirations as Economic Incentives in a Developing Economy—Taiwan" (unpublished paper).

37. ———. "Consumption of Modern Goods and Services and Their Relation to Fertility: A Study in Taiwan (unpublished paper).

38. ———. "The Relation of Economic Status to Fertility," *American Economic Review,* LIII, 3 (June, 1963), pp. 414–26.

39. Freedman, Ronald. "Norms for Family Size in Underdeveloped Areas," *Proceedings of the Royal Statistical Society,* CLIX, Part B (1963), pp. 220–45.

40. ———. "The Transition from High to Low Fertility: Challenge to Demographers," *Population Index,* 31, 4 (October, 1965), pp. 417–30.

41. Freedman, Ronald, and Lolagene Coombs. "Economic Considerations in Family Growth Decisions," *Population Studies,* XX, 2 (November, 1966), pp. 197–222.

42. Freedman, Ronald, Pascal K. Whelpton, and Arthur A. Campbell. *Family Planning, Sterility and Population Growth* (New York: McGraw-Hill, 1959).

43. Glass, D. V., and D. E. C. Eversley (eds.). *Population in History* (Chicago: Aldine, 1965).

44. Grabill, W. H., C. V. Kiser, and P. K. Whelpton. *The Fertility of American Women* (New York: Wiley, 1958).

45. Hansen, Alvin. *Fiscal Policy and Business Cycles* (New York: W. W. Norton, 1941).

46. Hickman, Bert G. *Growth and Stability in the Postwar Economy* (Washington: Brooking. Institution, 1960).

47. Hirschman, A. [illegible] O. *The Strategy of Economic Development* (New Haven: Yale University Press, [illegible]8).

48. Hughes, J. R. T. "[illegible]ndustrialization," *International Encyclopedia of the Social Sciences,* 7, 252–263 (Macmillan, 1968).

49. Kuznets, Simon. "Population and Economic Growth," *Proceedings of the American Philosophical Society,* III, 3 (June, 1967), pp. 170–93.

50. Lader, Laurence. *Breeding Ourselves to Death* (New York: Ballantine, 1971).

51. Leibenstein, Harvey. *Economic Backwardness and Economic Growth* (New York: John Wiley, 1957).

52. MacDonald, J. D. "Agricultural Organization, Migration, and Labour Militancy in Rural Italy," *Economic History Review,* XVI, 1 (1963), pp. 61–75.

53. Meade, J. E. "Population Explosion, the Standard of Living, and Social Conflict," *Economic Journal,* LXXVII (June, 1967), pp. 233–55.

54. Mincer, Jacob. "Market Prices, Opportunity Costs, and Income Effects," in *Measurement in Economics: Studies in Mathematical Economics and Econometrics in Memory of Yehuda Grunfeld* (Stanford: Stanford University Press, 1963).

55. Modigliani, Franco. "Fluctuations in the Savings–Income Ratio: A Problem in Economic Forecasting," *Conference on Research in Income and Wealth,* Studies in Income and Wealth, XI (New York: National Bureau of Economic Research, 1949), pp. 371–443.

56. Mukherjee, M. "A Preliminary Study of the Growth of National Income in India, 1857–1957," in International Association for Research in Income and Wealth, *Asian Studies in Income and Wealth* (New York: Asia Publishing House, 1965), pp. 71–103.

57. National Center for Health Statistics. *Natality Statistics Analysis: United States, 1965–1967* (Washington: U.S. Government Printing Office, 1970).

58. ————. *Monthly Vital Statistics Report.*

59. Ohlin, Goran. *Population Control and Economic Development* (Paris: OECD, 1966).

60. Olin, Ulla. "Population Growth and Problems of Employment in Asia and the Far East," in the United Nations, *World Population Conference, 1965,* IV (New York: U.N., 1967), pp. 314–17.

61. Okun, Bernard. *Trends in Birth Rates in the United States Since 1870* (Baltimore: Johns Hopkins Press, 1958).

62. Roberts, John M., Edwin Burmeister, and Richard F. Strand. "Preferential Pattern Analysis," in Paul Kay, ed., *Explorations in Mathematical Anthropology* (Cambridge: Massachusetts Institute of Technology Press, 1971).

63. Rosenthal, Jack. "Survey Finds 50% Back Liberalization of Abortion Policy," *New York Times* (October 28, 1971), pp. 1, 22.

64. Ryder, Norman B. and Charles F. Westoff. *Reproduction in the United States 1965* (Princeton: Princeton University Press, 1971).

65. Silver, Morris. "Births, Marriages, and Business Cycles in the United States," *Journal of Political Economy,* LXXIII, 3 (June, 1965), pp. 237–55.

66. Spengler, Joseph J. "The Economist and the Population Question," *American Economic Review,* LVI, 1 (March, 1966), pp. 1–24.

67. ————. "Values and Fertility Analysis," *Demography,* 3, 1 (1966), pp. 109–30.

68. United Nations. *The Determinants and Consequences of Population Trends* (New York: United Nations, 1953).

69. ————. "Inquiry Among Governments on Problems Resulting from The Interaction of Economic Development and Population Changes," United Nations Doc. E/3895/Rev. 1 (November 24, 1964), prepared for 1965 World Population Conference, Belgrade, Yugoslavia.

70. ————. *Preliminary Report on the World Social Situation* (New York: United Nations, 1952).

71. ————. "Recent Declines in Fertility in Developing Countries," Population Division Working Paper No. 26 (July 1968).

72. ————. *The World Population Situation in 1970* (New York: United Nations, 1971).

73. Taylor, Carl. "Five Stages in a Practical Population Policy," *International Development Review* (December 1968), pp. 2–7.

74. U.S. Bureau of the Census. *Current Population Reports. Population Estimates and Projections,* Series P-25, No. 476 (February 1972).

75. Westoff, Charles F., Robert G. Potter, and Philip C. Sagi. *The Third Child: A Study in the Prediction of Fertility* (Princeton: Princeton University Press, 1963).

76. ————, and Elliott G. Mishler. *Family Growth in Metropolitan America* (Princeton: Princeton University Press, 1961).

77. Whelpton, Pascal K., Arthur A. Campbell, and John E. Patterson. *Fertility and Family Planning in the United States* (Princeton: Princeton University Press, 1966).

78. Wolfe, Marshall. "Some Implications of Recent Changes in Urban and Rural Settlement Patterns in Latin America," in United Nations, *World Population Conference, 1965,* IV (New York: U.N., 1967), pp. 457–60.

79. Yasuba, Yasukichi. *Birth Rates of the White Population in the United States, 1800–1860* (Baltimore: Johns Hopkins Press, 1962).